Digital Course Materials

for

Practically Speaking

Third Edition

J. DAN ROTHWELL

Carefully scratch off the silver coating (e.g., with a coin) to see your personal redemption code.

This code can be used only once and cannot be shared.

Once the code has been revealed, this access card cannot be returned to the publisher. Access can also be purchased online during the registration process.

The code on this card is valid for two years from the date of first purchase. Complete terms and conditions are available at **oup-arc.com**

Access Length: 6 months from redemption of the code.

OXFORD
UNIVERSITY PRESS

Directions
Oxford University

P9-BVH-511

Your OUP digital course materials can be delivered several different ways, depending on how your instructor has elected to incorporate them into his or her course.

BEFORE REGISTERING FOR ACCESS, be sure to check with your instructor to ensure that you register using the proper method.

VIA YOUR SCHOOL'S LEARNING MANAGEMENT SYSTEM

Use this method if your instructor has integrated these resources into your school's Learning Management System (LMS)—Blackboard, Canvas, Brightspace, Moodle, or other

> Log in to your instructor's course within your school's LMS.

> When you click a link to a resource that is access-protected, you will be prompted to register for access.

> Follow the on-screen instructions.

> Enter your personal redemption code (or purchase access) when prompted on the checkout screen.

VIA OUP DASHBOARD

Use this method only if your instructor has specifically instructed you to enroll in a Dashboard course. **NOTE:** *If your instructor is using these resources within your school's LMS, use the Learning Management System instructions.*

> Visit **register.dashboard.oup.com** and select your textbook.

> Follow the on-screen instructions to identify your specific course section.

> Enter your personal redemption code (or purchase access) when prompted on the checkout screen.

> Once you complete your registration, you are automatically enrolled in your Dashboard course.

For assistance with code redemption, Dashboard registration, or if you redeemed your code using the wrong method for your course, please contact our customer support team at **dashboard.support@oup.com** *or 855-281-8749.*

Practically Speaking

"Absolutely love this book! It has helped me out in so many ways about how to speak in public. Thank you!"

—JOSÉ MENA

"I think the examples throughout the book are very simple and to the point. They helped a lot, especially when doing persuasive speaking."

—BRENDA V. MONTANEZ

Practically
Speaking

THIRD EDITION

J. DAN ROTHWELL

Professor Emeritus, Cabrillo College

New York   Oxford
OXFORD UNIVERSITY PRESS

Oxford University Press is a department of the University of Oxford.
It furthers the University's objective of excellence in research, scholarship,
and education by publishing worldwide. Oxford is a registered trademark of
Oxford University Press in the UK and certain other countries.

Published in the United States of America by Oxford University Press
198 Madison Avenue, New York, NY 10016, United States of America.

For titles covered by Section 112 of the US Higher Education
Opportunity Act, please visit www.oup.com/us/he for the
latest information about pricing and alternate formats.

Library of Congress Cataloging-in-Publication Data
Names: Rothwell, J. Dan, author.
Title: Practically speaking / J. Dan Rothwell, Professor Emeritus, Cabrillo College.
Description: Third Edition. | New York : Oxford University Press, [2019] |
    Revised edition of the author's Practically speaking, [2017]
Identifiers: LCCN 2019019033 (print) | LCCN 2019021751 (ebook) | ISBN
    9780190921057 () | ISBN 9780190080105 (ebook) | ISBN 9780190921033 (pbk.)
Subjects: LCSH: Public speaking.
Classification: LCC PN4129.15 (ebook) | LCC PN4129.15 .R68 2019 (print) | DDC
    808.5/1--dc23
LC record available at https://lccn.loc.gov/2019019033

9 8 7 6 5 4 3
Printed by LSC Communications, United States of America

To my lovely wife, Marcy.
No better partner in life could be imagined!

Brief Contents

Contents

CHAPTER 4 Gathering Material   67

CHAPTER 6 Attention: Getting People to Listen   102

CHAPTER 7 **Introductions and Conclusions**   121

CHAPTER 8 # Outlining and Organizing Speeches 139

CHAPTER 9 # Speaking Style: Using Language 162

CHAPTER 10   Delivering Your Speech   175

CHAPTER 11   Visual Aids   196

CHAPTER 12 Skepticism: Becoming Critical Thinking
Speakers and Listeners   219

CHAPTER **13**   Argument, Reasoning, and Evidence   235

CHAPTER 14   Informative Speaking   253

CHAPTER 15   Foundations of Persuasive Speaking   268

CHAPTER 16 **Persuasive Speaking Strategies** 287

Preface

Public speaking texts continue to take two main approaches. One could be called the all-you-can-eat buffet approach. These works are resplendent with almost every conceivable tasty feature that only the most dedicated and motivated students will ever sample. They can be wonderful books as a kind of "everything you ever wanted to know about public speaking, and then some" reference work, but public speaking novices may see them as daunting. A second is the cookbook approach. These works primarily offer a list of recipe steps for constructing and presenting a speech. Striving to cover "only the basics," they achieve this purpose, but few students are likely to find the recipe approach interesting reading.

Each approach has its merits and supporters. The significant success of the first two editions of *Practically Speaking*, however, suggests a clear desire by many to go in a different direction. *Practically Speaking* offers that different direction, one that was deemed worthy enough to receive the prestigious, peer-reviewed, 2018 **Textbook Excellence Award** from the Textbook and Academic Authors Association. Understanding this different approach can be ascertained by addressing key objectives for both students and teachers.

OBJECTIVES FOR STUDENTS

Practically Speaking aims to address four key objectives for students: (1) readability, (2) clarity, (3) applicability, and (4) affordability. Regarding the first objective—**readability**—the wisdom of Samuel Johnson seems apt: "What is written without effort is in general read without pleasure." Maximum effort has been devoted to writing a textbook that might ignite the interest of student readers, not induce a coma. Textbooks are not meant to read like spy thrillers, but they need not read like an instruction manual for setting up your new flat-screen TV. Therefore, I attempted to practice what I teach about gaining and maintaining attention by using the attention-getting strategies discussed in Chapter 6. The text includes novel and humorous examples, stories, quotations, photos, and cartoons; intense, dramatic, and poignant illustrations; colorful and vivid language and metaphors; and startling statistics and historical facts sprinkled throughout every chapter. The writing style is conversational, and the perpendicular pronoun "I" is used when relating personal narratives. First-person singular is more engaging than impersonal references such as "this author experienced" or "a student in the author's class," which makes me sound professorial and detached. Although it has been suggested that I employ the "editorial we" instead of the first-person singular, I tend to agree with Mark Twain, who said that "people with tapeworms have the right to use the editorial 'we'," but others should avoid it. I could use the passive voice instead, but that makes copy editors twitch and automatic grammar checkers become annoying nags. In addition, second-person pronoun references to "you" are employed frequently to address you, my readers, directly.

A second objective—**clarity**—is addressed in a variety of ways. The organization of each chapter follows the rules of good organizational logic presented in Chapter 8. Such logic can be examined by perusing the Table of Contents. In addition, headings and subheadings were carefully chosen and worded to produce maximum clarity as well as originality. Finally, numerous illustrations and explanations are provided to clarify all important public speaking concepts and processes.

A third objective—**applicability**—requires concerted effort to demonstrate the practical utility for students of becoming competent public speakers. The first chapter addresses in detail such applicability, opening with a discussion of the First Amendment guarantee of free speech, a subject of considerable currency. Numerous references to businesses and organizations, pop-culture references, and newsworthy events are used as illustrations throughout the text, reinforcing the applicability of competent public speaking for students.

A fourth objective—**affordability**—has become a national issue shared by students and faculty alike. An Oxford University Press national survey of 327 professors who teach public speaking at U.S. universities and community colleges revealed that almost 75% of respondents viewed price as an "extremely or very important" feature of a public speaking text. This view has only become more widespread in the ensuing years. Maximum effort has been exerted to make *Practically Speaking* an attractive but affordable alternative to other much more expensive choices. *Oxford University Press is a not-for-profit publishing company*, so this alone provides considerable price advantage for students surviving on tight budgets. The lean size of *Practically Speaking* also helps reduce the price.

OBJECTIVES FOR TEACHERS

Practically Speaking aims to address six different objectives for teachers of public speaking: (1) sound scholarship, (2) standard yet innovative coverage, (3) brevity, (4) recency, (5) logical organization, and (6) useful ancillaries. The first objective—**sound scholarship**—is critically important. Providing substantial theory and research to bolster the advice offered to novice student speakers counters the oft-heard, naive claim that public speaking is just "common sense." Without such theory and research, advice provided will appear as little more than the personal opinion of the author, easily trivialized or ignored, and often at odds with the opinions of others. It is bound to strike the more alert student readers that authors who insist on inclusion of research and evidence for student speeches, but include little research and evidence to support their advice offered in a textbook, seem contradictory. We never want students to equate relatively short texts such as *Practically Speaking* with being "lightweight" or insubstantial. The careful scholarship in *Practically Speaking* is evident in every chapter. *More than 500 references* are cited, and the communication competence model, carefully developed in Chapter 1, serves as the theoretical basis for all advice offered. In addition, *Chapter 12 on skepticism is the only chapter of its kind in public speaking texts that so thoroughly explains the theoretical underpinnings of the process of critical thinking for public speakers.* It is hard to imagine a more relevant discussion in the current polarized environment and troubling emergence of what a Rand report cleverly calls "truth decay" (Kavanagh & Rich, 2018).

A second objective for public speaking teachers—**standard yet innovative coverage**—is addressed in several ways. *All standard topics* found in any reputable public speaking text and identified in the Oxford survey previously referenced are thoroughly developed in *Practically Speaking*. Innovative coverage includes the opening *chapter on communication competence.* There is a *complete chapter on speech anxiety*, rarely offered in other public speaking texts. A full *chapter on gaining and maintaining attention*, a unique feature of *Practically Speaking*, emphasizes that speakers must do far more than merely gain the immediate attention of their audiences. The much greater challenge is to keep that attention throughout a lengthy speech. A full *chapter on skepticism (process of critical thinking)*, already mentioned, is yet another innovation of *Practically Speaking.* Finally, *two full chapters on persuasive speaking* provide both a theoretical explanation for how persuasion works generally and specific strategies for persuading public speaking audiences. Results from the Oxford survey showed that three-quarters of respondents believed that a chapter on foundations of persuasion is "extremely or very important." A chapter on persuasive speaking strategies was similarly embraced by 85% of respondents.

A third objective—**brevity**—was identified by 72% of respondents to the Oxford survey as variously "important" to "extremely important." A significant 85% of respondents in the same survey also noted that "preparing students to start speaking right away" is important. In standard, lengthy texts, students have to read hundreds of pages before they learn the basics for a simple first or second speech. Standard texts typically do not cover introductions and conclusions, for example, until almost 200 pages of text have been read. Students will reach the chapter in *Practically Speaking* on introductions and conclusions in far fewer pages. *Practically Speaking* gets students "up and running" quickly. A sample "first speech" even appears in Chapter 2. Another related concern in the Oxford survey identified by almost half the respondents was that students do not read the text. Reading a textbook of 500 pages, or ones disguised as shorter but formatted in hugely over-sized pages, can be daunting. *Practically Speaking* is about half the size of most standard public speaking texts. Its brevity is far less intimidating, and thus it is more likely to be read.

A fourth objective—**recency**—is always a challenge because of the lag period between finishing a manuscript and completing the textbook production process that typically takes months. As someone with a bachelor's degree in American history, I value the use of historical examples for illustrations. I also see the applicability of recent events to clarify concepts and processes in public speaking. I have included both, some examples as recent as 2019, the year this edition went into publication, and others that are centuries old. Great speakers and powerfully illustrative events do not appear in only one brief time period. We can learn from both the old and the new. This is true for references as well. Almost half of the more than 500 references are between 2014 and 2019, while some of the rest are more "classic" citations.

A fifth objective—**logical organization**—mirrors other public speaking texts. With the exception of Chapter 1 on communication competence, *all chapters can be moved to a different order if so desired.*

A final objective—**useful ancillaries**—is addressed in several ways:

- An **Instructor's Manual**, which I have carefully revised myself, contains dozens of unique activities and exercises, as well as almost 150 website links to a wide variety of speeches and video resources.
- A **Test Bank** that provides a multitude of questions from which to choose for construction of exams.
- **PowerPoint lecture slides** have been updated.
- **Speak Up** prompts, where students can record themselves and show what they've learned using **GoReact**, a speech recording interactive software. GoReact's easy-to-use video recording tool supports Communication courses by helping students practice and evaluate presentation skills in a fun and feedback-centered environment. Building confidence and skills, GoReact's effective peer-preview features and instructor evaluation tools save time and provide necessary student support.
- An **Occasional Newsletter** that briefly discusses recent research and issues relevant to public speaking and keeps *Practically Speaking* updated is offered to any interested party.

- The **Ancillary Resource Center (ARC)** at www.oup.com/he/rothwell-ps3e provides students with chapter summaries, practice exams, key term flashcards, student web speeches, video exercises, and speech topic ideas.
- **Course cartridges** for a variety of Learning Management Systems, including Blackboard, Canvas, Moodle, and D2L, allow instructors to create their own course websites integrating student and instructor resources available on the Ancillary Resource Center and Companion Website. Contact your Oxford University Press representative for access or for more information about these supplements or customized options.

NEW TO THIS EDITION

Many important changes have been made for this third edition.

1. More than **200 new references** have been added, and dozens of old references have been deleted. An abundance of **new studies, surveys, and statistics** on a wide variety of topics has been included throughout the text. The **scholarship** has also been thoroughly updated.
2. The photo package has been greatly expanded to include **many new photos**. Some less interesting photos have been deleted. Photos have been carefully chosen to show more than a commonplace variety of individuals merely speaking at a podium.
3. Copious new **examples, stories, humorous anecdotes, and pop culture references** also appear throughout the text.
4. Dozens of recent excerpts from **student speeches** have been added.
5. *New subject matter* has been included, such as:
    a. a lengthy discussion of **freedom of speech**;
    b. a substantial section that discusses **online speaking**;
    c. considerable new material on the "**death of expertise**" and the importance of credible sources;
    d. substantial additional analysis of "**truth decay**"—the deterioration of critical thinking practices;
    e. Appendix C on **group oral presentations**;
    f. detailed steps on **how to become a skeptic** both as a speaker and listener;
    g. new material on **gestures and cultural differences** in interpretation;
    h. additions to the discussion of **selective attention**;
    i. a segment on **startling audiences as speech openers**;
    j. a section on language and **abstract words**;
    k. an expanded and updated segment on **style in the electronic age**;

l. new material on **eye contact, voice quality,** and **vocal fillers;**
m. exploration of the difficulty students have **identifying biased sources;**
n. extended discussion of **analogical reasoning;**
o. development of **reframing** as a persuasion strategy;
p. expanded coverage of **anger** as a persuasive strategy;
q. more detail on **delivering a toast.**

6. Model informative and persuasive speeches, **Appendices A and B** have been completely **updated and significantly shortened.**
7. Some **material has been condensed** (e.g., humor as an attention strategy) and other material has been deleted (e.g., numerous political examples).
8. In aggregate, **more than 100 TED Talks and YouTube speech links** have been included at the end of chapters, many of them new additions, to provide valuable resources for students to see high-quality, and sometimes less than commendable, speeches for illustration and analysis.
9. **Critical thinking questions** have been added to the end of chapters.
10. *New chapter openings* have been provided for Chapters 1, 5, 7, and 8. Each opening provides a more engaging start to these chapters.

ACKNOWLEDGMENTS

My sincere thanks are extended to reviewers of this text. They include the following:

Brent E. Adrian, *Central Community College–Grand Island*
Kenneth R. Albone, *Rowan University*
Mary Beth Asbury, *Middle Tennessee State University*
Shirley Brownfox, *Laney College*
Amy Bryant, *Nashville State Community College*
Patrick Bungard, *Crafton Hills College*
Teresa Collard, *University of Tennessee*
Diana M. Cooley, *Lone Star College–North Harris*
Laura Crosswell, *Arizona State University*
Adrienne Hacker Daniels, *Illinois College*
Patricia Drevets, *Rogue Community College*
Jennifer Ehrhardt, *Pensacola State College*
Lilli Ann Linford-Foreman, *Central Oregon Community College*
Keith Forrest, *Atlantic Cape Community College*
Jeannine Foster, *Tarrant County College*

Tonya Forsythe, *Ohio State University*
Patrick Gagliano, *Newberry College*
Gina Giotta, *California State University–Northridge*
Gai Grannon, *Montclair State University*
Carla Harrell, *Old Dominion University*
Paul T. M. Hemenway, *Lamar University*
Daniel Hildenbrandt, *Owensboro Community and Technical College*
Curtis Hirsh, *St. Edward's University*
Lawrence A. Hosman, *University of Southern Mississippi*
Cynthia Irizarry, *Suffolk University*
Aubrie Johnson, *Salt Lake Community College*
Daniel Johnson, *Southwest Michigan College*
Laveda I. Joseph, *Columbus State University*
Tony Kemp, *Mercer University*
Rebecca M. Kennerly, *Georgia Southern University*
Susan Kilgard, *Anne Arundel Community College*
Heidi Kirkman, *Howard Community College*
Veronica Koehn, *Oregon Institute of Technology*
Antonia Krueger, *Eckerd College*
E. Grace Lager, *Eckerd College*
Jessica N. Lawson, *Wright State University*
Laureen LeFever, *Montclair State University*
Johnathan Marlow, *Tulsa Community College*
Leola McClure, *MiraCosta College*
Mumba Mumba, *Illinois College*
Daryle Nagano, *Los Angeles Harbor College*
Kekeli Nuviadenu, *Bethune-Cookman University*
David C. Oh, *Ramapo College of New Jersey*
Karen Otto, *Florida State College at Jacksonville*
Hilary Parmentier, *Florida Keys Community College*
Elaine Pascale, *Suffolk University*
Patricia Posthauer, *St. Joseph's College*
Evelyn Jean Pine, *Berkeley City College*
Julia Raz, *LA Mission College*
Patricia D. Richardson, *Cecil College*
Caryn D. Riswold, *Illinois College*
Betsy Rosenblum, *Quinnipiac University*
Kimberly Rosenfeld, *Cerritos College*
Theresa C. Shaton, *Kutztown University of Pennsylvania*
Joanna Showell, *Bethune–Cookman University*
Jo-Ann Sickles, *Everett Community College*

Cheryl Skiba-Jones, *Trine University*
Myron Skulas, *Cincinnati State Technical and Community College*
Janice Smith, *Pasco Hernando State College*
Richard Soller, *College of Lake County*
Sonja Stetzler, *Queens University of Charlotte*
Christy Takamure, *Leeward Community College*
Sharon Taxin, *St. John's University*
Dexin Tian, *Yangzhou University*
J. David Trebing, *Kent State University*
Fletcher Ziwoya, *University of Nebraska*
Elaine Zweig, *Collin College*

I also want to thank the many professionals at Oxford University Press who worked to bring *Practically Speaking* to the marketplace. They include Toni Magyar, acquisitions editor; Keith Chasse, executive editor for communication; and Alyssa Quinones, assistant editor.

I want to offer a special thanks to my wife, Marcy, for the wonderful *custom cartoons*. I gave her ideas and she produced beautiful, animated renderings. Artist, singer, writer, musician, computer program analyst—her talents seem boundless. I also want to thank the voters of my Santa Cruz county district for electing me to the Cabrillo College Board of Trustees by an overwhelming margin. The practical experience campaigning for public office was invaluable, and tantamount to a three-month migraine.

ABOUT THE AUTHOR

I am the former chair of the Communication Studies Department at Cabrillo College. I have a BA in American history from the University of Portland (Oregon), an MA in rhetoric and public address, and a PhD in communication theory and social influence, both from the University of Oregon. I have authored four other books in addition to *Practically Speaking*. They are *In Mixed Company: Communicating in Small Groups and Teams* (Oxford University Press), *In the Company of Others: An Introduction to Communication* (Oxford University Press), *Telling It Like It Isn't: Language Misuse and Malpractice* (Prentice Hall), and *Interpersonal Communication: Influences and Alternatives* (with James Costigan and published by Charles-Merrill).

I deeply appreciate receiving more than two dozen teaching awards during my lengthy academic career, including, among others, the 2010 "Ernest L. Boyer International Award for Excellence in Teaching, Learning, and Technology"; the 2010 Cabrillo College "Innovative Teacher of the Year"; the 2011 National

Communication Association "Community College Educator of the Year" award; a 2012 official "Excellence in Teaching" resolution by the California State Senate; and the 2014 Western States Communication Association "Master Teacher" award. Having never achieved one of my early life goals—to be a Hall of Fame major league baseball pitcher—these teaching awards, as much as I truly value them, will have to compensate for this one lifelong disappointment.

Practically Speaking

Communication Competence and Public Speaking

I t was October 1, 1964, on the campus of University of California, Berkeley. A graduate student, Jack Weinberg, defied a campus ban on political information tables. Campus police confronted him at his table where he was promoting the Congress of Racial Equality. As officers attempted to remove Weinberg, hundreds of students spontaneously sat down in front of the patrol car, preventing it from leaving campus. Weinberg sat in the stationary police car for 32 hours. This single event spawned what became known as the Free Speech Movement. Thousands of students joined the protest, giving highly political speeches over loudspeakers and bullhorns. The protest continued until about 800 students were eventually arrested. Charges were levied against the organizers of the sit-in, which sprouted an even larger student protest that mostly shut down the university. Eventually the campus ban on political speech was lifted. On the fiftieth anniversary of this iconic event, *San Jose Mercury News* reporter Katy Murphy (2014) summarized the importance of the movement this way: "The free speech movement made an unmistakable stamp on a campus that prides itself on its legacy of social activism, and its spirit of protest quickly spread to colleges across the nation" (p. A1).

Freedom of speech is the bedrock of a democratic society. There is an inherent recognition in the First Amendment to the U.S. Constitution that articulate speech can give voice to the voiceless and power to the powerless. Eloquence has

1

influenced the course of our history, as it did during the Free Speech Movement (*see access to links at end of chapter*). The oratory of Martin Luther King and others was a powerful instrument of the civil rights movement. Public speaking helped galvanize the Tea Party and the Occupy movements.

A wave of student protest, reminiscent of the Berkeley student uprising, has enveloped the United States in recent years ("Chasm in the Classroom," 2019). Ironically, the Berkeley campus in 2017 was a prominent venue for *restricting* free speech. Massive protests were aimed at preventing controversial right-wing firebrand Milo Yiannopoulos and conservative pundit Ann Coulter from speaking on campus. Roughly three-quarters of the efforts to "disinvite" controversial speakers have come from liberal students and faculty, with the remaining quarter emanating from conservatives (McLaughlin, 2017).

Years ago, Nat Hentoff (1992) wrote a carefully reasoned critique of arguments offered by those who, often with the best intentions, advocate banning certain kinds of speech. His book was titled *Free Speech for Me—but Not for Thee: How the American Left and Right Relentlessly Censor Each Other*. The challenges to free speech on college campuses have only become more vocal in years since Hentoff's defense of free speech (Chemerinsky, 2018). The mere threat of disruption from inviting controversial and provocative speakers onto college campuses can quash dissent—what Hentoff calls "the heckler's veto."

PHOTO 1.1: Mario Savio, a prominent student leader, giving a speech at UC Berkeley during the 1964 Free Speech Movement.

PHOTO 1.2: The Free Speech Movement Café on the Berkeley campus is a reminder of battles fought by students for the right to free expression.

Racist, sexist, homophobic, and xenophobic "hate speech" is repellant, and arguments supporting its restraint, especially on college campuses, can seem quite reasonable. For example, a national survey of college students revealed that a majority believe that "creating a positive learning environment for students by prohibiting certain speech" is more important than creating "an open environment where students are exposed to all types of speech and viewpoints . . . even if it means allowing speech that is offensive" (Villasenor, 2017). There is no consensus definition of hate speech, however. For example, one survey found that among those with college experience, 51% would ban a speaker who claims all White people are racists; 49% would bar a speaker who claims Christians are backward and brainwashed; 41% would ban anyone who says illegal immigrants should be deported; and 40% favor preventing anyone from proclaiming publicly that men are better at math than women (Crawford et al., 2015). Despite these results, survey data reveal that college students are less likely to support restricting free expression on college campuses than the general population ("Chasm in the Classroom," 2019).

Regardless of your personal beliefs about rhetorical censorship, the Supreme Court and federal courts have consistently ruled in favor of relatively unfettered public speech ("Speech on Campus," 2018). Campus codes that ban objectionable speech have been struck down (Chemerisnsky, 2018). Ironically, the hate speech code at the University of Michigan was used primarily against African

American students before the courts banned the code (Chemerinsky, 2018). As former ACLU president Nadine Strossen (2018) writes, such codes and similar laws "are predictably enforced to suppress unpopular speakers and ideas, and too often they even are enforced to stifle speech of the vulnerable, marginalized minority groups they are designed to protect."

The legal standard for banning speech is understandably high. "It is not enough to be hateful; it must be imminently injurious (a "true threat") or fall into a small class of exceptions such as child pornography . . . or the incitement of illegal behavior . . ." (Ceci & Williams 2018; see also Strossen, 2018). A majority of college students erroneously believe that the First Amendment to the U.S. Constitution does not protect hate speech, and that it is acceptable for student groups to shout down speakers to silence them (Chemerinsky, 2017). University of Chicago president Robert Zimmer (2016) counters these preferences for censorship of speech: "Universities cannot be viewed as a sanctuary for comfort. . . . Having one's assumptions challenged and experiencing the discomfort that sometimes accompanies this process are intrinsic parts of an excellent education."

Without diving deeply into the complexities of implementing the dictates of the courts, the simple answer to offensive speech is more speech. There is "no satisfactory alternative to free speech" (Ceci et al., 2018, p. 312). Recognizing this, UC Berkeley responded to the 2017 free speech controversies by changing policies and rules to permit freer dissent on campus, chiefly by designating the West Crescent area of the campus a "free speech zone" available for large-scale demonstrations at any time with minimal restrictions (Bauer-Wolf, 2018). The Southern Poverty Law Center, a non-profit organization that monitors hate groups, suggests ways to protect free speech but still express opposition. These include the following: ignore the controversial speakers because they need an audience to gain media attention; turn your backs on the speaker (do not shout them down); and hold a counter-demonstration on a different part of campus before, during, or even after the offending event, offering speeches that educate listeners on the relevant issues (Newman, 2017). One additional suggestion is that you could attend the offending speech, display protest signs, and engage in animated, but civil, debate during questioning periods.

Imagine if this critical right in a free society to speak your mind in public were taken from you? In earlier times, women did not have to imagine it; they had to fight for the right. In seventeenth-century colonial America, a woman who spoke publicly could be dunked in any available body of water. When raised, sputtering and breathless, she was given two choices—agree to curb her offending tongue or suffer further dunkings. In Boston during the same century, women who gave speeches or spoke in religious or political meetings could be gagged (Jamieson, 1988).

"Offensive speech" is a moving target. What once was banned is permissible today; what once was permissible is now under attack. Battles are waged over permissible public speech because we all sense its capacity for influencing our beliefs and values on issues of critical importance. Professor Steven Pinker (2015) of Harvard University asks: "How did the monstrous regimes of the 20th century gain and hold power? The answer is that groups of armed fanatics silenced their critics and adversaries."

There are many other important reasons to become a competent public speaker besides its powerful potential to produce often controversial societal change. College courses in diverse disciplines increasingly assign oral presentations. One massive survey revealed that 81% of first-year college students and 88% of seniors gave formal class presentations. A prodigious 92% of college seniors concluded that their knowledge and skills regarding "speaking clearly and effectively" were significantly enhanced by such training ("National Survey," 2018). *Those of you who do become proficient public speakers, if done early in your pursuit of a college degree, will enjoy an enormous advantage when giving class presentations.* Relatively few students, however, see themselves as proficient public speakers prior to training (Eagan et al., 2017). Whether viewing oral presentations with reluctance or relish, you will undoubtedly be required to give them in your classes, so, practically speaking, why not learn to do them well?

Teaching, law, religion, politics, public relations, and marketing also require substantial public speaking knowledge and skill. A Prezi/Harris survey reported that 70% of employed Americans found public speaking skills to be critical to their career success (Gallo, 2014). Employers, however, do not believe most job applicants possess such skills, mainly because applicants have received little or no training in public speaking (Grant, 2016).

Competent public speaking is useful in other circumstances as well. Average citizens are frequently called upon to give speeches of support or dissent at public meetings on utility rate increases, school board issues, and city or county disputes. Toasts at weddings or banquets, tributes at awards ceremonies, eulogies at funerals for loved ones, and presentations at business meetings are additional common public speaking situations.

Competent public speakers possess an impressive array of knowledge and skills. They know how to present complex ideas clearly and fluently, keep an audience's attention, analyze important issues, conduct research, make reasonable arguments, and support claims with valid proof. They entertain and also move people to listen, to contemplate, and to change their minds.

Given these bountiful benefits of effective public speaking, **the purpose of this chapter is to begin exploring public speaking from a communication competence perspective**. Toward that end, this chapter (1) defines both communication and communication competence in the context of public speaking, and (2) provides general ways to achieve public speaking competence as a basis for more specific exploration in remaining chapters.

DEFINING COMMUNICATION

Communication is a transactional process of sharing meaning with others. **Public speaking** is fundamentally an act of communication in which a clearly identified speaker presents a message in a more formal manner than mere conversation to an audience of multiple listeners on an occasion to achieve a specific purpose. Explaining how public speaking functions as a transactional process begins our journey.

Communication as a Transactional Process: Working with an Audience

To understand the ways in which public speaking, as a communication act, is a transactional process, some basic elements need brief explanation. When you give a speech in class, you are the *sender* who *encodes* your ideas by organizing and expressing them in a spoken language. The *message* is composed of the ideas you wish to express, such as what your college should do about rising tuition and fees. The *channel* is the medium used to share a message, such as a speech presented in person or remotely in a podcast or YouTube presentation. The *receivers* are your classmates who *decode* your message by interpreting your spoken words.

This decoding process is no small challenge given the multiple meanings of most words, as Groucho Marx once illustrated with his famous quip: "Time flies like an arrow; fruit flies like a banana." A *booty call* could be an invitation to a treasure hunt, or a search for something quite different. Consider actual newspaper headlines reported by the *Columbia Journalism Review*: "Prostitutes Appeal to Pope," "Students Cook and Serve Grandparents," "City Manager Tapes Head to District Attorney," and "Kids Make Nutritious Snacks." Imagine a non-native speaker of English trying to decode this sentence: "The woman was present to present the present to her friend, presently." Lexicographer Peter Gilliver calculated that the seemingly simple word *run* has 645 separate meanings, the most of any word in the English language (Liao, 2017).

Then there is *noise*, or any interference with effective transmission and reception of your message. This might be a loud cellphone conversation just outside the classroom, tardy students arriving in the middle of your speech, or that nauseating feeling the day after too much partying that can interfere

PHOTOS 1.3 & 1.4: Julián Castro's daughter provides an adorable distraction (noise) during his keynote address at the 2012 Democratic National Convention.

with the quality of your speaking performance. Consider Julián Castro, who was mayor of San Antonio, Texas, at the time, when he delivered the keynote address at the 2012 Democratic National Convention (*see access to link at end of chapter*). He spoke this line halfway through his speech: "*Que Dios te bendiga—* May God bless you." At that very moment, Castro's three-year-old daughter, sitting in the gallery with her mother, was shown on the giant television monitor behind Castro repeatedly flipping her hair. The crowd began to laugh at this adorable child's antic. Castro was clearly perplexed by this unexpected interruption. Afterward, Castro said that he was startled and thought, "What? You are not supposed to laugh at this part" (quoted in "Julian Castro's Daughter," 2012). This distraction was noise, an interruption in the effective transmission of Castro's message to his audience, illustrating that public speaking is truly a transactional process.

Defining communication as a **transactional** process means that the speaker is both a sender and a receiver, not merely a sender or a receiver. (Listeners are likewise sender-receivers.) As you give a speech, you receive *feedback* or responses, mostly nonverbal, from listeners. This feedback *influences* you while you are speaking. In Julian Castro's situation, he was distracted by the crowd's response to his daughter's hair-flipping. Transactional communication also means that there is more to a speech than the *content* (information) of your message. You develop a *relationship*, an association, with audience members as you present your speech. If they like you, they may listen to you; if they dislike you, they may not. For example, I had a Vietnamese student in one of my public speaking classes whose English was difficult to understand. He was genuinely enthusiastic when giving his speeches, however, and he was universally well liked by the class. So, whenever he gave a presentation, classmates would strain to discern what he was saying, and they always gave him a rousing ovation after each speech, even though I am certain only the gist of his message, at best, was comprehended.

Effective public speaking blends excellent content with a strong audience connection. Neither one by itself is sufficient. A well-constructed speech may fail if either you or your message does not resonate with listeners. Conversely, a strong connection with your audience may not compensate adequately for a poorly constructed, rambling, or indecipherable speech.

Communication as Sharing Meaning: Making Sense

Public speaking as a communication act requires more than the mere transmission of a message from a speaker to receivers. The speaker hopes to share meaning with his or her listeners. **Shared meaning** occurs when both the speaker and receivers have mutual understanding of a message (Anderson & Ross, 1994). Something is viewed as "meaningless" when it makes no sense. For example, consider the story of a Catholic nun lecturing to her third-graders and conducting standard catechism drills. She repeatedly asked her students, "Who is God?" Her students were to respond in unison, "God is a supreme being." Finally, she decided to test the fruits of her patient labor and called on one of the boys in the class. When asked, "Who is God?" he promptly and proudly replied, "God is a string bean." Words were transmitted, but meaning was not shared. "Supreme being" to a third-grader is difficult to grasp as an abstract concept, but a "string bean" is a concrete understandable object, even if applying it to the divinity is theologically mysterious.

Similarly, a Civic Science survey revealed that 56% of 3,200 Americans opposed teaching "Arabic numbers" to school children (McCrae, 2019). Arabic numbers are simply numbers from 0 to 9. Apparently, respondents did not know this (words were transmitted but meaning was not shared), so they responded to the word *Arabic* only, considering it to be a negative term.

Sharing meaning requires that you tailor your speech to your audience's ability to understand your intended message. Technical terminology or highly abstract presentations well beyond the knowledge and background of your listeners may merely confuse them, making your speech fairly pointless. "Geek speak" can leave the casual user of technology drowning in a sea of acronyms and jargon.

Sharing meaning between cultures poses its own unique problems. Accurate translations between languages are notoriously difficult. Electrolux, a Scandinavian manufacturer, discovered this when it tried to sell its vacuum cleaners in the United States with the slogan "Nothing sucks like an Electrolux." In preparation for the 2008 Summer Olympics in Beijing, China, notoriously poor translations featured on English signs had to be revised. "Beijing Anus Hospital" was changed to "Beijing Proctology Hospital," and "Deformed

PHOTO 1.5: Words matter, and in this case an incorrect, and weird, message might be shared. What do you think the intended message might be, because it certainly isn't to encourage swimmers to swallow water?

Man Toilet," thankfully, was changed to "Disabled Person Toilet" (Boudreau, 2007). Soon after the 9/11 terrorist attacks on the United States, George W. Bush observed during a press conference that "this crusade, this war on terrorism, is going to take a while." Bush used "crusade" to mean a vigorous action, but crusade is an explosively offensive word in the Muslim world, conjuring images of the historic clashes between Christians and Muslims. There was a huge outcry around the world from those who feared a renewed "clash of civilizations" provoked by the thought of a new crusade (Ford, 2001). Recognizing his verbal gaffe, Bush immediately dropped the term in future speeches and press conferences.

Sharing meaning nonverbally between cultures can be equally problematic (Cotton, 2013; Manolaki, 2016). World leaders, diplomats, and members of the business community have to be conscious of potentially embarrassing gestural misunderstandings when giving speeches. The A-OK and thumbs-up signs can be offensive gestures in many parts of the world. Raising the index finger to signify "one," as Americans often do to signify "We're number one," means "two" in Italy, so the gesture becomes "We're number two," a less satisfying source of celebratory pride. In Japan, however, the upright thumb means "five" (counting

PHOTO 1.6: The thumbs-up gesture does not have a universal meaning of "good job" or a sign of approval. In Australia, Greece, and much of the Middle East, it means the offensive "up yours."

begins with the index finger, and the thumb is the last digit). Nodding the head up and down means "yes" in the United States, and shaking it side to side means "no." In Bulgaria, Turkey, Iran, and Bengal, however, it is the reverse. In Greece, tipping the head back abruptly means "no," but the same gesture in India means "yes." (Nod your head if you understand all of this.)

In review, communication is a transactional process of sharing meaning with others. Public speaking as a communicative act is transactional because as a speaker you both send messages to listeners and receive messages (feedback) from your audience members. You influence your listeners and they influence you as this constantly changing, dynamic process of sharing meaning unfolds.

Identifying and explaining public speaking as an act of communication, however, does not tell you how to become a competent public speaker. Many books, both academic and mass market, have been written that attempt to do just that. What they often have in common is extensive recipes with a narrow focus for improving your public speaking, but they are devoid of a strong theoretical model for such proffered advice. *This makes the advice seem more personal opinion and individual taste than sound practice based on research.*

In contrast, the communication competence model is a well-conceived theoretical model grounded in solid reasoning and research. It should serve as your overarching guide to public speaking excellence. Defining what it is and how to achieve it generally are the next points of focus.

DEFINING COMMUNICATION COMPETENCE IN PUBLIC SPEAKING

Communication competence *is engaging in communication with others that is perceived to be both effective and appropriate in a given context* (Spitzberg, 2000). This section defines what it means to be both effective and appropriate when giving a public speech.

Effectiveness: Achieving Goals

Effectiveness is the degree to which speakers have progressed toward the achievement of their goals. In public speaking, you have general goals or purposes that you hope to achieve well, such as to inform, persuade, celebrate, entertain, inspire, or give tribute.

Degrees of Effectiveness: From Deficiency to Proficiency   Some of you would rather be dipped in molasses and strapped to an anthill than give a public speech in front of your peers. Yet giving a speech to an audience of strangers may invite no more than mild concern for success. Competence varies by degrees from highly proficient to severely deficient depending on the current set of circumstances. Thus, you may see yourself as moderately skillful giving a well-prepared informative speech, but woefully deficient giving an inspirational speech. We are more to less competent, not either competent or incompetent. Labeling someone a "competent speaker" makes a judgment of that individual's degree of proficiency *in a particular speaking context*, but it does not identify an immutable characteristic of that person.

Great speakers are not born that way; they become great, sometimes without realizing their potential until their hidden talent emerges unexpectedly. For example, a student in my public speaking class who experienced some trepidation about giving speeches gave a terrific persuasive presentation that argued for a smoking ban on campus. I encouraged her to present this speech to various decision-making bodies, which she did somewhat reluctantly. Her speech improved with each rendition, and it became so powerful that it provoked a campus-wide debate, and ultimately produced her desired result. When students express frustration at their perceived "powerlessness," I relate this story to exemplify the "power of one."

Even more astounding, Swedish teenager Greta Thunberg became an international sensation when her dogged attempt to alarm the world about climate change provoked worldwide youth demonstrations. What began as a one-person strike from school attendance displayed in front of the Swedish parliament building, six months later burgeoned into nearly 1.6 million young people in 133 countries demonstrating by leaving school as Thunberg encouraged (Haynes, 2019). Thunberg ultimately addressed the Houses of Parliament in London, the 2019 World Economic Forum in Davos, the United Nations COP24 conference, and the EU Parliament in Strasbourg, among other august bodies. She appeared on the cover of *Time* magazine, and she was nominated for a Nobel Peace Prize. One diminutive 16-year-old started a worldwide movement of protest (Knight, 2019). Never underestimate the potential power of public speaking (*see access to link of her speech at end of chapter*).

Audience Orientation: You Are Not Talking to Yourself   To be effective, the key focus of any speech has to be on your audience. Topics that interest you, for example, may cause your classmates to do a face plant onto their desks. A speaking style that is florid with colorful language and weighted with complicated sentence structure and sophisticated vocabulary may confuse and frustrate listeners whose native language is not English.

Audience orientation can be complicated by today's ready access to information through multiple forms of media transmission. You may be speaking to an immediate audience present in front of you, but your speech may be transmitted to additional remote audiences, especially if it is posted on YouTube. For example, University of Iowa college student Zach Wahls gave a powerful three-minute speech to the Iowa State Legislature that was subsequently posted on YouTube and viewed more than 19 million times (Grim, 2014) (*see access to link at end of chapter*). Wahls's speech became one of the most talked-about public addresses ever presented by a college student.

Your topic choice, your purpose in speaking, the organizational structure and development of your speech, your style and delivery, and your use of supporting materials all must keep a focus on your audience's needs, views, and expectations. For example, *your first class speech* might be to introduce yourself (*see an example speech on anxiety in Chapter 2*). Your student audience is unlikely to find a long, rambling speech interesting. Provide relevant, interesting information about yourself. Basic background, such as your age, place of birth, length of time in your present location, places you have visited, reasons why you are in college, educational major, what you consider to be fun, what makes you laugh, and what you plan for a career are just some possible disclosures you might share with your audience. You want to be brief, conversational in style and delivery, interesting, and organized, because that is what your audience likely expects. Also, definitely don't read your personal introduction. That only makes it appear that you are your own intimate stranger who can't remember basic details about your biography.

Appropriateness: Speaking by the Rules

Appropriateness is behavior that is perceived to be legitimate and fits the speaking context (Spitzberg, 2000). **Context** is the environment in which communication occurs. Context is composed of who communicates what to whom, why they are communicating a message, where it is presented, and when and how it is transmitted. For example, a religious leader is unlikely to use verbal obscenity during a sermon in a place of worship. To do otherwise would likely cause offense. A student leader, however, speaking to a student audience that has congregated in the campus quad may use some verbal obscenity to intensify his or her message without necessarily causing offense. Such language may even be viewed as more honest and credible (Feldman et al., 2017). When you change the elements of context, you change the rules that determine appropriateness.

Every communication context is guided by rules. A **rule** "is a prescription that indicates what behavior is obligated, prohibited or preferred in a given context" (Shimanoff, 2009, p. 861). For example, college instructors take for granted that students would not interrupt the flow of a lecture by talking inappropriately with fellow students. This is an implicit rule, meaning one that is assumed but not stated directly. Occasionally, however, this implicit rule has to be made explicit, identified directly, to students whose enthusiasm for casual conversation outweighs their ardor for the classroom task of listening to the professor's lecture.

The relationship between speaking context and rules is often very apparent but not always observed. Weddings, for example, all too often provide opportunities for members of the wedding party, relatives, or friends to offer cringe-worthy toasts to the bride and groom. Toasted on too much alcohol, they make sexually suggestive comments, use vulgar language, and generally

PHOTO 1.7: Comedian Michelle Wolf caused a huge controversy at the White House Correspondents' Dinner in 2018 regarding the appropriateness of her remarks (*See access to link at end of chapter*).

give an R-rated speech to a G-rated audience that usually includes young children. Despite obvious signals from offended listeners, the pickled presenters plod ever onward apparently unaware or unconcerned about their inappropriate behavior.

In general, competent public speaking requires both appropriateness and effectiveness. In the next section, global ways to do both are discussed.

ACHIEVING COMPETENT PUBLIC SPEAKING

The appropriateness and effectiveness of your public speaking can be improved in a variety of ways. This section offers five general ways (see Figure 1.1).

FIGURE 1.1: Communication Competence Model.

Knowledge: Learning the Rules

Achieving communication competence begins with knowledge of the rules that create behavioral expectations, and knowing what is likely to work effectively given the rules of the situation. There are no sacred, universal rules applicable to every speech situation, so such rules are contextual. In class, for example, rules operating for listeners typically include focusing on the speaker, not on your text messages, Facebook page, or social media; being an active listener; never heckling a classmate giving a speech lest you be given the same unwanted treatment; and not talking to classmates while a speech is being presented.

Rules, of course, can be changed. For example, research shows that rules regarding the use of swear words have changed dramatically. Swear words are 28 times more likely to appear in books recently published in English than books published in the early 1950s (Twenge et al., 2017). Whatever the prevailing rules, however, *communication becomes inappropriate if it violates rules when such violations could be averted without sacrificing a goal by choosing alternative communication behaviors.*

Skills: Showing Not Just Knowing

A **communication skill** is the ability to perform a communication behavior effectively and repeatedly. Clearly, fluently, concisely, eloquently, and confidently speaking to an audience are examples of such skill. Knowledge about public speaking without speaking skills will not produce competence. You can read this entire text and excel on every exam, but there is no substitute for skill gained by the practice and experience of speaking in front of an audience. Knowing that speaking with long pauses and vocal fillers such as *um, uh, like,* and *you know* is unskillful and ineffective does not automatically translate into an ability to speak fluently. You will continue using vocal fillers unless you hone your speaking skills with practice.

Sensitivity: Developing Receptive Accuracy

Can you accurately perceive the difference between a look of disgust, anger, joy, agreement, frustration, or contempt from members of your audience? **Sensitivity** is *receptive accuracy* whereby you can detect, decode, and comprehend signals in your social environment (Bernieri, 2001). Sensitivity can help you adapt your messages to a particular audience in an appropriate and effective manner (Hall & Bernieri, 2001).

A major aspect of sensitivity is being mindful, not mindless, about your communication. You are **mindful** when you think about your communication and concentrate on changing what you do to become more effective. You are **mindless** when you are not cognizant of your communication with others or simply do not care, so no improvement is likely (Griffin, 2012). This text encourages mindfulness at every stage of speech preparation and presentation.

Commitment: Acquiring a Passion for Excellence

Commitment is a passion for excellence—that is, accepting nothing less than the best that you can be and dedicating yourself to achieving that excellence. To exhibit commitment, *attitude is as important as aptitude.* In sports, athletes develop a high level of skill when they commit themselves to hard work, study, and practice. Academic success also does not come from lackluster effort. You make it a priority in your life. The same holds true for competent public speaking. You have to want to improve, to change, and to grow more proficient, and you must be willing to put in the effort required to excel. You do not wait until the last minute to think about your speech, and you do not try to "wing it" with no preparation. "Winging it" just means flying blind right into the mountaintop of failure.

Ethics: Determining the Right and Wrong of Speaking

Humans ponder the moral implications of their behavior. It is one of the characteristics that separates humans from the beasts-as-feasts daily killing field that occurs on the African Serengeti. Consequently, you should consider whether your communication in the public speaking arena is ethically justifiable. **Ethics** is a system for judging the moral correctness of human behavior by weighing that behavior against an agreed-upon set of standards that determine right from wrong.

Ethical Standards: Judging Moral Correctness of Speech   The National Communication Association's "Credo for Ethical Communication" identifies five ethical standards ("National Communication Association Reaffirms," 2017):

1. **Honesty.** "There is no more fundamental ethical value than honesty" (Josephson, 2002). Plagiarism—stealing someone else's words and ideas and attributing them to oneself—is clearly dishonest and is discussed in the next section.

2. **Respect.** Treating others as you would want to be treated is a central guiding ethical standard in "virtually all of the major religious and moral systems" (Jaksa & Pritchard, 1994, p. 101). Consequently, you should be respectful when others are speaking. Don't do an assignment for another class, for example, when other students are giving speeches.

3. **Fairness.** A debate in which one side was allowed to speak for 15 minutes but the opposing side was permitted only 5 minutes would be labeled as unfair. Fairness requires equal treatment and opportunity (Knights, 2016). "Playing by the rules" means avoiding favoritism. Whatever the rules, they should be applied without prejudice.

4. **Choice.** Our communication should strive to allow people to make their own choices, free of coercion (Cheney et al., 2011). Persuasion allows free choice among available options. Coercion forces decisions without permitting individuals to think or act for themselves. Shouting down speakers so they cannot give their speech is a bullying tactic that denies choice. The National Communication Association "condemns intimidation, whether by powerful majorities or strident minorities, which attempts to restrict free expression" ("National Communication Association Reaffirms," 2017).

5. **Responsibility.** You have an obligation to consider the consequences of your speeches on others (Jensen, 1997). Competent speakers must concern themselves with more than merely what works. For example, provoking listeners to engage in unlawful violence is irresponsible.

PHOTO 1.8: Heckling denies free choice by silencing the speaker. Can heckling ever be ethical?

In the abstract, these standards may seem straightforward and noncontroversial, but any list of standards for judging the ethics of public speaking, applied without exceptions, is bound to run into difficulty. For example, heckling a speaker is disrespectful, but is there never an occasion when heckling is the only means of communicating disagreement with a speaker? The Occupy movement's tactic in which an individual stands up in an audience during a speaker's presentation and calls out "mic check" has created quite a controversy since its common use in 2011–2012. As the original heckler barks out a sentence in protest to the main featured speaker, fellow protesters repeat each sentence to amplify their message. Congresswoman Nancy Pelosi was interrupted by the tactic in a September 19, 2017, news conference on the DACA immigration issue (see Sernoffsky, 2017, to access video of the event). On March 6, 2018, Lewis and Clark college students in Portland, Oregon, used the tactic to silence controversial ethics professor Christina Hoff Sommers (Soave, 2018). Protesters who use the mic check tactic argue that those individuals who are powerful easily gain access to the speaker's podium to express their ideas, while the less powerful must fight for the right to be heard (Kelp-Stebbins & Schifani, 2015). Targets of the mic check tactic repudiate it as blatant censorship.

This form of protest adds an ethical twist to the freedom of speech dialectic. The mic check tactic brings into focus a clash of ethical standards,

PHOTO 1.9: Some speeches are centered on ethical considerations. Here, former linebacker for the Super Bowl champion Baltimore Ravens, Brendon Ayanbadejo, an outstanding student of mine at Cabrillo College before he went on to UCLA and NFL All-Pro status, stands up for marriage equality based on fairness, respect, and choice. He was the first NFL athlete to take such a stand.

specifically: respect, freedom of choice, fairness, and responsibility. Applying ethical standards is not always clear-cut and obvious. Despite these difficulties, however, all five ethical standards are strong values in our culture, and they serve as important guidelines for ethical public speaking.

Plagiarism: Never Inconsequential   With the explosive growth of the Internet and the easy availability of whole speeches by others, student *plagiarism*, the dishonest theft of another person's words, has become a significant problem (Ali, 2016; Fields, 2017). As the ready availability of technological tools to lift material in whole or in part from the work of others increases, the likelihood that plagiarism will occur also increases (Roberts & Wasieleski, 2012).

There are essentially two kinds of plagiarism. The first is *selective plagiarism*, or stealing portions of someone else's speech or writings. That is bad enough, but a second kind, *blatant plagiarism*—when entire speeches are stolen and presented as one's own—is far more serious. Some instances of plagiarism can seem harmless. For example, you hear a speaker offer this bit of drollery at a graduation ceremonial speech: "Lord, help me to be the person that my dog thinks I am." It seems that you've heard this before. Then it hits you; it was on a bumper sticker. No big deal, right? Relatively speaking, this qualifies as a minor example of plagiarism, but the speaker still stole it even if the author cannot be cited. If someone in the audience recognizes that this unattributed bumper sticker humor is not original, it calls into question whether other parts of the speech were also pilfered, and the speaker's credibility may suffer. The speaker could simply state, "I saw a bumper sticker the other day that said . . . ."?

Also, be careful that when you *paraphrase*—when you put the ideas of someone else in your own words—that you are not merely changing a word or two. Such *pseudo-paraphrasing* is still plagiarizing the main structure of the quotation. For example:

Original quote: "I don't intend to give a long speech. Well, because Socrates gave a long speech and his friends killed him" (Taken from the movie *New Year's Eve*).

Pseudo-paraphrasing: "I don't plan to give a long speech because Socrates did and his friends murdered him." This is still plagiarism because only a few words have been replaced with synonyms. In a case such as this, just attribute the quotation to the movie script. Such citation of the source doesn't diminish the cleverness or utility of the line.

Stealing someone's words is pilfering a part of that person's identity. That is never an inconsequential act.

SUMMARY

Competent public speaking is an essential element of any democratic society. It also provides many practical benefits. The communication competence model serves as a theoretical guide throughout this discussion of practical public speaking. Public speakers must make choices regarding the appropriateness and likely effectiveness of topics, attention strategies, style and delivery, evidence, and persuasive strategies. When you are giving a speech, you must be sensitive to the signals sent from an audience that indicate lack of interest, disagreement, confusion, enjoyment, support, and a host of additional reactions. This allows you to make adjustments during the speech, if necessary. Finally, the effectiveness of a speech must be tempered by ethical concerns. Prepare in advance so there is no temptation to plagiarize as a shortcut.

TED TALKS AND YOUTUBE VIDEOS

Noise: "Julian Castro's Daughter Flips Hair during DNC Keynote Speech"; "Daddy's Girl! Julian Castro's Daughter, Carina Victoria, Flipping Hair during DNC Keynote Speech"

Free Speech Movement: "Mario Savio Speech: Berkeley, January 1964";

"Mario Savio Speech, short excerpt: December 2, 1964"

Audience Orientation: "Zach Wahls's: 'Two Mothers' Speech"

Appropriateness: "Michelle Wolf Complete Remarks at 2018 White House Correspondents' Dinner" (crude at times)

Power Of Public Speaking: "Greta Thunberg at UN Climate Change COP24 Conference"

Public Speaking And The Power Of One (Greta Thunberg): "Now I Am Speaking to the Whole World"

For relevant links to these TED Talks and YouTube videos, see the *Practically Speaking* Companion Website: www.oup.com/he/rothwell-ps3e. You can also gain access by typing the title of the speech reference into a Google search window or by doing the same on the TED Talks or YouTube sites.

CHECKLIST

- [ ] Gain knowledge of the rules underlying what works and what does not in specific public speaking contexts.

- [ ] Practice speaking skills.

- [ ] Strengthen your commitment to becoming a competent public speaker.

- [ ] Enhance your sensitivity to audience feedback by being mindful of apparent weaknesses that need correcting.

- [ ] Uphold ethical public speaking standards.

CRITICAL THINKING QUESTIONS

1. Should Holocaust deniers and White nationalists be banned from speaking at public colleges and universities? How about Muslim speakers, atheists, and those defending Black Lives Matter? Should any provocative speaker who incites strong emotions and risks potential violent reactions from an audience be banned from speaking?

2. What principle should guide any determination of who should be
    allowed to speak and who should be banned? Where do you draw the
    line between permissible and impermissible speech?

3. How should racist epithets uttered by a speaker during a campus event
    be handled?

NOTE: Online **student resources**, such as practice tests, flashcards, and other
activities, can be accessed at www.oup.com/he/rothwell-ps3e

Speech Anxiety

Rickey Henderson, longtime baseball star for the Oakland Athletics, fretted before giving a speech at the ceremony inducting him into baseball's Hall of Fame at Cooperstown on July 26, 2009. As he described it, giving a speech, especially of this magnitude, is like "putting a tie too tight around your neck . . . I've sweated to death about it and then wondered why" (quoted in Steward, 2009, pp. C1, C5). Henderson wisely sought help from speech instructor Earl Robinson at Laney College. He also received critiques from Robinson's students, who were taking a summer public speaking class and heard Henderson's speech. He practiced his speech for two weeks. One journalist, who listened to Henderson's 14-minute presentation at the Hall of Fame ceremony, offered this assessment: "He seized the stage in Cooperstown, N.Y., and commanded it as he did as a player. . . . He wasn't perfect, but he was pretty close. Moreover, he was gracious, highly effective, and suitably entertaining" (Poole, 2009, pp. 1A, 6A). Henderson "followed up his eloquent 2009 Hall of Fame speech in Cooperstown by nailing another address to the Coliseum crowd," in a ceremony to rename a major league park as "Rickey Henderson Field" in Oakland, California in 2017 (Steward, 2017).

The purpose of this chapter is to discuss speech anxiety as a potential problem that you can address effectively, as Henderson did. Toward that end, this chapter discusses (1) the magnitude of the challenge of speech anxiety, (2) its symptoms, (3) its causes, and (4) potential solutions.

SPEECH ANXIETY AS A CHALLENGE

Speech anxiety is fear of public speaking and the nervousness that accompanies that fear. Why address speech anxiety so early in this text and devote a chapter to it? There are two reasons. First, when a speech assignment is given, the immediate concern you may have is fear of speaking in front of an audience, especially to a gathering of your peers. This fear can negatively affect your academic performance, not just in a speech class, but in any class that assigns an oral presentation (Bodie, 2010). In fact, the instant a speech assignment is announced, many students manifest high levels of anxiety (Jackson et al., 2017). This anxiety can preoccupy your thoughts and adversely affect your ability to prepare your speech. Some students may drop a public speaking course early in the term if speech anxiety is not addressed promptly.

A second reason to address speech anxiety now is that managing it effectively requires specific preparation. If you wait until you actually give your speech before considering what steps need to be taken to manage your anxiety, it is usually too late. Simply put, you need a clear plan for managing your speech anxiety, one that is developed very early in the public speaking process.

Pervasiveness of Speech Anxiety: A Common Experience

Mark Twain once remarked, "There are two types of speakers: those who are nervous and those who are liars." Overstated perhaps, but fear of public speaking is widespread (Pull, 2012). A survey by Chapman University of 1,500 respondents puts the fear factor at 62% ("The Chapman University Survey," 2015). This same study also showed fear of public speaking as greater than fear of heights (61%), drowning (47%), flying (39%), and, yes, zombies (18%). The fear of public speaking holds true for both face-to-face and web-based, online speeches given to remote audiences (Campbell & Larson, 2012).

A substantial majority of experienced speakers also have anxiety before presentations. Famous speakers throughout history such as Cicero, Daniel Webster, Abraham Lincoln, Eleanor Roosevelt, Winston Churchill, and Gloria Steinem conquered their significant fear of public speaking by taking every opportunity to mount the speaker's platform. One study by Gordon Goodman of 136 experienced, professional actors found that 84% had suffered stage fright (Salomon, 2011). Actor Harrison Ford has feared public speaking his entire career. Even when the character he was playing in a movie was required to make a speech as part of the script (e.g., *Air Force One*), he admitted to feeling speech anxiety (Bailey, 2008), but he learned to manage it (*see access to Ford's 2018 "Global Climate" speech at end of chapter*). Other celebrities who experience performance anxiety include Adele, Ariana Grande, Beyoncé, Lady Gaga, Lorde, Katy Perry,

PHOTO 2.1: Actress Emma Watson admitted, "I was just terrified," when she gave her "gender equality" speech at the United Nations, but she was widely acclaimed for her moving presentation (*see access to link at end of chapter*). Speech anxiety can be effectively managed.

Rihanna, Sia, Jennifer Lawrence, Matt Damon, George Clooney, and Benedict Cumberbatch (Hickson, 2016). Even college instructors must manage it, and they do (Gardner & Leak, 1994).

Intensity of Speech Anxiety: Fate Worse Than Death?

Some surveys show that many people fear public speaking more than they fear death (Bruskin-Goldring Report, 1993; Thomson, 2008), prompting Jerry Seinfeld to quip that if you attend a funeral you would prefer being in the casket to delivering the eulogy. These "death before public speaking" survey findings, however, are dubious at best (Davies, 2011; Tuttar, 2019). Fear of public speaking might be on one's mind as a more immediate stressor than death, but if forced to choose between imminent death or an imminent public speech, who would really choose death? Nevertheless, some individuals' experience intense speech anxiety, and it should not be glibly diminished in importance. I experienced firsthand the challenge presented by speech anxiety (see **"First Speech"**), but I learned to manage my anxiety, and so can you.

CARTOON 2.1: The "death before public speaking" survey results are misleading. Who would actually choose death to avoid giving a speech? Nevertheless, irrational fear of public speaking can make it seem like a fate worse than death, and it should be taken very seriously. This makes it an issue worth addressing right away.

First Speech: Sample Narrative Speech of Introduction on Speech Anxiety

This sample speech seeks to accomplish two purposes: (1) to humanize the challenge of speech anxiety and its significance by telling a story of my own battle with this fear, and (2) to provide an example of a possible first speech of introduction to help you get started quickly without needing to read the entire text first.

Let's assume that your first speech's assigned *purpose* is to inform the class about a significant life experience. This may not be the exact purpose for your first assigned class speech, but no matter, because this sample identifies key points to note for any initial speech. This purpose calls for a narrative informative speech. A narrative speech tells a story and typically has three components: (1) *challenge,* (2) *struggle,* and (3) *resolution* (Friend, 2013), as you will see in this example.

(continued)

[CHALLENGE] I was a painfully shy child. Had the psychiatric diagnosis "social phobic" existed when I grew up, I am sure that I would have been thusly labeled. Strangers scared me. Just walking from elementary school sometimes turned into a tortuous trail to my home. If I saw a stranger walking toward me on the sidewalk, I would take a detour so I would not have to feel the mounting anxiety as the stranger approached. With enough strangers on my path home, the numerous detours could turn into a comical journey of abrupt twists and turns. My mom sometimes asked upon my eventual arrival, "What took you so long?"

My initial experience with public speaking starkly clashed with my social phobia. In eighth grade, my teacher assigned every student a five-minute speech in front of the class on one of the presidents of the United States. I agonized for two weeks before my presentation. I wrote my speech on cards, practiced it countless times, all the while hoping that a massive earthquake would hit Los Angeles, my residence at the time, forcing a cancellation of my speech. No such luck awaited me. Ultimately, I gave my speech, petrified but pleased that I didn't faint, vomit, or in any other way embarrass myself before my peers. I also vowed never to give another speech in my lifetime.

[STRUGGLE] My parents, however, foiled my plan. They felt that since I was so shy, joining the high school debate team would be a growth experience. I was stunned. I contemplated contacting Child Protective Services. Surely this qualified as child abuse. Acquiescing to their insistence that I join the debate team after much fussing and fuming, I showed up for the first meeting and was partnered with a first-year student named Jack. Turned out that he also hated the idea of participating on the debate team, so we devised what we thought was a foolproof strategy to sabotage our parents' plan for us. We would be so awful, so inept in our first debate, that the humiliation would engender compassion, and no small concern for the family's good name, and they would allow us to quit the team. It didn't work out that way. Oh, we were absolutely terrible in our first and only debate in a practice round against a terrific girls' team. Our opponents thrashed us, apparently feeling no pity for our pathetic performance.

[RESOLUTION] Embarrassed but weirdly triumphant, Jack and I showed our judge's ballot to our respective parents, fully expecting that after reading the voluminous negative comments, they would release us from our torment. Our plan failed. We were encouraged to "simply do our best." Jack and I decided afterwards that humiliating ourselves on a regular basis wasn't a particularly brilliant strategy after all, so we asked our school's senior team and our coach to teach us how to debate. Three weeks later, we participated in our first tournament and achieved unanticipated success. Who knew?

What's the moral of this story? Obviously, parents always know best! Okay, maybe not that. The real moral is that fear can act like a straitjacket restricting our choices. Had I not been required to face my fear of public speaking, unquestionably my life would have taken a much different path. I certainly would not have made speech and communication my life's profession. If, as a social phobic, I can overcome speech anxiety, so can any of you!

There are several key points to mention about this speech that warrant elaboration in ensuing chapters. The speech has a chronological organization— a specific sequence of events (see Chapter 8) that flows from its purpose (see Chapter 7). Several attention strategies are employed throughout, such as novelty and mild humor (see Chapter 6). Audiences respond when stories are well delivered (Karia, 2015). A conversational delivery works best for this type of personal, revelatory speech. It should not be delivered from a manuscript that can be disconnecting with listeners (see Chapter 10). Well-chosen examples that illustrate key points add vividness and texture to a speech (see Chapter 6). Finally, the length of the speech—approximately three minutes—is short and to the point (see Chapter 7). *This chapter will reveal the secrets of my success in overcoming severe speech anxiety.*

SYMPTOMS: FIGHT-OR-FLIGHT RESPONSE

Howard Goshorn observed, "The human brain is a wonderful thing. It operates from the moment you are born until you stand up to make a speech." "Going blank" is one of the most common concerns of novice speakers. Why does the human brain seem to stop working when giving a speech? Learning to manage your speech anxiety begins with identifying its common symptoms, and explaining why these symptoms occur. *Simply providing a laundry list of strategies for addressing speech anxiety offers no basis for understanding why some approaches work better than others, and why some commonly suggested approaches may be quite useless.*

Basic Symptoms: Your Body's Response to Threat

The physiological defense-alarm process triggered by stress is called the **fight-or-flight response** (Cannon, 1932). The fight-or-flight response produces a complex constellation of physiological symptoms. Some of the more pronounced symptoms are accelerated heartbeat and increased blood pressure that increase oxygen supply; blood vessel constriction in skin, skeletal muscles, and brain; increased perspiration; increased respiration; inhibited digestion; stimulated glucose release from the liver; increased blood flow away from extremities and to large muscles; stimulated adrenal gland activity; spleen release of red blood corpuscles; and bone marrow stimulation to produce white corpuscles (Cherry & Gans, 2018a).

Some of the more prominent corresponding verbal and nonverbal symptoms are quivering, tense voice and weak projection from constricted throat muscles; frequent dysfluencies such as "ums" and "uhs" and, of course, going blank from restricted blood flow to the brain causing confusion of thought; rigid, motionless posture from constricted muscles of legs and torso; and dry mouth from digestive system shutdown.

Appropriateness of Symptoms: Relevance to Public Speaking

The physiological symptoms of the fight-or-flight response make sense if you are about to grapple with a crazed grizzly or run with the bulls at Pamplona. Increased perspiration (cooling), respiration (oxygen), glucose (energy), and blood flow to major muscles (strength) would certainly help with the grappling and running. There are few times, however, in which fighting or fleeing would be an appropriate response to speech anxiety. Clothes saturated with perspiration, increased red and white corpuscles (for blood clotting and infection fighting), nausea, a pounding heart, a quivering voice, dry mouth, and rapid respiration are unnecessary and often distracting when making a speech—unless your life is in jeopardy, an unlikely classroom occurrence. Nevertheless, your sympathetic nervous system, which controls the fight-or-flight response, does not pick and choose relevant symptoms (Kuchinskas, 2008). When the response is triggered, you get the whole package. Thus, *the useful approach to speech anxiety is to moderate the fight-or-flight response, not hope to activate only selective symptoms.*

CAUSES OF DYSFUNCTIONAL ANXIETY

Dysfunctional speech anxiety occurs when the intensity of the fight-or-flight response prevents an individual from giving a speech effectively. **Functional speech anxiety** occurs when the fight-or-flight response is managed and stimulates an optimum presentation. *The degree of anxiety and your ability to manage it, not anxiety itself, determines the difference.* Low to moderate anxiety means you care about the quality of the speech. Anxiety can energize you and stimulate a more dynamic, exciting presentation (Star, 2018). Reframing your perception that speech anxiety can be beneficial can actually reduce your anxiety (Beltzer et al., 2014). So, if assessing how much anxiety is beneficial on a scale of 1 to 10, with 10 being you huddled in a corner of a room rocking in abject terror and 1 being a zombie-like state of complete indifference, you can benefit from about a 3 or 4 level of anxiety to begin your speech.

The first step in learning to maintain your anxiety at a functional level is to understand the causes of dysfunctional anxiety. Causes of dysfunctional speech anxiety fall primarily into two categories: self-defeating thoughts and anxiety-provoking situations.

PHOTOS 2.2 & 2.3: The fight-or-flight response is quite useful if you are running from the bulls at Pamplona, Spain. It is less useful when presenting a speech, unless managed effectively.

Self-Defeating Thoughts: Sabotaging Your Speech

Some individuals see giving a speech as a challenging and exciting opportunity, whereas others see it as an experience equivalent to being swallowed by a python. How you think about speaking to an audience will largely determine your level of speech anxiety (Bodie, 2010). *Self-defeating thoughts are grounded in the excessive concern that your audience will judge and reject you.* Turning down the volume of your dysfunctional self-talk is important.

Catastrophic Thinking: Fear of Failure   Wildly exaggerating the magnitude of potential failure is a common source of stress and anxiety (Ackrill, 2012). For example, minor problems of organization during a speech are magnified in the speaker's mind into graphic episodes of total incoherence and nonstop babbling.

Predictions of public speaking catastrophes are unrealistic because they are highly unlikely to occur. I personally have listened to more than 20,000 student speeches. I have witnessed some unimpressive presentations, but not more than a handful of these qualified as outright unforgettable disasters, and the obvious cause of the disaster in each case was a complete lack of preparation.

Catastrophic thinking, or catastrophizing as it is sometimes called (Legg, 2019), sees only failure, not an opportunity for exhilarating success produced by embracing challenges. Do not paralyze yourself with catastrophic, unrealistic thinking.

Perfectionist Thinking: No Mistakes Permitted   Perfectionists anguish over every perceived flaw, and they overgeneralize the significance of even minor defects (Jackson et al., 2017). For example:

"I tanked—I forgot to preview my main points."
"I feel so stupid. I kept mispronouncing the name of one of the experts I quoted."

CARTOON 2.2: Catastrophic thinking increases speech anxiety and magnifies minor mistakes into major mental meltdowns.

Flawless public speaking is an unreasonable goal. Even the most talented and experienced public speakers make occasional errors in otherwise riveting and eloquent speeches. Ironically, the imperfections so glaring to perfectionists usually go unnoticed by their audiences.

The Illusion of Transparency: Being Nervous about Looking Nervous   Speakers who experience high levels of anxiety often fall victim to the **illusion of transparency**—the overestimation of the extent to which audience members detect a speaker's nervousness (Dean, 2012). As difficult as it may be for you to believe, your anxiety is not as obvious as you may think it is (MacInnis et al., 2010). The speech by Zach Wahls referred to in the previous chapter is such a case. Wahls confessed on the *Ellen DeGeneres Show* that he was so nervous that he was shaking while presenting his "Two Mothers" speech to the Iowa state legislature (*see access to link at end of chapter*). You simply cannot tell this from looking at his speech on YouTube.

Nevertheless, this illusion of transparency greatly increases a speaker's anxiety. You become "nervous about looking nervous" (Savitsky & Gilovich, 2003, p. 619). Unlike telling a person not to be nervous about giving a speech, which

PHOTOS 2.4 & 2.5: Zach Wahls, despite considerable speech anxiety when he delivered his "Two Mothers" speech, learned to manage his fear and used his speaking skills to become a state senator from Iowa in 2018, garnering 78.5% of the vote (Garrand, 2018).

is unhelpful advice, informing a speaker about the illusion of transparency can free individuals from the cycle of anxiety and help them present better speeches because they worry less about appearing nervous (Jackson et al., 2017).

Desire for Complete Approval: Trying Not to Offend It is highly unlikely that you will please everyone who listens to your speech, particularly if you take a stand on a controversial issue. Few speeches are universally praised, even ones viewed as among the greatest speeches ever presented. Lincoln's Gettysburg Address, for example, was effusively praised by the *Springfield Republican* newspaper as "a perfect gem" that was "deep in feeling, compact in thought and expression, and tasteful and elegant in every word and comma" (quoted by Prochow, 1944, p. 17). The *Chicago Times*, however, editorialized: "The cheek of every American must tingle with shame as he reads the silly, flat and dishwatery utterances of the man who has to be pointed out to intelligent foreigners as the President of the United States" (quoted by Sandburg, 2002, p. 445).

Anxiety-Provoking Situations: Considering Context

Several anxiety-provoking situations are relevant to public speaking (Tsaousides, 2017a). There are three principal ones: novelty, conspicuousness, and types of speeches.

Novelty of the Speaking Situation: Uncertainty We often fear what is unpredictable or unfamiliar. For inexperienced speakers, the mere novelty of the speaking situation may trigger speech anxiety. Based on **uncertainty reduction theory,**

as you gain experience speaking in front of groups, the novelty wears off, uncertainty is reduced, and anxiety consequently diminishes because you gain a reservoir of knowledge from giving speeches that helps you handle almost any situation that might occur ("Uncertainty Reduction Theory," 2019).

Conspicuousness: The Spotlight Effect   When asked what causes their speech anxiety, most students identify being "on stage" or "in the spotlight." Being conspicuous, or the center of attention, can increase your anxiety (Cuncic, 2018a). Gaining confidence from experience speaking often to a variety of audiences large and small is a strong antidote for alleviating speech anxiety provoked by conspicuousness. This "spotlight effect" can also be mitigated by recognizing that there is a common tendency to overestimate the extent to which listeners are judging you while you speak (Jackson et al., 2017).

Types of Speeches: Varying Responses   Types of speeches combined with situational challenges affect whether you experience anxiety. Telling a story in front of a class of fellow students may give you no pause, but giving a lecture as a teaching demonstration while interviewing for an important job may be an anxiety-producing situation. Suddenly being asked to "say a few words" with no warning typically stirs greater anxiety than giving a more prepared speech (Witt & Behnke, 2006). Giving a speech to an audience hostile to your expressed point of view may also engender high levels of anxiety (Pertaub et al., 2002), but presenting in front of a highly supportive "classroom community" of students reduces anxiety (Swenson, 2011).

All of these causes of speech anxiety, both self-defeating thoughts and anxiety-provoking situations, can produce a spiraling effect that feeds on itself. *A key to managing your speech anxiety is to prevent the spiral of fear from ever occurring.* The next section takes a deep dive into the reservoir of effective strategies for preventing just such an occurrence.

STRATEGIES FOR MANAGING SPEECH ANXIETY

Many individuals, from famous actors to celebrities, have suggested strategies for managing speech anxiety. These include swearing at your audience backstage, sticking a pin in your backside (pain as diversion), and imagining members of your audience naked or clothed only in their underwear or in diapers. Although dubious solutions, these suggestions may work for you, but there is no good evidence that they have widespread application. If there were such evidence, speech instructors across the nation would be passing out pins to their anxious students.

These suggestions are unquestionably limited at best because they are diversionary tactics rather than strategies that directly address the primary causes of speech anxiety. This section discusses several substantial ways to manage your speech anxiety that are supported by research and address the main causes.

Prepare and Practice: Transforming Novelty into Familiarity

As in most social situations, whether making small talk with strangers at parties or playing a musical instrument in front of a crowd, you tend to be less anxious when you are confident of your skills. You fear making a fool of yourself when you do not know what you are doing. First and foremost, do not delay preparing and practicing your speech until the night before you give it. For some, in the words of author Rita Mae Brown, "If it weren't for the last minute, nothing would get done." Don't wait until the last minute because procrastination increases anxiety (Boyes, 2013a).

When you are adequately prepared, you have removed most of the novelty and uncertainty from the speaking situation. This reduces your anxiety. So prepare your speech meticulously. Begin the necessary research well in advance, organize and outline your speech carefully, and practice your presentation. Practice your speech while taking a shower. Give it in your car on your way to class. Give it to your dog; they are eager listeners (cats not so much). *Practice, practice, practice!* When you have practiced your speech "enough," practice it again. Do a dress rehearsal for friends or family members, or video record your performance and play it back so you can study parts to improve.

Giving speeches to a variety of audiences will gradually build your confidence and reduce your anxiety (Finn et al., 2009). Speaking experience, of course, will not reduce anxiety if you stumble from one traumatic disaster to the next. If you make speech after speech, ill prepared and untrained, your dread of public speaking will likely become dysfunctional.

Poor physiological preparation also will sabotage the most carefully prepared and practiced speech. You require appropriate nutrition to manage the stress of public speaking. Do not deliver a speech on an empty stomach. Complex carbohydrates such as whole grains, pastas, and legumes work well to stoke your energy, but eat lightly. You want blood traveling to your brain, not to your stomach. Avoid empty-calorie foods such as doughnuts. High intake of caffeine, simple sugars, and nicotine can stoke the physiological symptoms of fight-or-flight (increased heart rate, sweating). Alcohol and tranquilizers are also counterproductive solutions. Alcohol restricts oxygen to your brain and dulls mental acuity, resulting in poor performance (Stevens et al., 2017). Tranquilizers can send you on a Valium vacation in which you feel pleasantly numb but mentally dumb. You never want to take even a mild amphetamine. Speed kills a speech. It will increase your heart rate beyond what anxiety already induces.

Finally, preparation also can include physical exercise on a sustained basis. Research shows that making a habit of working out prepares your body to deal with stressors such as an impending speech (Reynolds, 2009).

There is no substitute for preparation and practice. If you do both, most of your anxiety will melt away, and your confidence will soar.

Gain Realistic Perspective: Rational Not Irrational Thinking

Understanding the progression of your speech anxiety can give you a realistic perspective on what is a reasonable amount to expect. It will improve naturally. There are four phases to speech anxiety symptoms (Witt et al., 2006). There is the *anticipation phase*, when your symptoms elevate just prior to giving your speech. The *confrontation phase* occurs when you face the audience and begin to speak. Here the fight-or-flight symptoms can increase. Next the *adaptation phase* kicks in, about 60 seconds into the speech. During this phase, anxiety symptoms steadily diminish, reaching a more comfortable level within a couple of minutes. Finally, there is the *release stage*—the 60 seconds immediately following the finish of the speech.

Recognizing that your anxiety will diminish dramatically and quickly as you speak should provide some comfort (see Figure 2.1). By learning to monitor your adaptation, you can accelerate the process. As you begin to notice your heart rate diminishing, mentally say to yourself, "It's getting better already . . . and better . . . and better." *Anxiety levels, even for the inexperienced, high-anxiety speaker, will diminish rapidly during the course of a speech.*

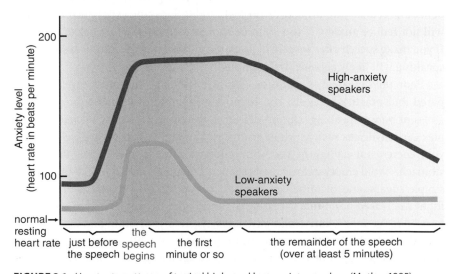

FIGURE 2.1: Heart rate patterns of typical high- and low-anxiety speakers (Motley, 1995).

Another aspect of gaining realistic perspective is learning to recognize the difference between rational and irrational speech anxiety. A colleague of mine, Darrell Beck, concocted a simple formula for determining the difference: *the severity of the feared occurrence times the probability of the feared occurrence.*

Severity is approximated by imagining what would happen if catastrophic failure did occur. Typically, when I ask my students for their worst imagined case of speech anxiety, they offer examples such as stuttering, sweating, knees and hands shaking violently, forgetting everything, even fainting or vomiting in front of the class. Imagine all of this occurring, not just one or two of these manifestations of catastrophic failure, but the entire mess. Would you hide from friends and family, afraid to show your face? Would you drop out of college? At most, you might drop the class, but even this choice is unlikely. Students are an understanding lot (this is not high school), and you will have other opportunities in class to redeem yourself. Disappointment or mild embarrassment is about as severe as the consequences get.

Then consider the probability of this nightmare scenario happening. It is highly improbable that all of these feared occurrences would transpire. No one has ever fainted or vomited in my classes despite the thousands of speeches I have witnessed. If you stutter and it is not an actual speech pathology, you can gain control by deliberately slowing your rate of speech and carefully enunciating your words. Other occurrences are mitigated with conscientious preparation and practice. When you consider the probability of the "worst-case scenario," you should realize that there is not much to concern you.

Even individuals for whom English is a second language will benefit from gaining a realistic perspective on their speech anxiety. Giving a speech in a second language can increase anxiety (Tan Chin Keok, 2010). There is an unrealistic expectation that English should be spoken perfectly. I have witnessed hundreds of speeches by non-native speakers of English. Never once has an audience of college students been rude to that speaker because his or her English was not perfect. Preparation and practice are especially critical for non-native speakers of English. *Very short speeches, even 30-second presentations on a small portion of a speech for class, given to friends or family members just for practice can be very helpful* (Seim et al., 2010). Working yourself into a lather over an impending speech simply lacks a realistic perspective.

Adopt a Noncompetitive Communication Orientation: Reframing

Desiring complete approval, engaging in perfectionist thinking, and fretting over your conspicuousness onstage all occur when you view public speaking as a **performance**—an attempt to satisfy an audience of critics whose members are focused on evaluating your presentation. No speech instructor expects silver-tongued oratory from novice speakers. You are expected to make mistakes, especially during your first few speeches. Speech classes are learning laboratories, not speech tournaments.

Reframe the performance orientation with a communication orientation. The **communication orientation** focuses on making your message clear and interesting to your listeners. You will perform more effectively as a speaker if you move away from the competitive performance orientation (Motley, 2011). Your speaking style and delivery will seem more natural, less forced and stiff. When conversing with a friend or stranger, you rarely notice your delivery, gestures, and posture. You are intent on being clear and interesting, even having some fun. Approach your speech in a similar way. Choking under pressure occurs most often when you overthink your performance while it is occurring (e.g., "vary your voice," "use gestures," "don't pace," "look at your audience," etc.). Scrutinizing your performance while speaking is counterproductive (Svoboda, 2009). Research on *attentional control* shows that high-anxiety public speakers concentrate on the threat associated with performance failure. Low-anxiety public speakers concentrate on that which does not heighten anxiety (Jones at al., 2012). *Simply concentrate on communicating your message clearly to your audience and the rest will follow if you have prepared and practiced.*

CARTOON 2.3: Giving a speech is not an Olympic event. The communication orientation concentrates on clarity of your message to address speech anxiety, not a performance orientation.

One way to develop the communication orientation is to practice your speech conversationally. Choose a friend or loved one with whom you feel comfortable. Find a private location and sit in chairs or on a couch. Using a conversational style, just begin describing the speech that you have prepared. Do not actually give the speech. Merely talk about the speech—what the speech covers and how you plan to develop it. Use notes if you need to, but refer to them infrequently. In subsequent practice sessions with your listener, gradually begin to introduce elements of the actual speech, such as an introduction. Eventually, deliver the entire speech while sitting down. Finally, present the entire speech standing, using only an outline of the speech for reference.

Does the communication orientation work? *When compared to other methods of anxiety reduction and control, the communication orientation is the most successful* (Motley, 2011). Simply concentrating on communicating with an audience, not impressing them, reduced anxiety levels of speakers from high to moderately low.

These methods for reducing and controlling your speech anxiety work so well that little else needs to be said. Nevertheless, here are some remaining methods you can use because they are your insurance policy.

Use Coping Statements: Rational Reappraisal

Negative self-talk leads to catastrophic thinking. If you stumble at the outset of your speech and say to yourself, "I knew I couldn't do this well" or "I've already ruined the introduction," you are immediately scrutinizing your performance. Negative, catastrophic thinking triggers high anxiety. A rational reappraisal can help you cope effectively with your anxiety (Ellis, 1995; Gallo, 2017). Try making coping statements when problems arise (mentally to yourself, of course, not out loud—which would be weird). "I'm past the tough part," "I'll do better once I get rolling," and "The best part is still ahead" are examples of positive coping statements. Coping statements shift the thought process from negative and irrational to positive and rational self-talk (O'Donohue & Fisher, 2008). Make self-talk constructive, not destructive.

Use Positive Imaging: Visualizing Success

Mental images can influence your anxiety either positively or negatively (Holmes & Mathews, 2005). Prepare for a speech presentation by countering negative thoughts of catastrophe with positive images of success, sometimes called **visualization** (Topper, 2015). This can be a very effective strategy for addressing your speech anxiety (Ayres, 2005). Novice speakers typically imagine what will go wrong during a speech. To avoid this pitfall, create images in your head that picture you giving a fluent, clear, and interesting speech. Picture your audience responding in positive ways as you give your speech. Exercise mental discipline and refuse to allow negative, disastrous thoughts to creep into your consciousness. Keep imagining speaking success, not failure.

Use Relaxation Techniques: Reducing Fight-or-Flight Response

A number of simple techniques can reduce physiological symptoms of the fight-or-flight response and produce a relaxation response (Scott, 2019). First, deep, slow, controlled breathing is very helpful (Wells at al., 2012). Five to seven such breaths per minute are optimum (Horowitz, 2002). Do not allow yourself to breathe in rapid, shallow bursts. This will likely increase your anxiety.

Relaxing your muscles through a series of tense-and-relax exercises also can be beneficial, especially right before giving a speech if you can be unobtrusive about it—perhaps backstage or outside. Lifting your shoulders slowly up and down, then rotating them slowly is relaxing. Wiggling your facial muscles by moving your cheeks, jaw, mouth, nose, and eyebrows and by smiling broadly may seem silly, but it loosens tight muscles. Even big, exaggerated yawns can help. Tensing then relaxing sets of muscles in your diaphragm, stomach, legs, and arms is another muscle relaxation exercise.

Try Systematic Desensitization: Incremental Relaxation

Systematic desensitization is a technique used to control anxiety, even phobias, triggered by a wide variety of stimuli (O'Donohue & Fisher, 2008). The technique operates on the principle that relaxation and anxiety are incompatible and do not occur simultaneously. Systematic desensitization involves incremental exposure to increasingly threatening stimuli coupled with relaxation techniques. This method of managing speech anxiety is very effective (Cuncic, 2018b). It is time-consuming, however, so you must be committed to this technique of anxiety reduction.

Applied to giving speeches, systematic desensitization involves making a list of perhaps 10 progressive steps in the speaking process, each likely to arouse increased anxiety. Find yourself a comfortable, quiet place to sit. Read the first item on your list (e.g., your speech topic). When you experience anxiety, put the list aside and begin a relaxation exercise. Tense your muscles in your face and neck. Hold the tensed position for 10 seconds, then release. Now do the same with your hands, and so on until you have tensed and relaxed all the muscle groups in your body. Now breathe slowly and deeply as you say the word "relax" to yourself. Repeat this for one minute. Pick up the list and read the first item. If your anxiety remains pronounced, repeat the process. If your anxiety is minimal, move on to the second item (e.g., gathering your speech material) and repeat the tense-and-relax procedure. Work through your entire list of 10 items, stopping when you are able to read the final item (e.g., beginning the introduction of your speech) without appreciable anxiety. Use systematic desensitization several days in a row before your actual speech presentation. Your anxiety level should fall to lower levels. The final step is exposure to the actual anxiety-provoking stimulus: giving the speech.

SUMMARY

Most people experience some speech anxiety. A key to managing your anxiety begins with understanding the fight-or-flight response to perceived threat and moderating the physiological symptoms through a variety of techniques and approaches. Self-defeating thoughts and anxiety-provoking situations are primary causes of dysfunctional speech anxiety, which can trigger intense fight-or-flight responses. Preparation, practice, and perspective are some important approaches to managing speech anxiety. In addition, you can try the communication orientation, coping statements, visualization, relaxation techniques, and systematic desensitization to fortify your management of speech anxiety.

TED TALKS AND YOUTUBE VIDEOS

Managing Speech Anxiety: "Terrified" Emma Watson UN Speech: "Emma Watson at the HeForShe Campaign 2014-Official UN Video"

Managing Speech Anxiety: "Harrison Ford: 2018 Global Climate Action Summit"

The Illusion Of Transparency: "Zach Wahls Talks about His Inspiring Speech"

Managing Speech Anxiety: Matt Abraham: "No Freaking Speaking: Managing Public Speaking Anxiety"

Good Basic Speech Anxiety Strategies: "How to NOT Get Nervous Speaking in Front of People"

Ted Talkers Fear Public Speaking: "TED Tackles Stage Fright: How 3 Notable Speakers Overcame Their Fear of Public Speaking"

For relevant links to these TED Talks and YouTube videos, see the *Practically Speaking* Companion Website: www.oup.com/he/rothwell-ps3e. You can also gain access by typing the title of the speech reference into a Google search window or by doing the same on the TED Talks or YouTube sites.

CHECKLIST

☐ Have I started preparing my speech well in advance of presenting it?

☐ Have I adequately prepared the substance of my speech?

☐ Have I practiced giving my speech repeatedly?

☐ Have I gained a proper perspective by realizing that catastrophizing is unwarranted?

☐ Have I tried practicing the communication orientation as explained?

☐ Have I tried relaxation techniques in advance of my presentation?

☐ Have I tried positive imaging?

☐ Have I done requisite physiological preparation?

CRITICAL THINKING QUESTIONS

1. What is the worst case of speech anxiety that you have experienced? What steps did you take to address it?

2. Have you ever experienced giving a speech without any anxiety? If so, why did you not experience speech anxiety?

NOTE: Online **student resources**, such as practice tests, flashcards, and other activities, can be accessed at www.oup.com/he/rothwell-ps3e

Audience Analysis and Topic Selection

Almost 2,500 years ago, Aristotle wrote: "Of the three elements in speechmaking—speaker, subject, and person addressed—it is the last one, the hearer, that determines the speech's end and object" (quoted by Cooper, 1960, p. 136). *Audience analysis and adaptation are critical elements of any public speech.* A speech's effectiveness is determined from the standpoint of the audience. "I gave a great speech, but the audience hated it" is uncomfortably close to "The surgery was a success, but the patient died" analogy. Think of audience analysis as the process of discovering ways to build bridges between yourself and listeners, to identify with their needs, hopes, dreams, interests, and concerns, and for listeners to identify with you. In general, you construct your speech with the audience always in mind. Thus, **the purpose of this chapter is to explore the essential role audience plays in constructing and presenting speeches**. Toward that end, this chapter addresses (1) types of audiences, (2) audience composition, (3) audience adaptation, and (4) topic choice.

TYPES OF AUDIENCES

Begin analyzing your audience by considering what type of audience will hear your speech. There are five general types of audiences: captive, committed, contrary, concerned, and casual. Each poses specific challenges for you, the speaker.

Captive Audience: Disengaged Listeners

A captive audience assembles to hear you speak because it is compelled to, not because listeners expect entertainment or intellectual stimulation. A required speech class is an example of a captive audience. Formal ceremonies, luncheon gatherings of clubs and organizations, and most meetings conducted in places of business are other examples. Listeners may attend a speech only because those with greater power (supervisors, teachers) insist.

Gaining and maintaining the interest of a captive audience is a primary consideration. Your sometimes ill-humored, captive listeners may prefer to be almost anywhere else than listening to a speech. Snaring their attention and keeping them listening to you is no small accomplishment. (Chapter 6 discusses attention strategies necessary to meet this challenge.)

Committed Audience: Agreeable Listeners

A committed audience voluntarily assembles because they want to invest time and energy listening to and being inspired by a speaker. A committed audience usually agrees with your position already and is presumably interested since they voluntarily appeared to hear your speech. Listeners who gather for Sunday sermons, political rallies, and social protest demonstrations are all examples of committed audiences. Gaining and maintaining the interest and attention of a committed audience is not nearly as difficult as doing the same with a captive audience. *Inspiring action, persuading, and empowering listeners to act decisively are primary challenges when speaking to a committed audience* (subjects for later discussion).

Contrary Audience: Hostile Listeners

You do not usually get to choose your audience, so sometimes the audience that forms is initially hostile to your position on issues. School board meetings, public meetings of the county board of supervisors, meetings on public utility rates, and political gatherings often attract hostile listeners ready to do battle. Listeners of this sort are more likely to engage in **ambushing**—looking for weaknesses in your arguments and preparing to pounce on perceived mistakes in your facts. It is vitally important in such circumstances that you have researched your topic and are well prepared. Your demeanor when addressing a hostile audience must remain unconditionally constructive. *Dealing with a hostile audience is adversarial. You want to defuse audience anger, not ignite it against you.* Be prepared for personal attacks, but resist personal counterattacks. Ask audience members who get rowdy to disagree without becoming disagreeable. (See discussion later in this chapter for more ways to address hostility.)

PHOTO 3.1: Emma González, a main speaker at the 2018 "March for Our Lives" in Washington, DC, is addressing an enormous, clearly committed audience inspired by her speech (see below).

PHOTO 3.2: Crowd shot from "March for Our Lives."

Concerned Audience: Eager Listeners

A concerned audience is one that gathers voluntarily to hear a speaker because listeners care about issues and ideas. A concerned audience is a motivated audience. Unlike a committed audience, however, listeners have not attended the speech to show commitment to a particular cause or idea. Concerned listeners want to gather information and learn. Listeners who gather for book and poetry readings or lecture series are examples of concerned audiences. *Your main considerations are to present new ideas and new information in a stimulating and attention-getting fashion.* Concerned listeners may eventually become committed listeners.

Casual Audience: Unexpected Listeners

A casual audience is composed of individuals who become listeners because they hear a speaker, stop out of curiosity or casual interest, and remain until bored or sated. When I was in Bath, England, I happened upon a street performer, or busker. He gathered an audience mostly with clever banter, corny jokes, audience interaction, and whimsical tricks. Curious about the gathering crowd, I joined the audience. Within minutes I was picked out of the crowd to "assist" the busker in performing one of his "daring" tricks. My job was to tie the busker's hands tightly behind his back with a chain, put a bag over his head, and count to 30 while the performer "escaped" from his confinement while on his knees with his head submerged in a two-gallon bucket of water. Not surprisingly, he performed this "underwater escape" successfully and garnered great laughter and applause from his casual audience.

Your primary consideration when addressing a casual audience is to connect with listeners immediately and create curiosity and interest. The busker did this well. Unlike a captive audience, members of a casual audience are free to leave at a moment's whim.

Each type of audience—captive, committed, contrary, concerned, or casual—presents its own challenges to a speaker. Each audience has its own expectations that a speaker must address both in preparing and presenting a successful speech.

AUDIENCE COMPOSITION

You should prepare your speech with your audience always in mind, so knowing something about your audience is critical. An initial place to begin is by trying to ascertain the attitudes, beliefs, and values of your listeners. An **attitude** is "a learned predisposition to respond favorably or unfavorably toward some attitude object" (Gass & Seiter, 2014, p. 42). "The critical notion in the definition of attitudes is evaluation" (Cooper et al., 2016, p. 5). Examples include "Lawyers are dishonest" or "Cross-country skiing is great if you live in a small country" (Steven Wright). A **belief** is what a person thinks is true or probable. "Women are more talkative than men" is a belief. This is an assertion of fact without evaluation. Objective evidence may contradict a belief. For example, women are not typically more talkative than men in mixed-sex groups (Swann, 2019). Talkativeness depends on the situation (Onnela et al., 2014). A **value** is the most deeply felt, generally shared view of what is deemed good, right, or worthwhile thinking or behavior. Values are general ideals that guide our lives. "Freedom" is a value that drives many competing attitudes on a wide range of topics, such as abortion, drug use, or health care.

You may have an opportunity to survey listeners and determine their basic values, beliefs, or attitudes. Often, however, you must make educated guesses about an audience based on **demographics**—characteristics of an audience such as age, gender, culture, ethnicity, and group affiliations. Even then *audiences these days tend to be composed of diverse members*, so often there are competing attitudes, beliefs, and values among listeners, making audience adaptation especially challenging. *Recognize that few audiences are entirely of one mind.*

Age: Possible Generation Gaps

The median age of an audience can provide valuable information for a speaker. College instructors, for instance, must speak to the experience of their students, and most of you were not even born until after 1995. This means that most of you have no direct experience of the Vietnam War, Watergate, eight-track tapes, ditto machines, manual typewriters, and cellphones the size of a brick used mostly by the rich and famous. You have not experienced a time when space travel was not possible, color television was not available, ATMs were not readily accessible, computers would not fit on a desktop or in your hand, and the Internet and social networking sites were unavailable.

Generalizations based on generational differences should be embraced cautiously, but a study by the Pew Research Center reported the largest generation gap in the United States in decades ("The Generation Gap," 2018). Viewpoints on a host of issues vary greatly between Millennials (anyone born between 1981 and 1996) and the Silent generation (anyone born between 1928 and 1945; see Dimock, 2018). The Pew study found that 79% of Millennials believe immigrants strengthen America, but only 47% of Silents hold this view. Millennials are mostly liberal, but Silents are mostly conservative. Most Millennials (62%) do not hold that belief in God is necessary to being moral, compared to 29% of Silents. A mere 18% of the younger generation views the United States as a country "above

PHOTOS 3.3 & 3.4: Audiences in the United States are much more likely to be heterogeneous (diverse) than homogeneous (similar).

all others"; 46% of the older generation holds this view. Legalization of marijuana reveals a huge gap between younger and older generations—71% support among Millennials but only 35% support among Silents. Views on gay marriage show an equally wide gap: 73% of Millennials favor gay and lesbian marriage; 41% of

Silents agree with this view. Finally, more recent Pew research shows a striking parallel between Generation Z (ages 13 to 21 in 2018) and Millennials. "On a range of issues, from Donald Trump's presidency to the role of government to racial equality and climate change, the views of Gen Z . . . mirror those of Millennials" (Parker et al., 2019). This means that the same gap between Millennials and older generations also exists between Generation Z and older generations.

Generational differences do pose significant challenges for public speakers. An audience composed of a mixture of older members, teens, and twenty-somethings makes it difficult to interest everyone in your topic. References to mutual funds and retirement accounts do not speak directly to the experience and interests of most younger audience members as they do with older members, and skateboarding won't likely galvanize interest among many older members of your audience. Conversely, do not assume older audience members are necessarily technologically proficient or enamored with the latest devices as younger generations. Pew Research surveys report that 95% of Generation Z and 92% of Millennials own a smartphone compared to 67% of Boomers (born between 1946 and 1964) and only 30% of Silents. A scant 23% of Silents use social media compared to 57% of Boomers and 85% of both Generation Z and Millennials (Anderson & Jiang, 2018; Jiang, 2018). Nevertheless, a topic on some aspect of technology, such as electric cars or solar energy, may bridge all generational groups. Stress management, immunity-boosting steps to improve health, and unusual vacations for the entire family are other possible topics that span generational interests and may appeal to a diverse audience.

Gender: Go Beyond Simplistic Stereotypes

Gender differences in perception and communication behavior do exist (Goman, 2016). Be careful, however, not to assume too much from these differences. For example, men generally find expressing feelings to be more difficult than passing kidney stones (Wong et al., 2006). However, men more easily express "negative emotions," such as anger or contempt, than "positive emotions," such as affection and joy. Women generally express emotions with greater ease, but they have more difficulty expressing negative than positive emotions (Chaplin, 2015).

Effective audience analysis means going beyond simplistic gender stereotypes ("women express feelings; men don't"). Stereotypes are broad generalizations about a group, which in some instances may be truer than not (Jussim et al., 2016), but they ignore individual differences of members within a group. Some men have little difficulty expressing the full range of human feelings, and some women are emotionally restricted.

Although some gender differences exist, develop your speech to include all audience members. A speech on sexual harassment, for instance, could be linked to both men and women by discussing effects on victims who are typically women but also men ("Charges Alleging Sexual Harassment," 2019). The consequences to the victims of sexual harassment should concern men and women alike. Consequences include psychological distress, depression, shame and embarrassment, diminished job performance, and even post-traumatic stress disorder ("Sexual Harassment in the Workplace," 2016). Why would anyone wish to ignore harassment of his or her partner, friend, or family member given such consequences?

In addition, sensitivity to an audience may require judicious attention to language when framing issues. Consistently referring to leaders as "he," "him," or "his," as in "A leader must inspire, and he must motivate his followers," excludes women. Similarly, referring to elementary school teachers as "she" or "her," as in "A third grade teacher works hard and she spends long hours with her students," excludes men.

Is sexist language merely "political correctness," as some derisively attest? Substantial research refutes such a claim (Menegatti & Rubini, 2017). Gender-biased language promotes inaccurate sexist stereotypes, makes women (and sometimes men) virtually invisible when forming mental images, and can negatively affect employment opportunities (Budziszewska et al., 2014; Douglas &

CARTOON 3.1: Sexist language is inappropriate. For example, 11% of registered nurses, more than 350,000 individuals, are male (Auerbach et al., 2017). Be inclusive, not stereotypic.

Sutton, 2014). Try to speak in more inclusive, nonstereotypic terms, using "him or her" or plural forms such as "doctors . . . they."

Ethnicity and Culture: Sensitivity to Diversity

According to the U.S. Census Bureau, a third of the population of the United States is non-White. By 2045, minorities composed largely of Latinos and Mexican Americans, African Americans, and Asian Americans will constitute the majority of the population (Frey, 2018). Students who fail to analyze the multicultural makeup of college audiences can create embarrassing speaking situations. Despite my efforts to encourage sensitivity to individuals from diverse cultures, I have witnessed several student speeches that ignited awkward, even hostile, moments in class. One Jewish student referred to Palestinians as "terrorists and war mongers." This did not sit well with several Arab students in the class. Policies and issues can be questioned and debated without resorting to insults and sweeping generalizations that offend audience members.

One important hazard to avoid is **ethnocentrism**—the belief that customs, practices, and behaviors of your own culture are superior to any other culture. Difference does not equal deficiency unless basic human rights are jeopardized. Avoid disparaging the customs, practices, and behaviors of cultures different from your own.

Group Affiliations: A Window into Listeners' Views

The groups we belong to tell others a great deal about our values, beliefs, and attitudes. Membership in Save Our Shores indicates a strong belief in protecting our ocean environment. Working with Habitat for Humanity indicates an interest in charitable work and a concern for poor people with inadequate housing. Membership in the National Rifle Association reveals viewpoints on gun ownership. Membership in clubs, sororities, fraternities, national honorary societies, or educational groups provides information about your listeners that can be helpful in shaping your speeches.

Be cautious, however, not to assume too much and stereotype all members of a group. Group affiliations suggest possible aspects to consider about your audience, but religious affiliations, for example, can be tricky. One survey of U.S. Catholics found only 17% agreed with the Vatican's ban on birth control ("2018 National Survey"). A Pew Research survey found that a significant majority of U.S. Catholics support same-sex marriage (76% of Catholic Democrats; 59% of Catholic Republicans) (Linka & Smith, 2019). In May 2015, Ireland, a strongly Catholic country, held a referendum in which that country's ban on gay marriage was voted down overwhelmingly (62% to 38%). Ireland became the first nation to eliminate the ban on gay marriage by popular vote (McDonald, 2015). In 2018, Ireland also voted overwhelmingly to legalize access to abortion, and in 2019 restrictions on divorce were loosened substantially. Who would have guessed this, if judging only by religious affiliation?

Additional audience composition factors, such as sexual orientation, income, and education level, also can affect your audience analysis. With some exceptions, however, these may not be so apparent. Some people purposely hide their sexual orientation or consider it nobody else's business, and others consider it rude to ask or discuss income level. Nevertheless, be sensitive to these elements of audience composition.

ADAPTING TO DIVERSE AUDIENCES AND SITUATIONS

Analyzing your audience and breaking it into its constituent parts is only half the battle. The other half is taking this analysis and adapting effectively to audiences and situations.

Establish Identification: Connecting with Your Audience

Identification is the affiliation and connection between speaker and audience. As discussed in the opening chapter, transactional communication means that as a speaker, you establish a relationship with your audience. You want this relationship to be a positive one.

Likability: I Can Relate to You   A key element of identification is the likability of the speaker. Even when your audience is composed of highly diverse members, if your listeners grow to like you, they are more inclined to listen. Compliance and assent on controversial positions are more probable if you are liked than if you are not liked (Perloff, 2017). How do you enhance likability? Praising and complimenting your audience ("This class did better on the exam than any previous class"), saying you like your audience ("What a great group"), and expressing genuine concern and showing empathy for problems and pain faced by audience members are just some quick ways (Goldstein et al., 2008). Using humor that doesn't offend improves likability (Covin, 2011). Telling stories well is also a very effective means of creating likability, especially personal stories that resonate with audiences, such as tragedies faced and self-deprecating stories about funny mistakes that make you seem more human. Substantial research shows that storytelling promotes **social cohesion**—it binds us together in mutual

PHOTO 3.5: Ellen DeGeneres typically uses gentle humor, even on controversial topics, that enhances her likability with diverse audiences. For example, "Do we have to worry about who's gay and who's straight? Can't we just love everybody and judge them by the car they drive?" (quoted by Connors, 2016). A 2013 survey by iHeartRadio rated Ellen "most likable woman in Hollywood" ("Ellen DeGeneres Named," 2013).

liking (Hogan, 2003). Our brains even seem to be wired to relish good stories. "Storytelling is one of the few human traits that are truly universal across culture and through all of known history" (Hsu, 2008, p. 46). An audience can be highly diverse, but who does not love a great story and like the person who tells it well? "We humans have been communicating through stories for upwards of 20,000 years, back when our flat screens were cave walls" (Monarth, 2014).

Stylistic Similarity: Looking and Acting the Part   We tend to identify more closely with those individuals who appear to be similar to us (O'Keefe, 2016). One way to appear similar is to look and act the part. This is called **stylistic similarity**. For example, when you go for a job interview, you should dress, look, and speak as an interviewer would expect from someone worthy of the job. Showing up in baggy pants and a T-shirt emblazoned with an imprint of your favorite local rock band when applying for a teaching job is unlikely to work in your favor. Using verbal obscenity during a teaching demonstration also is unlikely to charm an interview panel.

When the situation is formal, such as a valedictory speech at a graduation ceremony, dress and speak formally. Slang and offensive language should be avoided.

When the situation is less formal, such as some classroom speeches, county fair presentations, student rallies, and many protest marches and public gatherings, however, you need to shift styles and speak, dress, and act more casually so your audience can relate to you.

Finding the appropriate level of formality can be tricky when the situation does not call for a clear-cut choice. For example, as a student, how do you respond to your instructor dressing formally, insisting you address him or her as "Professor" or "Doctor" so-and-so, and being required to always raise your hand to be recognized before speaking? Would you relate better if your instructor were more casual, or do you appreciate the formality?

A formal style communicates the seriousness of your intent and the significance of the event. An informal style communicates less seriousness, perhaps even playfulness, and sets a more casual atmosphere that encourages student participation. Your style needs to match your expectations and goals. Teachers make choices about formality or informality based on their goals for the class.

In June 2009, comedian Stephen Colbert exhibited the power of stylistic similarity in producing identification with an audience when he took his *Colbert Report* to Iraq and performed four shows for the troops. He dubbed the series of shows *Operation Iraqi Stephen: Going Commando*. To great applause and laughter from the assembled troops, Colbert marched on stage dressed in a camouflage business suit and tie. Later he had his head shaved by Gen. Ray Odierno to exhibit solidarity with the soldiers. The crowd roared its approval. One soldier, Ryan McLeod, remarked afterward, "Definitely the highlight was seeing him sacrifice his hair." Later Colbert declared, "By the power vested in me by basic cable, I officially declare we have won the Iraq war" (quoted in Baram, 2009).

Substantive Similarity: Establishing Common Ground   Highlighting similarities in positions, values, and attitudes also encourages identification. This **substantive similarity** creates identification by *establishing common ground* between speaker and audience. If listeners can say, "I like what I'm hearing," they can identify with the speaker. If you are speaking to a contrary audience, it is helpful to build bridges by pointing out common experiences, perceptions, values, and attitudes before launching into more delicate areas of disagreement. Listeners will be more inclined to consider your more controversial viewpoints if they initially identify with you.

As the Republican Governor from South Carolina, Nikki Haley was given the responsibility to offer a rebuttal speech to President Obama's 2016 State of the Union (*see access to link at end of chapter*). Typically, these rebuttal speeches in the past have been one-sided bashings of the president. Haley took a different, and unexpected, tack. She began with a mild criticism but quickly veered

PHOTO 3.6: Stephen Colbert's head shaving and camouflage suit created a strong identification with his audience of American soldiers in Iraq.

into a most unusual statement: "We need to be honest with each other, with ourselves: while Democrats in Washington bear much responsibility for the problems facing America today, they do not bear it alone. There is more than enough blame to go around. We as Republicans need to own that truth. We need to recognize our contributions to the erosion of the public trust in America's leadership. We need to accept that we've played a role in how and why our government is broken" (Engel, 2016). Although some strong conservatives in her party were less than thrilled with her common-ground, substantive similarity approach, Republican consultant and pollster Frank Luntz noted that Haley's speech rated higher with his focus group composed of individuals from both parties and independents than Obama's speech, and was the most favorably rated State of the Union rebuttal he had ever tested (Engel, 2016).

Appealing to broadly accepted rights and values also works well to create identification in a broad range of situations. The United Nations Universal Declaration of Human Rights, originally adopted on a 48 to 0 vote with 8 nations abstaining, claims that every human being has the right to life, liberty, security, freedom of speech and belief, equal protection under the law, participation in the political process, a decent standard of living, necessary social services,

PHOTO 3.7: As Republican Governor of South Carolina, Nikki Haley delivered a rebuttal to Obama's 2016 "State of the Union" based on a superb common-ground identification strategy.

and education (Harrison, 2000). Although not entirely without controversy, these values bind most nations and cultures. As Harrison (2000) notes, "The vast majority of the planet's people would agree with the following assertions: life is better than death, health is better than sickness, liberty is better than slavery, prosperity is better than poverty, education is better than ignorance, and justice is better than injustice" (p. xxvi). Here is your common ground.

As Secretary of State, Hillary Clinton made such appeals to the common ground of universal human rights in a well-received December 6, 2011, speech in Geneva, Switzerland, to celebrate International Human Rights Day: "It is a violation of human rights when people are beaten or killed because of their sexual orientation." She continued, "Violence toward women isn't cultural; it's criminal. Likewise with slavery, what was once justified as sanctioned by God is now properly reviled as an unconscionable violation of human rights." She also noted, "Combating Islamaphobia or anti-Semitism is a task for people of all faiths" (Clinton, 2011).

All elements of identification interact. Being likable alone does not necessarily negate strong substantive disagreements listeners may have with your positions, and agreement on substance may be negated by being disliked. As a student interviewing for a job, you may be viewed quite positively on likability and both stylistic and substantive similarities. Credibility, however, may be an issue, and it is yet another element that must be added to the audience adaptation mix.

Build Credibility: Establishing Believability

O'Keefe (2016) defines **credibility** as "judgments made by a perceiver (e.g., a message recipient) concerning the believability of a communicator" (p. 347). In *Rhetoric*, Aristotle identified the ingredients of credibility, or **ethos** in his terminology, as "good sense, good moral character, and good will." Recent research affirms Aristotle's observation and expands the list of dimensions somewhat. The primary dimensions of credibility are competence, trustworthiness, dynamism, and composure (Gass & Seiter, 2014; Pornpitakpan, 2004). All four are developed throughout a speech.

Competence refers to the audience's perception of the speaker's knowledge and experience on a topic. Competence addresses the question "Does this speaker know what he or she is talking about?" You can enhance the perception of your competence when you identify your background, experience, and training relevant to a subject. Citing sources of evidence, speaking fluently, and avoiding vocal fillers such as "um" and "you know" also enhance perceptions of competence (Carpenter, 2012; O'Keefe, 2016).

Trustworthiness refers to how truthful or honest we perceive the speaker to be. Trustworthiness addresses the question "Can I believe what the speaker says?" We hesitate to buy anything from a salesperson we perceive to be dishonest. One way to increase your trustworthiness is to argue against your self-interest (Pratkanis & Aronson, 2001). If you take a position on an issue that will cost you money, a job, a promotion, or some reward or benefit, most listeners will see you as presenting an honest opinion. Advocating a tuition increase while attending college is an example.

Dynamism is a third dimension of credibility. It refers to the enthusiasm, energy, and forcefulness exhibited by a speaker. Sleepy, lackluster presentations lower your credibility. Over-the-top enthusiasm, however, can be equally problematic. Those who pitch products on infomercials are invariably enthusiastic, sometimes bordering on frenzied. Former Michigan governor Jennifer Granholm's 2012 speech before the Democratic National Convention reminded some of Howard Dean's disastrous 2004 "I Have a Scream" speech (*see access to link at end of chapter*). Although Granholm's speech whipped the partisan crowd into a frenzy, many critics on both sides of the partisan aisle mostly agreed that her delivery was too manic. She rocked her immediate audience, but the remote television audience was likely split on the effectiveness of her speech (*see access to link at end of chapter*). Granholm admitted afterward that "I probably shouldn't have gotten so worked up" (quoted by Eggert, 2012). Apparently, oblivious to Granholm's excesses, Rudy Giuliani seemed to repeat Granholm's mistaken notion that screaming one's speech is effective when he delivered a primetime oration at the 2016 Republican National Convention (*see access to link at end of chapter*). Similar to Granholm's speech, Guiliani seemed to ignite the immediate crowd in the arena, but critics across the partisan divide were largely disparaging about his shrill performance. Too little dynamism can diminish your speech, but too much can backfire.

PHOTO 3.8: Jennifer Granholm, an accomplished public speaker, was nevertheless, by her own admission, probably overly animated in her delivery when speaking at the 2012 Democratic National Convention.

PHOTO 3.9: Rudy Giuliani followed in the footsteps of Jennifer Granholm by striving for dynamism but sometimes appearing out of control at the 2016 Republican National Convention.

A final dimension of speaker credibility is **composure**. Audiences tend to be influenced by speakers who are emotionally stable and appear confident and in control of themselves. Cable news shows are notorious for shouting matches between political adversaries. To some, these episodes are entertaining, but it is doubtful that any listeners are impressed by witnessing two verbal combatants savage each other with cross-talk to the point where unleashing fire hoses on them to dampen their tempers seems almost appropriate.

Displaying emotion overtly, however, does not always destroy a speaker's credibility. Too much composure may be perceived as hard-heartedness or insensitivity. Shedding tears while delivering a eulogy at a funeral or expressing outrage at an atrocity, as Barack Obama did on January 5, 2016, in a speech on gun violence that referenced the Sandy Hook massacre of 20 elementary school children and 6 adults, may enhance your credibility. "First graders in Newtown. First graders," Obama said as tears rolled down his face. "Every time I think about those kids, it gets me mad" (quoted by Wheaton & Gass, 2016). Award-winning CNN news commentator Mel Robbins (2016) articulated the reaction most people had to Obama's show of emotion, "Weeping over the shooting of children—of anyone—is appropriate and important." *The appropriateness of displaying composure depends on the situation.* Most people expect at least some display of emotion when a tragedy occurs.

Similar to identification, the four elements of credibility interact. As a student speaker, for example, you may appear to your listeners as trustworthy, dynamic, and composed, but your competence may be questioned if you are speaking on a technical topic with little or no experience. Identification and credibility can also interact. One study asked college professors to assess an email message from a student that read "R U Able to Meat Me?" Professors especially disliked the "R U" acronym for "are you" as overly casual (stylistic similarity issue), and using "meat" for the correct "meet" raised concerns about the student's competence (ability to spell or diligence in proofing messages) (Stephens et al., 2009).

Adapt to the Situation: Influence of Circumstances

Situations vary. Are you speaking outdoors or indoors? Is this an online or in-person presentation? Are you speaking in a small classroom or a large auditorium or even a stadium? Outdoor venues require constant adaptation to a variety of possible interruptions or noise. Speaking to a group of 30 people in a park, for example, may compete with children playing loudly nearby, perhaps traffic noise adjacent to the park, or people walking by and conversing. Using visual aids is hindered when outdoors because of sunlight or darkness. An amplifying system

PHOTO 3.10: Which elements of identification and credibility are evident from this photo of LeBron James addressing a crowd of students, parents, local officials, and sponsors at the grand opening of the I Promise school in Akron, Ohio, partially funded by his James Family foundation?

may be required to be heard. That requires some practice using a microphone. Indoor venues are usually quieter, more controlled, intimate settings. A small conference room is more informal than a large lecture hall, and it is easier to connect with listeners directly in smaller indoor settings. The key to adapting to variations in physical settings and the size of your audience is to remain flexible. Checking the site where you will be speaking, of course, is always a good idea to make sure the setup is appropriate.

Adapt While Speaking: Exhibit Sensitivity

In Chapter 1, sensitivity was identified as a key element of how to become a competent public speaker. Sensitivity means receptive accuracy—picking up the signals being sent by your audience. Although audience adaptation is largely an issue of preparation, it also needs to occur while you are presenting your speech. Inexperienced public speakers find this challenging. It is difficult to alter your speech on the fly when you have little experience doing so. Nevertheless, as you become more experienced, adapting to your audience while speaking becomes easier.

Public speaking is a transactional process, so your listeners are providing feedback indicating how your speech is being received. When your listeners seem to be losing interest, crank up your delivery by showing greater enthusiasm and animation. You may want to tell an interesting or humorous story much sooner, even though planned for later in the speech. Some details may need to be dropped if you are running short on time. You do not want to increase the pace of your delivery to race through prepared material. When listeners appear confused, offer an additional example for clarification or explain your point in different, simpler terms. Adapting while presenting your speech is discussed in subsequent chapters, but for now, realize that with experience you can learn to respond to the unique circumstances every speech situation offers.

TOPIC CHOICE AND AUDIENCE ADAPTATION

If you become an expert on some subject, you may be asked to speak on that topic. Here the speech topic is chosen for you. In a speech class, however, the choice, within broad limits, will likely be up to you. In this section, how to choose a topic that is adapted well for you, your audience, and the occasion is discussed.

Exploring Potential Topics: Important Choice

Choosing bad topics produces bad speeches; choosing great topics is the first step toward producing great speeches. There are four primary ways to explore potential speech topics systematically.

Do a Personal Inventory: You as Topic Source   Begin your exploration of appropriate topics by looking at your own personal experiences and interests. Make a list. Do you have hobbies, such as woodworking, scrapbooking, or stamp collecting? What sports do you play? List any unusual events that have occurred in your life, such as getting caught in a tornado or witnessing a bank robbery. Have you done any volunteer work for charitable organizations? What form of entertainment interests you—romantic movies, rap music, dancing, rodeo, or car shows? Do you have any special skills, such as surfing, cooking, carpentry, or sewing? Have you traveled to any interesting places, such as Ayers Rock or Machu Picchu? Have you met any exciting people, such as a rock star, professional athlete, or famous actor? What is the worst thing that has happened to you? What is the best? This list contains many possible choices for a speech topic.

Brainstorm: New Possibilities   You may need to brainstorm additional topic possibilities beyond your personal inventory. Take your personal list, examine it, and then choose five topics that seem most promising. Write down each topic on a separate list, and brainstorm new possibilities for each topic. For example, brainstorm "trip to London" by letting your mind search for related topics, such as double-decker buses, driving on the left side of the road, the British accent, Parliament, royalty, Hyde Park, British money, and British rock groups. Now consider each of these and try to brainstorm a more specific topic. British money, for example, might lead to a comparison of British and American currency. Driving on the left could lead to why the British drive on the left but we drive on the right. Parliament could trigger a comparison between the U.S. Congress and the British Parliament.

Crowdsourcing for Topics: Group Wisdom   If you are struggling to find a suitable topic, you might solicit ideas from fellow classmates and have suggestions posted on a shared Google doc or on your Facebook page. Gavin Newsom, California Lt. Governor at the time, used this very technique, known as crowdsourcing, to generate ideas for his commencement address at San Francisco State University in May 2015. "Don't want to give a speech that will bore the graduates and their families," Newsom wrote on his Facebook page (Garofoli, 2015).

Scanning for Topics: Quick Ideas   Scanning books can help generate additional ideas for speech topics. Access Amazon.com and scan the latest nonfiction bestsellers. This process can produce some real surprises. My own casual search for interesting books to read led me to *Spinglish: The Definitive Dictionary of Deliberately Deceptive Language*, by Henry Beard and Christopher Cerf (2015). The authors present an impressive list of deceptive euphemisms, such as calling a box of Kleenex a "disposable mucus recovery system" (enabling hospitals to charge patients $15 or more), disguising an airplane crash as a "controlled flight into terrain," camouflaging massive layoffs of workers as "rightsizing" and firing as "involuntarily leisured," masking lying as "reality augmentation," and concealing death by a physician's malpractice as a "negative patient care outcome." This book could serve as a solid starting point for a great speech on the power of language to shape false perceptions.

Scan magazines, such as *Time, Consumer Reports, Ebony, Sports Illustrated, People, Psychology Today, O Magazine, Ms., Men's Health*, or *Scientific American*. Look at the table of contents, and leaf through the articles. Do not spend time reading them. If you see a promising topic, write it down or take a photo with your smartphone and note the magazine, the article, and the date.

Do the same with newspapers. Finally, scan blogging sites such as *Huffington Post*, which has a potpourri of articles and opinion columns on politics, sports, news items, gossip, comedy, business, entertainment, and fashion. If you cannot find a topic of appropriate interest after scanning this site, you are not looking hard enough.

Appropriateness of Topic: Blending Topic and Audience

Choosing a topic that is inappropriate for a particular audience virtually guarantees that your speech will be ineffective. Appropriateness is contextual. A speech topic that works in one instance may be an abysmal failure in another. There are three central elements to consider when analyzing the appropriateness of your topic choice: speaker, audience, and occasion.

Speaker Appropriateness: Suitability for You   If you find a topic uninteresting, then it is not appropriate for you, the speaker. It is a rare individual who can take a topic that he or she finds dull and successfully fake interest to an audience. If you think the subject is dull, what must your audience think? Choose a topic that interests or excites you.

Avoid choosing a topic that is a poor fit for you. A White person speaking about the "Black experience in America" is a poor fit, even potentially offensive. Similarly, young people talking about "what it's like being old" sounds goofy. Men speaking about female menopause or women discussing proper care of the male prostate is awkward. Describing what it is to be a Muslim in America when you have never been one lacks credibility. No matter how gifted you are as a speaker, some topics will sink your chances of presenting an effective speech.

Audience Appropriateness: Suitability for Your Listeners   Over the years, my colleagues have shared many horror stories about student speeches on topics that were startlingly inappropriate, such as "how to assassinate someone you hate," "spitting for distance," "harassing the homeless," "proper methods of inducing vomiting after a big meal" (with demonstration), "opening a beer bottle with your teeth," "constructing a bong," and "shoplifting techniques that work." These topics are inappropriate because they are offensive, trivial, demeaning, or they encourage illegal, unethical behavior. Most are pointless, adolescent silliness.

There are other reasons why a topic might be inappropriate. An audience may find a topic choice difficult to relate to or appreciate. Giving a speech on how to surf to an audience living in Kansas is a bit weird. A topic can

CARTOON 3.2: Some topics are inappropriate because they are trivial and offensive.

also be too technical or complex. I once had a student try to explain string theory, a developing branch of theoretical physics, in a 5-minute speech. Not surprisingly, the speech was more confusing than clarifying for her audience unschooled in such things. A topic may also be overused. I have heard many reasons to legalize marijuana in several hundred student speeches over many years. Although I am ambivalent on the topic, for me the strongest reason to legalize marijuana nationally is to put an end to all speeches on the subject (although outlawing marijuana would undoubtedly become the new hue and cry). Be wary of shopworn topics that might bore your instructor and your classmates.

Occasion Appropriateness: Suitability for the Event   The occasion usually defines the general purpose of your speech, so topic choice should be suited to that general purpose. A **general purpose** identifies the overall goal of your speech—to inform, describe, explain, demonstrate, persuade, celebrate, memorialize, entertain, or eulogize.

If you are asked to give a persuasive speech in class, merely explaining how to be successful when taking an online class, for example, is not appropriate. You have to promote a controversial position, such as arguing that online classes are inferior to traditional classes. A graduation ceremony invites topics such as "employment possibilities for the future," "skills for success," and "thinking in the future tense," not an unrelated series of jokes meant to entertain but not provide insight or inspiration for graduates. A sermon at a religious service warrants a topic related to moral behavior, not a political speech of advocacy, the very issue that arose from a eulogy delivered at Aretha Franklin's funeral in September 2018. "We feel that Rev. Jasper Williams, Jr. used this platform to push his negative agenda, which as a family, we do not agree with," was a statement issued by Vaughn Franklin, the singer's nephew, on the family's behalf ("Aretha Franklin's Family Criticizes," 2018). The occasion and its general purpose dictate the appropriateness of a topic choice.

Narrowing the Topic: Making Subjects Manageable

Sometimes you are given a very broad topic on which to speak. Narrowing your topic to fit the audience and the occasion is a significant task for the competent speaker. Time constraints dictate to what extent a topic must be narrowed. President Woodrow Wilson took his public speaking very seriously. A reporter interviewed him once regarding his speech preparation. "How long do you spend preparing a 10-minute speech?" Wilson was asked. He replied, "About 2 weeks." "How long do you spend preparing an hour-long speech?" the reporter queried. "About a week," answered Wilson. Surprised, the reporter then asked Wilson how long he prepared for a 2-hour speech. He replied, "I could do that now." Giving a long-winded speech takes less effort than narrowing the speech to fit into a shorter time allotment.

Once you have settled on a general topic that is appropriate for you the speaker, your audience, and the occasion, begin narrowing the topic to fit your time limit. A 5-minute speech obviously requires much more narrowing than a 15-minute speech. Take the general topic and brainstorm more specific subtopics. For example, a broad topic such as "the cost of a college education," could be broken into these more specific subtopics: problems with financial aid, how to get a scholarship, part-time student employment, the high cost of textbooks, room and board fees for campus living, college tuition, and college fees. Each of these subtopics could be developed into an effective 5-minute presentation.

Staying within your time limit is critical. If you are asked to give a 15-minute address at a luncheon meeting of a civic organization, you will be addressing a roomful of empty chairs if you go much beyond the time limit. People attending luncheon meetings often have only an hour, of which your speech is but a small part.

Abraham Lincoln's Gettysburg Address, considered one of the great American speeches, lasted a little more than *2 minutes*. Famed orator Edward Everett, who preceded Lincoln, gave a 2-hour-plus speech. He later wrote Lincoln: "I shall be glad if I could flatter myself that I came as near to the central idea of the occasion in two hours as you did in two minutes" (quoted in Noonan, 1998, p. 65). Although Barack Obama's State of the Union speeches were lengthy (for a comparison to other presidents, see Woolley & Peters, 2017), he wisely patterned his January 20, 2009, inaugural address along the lines of Lincoln. His first speech as president, delivered outdoors to a massive crowd whose members endured frigid weather, lasted a mere 18 minutes. His second inaugural address delivered on January 21, 2013, was equally brief. Donald Trump also followed suit and spoke for a mere 15 minutes at his 2017 inaugural address. On these occasions, heeding the advice of another president, Franklin Roosevelt, is warranted: "Be sincere; be brief; be seated."

SUMMARY

Audience analysis is an essential component of competent public speaking. Analyzing your audience begins with knowing the five types of audiences, discerning the composition of your audience, and then adapting your topic choice and development to meet the expectations and needs of your audience. You want to establish your likeability, credibility, and identification with your audience. Your topic choice should be appropriate for you as speaker, for your audience, and for the occasion. Narrowing your topic to fit the time limit of your speech is also important.

TED TALKS AND YOUTUBE VIDEOS

Storytelling and Identification: Ann Romney's 2012 Convention speech— "Raw Video: Ann Romney's Speech at the RNC"

Storytelling and Identification: Michelle Obama's 2012 Convention speech—"First Lady Michelle Obama's Full Speech from the 2012 Democratic National Convention—HD Quality"

Generation Gap: "Millennials Show Us What 'Old' Looks Like"

Committed Audience: "Emma Gonzalez's Powerful March for Our Lives Speech in Full"

Excessive Dynamism: "Gov. Jennifer Granholm 2012 Democratic National Convention Speech"

Appropriate Dynamism: Gov. Jennifer Granholm 2013 TED Talk: "A Clean Energy Proposal: Race to the Top" (compare to her convention speech)

Excessive Dynamism: "2004: The Scream That Doomed Howard Dean"

Excessive Dynamism: "Full Speech: He's Fired Up for Trump! Rudy Giuliani—Republican National Convention"

Really Excessive Dynamism: "Phil Davison Gives a Crazy Speech"

Substantive Similarity (effective common ground strategy): "Nikki Haley Delivers GOP Response to the State of the Union Address"

Appropriate Dynamism/Common Ground/Stylistic Similarity: "The Speech That Made Obama President"

Likability, Common Ground, Humor (identification): Ellen DeGeneres: "Ellen Slams Mississippi's Anti-LGBT Law in Powerful Monologue"

For relevant links to these TED Talks and YouTube videos, see the *Practically Speaking* Companion Website: www.oup.com/he/rothwell-ps3e. You can also gain access by typing the title of the speech reference into a Google search window or by doing the same on the TED Talks or YouTube sites.

CHECKLIST

☐ Do an audience analysis profile to prepare for your speech.

☐ How well do you know your audience? Are they mostly strangers? Classmates? Highly diverse group (age, gender, culture, political viewpoints)? If diverse, your approach will need to be more inclusive than if you are speaking to a more homogeneous group.

☐ How will you attempt to identify with your audience? Dress the part? Speak like them? Find common ground on issues and experiences? Use humor?

☐ Is your topic appropriate for the audience, yourself as speaker, and the occasion?

CRITICAL THINKING QUESTIONS

1. Can you ever strive too hard to identify with an audience?

2. What identification strategies would you use with a hostile audience composed of individuals from a markedly different generation and ethnicity from your own?

3. Can all topics be made interesting to any audience with the right strategies?

NOTE: Online **student resources**, such as practice tests, flashcards, and other activities, can be accessed at www.oup.com/he/rothwell-ps3e

CHAPTER

4

Gathering Material

The advent of electronic technologies has ushered in the Information Age. You have greater access to information than at any other time in human history. This makes gathering credible material for your speech topic especially challenging. The research firm IDC (International Data Corporation) forecasts that the total global digital data available in 2025 will be 175 zettabytes, an increase from 33 zettabytes in 2018 (Reinsel et al., 2018). To provide some perspective, 1 gigabyte can store 960 *minutes* of music, but 1 zettabyte can store *2 billion years* of music ("How Big Is a Zetabyte?," 2016). The Internet provides ready access to a cornucopia of information. Technology entrepreneur Mitchell Kapor once noted, "Getting information off the Internet is like taking a drink from a fire hydrant." The widespread use of cellphones further magnifies the problem. "Our smartphones have become Swiss army-knife-like appliances . . . They're more powerful and do more things than the most advanced computer at IBM corporate headquarters 30 years ago" (Levitin, 2015).

The word *staggering* does not seem sufficient to capture the size of the challenge we face in coming years with information overload. As Nate Silver (2012) notes, most of this abundance of information is useless noise—a distracting accumulation of fabrications, speculations, and conspiracy theories. Your challenge is to mine the nuggets of credible information for your speech that are buried in the cavernous refuse of misinformation and trivialities.

Gathering useful information for your speech takes effort and know-how. Consequently, *the purpose of this chapter is to provide advice and insight on how to research speech topics effectively.* Toward that end, this chapter discusses

(1) using the Internet for finding quality research, (2) evaluating Internet research and information, (3) using libraries effectively, and (4) conducting interviews to generate your own relevant information.

THE INTERNET: ONLINE RESEARCH

The Internet has become a primary source for research by college students. A UCLA survey of more than 171,000 first-year college students revealed that the vast majority frequently used the Internet for research (Eagan et al., 2017). Unfortunately, a University College of London study found that Internet users are increasingly becoming "power browsers" who scan instead of devoting time to actually "evaluating information, either for relevance, accuracy or authority" (Rowlands et al., 2008). This section briefly discusses various Internet tools to help in your search for relevant speech material. Analyzing information found on the Internet is also addressed.

PHOTO 4.1: Although the Internet is a vast repository of useful information and a research tool of unprecedented potential, it can also be a vast wasteland of misinformation. Not everyone embraces its positive potential. Dorothy Gambrell, for one, says "the Internet is a drunk librarian who won't shut up." *New York Times* columnist Frank Bruni views the Internet as "a sinkhole for the gullible. It renders everyone an instant expert. You have a degree? Well, I did a Google search!" Exercise extreme caution when using the Internet for speech research.

Search Engines

You are undoubtedly familiar with search engines that generate indexes of Web pages that match, or link with, keywords typed in a search window. A comprehensive list of search engines can be found at the Library of Congress website (http://www.lcweb .loc.gov/global/search.html). These are some of the more popular search engines:

Google (http://www.google.com): Created at Stanford University in June 1998 by students Sergey Brin and Larry Page, Google has become synonymous with the Internet search, as in "Google it." In mid-2019, Google had 88% of the U.S. search market share. It is often the first, and unfortunately, the only research tool used by college students. Dare to be different and expand beyond Google.

Bing (www.bing.com): Launched in 2009 as an upgrade of Microsoft's previous search engine, MSN Search, Bing had 6.4% of the U.S. market share in mid-2019.

Yahoo (http://www.yahoo.com/): Formerly a major search leader, Yahoo fell on hard times in 2012. Yahoo had 4.15% of the U.S. market share mid-2019 ("Search Engine Market Share," 2019).

Google Scholar (http://scholar.google.com): Google Scholar indexes an extensive list of full-text, scholarly literature across a multitude of publishing formats and disciplines.

To increase the efficiency and relevance of your research using search engines, employ a few simple steps. First, narrow your search. Typing *smoking*, for example, into the Google search window produced 495 million hits when last checked. Try a narrower search, such as *college smoking policies*. Second, change your search terms if you don't find relevant sites and information. You might have to search for college smoking *regulations* instead of policies. Third, be concise in your phrasing. A lengthy sentence may provide zero hits, but a short phrase may produce many relevant sites. Finally, articles, pronouns, conjunctions, and prepositions should be avoided for a smoother search.

Virtual Libraries

Because much on the Internet is irrelevant, misinformed, or plain nutty, virtual libraries have been created to provide more selective, higher quality information. A **virtual library**, or digital library, is a search tool that combines Internet technology and standard library techniques for cataloging and appraising information. Virtual libraries are usually associated with colleges, universities, or organizations with strong reputations in information dissemination. Your college library may have such an information tool. Unlike other search tools, virtual libraries provide fewer websites and a narrower focus, but the information has been carefully screened so it is more credible. Here are three of the more popular virtual libraries:

Universal Digital Library (www.ulib.org)
Digital Public Library (https://dp.la/)
Internet Public Library, Library of Congress (https://www.loc.gov/item/2003556257/)

Government Sites

Gaining access to government documents and publications can be enormously helpful when you research your speech topics. Two key government sites are as follows:

United States Census Bureau (www.census.gov): Provides abundant statistical information on political, social, and economic elements relevant to life in the United States.
USA.gov (www.usa.gov): Provides primary access to a broad source of U.S. government information on the Internet.

Survey Sites

Survey results from credible sources can add real punch to your speeches. Here are two very valuable sites for obtaining such useful information:

Pew Research Center (http://www.pewresearch.org/): This is an excellent source for surveys of public opinion on a multitude of topics.
Gallup (http://www.gallup.com/home.aspx): A classic, reliable survey organization that measures opinion on a wide range of topics, both national and international.

Wikipedia: Credible Scholarship or Mob Rule?

Wikipedia, the online collaborative encyclopedia, is the most widely used general reference source on the Internet (Smith, 2019). As Association for Psychological Science President Mahzarin Banaji (2011) noted, "It is the largest collaboratively produced knowledge repository that has ever existed."

One serious problem with *Wikipedia*, however, is that it takes contributions from almost anyone willing to make entries. Information can be unreliable, even wrong (Kolbe, 2018). Sources of articles contributed are often omitted. Even though *Wikipedia* articles often include links to valid and credible sources, and some articles are first-rate scholarly works, nevertheless you may be quoting merely an interested party with no expertise and a decidedly biased view. Ironically, administrators at *Wikipedia* caution against using it as a primary source because "anyone in the world can edit an article, deleting accurate information or adding false information" ("*Wikipedia*: Citing *Wikipedia*," 2017). It is best to use it as one possible starting point for your research but not as a primary, reliable reference.

News and Blogging Sites: Be Very Choosy

Although of limited breadth, some blogging sites can be useful as sources of very recent political news, world events, and popular culture stories and issues. These sites are usually accessible from computers in your college library, even on your smartphones. The opinions offered by bloggers are sometimes interesting, even amusing, and often incendiary, but they are not credible sources of information. Many blogging sites, however, include detailed articles by reputable authors with frequent links to online newspapers, magazines, and scholarly articles. Potentially useful blogging sites include the following:

CNN Politics (http://www.cnn.com/politics)
Daily Kos (http://www.dailykos.com/)
Huffington Post (www.huffingtonpost.com)
National Review (www.nationalreview.com)
Politico (www.politico.com)
Real Clear Politics (http://realclearpolitics.com)
Salon (http://www.salon.com)
Slate (http://www.slate.com/)

Be very careful using these blogging sites, however. To greater or lesser extent, they all have a certain political leaning. They are best for getting you started on recent political and social events and news items, but they are not credible sources in and of themselves. You should not offer *Huffington Post*, for example, as your primary source. Look for credible sources who write articles included on the site (e.g., experts in their fields).

Famous Quotation Sites: The Wisdom of Others

Famous quotations can often add spice and interest, and sometimes humor, to your presentation. There are several useful, non-subscription (free), online sites for finding relevant quotations, such as the following:

Brainyquote (http://www.brainyquote.com/)
Bartlett's Familiar Quotations (http://www.bartlettsquotes.com/)
YourDictionary (http://quotes.yourdictionary.com/)

Evaluating Internet Information: Basic Steps

The Internet can be a phenomenal resource for finding high-quality information, but it also provides a monsoon of misinformation. For example, I received from a friend the following attachment in an email:

> These are actual comments made on students' report cards by teachers in the New York City public school system.
>
> 1. Since my last report, your child has reached rock bottom and has started to dig.
> 2. I would not allow this student to breed.
> 3. Your child has delusions of adequacy.
> 4. Your son is depriving a village somewhere of an idiot.
> 5. Your son sets low personal standards and then consistently fails to achieve them.
> 6. The student has a "full six-pack" but lacks the plastic thing to hold it all together.
> 7. This child has been working with too much glue.
> 8. When your daughter's IQ reaches 50, she should sell.
> 9. The gates are down, the lights are flashing, but the train isn't coming.
> 10. If this student were any more stupid, he'd have to be watered twice a week.
> 11. It is impossible to believe that the sperm that created this child beat out 1,000,000 others.
> 12. The wheel is turning, but the hamster is definitely dead.

Confident that public school teachers would not have written these "actual comments," especially on a report card, I used the Internet to check on the credibility of this report. I chose one of the comments, typed it verbatim into the Google search window, and located websites that printed the same list of comments but claimed that the list was garnered from British military officer fitness reports, employee performance evaluations, military performance appraisals, and appraisals of federal employees. There were 672 Google hits that printed this list of comments attributed to various sources. The list is almost certainly fabricated. How would anyone have gathered these comments? Who has unfettered access to student report cards, and what teacher would be foolish enough to make such objectionable comments on a report card sent home to parents, risking legal action or termination of employment? Consider whether claims made on Internet sites are even plausible (see Chapter 12 for elaboration).

Then there is the oft-repeated Internet hoax that Congress is considering passage of the "Americans with No Abilities Act." The act would defend millions of

CARTOON 4.1: As humorist Will Rogers reportedly said, what gets us into real trouble is "what we know that ain't so." Consult snopes.com to correct urban myths and misinformation, such as the spiders and sex statistics that "ain't so."

Americans who "lack any real skills or ambition." Originally a political satire published by *The Onion* in June 1998 that lampooned the Americans with Disabilities Act, the satirical piece has been circulating for two decades on the Internet as a serious news story constantly "updated" (see "Democrats Introduce Americans with No Abilities Act," 2017). It is a joke! How could it be otherwise? Despite the low opinion most Americans have of Congress, it is totally implausible that such a silly piece of legislation would ever be proposed by members of either major political party.

The Internet is a rich source of rumor, gossip, and hoaxes, so you should exercise extreme caution when using it for serious, credible research. How do you separate the high-quality information on the Internet from the hokum? In general, follow four easy steps (see "Evaluating Internet Resources," 2019).

1. **Consider the source.** The specific source of the information is not always clear from accessing a website. Are you looking at medical information from the Mayo Clinic or from an anonymous source? If no source is evident other than the name of a website, be very suspicious. Even an author's name

without accompanying credentials is dubious. You may be able to find the credentials of an author by consulting *Biography Index*. Simply typing the author's name in the Google search window will often reveal whether the person has strong credentials or is a sketchy source associated with biased or questionable affiliations. If you can't verify an author's credentials, don't use the source. Check to see if references are cited in the article, and make a quick check of some of them to see if they exist or are from reputable sources.

2. **Consider source bias.** No matter the source, if the website uses a hard sell to peddle products, therapies, or ideas, be wary. Look for sites that have no vested interest, no products to sell, and no axe to grind. Look at the website address. If it ends in *gov* or *edu*, the website is sponsored and maintained by a governmental or an educational institution with a reputation to protect. If the address ends in *com*, it is a commercial site with varying levels of credibility. If such sites are offering fact-checking information, then their credibility and profitability are dependent on accuracy. Website addresses ending in *org* are sponsored by organizations and also have varying credibility depending on the reputation of the organization.

3. **Determine document currency.** Not everything on the Internet is recent. Look for current information. Websites sometimes indicate when the site was last updated. Many documents indicate the date at the top or at the end of the document. You can also make a rough estimate of the currency of the document from the currency of the information contained in the article and from any sources cited in the article. If the source references are all outdated (at least five years old or older), you can deduce that the site has not been updated recently. We live in a fast-changing world. You will want to use the most recent information, not what may have been true at one time but may no longer be true now.

4. **Use fact-checking sites.** The validity of many claims can be checked for accuracy at a number of sites. Potential urban myths and hoaxes, such as "marijuana contains alien DNA from outside our solar system" (a factually ridiculous article posted to show people's tendency to share articles without reading them); "90% of people in the U.S. marry their high school sweethearts," and "Coca-Cola is an effective spermicide" can be checked at Snopes (www.snopes.com). Most political claims, especially when made in the heat of a political election, can be checked for accuracy at nonpartisan sites such as PolitiFact (https://www.politifact.com), FactCheck (https://www.factcheck.org), and The Fact Checker (http://www.washingtonpost.com/news/fact-checker/). Medical claims can be checked for accuracy at sites with a long history of credibility, such as Centers for Disease Control

and Prevention (www.cdc.gov), Mayo Clinic (MayoClinic.com), American Cancer Society (cancer.org), American Heart Association (americanheart .org), and the American Diabetes Association (diabetes.org). News events can be checked at reputable news agencies' sites such as *The New York Times* (https://www.nytimes.com), CNN (www.cnn.com), *The Wall Street Journal* (https://www.wsj.com/), and *The Christian Science Monitor* (https://www .csmonitor.com/).

LIBRARIES: BRICKS-AND-MORTAR RESEARCH FACILITIES

The Internet is a wonderful virtual resource, but the bricks-and-mortar library buildings still house books, documents, and reference works that cannot be found on the Internet. College libraries also are computerized, and most allow students to access the Internet on library computers. Thus, college libraries provide "one-stop shopping" for information on speech topics. A huge majority of Americans view libraries as an excellent repository of trustworthy and reliable information. Millennials especially (87%), according to a Pew Research study, are the most supportive of any age group (Geiger, 2017).

Every college library offers one or more tours of its facility. Take the tour. Even if you are already knowledgeable about using a library, the tour will familiarize you with where materials are located in a specific library.

Librarian: Expert Navigator

Begin researching early. A frenzied attempt to research your speech topic in the library the night before your presentation will jump-start your anxiety and prove to be a less than satisfactory experience. If you do not know quite where to begin, ask the librarian; there is no better single source of information on researching a speech topic. Your librarian is the expert on information location. Do not expect the librarian to do your research for you, but he or she will guide you on your journey through the maze of information if you get stuck.

Library Catalogues: Computer Versions

For decades, the card catalogue was a standard starting point for most research. The card catalogue, listing all books contained in the library on 3 × 5 cards by author, title, or subject, has become antiquated. The old card catalogues have been computerized in almost all libraries in the United States.

PHOTO 4.2: The Library of Congress is the world's largest library, housing more than 167 million items in 470 languages. About 10,000 items are added to the collection *each day*. Conveniently, many of the Library's resources (and these facts) are available online at www.loc .gov. "I couldn't find anything on my speech topic" is hardly a plausible excuse these days. Do not ignore traditional libraries in your search for high-quality information for your speeches. As Neil Gaiman notes, "Google can bring you back 100,000 answers. A librarian can bring you back the right one."

The computer catalogue, like its predecessor, lists books according to author, title, and subject. An important distinguishing characteristic of the computer catalogue is that you can do a keyword search. Type in "mountain climbing," and a list of titles appears related to this subject. You can also keyword search by author names. Computer catalogues also indicate whether the book is available or checked out, saving you time.

Periodicals: Popular Information Sources

The Reader's Guide to Periodical Literature provides current listings for articles in hundreds of popular magazines in the United States. Articles are listed by both author and subject, *and there is a computer version* titled *Reader's Guide Abstracts and Full Text*. This computer version is faster to use, and it includes a brief abstract, or summary, of the listed magazine articles and full-text articles from more than 100 periodicals. There are many other periodical indexes. Check with your librarian to discover which are available at your college library.

Newspapers: An Old Standby

Despite their recent economic struggles, newspapers are still one of the richest sources of information on current topics. Your college library will undoubtedly subscribe to the local newspaper. Database indexes for newspapers include Newsbank Index, the InfoTrac National Newspaper Index, and UMI's Newspaper Abstracts. In addition, every major newspaper (e.g., *The New York Times, Los Angeles Times, USA Today, The Boston Globe, Chicago Tribune, The Wall Street Journal*) has its own website that includes major news stories online each day for up-to-the-minute information on breaking news and an archive of past articles on topics.

Reference Works: Beyond *Wikipedia*

General reference works available in most college libraries are *Statistical Abstracts of the United States, World Almanac, Monthly Labor Review, FBI Uniform Crime Report, Vital Statistics of the United States, Facts on File, The Guinness Book of World Records,* and *Who's Who in America.* References for government related information include *Monthly Catalogue of United States Government Publications, Congressional Quarterly Weekly Report, The Congressional Record, The Congressional Digest,* and *The Congressional Index.*

Databases: Computerized Collections of Credible Information

Databases can be extremely helpful resources for researching speech topics. There are many such databases, and your library may subscribe to some or all of the following:

ProQuest (http://www.proquest.com/): This database makes thousands of periodicals and newspapers available for research.

Social Science Research Network (http://www.ssrn.com/en/): SSRN consists of two parts: an abstract database of more than 810,000 scholarly papers and an Electronic Paper Collection of almost 600,000 downloadable full-text documents in PDF format.

LexisNexis Academic (https://academic.lexisnexis.eu): This provides full-text access to thousands of magazine articles, newspapers, legal documents, and transcripts of television programs.

Academic Search Complete (EBSCO) (https://www.ebsco.com /products/research-databases/academic-search-complete): This is a leading resource for scholarly research; one of the world's largest educational databases.

INTERVIEWING: QUESTIONING EXPERTS

Research interviews are sometimes a very productive resource for your speeches. Interviewing local artists about painting techniques or about standards for determining the difference in quality between a Picasso painting and a three-year-old's crayon drawing could be quite useful. Interviewing an expert on hybrid car technology might be a great place to begin your research on this topic. Experts can often guide your search by telling you where to search and what to avoid.

Student speakers often assume that no expert would want to be interviewed by just a student. That is usually untrue, especially when you consider how many experts are college professors on your campus. If your topic is a campus issue, such as parking problems or theft of car stereos, an interview with the campus chief of security could provide valuable information.

Interview Plan: Be Prepared

No research interview should be conducted without a specific plan of action. Your plan should include what you hope to find, whom you will interview and why, a specific meeting time and place arranged with the interviewee, and prepared questions that will likely elicit helpful information. Avoid questions that

PHOTO 4.3: Don't assume that experts, in this case a college professor, are uninterested in being interviewed by a student.

ask the obvious or tell you what you already know. Also avoid leading questions such as "You couldn't possibly believe that this campus has no parking problem, could you?" In addition, avoid hostile or belligerent questions such as "When you screwed up the arrest of that student accused of stealing car stereos on campus, did you make the arrest because you are biased against Middle Eastern people?" Ask difficult questions if you need to, but be respectful to the interviewee. Open-ended questions are usually a good way to begin a research interview. Consider a few examples:

> Do you believe we have a parking problem on campus?
> What actions have been taken to address the parking issues on campus?
> What more should be done about campus parking?

Interview Conduct: Act Appropriately

The manner in which you conduct yourself during the interview will usually determine whether the interview will be a success and provide useful information. Dress appropriately for the interview. Sloppy or bizarre dress will likely insult the interviewee. Always be on time for your meeting. If you are late, the interview may be cancelled. Never record your interview without the expressed permission of the interviewee. This is not ambush journalism or an undercover operation with hidden cameras trying to catch an interviewee telling a lie. Stay focused and avoid meandering into unfruitful side discussions. Take careful notes. Stay within the allotted time for the interview. Thank the interviewee for answering your questions. Review your notes after the interview, and write down any additional clarifying notations that will help you remember what transpired during the interview.

Interviewing by Email: Surprise Yourself

Not all interviews need to be in person. You might be surprised by how readily experts from around the world are happy to answer a few short questions posed to them by inquiring, eager students. Students from various places in the United States and even from distant countries have contacted me by email to ask a few pertinent questions regarding communication concepts and issues. I am always flattered to be contacted and willing to respond. Many experts have home pages with an email address. Make a short, initial inquiry about being interviewed. Lengthy emails may go unread. If the expert agrees to answer questions, be brief and concise. Ask only a few well-phrased, precise questions. Proofread every email for proper spelling and grammar. Fewer questions are more likely to get answers than a lengthy survey.

SUMMARY

Gathering relevant, credible material for your speech is not a casual event. You should begin early and have a focused plan of attack. Although the Internet is an amazing, plentiful source of information, it is also a source of abundant misinformation, hoaxes, gossip, and questionable opinions by all sorts of individuals, some identified and others anonymous. The library is still a major resource for speech research. Knowing how to use it efficiently and effectively can save you time and prove enormously productive. In some instances, you can generate your own information by interviewing experts.

TED TALKS AND YOUTUBE VIDEOS

Empowerment and Technology: "How to Get Empowered, Not Overpowered, by AI"

Power of the Internet: "What Everyday Citizens Can Do to Claim Power on the Internet"

Wikipedia: "Is Wikipedia a Credible Source?"

For relevant links to these TED Talks and YouTube videos, see the *Practically Speaking* Companion Website: www.oup.com/he/rothwell-ps3e. You can also gain access by typing the title of the speech reference into a Google search window or by doing the same on the TED Talks or YouTube sites.

CHECKLIST

When evaluating Internet information, did you remember to

☐ Consider the credibility of sources?

☐ Consider possible source bias?

☐ Determine document currency?

☐ Use fact-checking sites?

☐ See Chapters 5 and 13 for additional tips on evaluating sources of information.

CRITICAL THINKING QUESTIONS

1. Is there any potential bias in government sites, such as the U.S. Census Bureau?

2. Are fact-checking services unbiased? Some have won Pulitzer Prizes; does this make them impervious to claims of some bias?

3. Is it possible to be completely objective when fact checking?

NOTE: Online **student resources**, such as practice tests, flashcards, and other activities, can be accessed at www.oup.com/he/rothwell-ps3e

Using Supporting Materials Effectively

Faux conservative Stephen Colbert, a self-described "well-intentioned, poorly informed, high-class idiot" (quoted by Solomon, 2005), pretended to be contemptuous of facts while favoring "truthiness," that is, asserting what one wishes were true even though it is not. As Colbert amusingly noted on his now defunct Comedy Central show *The Colbert Report*, "I'm not a fan of facts. You see, facts can change, but my opinion will never change, no matter what the facts are" (quoted by Peyser, 2006). Unlike satirist Colbert's fake character, one of your chief concerns should be the facts and the supporting materials that bolster your facts. Case in point: On December 4, 2016, 28-year-old Edgar Maddison Welch walked into the Comet Ping Pong pizzeria in Washington, DC, and discharged his firearm in the mistaken belief that he was rescuing abused children held captive in a sex-slave ring housed in the pizzeria's basement (Debies-Carl, 2017). The pizzeria had no basement and no abused children imprisoned. He fell for an absurd, fact-free conspiracy theory promulgated widely on the Internet. As Voltaire is reputed to have said long ago: "Those who can make you believe absurdities can make you commit atrocities." Fortunately, in the "Pizzagate" incident, quick response from law enforcement prevented a potential atrocity.

Without supporting materials, you would have the mere shell of a speech—empty, insubstantial, even dangerous. **Supporting materials** are the examples, statistics, and testimony used to bolster a speaker's assertions. Chapter 13 explains the fallacious (erroneous) use of examples, statistics, and testimony that serves "truthiness" in the more complex context of developing arguments. This chapter, however, focuses on the more fundamental issue of how to use supporting materials constructively. Thus, ***the purpose of this chapter is to identify types of supporting materials and their effective use.*** Toward that end, this chapter discusses (1) competent use of examples, (2) competent use of statistics, and (3) competent use of testimony as supporting materials.

Using supporting materials is an audience-centered process. The three primary questions your listeners are likely to ask, and you need to answer during your speech, are "What do you mean?," "How do you know?," and "Why should we care?" Thus, *supporting materials accomplish four specific goals: to clarify points, to support claims, to gain interest, and to create impact.*

USING EXAMPLES COMPETENTLY

Examples are specific instances of a general category of objects, ideas, people, places, actions, experiences, or phenomena. The principal purposes of examples are to improve understanding and to support points made in your speeches. This section discusses the types of examples used in speeches and how to use them appropriately and effectively.

Types of Examples: Specific Illustrations

The well-chosen example makes your speech memorable, and it may have a great impact on listeners. There are four main types of examples: hypothetical, real, brief, and extended.

Hypothetical Examples: It Could Happen   A **hypothetical example** describes an imaginary situation, one that is concocted to make a point, illustrate an idea, or identify a general principle. Hypothetical examples help listeners envision what a situation might be like. They tap into similar experiences listeners have had without having to cite actual occurrences or historical events that may not be readily available. *As long as the hypothetical example is consistent with known facts, it will be believable.* A hypothetical example can also help an audience visualize what might occur. Imagine what it would be like to experience a hurricane, tornado, or tsunami. In what ways would your life be changed if you suddenly lost your job, were laid up in a hospital for three months, or became permanently disabled? These hypothetical examples help listeners picture what might happen, and they motivate listeners to take action that might prevent such occurrences. When a real example is not available, a hypothetical one can be a useful substitute. It's the difference between "when you lost your job" and "if you lost your job."

Real Examples: It Did Happen   Actual occurrences are **real examples**. A chief benefit of using a real example is that it cannot be easily discounted by listeners as simply "made up" or that it "won't occur." In November 2018, a raging wildfire completely destroyed the town of Paradise, California, a community of about 27,000 people. Imagine what residents who survived this firestorm must have endured. The destruction of an entire town of this size may have seemed unimaginable until it happened.

Unlike hypothetical examples, real examples can sometimes profoundly move an audience. For example, during the tumultuous protests in Iran following the disputed presidential election in June 2009, 26-year-old Neda Agha-Soltan stepped from her car to get fresh air while caught for an hour in traffic clogged by mass protests. Within seconds she was shot in the chest by a suspected government sniper ("Who Was Neda?," 2009). Caught on a video cellphone by a bystander, her agonizing death almost instantly became a rallying cry for the antigovernment protesters in the streets. The video was posted on YouTube and was seen by millions around the world. Protesters brandished copies of a picture showing her last moment of life. Mehdi Karroubi, an opposition leader and presidential candidate, called Neda a martyr. "A young girl, who did not have a weapon in her soft hands, or a grenade in her pocket, became a victim of thugs who are supported by a horrifying intelligence apparatus," he wrote (quoted by Fathi, 2009). Neda Agha-Soltan became a symbol of the Iranian uprising.

PHOTO 5.1: Protests erupted around the world when Neda Agha-Soltan was shot and killed during the Iranian uprising in 2009. This one occurred in Los Angeles. Real examples can be quite powerful.

Real examples have immediacy and genuineness that hypothetical examples typically lack. Just picture the different response you would have to "I could become an alcoholic and so could you" and a speaker saying, "I am an alcoholic, and if it happened to me, it could happen to you." Real examples have more credibility and impact than hypothetical examples. The firestorm that wiped out the town of Paradise negates anyone from arguing, "That would never happen." It can, and it did!

Brief Examples: Short and to the Point   Sometimes you can make a point quickly with a **brief example.** "The Golden Gate Bridge was viewed as an 'upside-down rat trap' that would mar the beauty of the San Francisco Bay and was opposed by over 2,300 lawsuits. Today, the Golden Gate Bridge is not only considered one of the world's most iconic landmarks, it is also a symbol of engineering ingenuity" (Diridon, 2018, p. A6). This brief example makes the point that large infrastructure projects are almost always met with significant opposition because change can be an ordeal. With short attention spans and information overload, brief examples work well to maintain your audience's interest.

Extended Examples: Telling a Story   Sometimes a story is so profound and so moving that only a detailed, **extended example** can do it justice. Consider this extended, real example:

> Genie was 13 years old when she was discovered in a suburb of Los Angeles in 1970. From the time she was 20 months old, Genie had been imprisoned in a bare room with the curtains drawn. She was strapped naked to a potty chair and sometimes tied in a makeshift straitjacket by her abusive father. Genie had minimal human contact. If she made noise, her father did not speak to her but literally barked or growled, or beat her with a stick. Genie's mother, almost blind and fearing her husband's brutality, left Genie isolated and deprived.
>
> When Genie was discovered, she could not walk, talk, stand erect, chew solid food, or control her bodily functions. She was about four-and-a-half feet tall and weighed about 60 pounds. Despite years of intensive training, Genie never lost her unnatural voice quality, and she never learned to master language. Her very ability to communicate with other humans was forever impaired. *(Carroll, 2016)*

A briefer version of this touching, tragic story could be told, but which details would you delete and with what effect? A story's length must fit the time constraints for your speech, but for full impact a story sometimes must have at least minimal elaboration.

Using Examples Effectively: Choose Carefully

Using examples effectively requires skill. The well-chosen example can make a speech come alive. Here are some basic tips.

Use Relevant Examples: Stay on Point   Examples must be relevant to the point you make. A young Abraham Lincoln, acting as a defense attorney in a courtroom trial, explained what "self-defense" meant by using a relevant story to clarify his point. He told the jury about a man who, while walking down a country road with pitchfork in hand, was attacked by a vicious dog. The man was forced to kill the dog with his pitchfork. A local farmer who owned the dog asked the man why he had to kill his dog. The man replied, "What made him try to bite me?" The farmer persisted, "But why didn't you go at him with the other end of the pitchfork?" The man responded, "Why didn't he come at me with the other end of the dog?" (cited in Larson, 2012). Lincoln made his point that the degree of allowable force is dependent on the degree of force used by the attacker.

Choose Vivid Examples: Create Images   Examples usually work best when they are vivid. A vivid example triggers feelings and provokes strong images (Pratkanis & Aronson, 2001). Student Kittie Grace (2000) uses a vivid example to evoke a strong image on her main theme that hotels in America are unsanitary:

> According to the August 8, 1999 *Hotel and Motel Management Journal* or *HMMJ*, in Atlantic City, New Jersey, two unsuspecting German tourists shared a motel room which had been cleaned that morning, but a foul smell permeated through the room. After the third complaint, housekeeping cleaned under the bed finding the body of a dead man decomposing, all because housekeeping failed to clean under the bed in the first place. *(Grace, 2000, p. 86)*

This example is so vivid that it quite likely will come to mind the next time you stay at a hotel.

Use Representative Examples: Reflect What Is Accurate   Examples should be representative. Was the example of the dead body under the hotel bed representative? Kittie Grace presented voluminous evidence that significant numbers of people are getting sick and dying from unsanitary conditions in hotels in the United States because of negligent housekeeping. The example of the dead body graphically represents just how negligent the housekeeping can be. She does not claim that dead bodies will be found under hotel beds on a regular basis, or even imply such. Nevertheless, its representativeness can be called into question. Most of us do not discover dead bodies under hotel beds in our entire lifetime. For this we can be thankful.

When vivid examples are unrepresentative, they have the power to distort the truth. The graphic, gruesome, and grand event can certainly galvanize our attention. Television producer Gary David Goldberg once sardonically observed, "Left to their own devices, the networks would televise live executions. Except Fox—they'd televise live naked executions" ("TV or not TV," 1993, p. 5E). When an outrageous, shocking, controversial, and dramatic event gains our attention but distorts our perceptions of the facts, this is called the **vividness effect** (Glassner, 1999). The shocking example can erroneously negate credible, contradictory evidence (Sunstein & Zeckhauser, 2009). For example, a single

PHOTO 5.2: The vividness effect is illustrated by a dramatic event. The crash of Asiana Flight 214 at the San Francisco International Airport on July 6, 2013, is such an event.

airline disaster can provoke fear of boarding a jetliner and induce many people to choose driving their automobile instead. Yet the odds of perishing in a plane crash are 1 in 11 *million*, whereas the odds of dying in a car crash in the United States are 1 in 5 *thousand* (Ropeik, 2008).

Stack Examples: When One Is Not Enough   Sometimes a single example does not suffice to make a point clear, memorable, interesting, or adequately supported. Note the value of using plentiful examples stacked one on top of another in the following presentation:

Words are human creations. You have the power to invent new words. For example, in the late 1800s, male residents of Boonville, California, created a lingo of their own called Boontling, mostly to talk around women without them understanding what was being said. The rules for Boontling with its more than 1,300 words are those of English. Those individuals who *harp Boont* (speak Boontling) concocted some colorful words. Examples include: *grey-matter kimmie* (college professor), *tongue-cuppy* (vomiting), *scotty* (heavy eater), *wheeler* (lie), *shoveltooth* (medical doctor), and *high-split* (very tall, slender man). Knowing just these few

Boont words gives you the ability to translate this sentence: "The high-split, grey-matter kimmie told a wheeler to the local shoveltooth about his supposed tongue-cuppy experience resulting from being a scotty." There are still a few speakers of Boontling, but most have *piked to the dusties* (died).

In this instance, using only one or two examples of Boontling would not adequately clarify the main point, create much impact, support the claims, or spark much interest.

Choosing apt examples and using them competently can mean the difference between a mediocre or memorable speech. *Never underestimate the importance of picking your examples for maximum clarity, accuracy, and impact.*

USING STATISTICS COMPETENTLY

Statistics are measures of what is true or factual expressed in numbers. Statistics can provide magnitude and frequency and allow comparisons. For example, in a speech on the history of the Internet, you could note that the first Internet website was info.cern.ch, created by Tim Berners-Lee in December 1990 ("How We Got," 2008). The number of websites (not Web pages) worldwide jumped to *24 million* by 2000. The number reached more than 1.5 billion in 2018 ("Total Number of Websites," 2019). The magnitude of the Internet today and its astronomical growth in just slightly less than 30 years (comparison) are exhibited by these statistics.

A well-chosen statistic can support claims, show trends, correct false assumptions, validate hypotheses, and contradict myths, perhaps not as dramatically and memorably as a vivid example, but often more validly and effectively (Lindsey & Yun, 2003).

You should be cautious, however, not to take statistics at face value. For example, British physician Andrew Wakefield coauthored an article in the highly renowned British journal *The Lancet* in 1998, asserting that 12 normal children became autistic after receiving the measles, mumps, and rubella vaccine. First, the sample size was ridiculously small, so that should have signaled extreme caution. Second, several efforts to replicate Wakefield's results found no such correlation between the vaccination and autism. Third, it was discovered that three of the "previously normal" children in Wakefield's sample who supposedly became autistic didn't actually become autistic, and five other children had documented developmental problems before taking the vaccine. Wakefield's article resulted in a mass refusal by parents in Britain and the United States to give their children the necessary vaccination, resulting in significant outbreaks of disease among children. *The Lancet* retracted the article in 2010, declaring it "an elaborate fraud" and concluding: "It was utterly clear, without any ambiguity at all, that the statements in the paper were utterly false" (see Smith, 2015, and "Do Vaccines Cause Autism?" 2019).

Statistical fallacies, or errors, in the use of statistics are discussed in detail in Chapter 13. This section, however, addresses basic ways to use statistics competently and without error.

Choose Statistics for Effect: Beyond Numbing Numbers

Statistics do not have to be dull and mind numbing. In fact, research shows that they can be very persuasive when used properly (Perloff, 2016). For example, in April 2018, Nebraska State Police seized illegally obtained fentanyl, an opioid more than 30 times more potent than heroin. A single two-milligram dose can be fatal. *USA Today* calculated that this single drug bust of 118 pounds of fentanyl was capable of killing more than *26 million people* from overdosing (Shannon, 2018). These statistics are stunning, and they spotlight the catastrophic danger of opioid abuse in America.

Use Accurate Statistics Accurately: No Distorting

A statistic itself should be accurate, but the speaker should also use an accurate statistic carefully to avoid misleading an audience. Consider, for example, a major study that found the national average teacher salary for public elementary and secondary schools was $58,950 in 2017, a $17,143 improvement from the average salary in 2000. When adjusted for inflation, however, teachers' purchasing power *declined* by 1.6% ("Digest of Education Statistics," 2018). The $17,143 salary increase is an accurate statistic, but it would not be accurate to claim from this statistic that teacher salaries improved substantially in the decade-and-a-half period based only on raw salary increases.

Make Statistics Concrete: Meaningful Numbers

Large statistics do not always communicate meaning to listeners. For example, the difficulty in sending a spaceship to Alpha Centauri, the nearest star system to Earth, is its distance—4.3 light years from our sun. That is equal to about 26 trillion miles (Angier, 2002). These statistics are so large that they have little meaning beyond "really big." To bring it down to Earth a bit more, consider that the fastest spacecraft ever launched is NASA's New Horizons, which travels at 36,373 miles per hour. If New Horizons were targeted at Alpha Centauri, it would take approximately 78,000 years to get there ("How Long Would It Take," 2015). Providing this concrete description of a number beyond big helps make the numbers meaningful to the average person.

Make Statistical Comparisons: Gaining Perspective

Making a meaningful statistical comparison can provide real perspective for your audience. Student Davis Vaughn (2013), in his speech at the Interstate Oratorical Association contest, makes this comparison: "The *American Journal of Public Health*'s May 2012 issue details, while LGBT youth only make up 3.5% of the total adolescent population, they disproportionately represent almost 40% of homeless youth across the country" (p. 11). Student Audrey Baker (2018), also speaking at the annual Interstate Oratorical Association contest, citing a March 14, 2017 PEW Charitable Trust report, notes this comparison regarding compensating the wrongfully imprisoned: "Texas offers $80,000 for every year spent in prison. Wisconsin, on the other hand, pays $5,000 for every year spent in prison, capped at a maximum of $25,000. So, a person in a state like Wisconsin could be wrongfully imprisoned for 25 years and receive less than a third of what a person in Texas would receive after one year" (p. 58). These statistical comparisons provide needed, powerful perspective.

CARTOON 5.1, PIGGY BANKS: According to the AFL-CIO 2019 "Executive Paywatch" report, CEOs at S&P 500 companies average "287 times more money than the average U.S. rank-and-file worker" (Shuler, 2019). Statistical comparisons can provide important perspective.

Use Credible Sources: Build Believability

Biased sources diminish the quality and the credibility of a statistic. *Objectivity* and *accuracy* are essential for sources to be credible. Sources exhibit objectivity by having no stake in the outcome of their inquiries. They just want to report the facts accurately with no agenda to advance.

Speakers often cite credible sources for some, but not all, statistics used. Make it an automatic practice that *every time you use a statistic you cite a credible source for that statistic* unless the statistic is common knowledge, such as the United States has 50 states. Listeners should never be given the opportunity to wonder, "Where did the speaker get that statistic?"

Stack Statistics: Creating Impact

A particularly effective strategy is to stack statistics, especially statistics that also show comparisons. Student Caleb Rawson (2013) provides an example:

> Retirement savings woes are affecting every American. According to a report published by the Employee Benefit Research Institute this March, since 2007 the percentage of Americans "not at all confident" that they will have enough money for retirement has increased from 10% to 28%. The percent of those who are confident has decreased from 27% to 13%, and with good reason. Only 66% of American workers have anything set aside for retirement and 57% of workers have less than $25,000 set aside for retirement. *(p. 29)*

Stacking statistics, however, should be used sparingly and only to create an impact on the central points in a speech. An audience will quickly tune out if you stack a mountain of statistics repeatedly.

Statistics can be enormously useful, even powerful, as a supporting material for your speeches. Choosing the most apt statistic and using it competently, however, are key concerns. Note how the following example combines strategies for competent use of statistics:

> Science writer Steve Mirsky, in a June 2017 *Scientific American* article, notes that on the basis of 65 studies, researchers estimate that the world has approximately 25 *million metric tons* (55.1 billion pounds) of spiders—half the estimated weight of the Great Wall of China, according to the Guinness Book of World Records. The world's entire human population weighs less than 300 million metric tons. There are either really enormous spiders out there lurking, tipping the scales, or the spider population vastly outnumbers humans. Mirsky quotes American Museum of Natural History arachnologist

Norman Platnick to sum up the worldwide prevalence of spiders: "Wherever you sit, a spider is probably no more than a few yards away." Mirsky offers the somewhat unsettling observation, "As most spiders have eight eyes, it's probably looking at you, too."

Here the stack of statistics provides an effective comparison, is attention grabbing, accurate, concrete, and substantiated by three credible sources.

Use Visual Aids: Clarify Statistical Trends and Analysis

Displaying complex statistical trends and analysis can be clarified by using visual aids. Simply reciting lots of statistics may leave your audience baffled and frustrated. A simple graph (see Chapter 11 for several types) can make statistics more comprehensible. Cluttered depictions of complex statistics, however, don't work well oratorically. If while reading you can view the visual aids close up, and you have time to study each one, then complex graphics might be useful. When

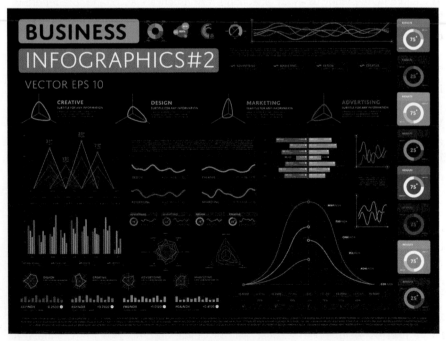

PHOTO 5.3: Displaying statistical comparisons and analysis with a visual aid can provide clarification and understanding, but be careful not to overwhelm your audience with abundant graphs in a single image. Don't clutter your visual aid; keep it simple. Break complex statistical analysis into several separate visual aids if necessary.

giving a speech, however, your audience usually cannot carefully examine each statistical graph because of time limits and restrictions on displaying statistical graphs large enough to be seen by your entire audience, so your visual aid may be more a visual hindrance. When displaying statistics, of course, you need to explain your graphs, not assume that they speak for themselves. (See Chapter 11 for more detail on displaying statistics visually.)

USING TESTIMONY COMPETENTLY

Testimony, derived from the Latin word for *witness*, is a firsthand account of events or the conclusions offered publicly by experts on a topic. In this section, several kinds of testimony that you can use to support your points are discussed, and ways to use testimony competently are explored.

Types of Testimony: Relying on Others

There are three principal types of testimony you can use as supporting material. Testimony of experts is probably the most commonly used, but testimonies of eyewitnesses and non-experts are also effective.

Testimony of Experts: Relying on Those in the Know   Tom Nichols (2017), in his provocative book *The Death of Expertise*, pointedly argues: "I fear we are witnessing the death of the ideal of expertise itself, a Google-fueled, Wikipedia-based, blog-sodden, collapse of any division between professionals and laypeople, students and teachers, knowers and wonderers—in other words, between those of any achievement in an area and those with none at all." He continues: "Ignorance has become hip, with some Americans now wearing their rejection of expert advice as a badge of cultural sophistication."

Testimony of experts is a critical aspect of supporting your claims, especially if those claims are controversial. To denigrate expertise is to repudiate the value of seeking advice from medical doctors who spend years studying disease and potential cures as opposed to others who tout superficially acquired "wisdom" from "the University of Google" (e.g., Jenny McCarthy). When we step into an elevator, we expect the elevator has been checked for safety by an expert steeped in the mechanics of this vehicle that sends us up and down dozens of floors in hotels and skyscrapers. We prefer not to plummet to our death if at all possible. We don't, presumably, trust the safety of any elevator on the mere say-so of the hotel concierge, for example. As Nichols notes, "Experts are the people who know considerably more on a subject than the rest of us, and are those to whom we turn when we need advice, education, or solutions in a particular area of human knowledge." They are not infallible, but they are far more likely to be knowledgeable and correct, helping us to understand complex issues, than those who presume to speak with authority but have no substantial background to support their credibility. Do we want to listen to those who believe that Abraham Lincoln was the first president of the United States who "emaciated slaves" and that Socrates was a "great Indian chief" (Nichols, 2017), or do we value historians who can correctly identify and interpret historical facts for useful perspective on current events?

Experts can help laypeople sort fact from fantasy. Should you worry about heart disease before you reach 30 years old? Listen to the experts at the American Heart Association. Worried about the Zika virus or any new disease that emerges? Consult the Centers for Disease Control and Prevention, an organization known worldwide for relevant knowledge and accuracy.

Eyewitness Testimony: You Had to Be There   Using the testimony and accounts of those who have observed some event or activity is a staple of criminal and civil trials. Eyewitnesses support factual claims for both sides in the courtroom, and their testimony is often critical to the outcome of a case. Eyewitnesses can also be a source for news events. In the June 2009 disputed presidential election in Iran, hundreds of thousands of protesters hit the streets of Tehran in defiance of the ruling regime. In an attempt to control global perceptions of these exploding events, the Iranian government expelled foreign journalists. Major news networks and cable shows scrambled for any bits of news that they could garner. Twitter became an important source of eyewitness messages from protesters clashing with the police and the government (May, 2009). Twitter was scheduled to be shut down for maintenance, but the U.S. State Department made the highly unusual request that Twitter remain in service to keep the limited information from Iran flowing (Hannah, 2009). Protesters sent tweets continually as events were occurring to counter the spin coming from official news sources within the Iranian government.

Similarly, uprisings across the Middle East and North Africa arose, starting in Tunisia in December 2010 and spreading to Egypt, Yemen, Algeria, Morocco, Libya, and other countries. These "Arab Spring" protests were fanned by cellphone videos posted on YouTube and Facebook and by Twitter tweets sent to the outside world. A study at the University of Washington of these firsthand accounts from protesters concluded, "The Arab Spring had many causes. One of these sources was social media and its power to put a human face on political oppression" (Howard et al., 2011).

Testimony of Non-Experts: Ordinary Folks Adding Color to Events   You do not have to be an expert or an eyewitness to world events to add compelling testimony to your speech. Follow the example of newspapers, television news media, and documentary films. They all use interviews with "common folks" to spice up a story and personalize coverage of events. When the water supply in Flint, Michigan, was discovered to contain toxic levels of lead in 2015, it was mostly ordinary citizens who sought media coverage when government seemed to turn a blind eye.

How to Use Testimony Effectively

When you cite testimony to support your speech, you have to decide whether to quote exactly or merely paraphrase. Typically, you use a direct quotation when the statement is short, is well phrased, and communicates your point more eloquently or cleverly than you can. Paraphrasing is appropriate when a direct quotation is not worded in an interesting way, such as in most government documents, or when a quotation is very lengthy and needs to be shortened. Whether quoting directly or merely paraphrasing, there are a couple of ways to present testimony appropriately and effectively during your speech.

Quote or Paraphrase Accurately: Consider Context   It is imperative that you not misquote or inaccurately paraphrase either an expert or an eyewitness supporting your claims or an opponent in a debate or discussion. When quoting someone's testimony, do not crop the quotation so it takes on a different meaning than communicated in context. Do not delete important qualifiers from any statement. This is an all-too-common practice in politics on all sides of the political spectrum.

Use Qualified Sources: Credibility Matters   *Testimony from non-experts and eyewitnesses can be highly unreliable.* Non-experts can provide color and even drama to events, but they should not be quoted on topics that require technical knowledge or careful study. Abundant research also shows the unreliability of eyewitness testimony ("Eyewitness Testimony Is Often Unreliable," 2018; Wright et al., 2009). The tweets from Iranian "eyewitnesses" on the 2009 uprising could not be verified. News organizations often took these accounts as factual, yet some of these tweets could have been government plants trying to confuse the issue and create seeds of doubt for outsiders. Others may only be reporting gossip or hearsay, not direct observations of events. As Mark Glaser, host of PBS's online show *Media Shift*, observed about the Twitter phenomenon in Iran, "I feel like I'm not getting what I get at the BBC's site with confirmed sources" (quoted by May, 2009).

GENERAL CONSIDERATIONS ACROSS TYPES

There are several basic tips for using supporting materials effectively that apply to all types. They are as follows: choose interesting supporting materials, cite sources completely, abbreviate repetitive source citations, and combine types of supporting materials.

Choose Interesting Supporting Materials: Counteracting Boredom

Your first consideration when choosing supporting materials should be their credibility and strength. Nevertheless, *strong, credible, but also interesting supporting materials are the best of all choices.* Do as student Ted Dacey (2008) does when speaking about bottled water:

> Rocky Anderson, mayor of Salt Lake City, Utah, detailed the true cost of bottled water to NPR's *Talk of the Nation* on July 23, 2007. He explained: "We're told we should drink eight glasses of water a day. If you filled that glass from a tap in any major city, it will cost you about 49 cents a year. To get that same amount of bottled water, it will run around $1400 every year." *(p. 54)*

That fact is startling, and it is an interesting comparison from a credible source. He follows this with another interesting comparison from a credible source: "According to *Business Week* of April 14, 2008, to produce a 1 year's supply of

CARTOON 5.2: Vague references to "studies" and "research" are incomplete citations. What studies and whose research support the speaker's claims?

water bottles for the American market, it takes 17 billion barrels of oil each year, or enough to fuel 1 million cars for an entire year" (p. 55). He provides credible but also interesting supporting materials.

Cite Sources Completely: No Vague References

Every statistic that is not mere common knowledge, every controversial assertion of facts, and any testimony used to support claims made in speeches should have a credible source. Otherwise, dangerous nonsense can parade itself as significant truth. Unlike an essay or journal article, audience members do not typically have access to a bibliography. So you must provide sufficient information orally to build credibility.

Credible source citation should include, as a minimum:

1. the name of the source;
2. the qualifications of the source if not obvious;
3. the specific publication or media citation where the evidence can be found; and
4. the relevant date of the publication.

See **Table 5.1** for examples of complete citations of various sources.

Student Joshua Freed (2015), while citing his sources, fails to provide complete references in an otherwise strong speech on "the criminal debt penalty": "Terry Aladjem, professor at Harvard University, called this broken 'justice' system a charade. . . ." This is a nebulous citation. Is Aladjem a professor of criminology or sociology, or perhaps a professor of English or computer science with no expertise on the criminal justice system? Also, is this a current stated view of Aladjem or one offered a decade or two ago? Experts sometimes change their minds, so currency is important. *A complete citation of the source of your information enhances your credibility and persuasiveness as a speaker if your source is qualified, current, and cited completely.*

Abbreviate Repetitive Source Citations: Oral Reference Reminders

The initial oral citation of a source should be complete, but subsequent references to the same source can be abbreviated to avoid tedious repetition, unless the abbreviation might cause confusion, such as two articles from the same magazine. Student Sharon Chen (2015) abbreviates this way in her speech: "The previously cited *Asian-Pacific Law and Policy Journal* article . . ." (p. 96). Student Alexander Trent (2017) abbreviates this way in his speech: "The aforementioned Associated Press article . . ." (p. 18). Abbreviating repetitive, secondary citations makes your speech flow more smoothly.

TABLE 5.1

Oral Citation of Sources

Here are some examples from student speeches presented at the annual Interstate Oratorical Association contest that illustrate how to cite a variety of sources concisely and effectively during your speeches:

Expert Source	"Susan Dooha, Executive Director of the New York Center for Independence of the Disabled, told NPR on November 9, 2013, . . ." (Galloway, 2014, p. 39).
Website	"According to the [Gun Free Schools] Act's text listed at Congress.gov and accessed December of 2017 . . ." (Bridges, 2018, p. 52).
Academic Journal	"[Law] Professor Robin Feldman explains in the *Stanford Technology Law Review* on January 23, 2012 that . . ." (Lese, 2012, p. 161).
Television Program	"CNN of February 5, 2018 argues . . ." (De Luna, 2018).
Magazine	"U.S. News and World Report explained November 2, 2017 that . . ." (Perry, 2018, p. 67).
Personal Interview	"In an interview I had with Colin Miller, law professor at the University of South Carolina, on September 14, 2017 . . ." (Ody, 2018, p. 19).
Newspaper	"The New York Times of March 8, 2017 notes that . . ." (Rich, 2018, p. 22).
Organization	"The National Bureau of Economic Research published a study in May 2017 concluding . . ." (Kamen, 2018, p. 92).
Book	"In her 2016 book, *A Prescription for Alcoholics*, author Linda Burlison reminds us . . ." (Perry, 2017, p. 109).
Newsletter	"Harvard University Kennedy School of Government's newsletter of July 6, 2017 reveals . . ." (Gonzalez, 2018, p. 94).
TED Talk	"As software engineer Brian Olsen explains in his June 2016 TED TALK . . ." (Gonzalez, 2018, p. 95).

Combine Examples, Stats, and Quotes: The Power of Three

Sometimes you can combine examples, statistics, and quotations to provide real impact. For example, a case that texting among teens has become excessive was made in 2010 as follows:

> Reina Hardesty, a California teenager, accumulated a staggering 14,528 text messages in a single month. Her online statement from AT&T ran 440 pages, according to a January 11, 2009, *New York Post* article. Reina "explained" her 484 text messages per day or 1 every 2 minutes of her waking hours with "It was winter break and I was bored." A 2010 survey by Nielsen Media Research found that most teenagers do not reach the heights of Reina, but they do average 3,339 text messages per month. Katie Keating, a representative of AT&T, responded to inquiries about Reina's prodigious texting with this observation cited in the January 7, 2009, *Orange County Register*: "Texting is becoming more and more popular, and growing at a spectacular rate. Text-messaging is now hard-wired into our culture."

In a short space, a specific and dramatic example was offered, specific statistics were provided, and two direct quotes were used from reputable sources. Combining three types of supporting materials makes a nice package.

SUMMARY

There are four primary reasons to use supporting materials generously in your speeches: to clarify points, support claims, gain interest, and create impact. There are three chief forms of supporting materials: examples, statistics, and testimony. Each has its strengths and weaknesses. Examples can be very vivid and powerful but limited in applicability. Statistics can establish the magnitude of a problem or event and provide perspective, but they can also seem dull and tedious and distort the facts. Testimony can personalize problems and issues, but it can also be inaccurate and unreliable. In each case, consider the many tips offered for using each supporting material effectively.

TED TALKS AND YOUTUBE VIDEOS

Statistical Comparisons but Missing Citation: Chris Jordan: "Turning Powerful Stats into Art"

Using Statistics: Sebastian Wernicke: "Lies, Damned Lies and Statistics"

Misuse of Statistics: "Bill Maher: Fun with Statistics" (Warning: rough language)

Student Speech/Supporting Materials: "Informative Speech: The Causes of Homelessness" (abundant sources not always cited completely)

Use of Statistics: "The End of Average: Todd Rose '8 for 8'"

For relevant links to these TED Talks and YouTube videos, see the *Practically Speaking* Companion Website: www.oup.com/he/rothwell-ps3e. You can also gain access by typing the title of the speech reference into a Google search window or by doing the same on the TED Talks or YouTube sites.

CHECKLIST

☐ Have you chosen the most appropriate supporting material to support your claims?

☐ Are your supporting materials representative, or are they biased and out of the ordinary?

☐ Are your supporting materials accurate, and do they meet criteria for effectiveness?

☐ Do you have a credible source for each supporting material, especially for statistics and testimony?

☐ Have you cited your sources completely?

☐ Are your sources current?

☐ Have you chosen interesting supporting materials?

☐ Are you mixing supporting materials for optimum effect?

CRITICAL THINKING QUESTIONS

1. Why do you think that there is a growing trend to brand experts as "elitists?" Is this characterization ever justified? Are experts more likely to accurately predict future trends than a layperson?

2. Can you ever use too many supporting materials in your speech? If so, how would you determine when you have reached the point of diminishing returns?

3. Can non-experts ever be more accurate than experts?

NOTE: Online **student resources**, such as practice tests, flashcards, and other activities, can be accessed at www.oup.com/he/rothwell-ps3e

Attention: Getting People to Listen

erry, my close friend and colleague at Cabrillo College, had just finished lecturing in his general psychology course. Several students engaged him afterward, asking questions about points he had presented. As Terry finished and turned to gather his materials and leave, he heard a shout, turned, and was hit in the face with an ax handle by a former student. Armed with a squirt bottle with some unknown liquid, the former student waved the bottle as if to spray anyone daring to disarm him. Three courageous male students, despite not knowing what was in the bottle (it was oil and kerosene), jumped Terry's attacker and immobilized him until police officers arrived. Terry was badly wounded, bleeding profusely from his cheek that had been crushed by the blow from the ax handle, but in his dazed state he pleaded with his three students who had immobilized his attacker not to hurt him because "he has a mental disorder." Terry recovered after plastic surgery to reconstruct his cheek. Understandably, the entire campus was shaken by this event. The college held an all-day conference on implementing safety measures to prevent any such violent acts in the future.

This is a true story. Did it grab your attention? If so, is it because this event really happened, that it occurred on a college campus, and that the victim was a teacher? Is it because the story is shocking, unusual, and disturbing? Does it resonate because violence on college campuses sadly has become increasingly commonplace? Are unpleasant, intense examples such as this one always appropriate to gain an audience's attention, or should they be avoided? These and other questions are addressed in this chapter.

Gaining attention in any circumstance is challenging but critical. One national survey of individuals from a wide variety of professions revealed that the top-ranked skill for preparing and delivering a speech was keeping an audience's attention (Engleberg, 2002). Corporate media consultant Steve Crescenzo (2005) observes, "In today's short-attention-span, sound-byte society, the one thing people cannot afford to be is boring" (p. 12). A national study of first-year college students showed that almost two-fifths of respondents were often bored in class (Eagan et al., 2017). When Ellen DeGeneres hosted the Academy Awards, she put it succinctly: "Let's be honest. It's not that we don't have time for long speeches. It's that we don't have time for boring speeches" (quoted by Folk, 2014).

If your audience is not attentive, then you are talking to yourself. You want your listeners excited, engaged, touched, and anxious to hear what comes next. You do not want them yearning for those signal words "In conclusion." It is a lesson every teacher learns when lecturing to students for an entire class period and every religious leader comprehends when delivering a sermon or homily to a congregation. Most speeches are not meant to be purely entertainment, but if listeners are bored when you speak to them about significant issues, then your substantial ideas will not rouse lethargic listeners from slumber.

The next chapter addresses very specific ways to gain attention during the introduction to your speech that extend from this chapter's discussion. It is

PHOTO 6.1: Gaining audience attention is a good start, but maintaining that attention of listeners throughout your speech is a huge challenge.

important to note here, however, that grabbing the attention of your audience during your introduction but losing their attention during the rest of your speech is tantamount to a sprinter flying out of the starting blocks but flopping on the ground a few meters into the race. Getting off to a fast start on your speech by grabbing attention, *but then ignoring the far more challenging task of maintaining that attention throughout your entire speech, is a formula for failure.* Whether for 5 minutes or 55, keeping your listeners' rapt attention is a supremely difficult task, making it a topic worthy of considerable discussion and illustration that goes far beyond isolating it as a requirement only for an effective introduction to your speech.

Capturing and holding the attention of your audience has to be an integral part of your speech development. Thus, **the purpose of this chapter is to explain ways that gain and maintain the attention of your listeners while presenting your speech.** Toward that end, this chapter discusses (1) the nature of attention and the challenges it presents for both speakers and listeners, and (2) rhetorical strategies that can ignite audience attention from the beginning of your speech to its conclusion.

NATURE OF ATTENTION: A TRANSACTIONAL PROCESS

An enormously popular British ad that featured a sexy model acting seductively as she climbed inside a sleek automobile drew attention to the wrong stimulus. A study of this ad showed that the attractive model commanded attention while the automobile being advertised was virtually invisible to almost everyone watching (Clay, 2002). As a speaker, being seen in our kaleidoscopic world of images and heard above the clamoring din is your great task. As a listener, your task is to act mindfully, even if the speaker is not adept at maintaining your attention. *The nature of attention, therefore, is a transactional process in which speakers and listeners work together to create a captivating experience.* Therefore, this section explores the challenges you face as a speaker when trying to gain and maintain the attention of your listeners, and the role listeners play in assisting speakers in this endeavor.

Selective Attention of Listeners: Filtering Stimuli

Attention is unavoidably selective. **Attention** is the act of focusing on a specific stimulus to the exclusion of competing stimuli (*see access to "Volkswagen" link at end of chapter*). Herein lies the challenge for any speaker. Minds easily wander,

PHOTO 6.2: Texting in class is the number-one classroom distraction. Texting in class sends the message: "I don't care enough to pay attention to the instructor presenting a lecture."

every chance they get (Wang et al., 2018). One study reported that almost 97% of college students use their phones during class for non-educational purposes. Almost 90% of survey respondents also reported that texting is the number-one classroom distraction, followed by 70% reporting use of social media, and 40% browsing the Internet (Reid, 2013; "Study," 2016). Distractions impede effective listening. We can't comprehend and retain messages that never penetrate our awareness.

From a speaker's standpoint, the challenges of attracting attention to your message and avoiding distractions are complicated by the fact that *listeners cannot attend to two competing stimuli simultaneously* (Sma et al., 2018). When audience members are texting while hearing a speech, their minds are weaving back and forth between two incompatible tasks. *Ironically, frequent multitaskers believe they are good at balancing two tasks at once, but research shows that they are typically the worst.* As Stanford psychologist Clifford Nass notes, "It turns out multitaskers are terrible at every aspect of multitasking. They're terrible at ignoring irrelevant information; they're terrible at keeping information in their head nicely and neatly organized; and they're terrible at switching from one task to another" ("Interview: Clifford Nass," 2010). Selectivity of listeners' attention highlights the magnitude of the challenge you face gaining and maintaining your audience's focus on you, the speaker.

How to Be a Mindful Listener: Assisting the Speaker

The speaker has the primary task of generating an audience's attention, but listeners also play an important role. Imagine speaking to an audience whose members are mostly texting, updating their Facebook page, or surfing websites. The transactional nature of public speaking means that a speaker is significantly impacted by the attentiveness of his or her audience. Inattentive listeners can drain the enthusiasm from even the most talented speakers, transforming them into dull presenters just going through the motions of public speaking until they can escape the whole dreadful experience. Have you ever witnessed a comedian who couldn't get his or her audience to laugh? It's torture to watch.

Generally, listeners should be *mindful*—careful attention is given to a speaker's message. *Mindful listening is active listening*; you are engaged in the communication transaction with speakers. You are not merely a passive observer. As the old adage goes, "You have one mouth for speaking but two ears for listening." Management consulting firm Accenture surveyed 3,600 professionals from 30 countries (half men; half women) and found that nearly all respondents considered themselves to be good listeners, yet they admitted to spending much of their time exhibiting bad listening habits that included being easily distracted and multitasking (Cole, 2015). Even the possibility that a person's cellphone may ring can diminish comprehension of messages from others by 20% (Sullivan & Thompson, 2013).

Here are some tips on how you can assist a speaker by being a mindful listener.

1. *Come prepared to listen to speakers.* Even if you are part of a captive audience, don't show disdain, boredom, or antagonism toward the speaker.
2. *Avoid distractions.* Shut off any electronic device that will divert attention from the speaker and his or her message. Don't multitask. You don't learn if you are inattentive.
3. *Be an active listener.* Active listening is effortful not effortless. Focus your attention and concentrate on listening carefully for the speaker's theme and main points. Try to comprehend the speaker's core message, not every detail.
4. *Take notes if practical.* Writing down the speaker's theme and main points helps you remember them later. Provide only necessary detail that helps you understand and recall main points. If possible, review your notes for just 10 minutes within 24 hours of hearing the speech, and then review your notes for 5 minutes a week later. Research shows that this will vastly improve retention (Hoffman, 2014).

PHOTO 6.3: Multitaskers are inattentive, distracted listeners. Ironically, those who are most confident that they can "do two things at once" effectively are the least effective listeners.

5. *If the speech is informative, jot down any detail that is new information.* If the speech is argumentative/persuasive, first listen to understand the main points before evaluating each point.

6. *Listen critically for solid reasoning and strong evidence* to bolster main claims (discussed in later chapters in detail).

7. *Be ethical.* Listen respectfully, even if you strongly disagree with the speaker. Don't let your emotions (anger, frustration, etc.) cloud your thinking. Jot down any questions you might ask the speaker if given an opportunity.

SPEAKER'S ATTENTION STRATEGIES: TRIGGERING LISTENING

To meet the challenges of gaining and maintaining the attention of listeners who may not always be mindful, certain strategies can be extremely helpful. Attention is both a voluntary and an involuntary activity. A sudden shrill scream will command your instant attention. That is involuntary. It is unexpected and unavoidable. Choosing to pay attention to a speaker whose topic may not interest you initially is voluntary. Key stimulus triggers that can ignite attention involuntarily include appeals to that which is novel, startling, vital, humorous, changeable, or intense (Passer & Smith, 2016). *When direct effort is made by you to exploit such triggers, they become attention strategies.*

The Vital Appeal: Meaningfulness

You attend to stimuli that are meaningful to you, and you ignore stimuli that are relatively meaningless (Ruiter et al., 2006). Problems and issues that vitally affect your lives are meaningful. In this sense, audiences tend to be self-oriented. Listeners heed warnings when a societal problem affects them personally, or they think it does. When the Ebola virus hit West Africa and spread rapidly in 2014, most Americans were unaware and inattentive. When two American health workers became ill with the virus, however, panic spread. A *Washington Post/ ABC News* poll found as a result that almost two-thirds of respondents expressed concern about an Ebola epidemic in the United States (Ahmed & Mendoza, 2014).

Instead of making a general appeal to the vital, citing the seriousness of the problem for nameless, faceless citizens, *personalize the appeal to all of your listeners.* Student Jake Gruber (2001) did exactly this when he stated in his speech on heart disease in women:

> Whereas one in 28 women will die of breast cancer, one in five will die of heart disease. And guys, before you take the next nine minutes to decide what you'll eat for lunch, ask yourself one question: what would my life be like if the women who make it meaningful are not there? Clearly, this is an issue that concerns us all. *(p. 16)*

Novelty: The Allure of the New

Novelty attracts attention (Poldrack, 2010). Audience members are naturally drawn to the new and different. Conversely, the commonplace can produce a stupor. Recognizing this means never beginning your speech with a snoozer, such as "My topic is . . ." or "Today I'd like to talk to you about . . . ." Stimulate interest in your subject. There are several ways to make novel appeals to stimulate attention.

Unusual Topics: Choosing Outside the Box   In this age of high-tech weapons systems and sophisticated counter-terrorism tactics, sometimes it is the low-tech solutions that save lives. American troops in the Iraq War were constantly faced with potential booby-trapped dwellings. A solution? Shoot Silly String across a room before entering to locate possible tripwires attached to bombs.

PHOTO 6.4: This is a most unusual sign. Novelty can draw attention.

This is an unusual topic for a great speech: low-tech creative solutions to significant problems. It is much easier to attend to unusual topics on substantial issues.

Unusual Examples: The Anti-Sedative   Sprinkle your speech with unusual examples that illustrate important points. For instance, consider using real examples such as these pulled from a newspaper story:

> "The check is in the mail" used to be the standard ploy to ward off bill collectors. Not so anymore. Delinquent customers have adopted more original stalling tactics. One woman claimed that she had run over her husband with a car, breaking both of his arms thereby making it impossible for him to write checks or pay by computer. A flower-shop owner insisted that she could not pay her bills until someone died and had a funeral. "Business should pick up soon," she said hopefully. These are silly excuses for failing to pay one's bills, but mounting personal debt is no laughing matter.

Compare this opening to the more commonplace "I want to talk to you about how to handle personal debt." The more novel opening with unusual examples invites attention. The commonplace opener does not.

Unusual Stories: Compelling Attention   Storytelling can jazz up a potentially tedious speech. Media are filled with novel stories that can be used to snare listeners' attention. For example:

> Doctors who examined Hall of Fame Pittsburgh Steelers' center Mike Webster estimated that he suffered the equivalent of 25,000 car crashes without a seatbelt in the 25 years he played football from high school through the NFL. After retiring, he experienced amnesia, dementia, and depression from his football-induced head trauma. He was featured in the 2015 Will Smith movie *Concussion* about chronic traumatic encephalopathy (CTE) resulting from repetitive head injuries while playing professional football. Webster's experiences reflect a serious problem that until recently has received relatively little attention. Football at all levels, from high school to the NFL, is hazardous to your brain. Stronger regulation of football injuries must be implemented.

Unusual stories invite attention because they are not trivial, commonplace episodes we have heard many times. They make us sit up and take notice.

Unusual Phrasing: Wording Matters   Colorful phrasing or unusual wording can transform an ordinary statement into a novel, memorable one. For example:

Ordinary: Most books are carried fewer than 60 days by bookstores unless they become bestsellers.
Novel: The shelf life of the average book is somewhere between milk and yogurt. (Calvin Trillin)
Ordinary: Our office was way too small.
Novel: He and I had an office so tiny that an inch smaller and it would have been adultery. (Dorothy Parker)
Ordinary: Sometimes you're the villain; sometimes you're the victim.
Novel: Sometimes you're the windshield; sometimes you're the bug. (Mark Knopfler)

Unusual Presentation: Song and Dance   The airline industry recognizes that focusing an audience's attention on an important message can be very challenging. In an effort to get passengers to listen carefully to safety instructions at the beginning of flights (critical information if an emergency were to occur), flight attendants have tried singing the safety message accompanied by a ukulele, impersonating famous people while reciting the instructions, and even performing a rap version of the safety message.

Flight attendants have also added a little humor to their standard safety instructions, such as: "Your seat cushions can be used for flotation, and in the

PHOTO 6.5: Clever wording can help grab attention.

event of an emergency water landing, please take them with our compliments" or "To activate the flow of oxygen (to the mask), simply insert 75 cents for the first minute" (*see access to link at end of chapter*). Presenting your message in an unusual way can be a very effective, novel attention strategy as long as it stays within the bounds of appropriateness.

Humorous Appeal: Keep Listeners Laughing

"We've childproofed our house, but they keep finding a way in." This ironic, anonymous quip has been circulating on the Internet for years. Its humor gives it staying power. Humor is a superior attention strategy if used adroitly, probably the very best antidote to boredom (Banas et al., 2011). Actor Ryan Reynolds regularly spices up his interviews with humor. For example, when asked about plane rides with his two young kids, he replied: "Usually when I'm on an airplane with my kids, at some point I get up and ask the flight attendants if I can leave the aircraft. Ninety-nine percent of the time they say, "No, please stay seated!" So I just sit back down and long for the sweet release of death" (quoted by McNiece, 2019).

Using humor effectively, however, can be very dicey. It requires far more than chirpy advice such as "Be funny." Complex issues of appropriateness and effectiveness are always present because "almost all forms of humor involve ridicule

PHOTO 6.6: Humor is challenging. Some listeners may find your attempt to be funny uproarious, others may exhibit mild laughter, and others may show a tepid, bored, or even a hostile response.

of something—a person, behavior, belief, group, or possession—at some level" (Greengross & Miller, 2008, p. 394). There are several guidelines for using humor competently as an attention strategy.

Do Not Force Humor: Not Everyone Is Funny   If you have never told a joke without flubbing the punchline, avoid humiliating yourself. Listening to a speaker stubbornly try to be funny without success can be an excruciatingly uncomfortable experience for all involved. Nevertheless, you can still use humor. Use humorous quotations; tell funny stories or amusing occurrences to amplify or clarify points. *Do not telegraph stories as intentionally humorous*, however, by using a risky lead-in, such as "Let me tell you a really funny story." Such a lead-in invites embarrassment if your listeners do not laugh. Simply tell the story and let audience members laugh if they are so inclined.

Use Only Relevant Humor: Stay Focused   Humor should amuse listeners while making a relevant point. It should not be an opportunity to insert an irrelevant political aside or merely to "loosen up" your audience with laughter. *Tie the humor directly to a main point or principal theme.* For example: "Someone once said, 'I want to die peacefully in my sleep like my grandfather, not screaming in terror like his passengers.' You've all experienced it—the nerve-wracking anxiety every time you see an elderly person driving a car. I want to convince you that greater restrictions on elderly drivers should be instituted." The humor is simple and it leads directly to the purpose of the speech.

Be Sensitive to Audience and Occasion: Humor Can Backfire   Don West, defense attorney for George Zimmerman in the Trayvon Martin murder case in 2013, began his opening statement to the jury with a knock-knock joke. The jury, not surprisingly, was not amused. The murder of a loved one is hardly a laughing matter, and West, an experienced lawyer, should have realized that his lame joke was inappropriate. West later apologized to the jury.

Humor can be tricky business (Warren & McGraw, 2015). Sexist, racist, and homophobic "jokes" exhibit poor taste and lack of ethics. Coarse vulgarities, obscenities, and sick jokes are not everyone's idea of amusement. Humor that ridicules and demeans groups or individuals usually backfires (Frymier et al., 2008). Humor that is negative or hostile may alienate vast sections of an audience, unless it is an official "roast" (Banas et al., 2011).

Considering the common multicultural composition of audiences, knowing what amuses individuals in different cultures and what might offend them is important. An Internet study called LaughLab tried to determine the world's funniest joke (Wiseman, 2007). A favorite among American respondents, especially men, was this joke:

Texan: Where are you from?
Harvard graduate: I come from a place where we do not end our sentences with prepositions.
Texan: Okay, where are you from, jackass?

The French liked: "You're a high-priced lawyer. If I give you $500, will you answer two questions for me? The lawyer responds, 'Absolutely! What is the second question?'"

Humor is subjective, and you may find these jokes less than thigh-slappingly funny, but LaughLab does not have to be representative of everyone's taste. It highlights that there are cultural differences, so be careful (Yue et al., 2016; Zhang, 2005). Generally speaking, sick jokes or dark humor do not travel well from culture to culture or even person to person. Sarcasm, satire, and parody of others are usually unappreciated by Asians who usually value politeness and harmony. Jokes about religion, sex, and the underprivileged can also cause deep offense (Lewis, 1996). *Humor that is gentle or self-deprecating usually travels best* (Rudlin, 2014).

Consider Using Self-Deprecating Humor: "I'm Not Worthy"   Humor that makes gentle fun of your own failings and limitations, called **self-deprecation**, can be quite appealing because it communicates that you have enough confidence to recognize and note your flaws and to exhibit some modesty. Self-deprecation can be disarming. During the famous Lincoln–Douglas debates, U.S. Senator Stephen Douglas called Abraham Lincoln "two-faced," whereupon Lincoln calmly replied, "I leave it to my audience. If I had another face, do you think I would wear this one?"

Making fun of yourself instead of other people can work well with an audience, but, again, the advice is more complicated than simply "be self-deprecating" (Baxter, 2012). If you are self-deprecating during a job interview and teaching demonstration, you may handicap yourself compared to other job applicants who present a more capable image. Nevertheless, gentle self-deprecation can be attractive if not overdone.

Startling Appeal: Shake Up Your Listeners

The startle response is hardwired into our brains as a defensive reflex that protects us from immediate threats (Lakhan, 2016). Although you can capitalize on this natural tendency to startle from abrupt stimuli during your speech by shouting suddenly, slamming a book onto a podium, or whipping out an air horn and blasting it at your audience to arouse them from slumber, there are less obnoxious and more relevant ways to startle your audience into attending to your message.

Startling Statements, Facts, or Statistics: The "Oh WOW" Effect   A startling statement, fact, or statistic can rouse audience attention. Student Kathy Levine (2001) offers this startling revelation in her speech on dental hygiene:

> As the previously cited *20/20* investigation uncovered, the water used in approximately 90% of dental offices is dirtier than the water found in public toilets. This means 9 out of 10 dental offices are using dirty water on their patients. Moreover, the independent research of Dr. George Merijohn, a periodontist who specialized in dental waterlines, found that out of 60 randomly selected offices from around the nation, two-thirds of all samples taken contained oral bacteria from the saliva of previous patients. *(p. 77)*

Startling statements, facts, and statistics can be unsettling. They are meant to alarm, shock, and astonish an audience into listening intently to what you have to say. Here's a truly startling statistic, for example: the 26 richest people in the world have as much accumulated wealth as the poorest 3.8 billion people (almost half the globe's total population) (Quackenbush, 2019). This dramatically high-lights the problem of income inequality and would be a great opener for a speech on this topic.

Inappropriate Use: Beware Bizarre Behavior   Startling an audience should enhance your speech and your personal credibility with the audience, not de-tract and distract from these goals. Inappropriate use of the startling appeal can backfire. Every speech teacher remembers notable examples of student mis-calculations when using a startling appeal. For instance, one student punched himself so hard in the face that he momentarily staggered himself and produced a large bruise under his eye (the speech was on violence in America). Another student screamed obscenities to her stunned audience (the topic was the First Amendment). Sometimes speakers in a classroom situation need to be inter-rupted because they have clearly crossed beyond the boundaries of good taste and common sense.

The competent public speaker exercises solid judgment when choosing to startle his or her listeners. *Your goal should not be to gain attention by being out-rageous, being irresponsible, or exercising poor judgment.* You should consider the implied or stated rules of a speech context when choosing attention strategies. An audience can turn on you when angered or offended. Startle an audience, but be appropriate.

PHOTO 6.7: You can bring an audience to its feet with a stunt such as giving a speech naked, but is this ever appropriate for a public speech? Explain.

Movement and Change: Our Evolutionary Protection

Attention to change is built into our brains. You do not pay attention to that which is static. "Is the carpet still the same?" "Is the paint on the walls unchanged?" "Has the TV been moved?" These are not the questions we ask each day unless change occurs (the TV is gone). Why? Because change carries new information.

Fast change especially provides important information. It warrants greater attention because it may indicate a potential threat to our well-being. Predatory animals move very slowly or remain still for long periods of time while stalking prey. If they move too fast before they are close enough to pounce, the prey notices and bolts. I'm not suggesting that you view your audience as prey, but the analogy is apt because movement represents change and you attend to it (von Muhlenen et al., 2005).

Too little movement when speaking can anesthetize an audience. A speaker stands before an audience, grabs the podium in a vise-like grip (white knuckles clearly visible to everyone), assumes an expressionless face reminiscent of a marble statue in a museum, and appears to have feet welded to the floor.

CARTOON 6.1: Immobility when speaking can act like a sedative. Movement produces change, and change creates attention.

This is an example of too little body movement and change. Aimlessly pacing like a caged panther, wildly gesticulating with arms flailing in all directions, or awkwardly wrapping legs and arms around the podium are examples of excessive body movement. Essentially, strive for balance in movement when speaking. Be animated, but not frenetic.

Intensity: Extreme Degree of a Stimulus

You attend to the intense (Cherry & Gans, 2018b). **Intensity** is concentrated stimuli. It is an extreme degree of emotion, thought, or activity. Relating a tragic event, a moving human-interest story, or a specific instance of courage and determination plays on the intense feelings of your audience.

The opening to this chapter told the story of my friend, Terry, who was violently attacked by a mentally ill student. This was an intense, traumatic event for the campus community. Understandably, it riveted everyone's attention and became the subject of much discussion and debate. This event, however, was unpleasant, even disturbing. This raises an important issue: *Should speakers use unpleasant examples to capture attention?* Might your listeners be repelled by such stark, negative examples? There is often a potential risk when you employ intensity as an attention strategy. Any time deep human emotion is aroused, your listeners may respond in a variety of ways, both positive and negative. Nevertheless, research shows that very unpleasant stimuli can be highly interesting and attention grabbing, while highly pleasant stimuli can be so uninteresting that attention is easily diverted (Turner & Silvia, 2006).

Whether to use an unpleasant yet intense example is a judgment. Unpleasant examples are likely to work most effectively when they are used occasionally. A steady diet of unpleasantness can be mind-numbing and counterproductive. Nevertheless, the extremely difficult challenge you face as a speaker to gain and maintain the attention of your audience may require moving beyond just happy stories and uplifting examples, as pleasant and comforting as these can be. Human interest runs the gamut from pleasant to unpleasant, so do not restrict yourself just to one or the other. Sometimes the two, pleasant and unpleasant, seem to blend. Consider this example:

What is love? There's romantic love with passion ignited. There's the love of a friend or companion. Then there's the simple, childlike love seen in the story of a four-year-old boy whose next-door neighbor had recently lost his wife. The man was crying in his backyard. The little boy came over, sat on the grieving man's lap. Asked later by his mother what he'd said to the man, the little boy replied, "Nothing, I just helped him cry."

The story of the grieving neighbor is unpleasant, but the little boy's act of love is pleasantly poignant.

Sometimes you can blend intensity with other attention strategies to mitigate the unpleasant without losing impact. For example:

> On April 9, 2017, Dr. David Dao, a passenger on United Airlines flight 3411, was forcibly removed from the plane by Chicago Department of Aviation officers. A computer randomly picked him to disembark because the flight was over-booked. Dao insisted that he could not "volunteer" to leave the overbooked flight because he had patients to see the next morning. Dao refused to comply with the officers' demands that he leave the airplane, so they dragged him from his seat, inflicting numerous injuries, including a concussion, broken nose, and the loss of two front teeth. Cellphone video by another passenger of this as-tonishing event went viral. The response from the Twitterverse was swift. One person tweeted, "United: You may be asked to vacate or be taken off the plane by force, but for $49.99 you can upgrade to trial by combat." Another tweeted, "In the unlikely event of an overbooking, please assume the crash position whilst we hunt down volunteers." Yet another individual offered this sardonic take on the event, "United: Putting the hospital in hospitality."

This example blends several attention strategies: novelty, the startling, intensity, and humor.

SUMMARY

Gaining and maintaining the attention of your audience are critical challenges for any speaker. Attention does not just happen; you have to plan it carefully. Although voluntarily making an effort as a listener to attend to a speaker's message is important, responsibility for attention resides mostly with the speaker. Involuntary stimulus triggers, such as appealing to what is novel, startling, vital, humorous, changeable, and intense, can provoke audience interest and keep listeners paying attention to your speech.

TED TALKS AND YOUTUBE VIDEOS

Mindful Listening: "Hilarious Southwest Flight Attendant"

Excessive Intensity: "Steve Ballmer Going Crazy on Stage"

Focused Attention: "Volkswagen: Eyes on the Road"

Intensity: "The Greatest Movie Speeches: Mel Gibson *Braveheart* Speech"

Inspiration: "Best Inspirational Speech Ever: Motivational Video"

Self-Deprecating Humor: "Dan Pink: 'The Puzzle of Motivation'"

Self-Deprecating Humor: "Tina Fey: The Mark Twain Prize Speech"

Self-Deprecating Humor: "Mark Twain Prize: Ellen DeGeneres's Full Acceptance Speech"

How Humor Works: "More Than Funny" (Michael Jr.: TED x University of Nevada)

For relevant links to these TED Talks and YouTube videos, see the *Practically Speaking* Companion Website: www.oup.com/he/rothwell-ps3e. You can also gain access by typing the title of the speech reference into a Google search window or by doing the same on the TED Talks or YouTube sites.

CHECKLIST

Attention Strategies

- [ ] Novelty: use unusual topics, examples, stories, and phrasing.

- [ ] Startling appeal: use startling statements, facts, and statistics.

- [ ] Vital appeal: make your speech meaningful for your audience. Answer the question, "Why should they care?"

- [ ] Humorous appeal: do not force humor; use only relevant humor; be sensitive to your audience and occasion; use self-deprecating humor in some circumstances.

- [ ] Movement and change: be animated in delivery and move; don't just stand there immobile.

- [ ] Intensity: we are drawn to the riveting, dramatic, graphic, vivid example, story, or fact.

CRITICAL THINKING QUESTIONS

1. What makes a story attention-getting? What would make a story uninteresting?

2. Is it easier to gain the immediate attention of listeners than to keep interest throughout a speech? Explain.

3. G. K. Chesterton is reputed to have said: "There are no uninteresting topics, only uninteresting people." Do you agree? Can every topic be made interesting to any audience if the right attention strategies are used?

NOTE: Online **student resources**, such as practice tests, flashcards, and other activities, can be accessed at www.oup.com/he/rothwell-ps3e

CHAPTER

7

Introductions and Conclusions

The beginning and ending can be as important as the body of your speech. Creating a favorable first impression alerts your audience to expect a quality presentation. A limp introduction can encourage audience members to whip out their cellphones and exercise their thumbs. Ending with a bang leaves a lasting, favorable impression on your listeners. A weak, lifeless conclusion, however, can neutralize an otherwise impressive speech. Just imagine Martin Luther King ending his historic "I Have a Dream" speech with this conclusion: "I hope we all will finally be free. Thanks for listening." Ho-hum! (See how to access his actual, masterful conclusion at the end of this chapter.)

Student Kerry Konda (2006) gave this gripping introduction to her speech delivered at the Interstate Oratorical Association contest:

> On the roof of an old airport hangar outside of Fallujah, the Marine credo, "No One Left Behind" is spelled with crudely arranged sandbags. Inside this hangar was where Marine Sgt. Daniel Cotnoir, father of two, tried to put that credo into practice. His job on the mortuary unit was to crawl along, sifting through the blood-soaked debris of blast areas, finding pieces of his fallen comrades, and then, put them back together. For his outstanding service in Iraq, the Marine Corps Times honored him as "Marine of the Year." However, this glory quickly faded. According to the *Boston Herald* on August 15, 2005, Cotnoir pointed a 12-gauge shotgun out his second-floor window and fired a single shot into a crowd of noisy revelers who were leaving a nightclub and nearby restaurant in retaliation for a bottle that was thrown through his window. After police arrived, Cotnoir broke down crying, saying he had to protect his family. Cotnoir is just one of the many

121

> soldiers returning from Iraq, who in military terms, has "temporary adjustment disorder," but in reality is suffering from something far greater. That something is PTSD, posttraumatic stress disorder. *(p. 74)*

This is a very compelling beginning to a speech. The story is novel, startling, and intense. Kerry's conclusion, however, is equally noteworthy:

> Claiming posttraumatic stress disorder is just a temporary adjustment soldiers must go through is unacceptable. Our soldiers, like Daniel Cotnoir . . . made it through the hell that is war, but we cannot lose them to the battles that still rage in their minds. As Americans, we cannot sit idly by and deny them the right to lead a normal life when they sacrificed so much. Instead, we must do what is humanly possible and answer the call in their time of need; we must follow the example of Sgt. Daniel Cotnoir and leave no one behind. *(p. 76)*

Tying the introduction and conclusion together with the Marine slogan "Leave no one behind" neatly packages the speech. The speech ends as powerfully as it began.

Recognizing the impact a well-constructed beginning and ending to your speech can have on your audience, ***the purpose of this chapter is to explore ways to construct effective speech introductions and conclusions***. Toward that end, this chapter discusses (1) achieving objectives for competent introductions and (2) achieving objectives for competent conclusions.

OBJECTIVES FOR COMPETENT INTRODUCTIONS

There are five principal objectives for a competent introduction to a speech: gain attention, make a clear purpose statement, establish the significance of your topic, establish your credibility on the subject, and preview your main points. Please note that *these objectives are not rigid rules that must be followed without variation.* A wedding toast, a eulogy, a short acceptance speech, or a presentation that introduces another speaker, for example, usually does not need you to establish your credibility or preview your main points. Also, your purpose may already be clear. Some occasions also make a direct reference to significance unnecessary because the audience has assembled in recognition of the importance of the topic. A graduation ceremony and a commemoration for the victims of the 9/11 terrorist attacks are examples. Nevertheless, these five objectives are especially important for most informative and persuasive speeches.

Gain Attention: Focusing Your Listeners

In the previous chapter, general attention strategies were discussed that should be incorporated throughout your entire speech. For the introduction to your speech, however, more specific suggestions should be helpful.

Begin with a Clever Quotation: Let Others Grab Attention   Opening with a clever quotation can capitalize on the wit and wisdom of others. Any such quotation, of course, should be directly relevant to your purpose statement (see ensuing discussion). For example:

> President John F. Kennedy, in a speech at a White House dinner honoring several Nobel Prize winners, said: "I think this is the most extraordinary collection of talent, of human knowledge, that has ever been gathered together at the White House with the possible exception of when Thomas Jefferson dined alone." President Kennedy deftly complimented his esteemed honorees without becoming effusive in his praise. Complimenting others is an important but often overlooked way to cement interpersonal relationships, build teamwork, and promote goodwill among coworkers and friends. Giving compliments unskillfully, however, can provoke embarrassment and awkwardness between people. Today I will explain how to give compliments effectively.

Note that the quotation not only grabs attention with ironic humor, a nice attention strategy in its own right (see Chapter 6), but it necessarily introduces the topic to listeners and leads smoothly to the purpose statement.

Startle Your Audience: Surprise Opener   In the previous chapter, the startle response was explained as a potential attention strategy to gain and also maintain audience interest. Capitalize on this to grab your audience's attention as the opener to your speech. For example:

- Football can kill you!
- A staggering 37 gallons of water are used, and wasted, to produce a single cup of coffee!
- Americans are 4.4% of the world's population, but they own 42% of the world's guns!
- Smartphones are killing people; no, not from radiation exposure, but from death by distraction.
- They have been dubbed "donor-cycles" in emergency rooms across the country! Death by motorcycle is a serious and rising problem.

Each of these startling statements, facts, and statistics can and should be supported by credible sources, but startling your audience immediately makes listeners want to know more, and that opens the door for evidentiary support of these startling openers and further exploration of your topic.

Use Questions: Engage Your Listeners   Asking questions of your audience can be an effective technique for gaining listeners' attention immediately. A question asked by a speaker that the audience answers mentally, but not out loud, is called a **rhetorical question**. Consider this example:

> The Scottish dish called haggis is a mixture of sheep innards blended with chunks of sheep fat, seasonings, and oatmeal, all cooked in the animal's stomach. If a Scottish friend offered this to you for dinner, would you eat it or would you try to politely decline the dish? Local tribesman in East Africa enjoy a tall drink of fresh cow's blood. Would you down a glass if offered? Some cultures find insects tasty. Would you try these crunchy little creatures? Let me explain why cultures vary dramatically in their food choices.

These rhetorical questions engage an audience by inviting listeners to imagine what they would eat, and they create curiosity about what constitutes edible or desirable food throughout the world.

Rhetorical questions can also be quite powerful triggers of thought and emotion. "Who will be last to die for a mistake?" is a biting rhetorical question that challenges the very purpose served by continuing a flawed war policy that sacrifices human lives.

Make sure, however, that rhetorical questions are meaningful, not merely a commonplace device to open a speech. "Have you ever wondered why our college doesn't have a chess team?" may produce a "not really" mental reaction from the audience with a corresponding headshake. The question does not spark interest if interest is already lacking.

You may want to ask **direct questions** that seek overt responses from listeners. This active participation requires listeners to become engaged. "How many of you have attended a rock concert—raise your hands?" or "Let's see a quick show of hands—have you tried an exercise program in the last year?" are examples. Student Daniel Hinderliter (2012) opened his speech at the Interstate Oratorical Association contest with these direct questions:

> By a show of hands, how many of your families have a hammer at home? If you think your neighbors to your left have a hammer, keep your hand up. Keep your hand up if you think your neighbors on your right have one. How about your neighbors across the street? That's four hammers, none of which, I'd be willing

to bet, get used on a daily basis; the purchased quantity far outstrips any actual need. This disparity between need and ownership is emblematic of hyper-consumerism. *(p. 140)*

Polling an audience can be engaging, even amusing. For example:

How many in this audience have used a dangerous, illegal drug in the past six months? Whoa, some of you actually raised your hand; that's a first. You might want to check the Fifth Amendment protections against self-incrimination. Americans revere the Bill of Rights, but how many of you can even identify the first 10 amendments to the U.S. Constitution?

This example uses both direct and rhetorical questions to engage the audience. *Expecting listeners to respond overtly to a question can be risky business.* Asking an audience to cop to illegal behavior is questionable in its own right, even if it offers an opportunity for humor and playfulness with the audience. It could also easily produce an awkward silence with no hands raised. Conversely, you may expect (and hope) no hands are raised. A student began her speech this way: "How many of you have ever sewn your own clothes?" Almost every

CARTOON 7.1: Is this a rhetorical or a direct question? Although questions can engage listeners, they also may invite smart-aleck listeners to make abusive remarks. If you are uncomfortable with unexpected responses from an audience, use a different attention strategy.

student raised a hand. "Wow, I didn't expect that response," she blurted. Speakers faced with unexpected answers to questions may sputter or become annoyed with the audience. Some listeners may see your question as an opportunity to heckle or ridicule you. "How many of you have difficulty losing weight?" might trigger "Not as much trouble as you seem to have." Only certain audiences would likely be so boorish (high school comes to mind), but *skip polling your audience unless you feel comfortable ad-libbing quick responses.* Anticipate potential answers to your direct questions, and be prepared to make those answers relevant to your speech.

Tell a Relevant Story: Use Narrative Power   A speaker was invited to address the campus community at Cabrillo College. She opened with a personal story that illustrated the importance of acts of kindness. When driving from the cemetery after visiting the grave of her five-year-old son, through tears from unimaginable sadness, she inadvertently ran a stop sign, pulling in front of another driver who had to brake hard to avoid a collision. The driver who screeched to a halt was a highway patrolman. The grieving mother pulled over to the curb. The officer got out of his patrol car and walked up to the passenger side of her vehicle. He tapped, indicating for her to roll down her window. He leaned over and asked, "May I get in?" She nodded her head, continuing to sob. The officer sat in the passenger seat for a few moments without saying a word, then he asked, pointing to the cemetery, "Do you have someone in there?" Her eyes welled with tears, but she found comfort in telling him about her little boy. When she finished, the officer asked her how far away she lived, and then he offered to follow her home to be sure she got there safely. He never mentioned the traffic violation.

Almost everyone who listened to the personal story of the grieving mother and the kindly highway patrolman subsequently admitted being profoundly moved. This was a powerful opening narrative, and it set up the remainder of her speech that explored why kindness matters in a world too often immersed in cynicism and swamped in hatred.

A short, entertaining, real-life story is called an **anecdote**. Anecdotes, such as this one, can be particularly captivating because they are human interest stories.

Begin with a Simple Visual Aid: Show and Tell   A simple visual aid can spark immediate interest. For example, you could hold a smartphone for your audience to see, then note the following:

This tiny device has more computing power than the supercomputers of only 40 years ago that filled a large portion of a room. So why hasn't there been an equivalent downsizing of solar cells and enhancement of solar power in the

PHOTO 7.1: Imagine this Flint, Michigan, resident holding up this polluted, lead-contaminated water and beginning a speech, "Would you drink this water?" Sometimes a simple visual aid can command instant attention.

same time period? Shouldn't we be able to replace huge, bulky solar panels with smartphone-size solar cells with the capacity to power an entire house? I'm going to explain why this hasn't occurred and what can be done to make greater progress.

Beginning with a simple visual aid can draw in your audience and, importantly, create curiosity about why solar technology has not advanced as rapidly as we may have desired.

Refer to Remarks of Introduction: Acknowledging Praise   If you are introduced to an audience, you may need to respond briefly before launching into your prepared speech. A simple, clean reference to those remarks is sufficient, and a bit of humor adds a little spice. Walter Mondale, former U.S. senator from Minnesota, had a standard response when he was extravagantly introduced to an audience: "I don't deserve those kind words. But then I have arthritis and I don't deserve that either." Former President Lyndon Johnson also had a standard line prepared if the introduction of him to an audience was effusive in its praise: "That was the kind of very generous introduction that my father would have appreciated and my mother would have believed" (quoted by Noonan, 1998, p. 148). The humor is gentle and appealing as an opener. It enhances likability.

Make a Clear Purpose Statement: Providing Intent

As explained in Chapter 3, a **general purpose** identifies the overall goal of your speech. It tells the audience that you plan to inform, describe, explain, demonstrate, persuade, celebrate, memorialize, entertain, or eulogize someone or something. The general purpose will be given to you if your speech is a classroom assignment (e.g., give a demonstration speech). If provided no direction from others, choose an appropriate topic (see Chapter 3 discussion), then decide what general purpose best suits the audience and occasion.

Next, formulate your specific purpose. A **specific purpose statement** is a concise, precise statement composed of simple, clear language that both encompasses the general purpose and indicates what the speaker hopes to accomplish with the speech. For example:

TOPIC: Cost of a college education
NARROWED TOPIC: The high cost of textbooks
GENERAL PURPOSE: To inform
SPECIFIC PURPOSE STATEMENT: I will explain why textbooks are so expensive.

Once you have constructed your specific purpose statement, test its appropriateness and likely effectiveness. Ask the following questions:

1. **Is your purpose statement concise and precise?** A long, wordy statement will confuse listeners. You should be able to phrase an effective purpose statement in about 15 or fewer words. If your purpose statement is much beyond 15 words, rephrase it until it is more concise.

2. **Is your purpose statement phrased as a declarative statement?** Phrasing a purpose statement as a question, such as "Why are textbooks so expensive?" asks your listeners to provide the answers. Typically, you begin with your general purpose, such as to explain, to inform, to persuade, to celebrate, to teach, to demonstrate, or to eulogize. Then you declare the direction of your speech by providing your specific purpose. For example: "I will explain why textbooks are so expensive" is a declarative, specific purpose statement.

3. **Is your purpose statement free of colorful language?** Keep your purpose statement plain and direct. Colorful language is fine for the body of your speech, but it can be confusing in a purpose statement. For example, "You will learn why textbooks are the golden fleece of education" is a purpose statement that is likely to leave some of your listeners scratching their heads and thinking "huh?"

4. **Is your purpose statement more than simply a topic?** "To inform you about the cost of textbooks" is a topic statement, not a specific purpose

statement. Listeners are provided with no direction. Tell them specifically what you seek to accomplish. "I will discuss the feasibility of a textbook rental program on campus" is a purpose statement with a direction.

5. **Is your purpose statement practical?** Can your listeners accomplish what you ask them to do? "I want to teach you to be a top-notch computer programmer" will not happen in a single speech, even a lengthy one. It is too technical and complex, especially if audience members are mostly uninformed on the topic. Make your specific purpose statement practical: "I want to convince you that taking a computer programming course is worthwhile."

The specific purpose statement provides clear direction for your entire speech, guiding the audience members as they listen to the points you make. Imagine a classmate giving this introduction, and notice the blending of the opening attention strategy and the purpose statement:

> The Westboro Baptist Church regularly holds small protests at funerals for dead soldiers, holding signs and shouting "God Hates Fags" and "Thank God for Dead Soldiers." Following the massacre of 49 gay nightclub partiers in Orlando, Florida, in June 2016, Pastor Roger Jimenez from the Verity Baptist Church in Sacramento, California, told his parishioners, "The tragedy is that more of them (gays) didn't die. The tragedy is—I'm kind of upset that he (the shooter) didn't finish the job . . . I wish the government would round them all up, put them up against a firing wall, put a firing squad in front of them, and blow their brains out."
>
> The vileness of this kind of hate speech may incline us to support laws that ban it, and that's understandable. Hate speech is repugnant. I hope to convince you, however, that outlawing hate speech, no matter how venomous, produces significant disadvantages.

This introduction accomplishes two critical objectives: it gains attention, and it provides a clear purpose statement.

The **theme**, or *central idea*, identifies the main concept, point, issue, or conclusion that you want the audience to understand, believe, feel, or do. The theme becomes the one concise thought, separate from all the details provided in the speech, that audience members hopefully remember. A theme is typically determined once you have investigated your specific purpose statement sufficiently to provide details. The gay bashing examples used to ignite attention in the speech introduction just presented never get to the theme, which is identifying the particular disadvantages of banning hate speech, such as that it drives hate speech underground, stifles freedom of speech, and so forth. The theme for the purpose statement "to explain why textbooks are so expensive" would be: "Textbooks are expensive because of used books, ancillaries, and costly graphics." *You want to keep your theme uppermost in your mind as you prepare your speech.* The theme guides speech development.

Establish Topic Significance: Making Your Listeners Care

As noted in Chapter 3, don't choose a trivial topic. By definition, it won't have significance to an audience. Also, avoid overly technical topics beyond the audience's grasp. Clearly establish the basis for why listeners should care about the problem, information, or demonstration central to your purpose. Listeners typically want to know "How does this affect me?" If you are an avid card player, quilter, or woodworker, your audience will see your enthusiasm for your topic. Why should audience members be enthusiastic, though, if they have never tried such activities or if they proved to be embarrassingly inept when they did try?

Consider this example that ties the purpose statement to an audience's need to know its importance:

> Mark Twain once said that golf is a good walk spoiled. I beg to differ. Golf is a good walk, but it is only spoiled if you lack knowledge of the strategy behind the game and your skill level is embarrassingly bad. Understanding the strategy and learning to play golf well can make for an extremely enjoyable few hours of recreation in the bright sun and fresh air. Millions of dollars' worth of business are negotiated on the golf links every day. To put it succinctly, golf can be entertaining, and it can enhance your life physically, psychologically, economically, occupationally, and politically.
>
> I can't teach you to play golf well in a five-minute speech. You'll want to find a qualified golf instructor to help you do that. I can, however, briefly explain important qualities to consider when choosing a golf instructor.

Some topics are more challenging to make relevant to an audience's interests than others. Nevertheless, without relevance, listeners will quickly tune out and let their minds wander freely.

Establish Your Credibility: Why Listeners Should Believe You

Establishing your credibility is a process that develops over the course of an entire speech. Nevertheless, it is an important requirement of effective introductions for most speeches (eulogies, "roasts," and some other special-occasion speeches may be exceptions). When you have real expertise on a subject, do not hide that fact.

Do not begin by apologizing to your audience, however, if you lack expertise. "I'm really not an expert on this topic," or worse, "I'm not a very good speaker" are pointless disclaimers that immediately diminish your credibility. This just presents a reason for your listeners to ignore your speech.

In Chapter 3, elements of credibility—*competence, trustworthiness, dynamism*, and *composure*—were explored in detail. There are many ways to capitalize on these elements. Mentioning to your audience that you have surfed for 10 years, worked as an auto mechanic for three years, or have a degree in nursing, for example, would likely induce your listeners to grant you credibility on those subjects (competence). Presenting a commanding presence by exhibiting a confident, fluent, energetic delivery (competence and dynamism), sharing personal experiences that offer insight on a problem from an insider's viewpoint (competence and trustworthiness), or citing authoritative sources of initial information all can build credibility.

Consider, for example, how Ricardo, a former long-time gang member, establishes his credibility:

> I got my first tattoo when I was 11 years old—a skull. At 14, I had a Chinese character tattooed on my right forearm. It meant "trust no one." A dozen or more tattoos were added until, at 18, an ornate cross and rosary that memorialized my dead older brother killed in a rival gang hit was added to my left hand. Most of these tattoos symbolized transitional points into gang life. When my brother died, I vowed to leave gang life and find a productive path. When I searched for a job, however, my gang tattoos made employers wary of me. They would never come right out and say so; instead they would say, "Sorry, we don't have any openings," even though I knew they did. A Harris poll last month showed that 17% of tattoo wearers regret getting them. I speak from experience—be very cautious before getting any tattoo.

Ricardo establishes his credibility by identifying his personal experience with tattoos and by citing a reputable study. Credibility can also be established even if you have no particular expertise or relevant experience on a subject. Here is an example:

> I've always been in favor of alternative sources of energy—biofuels, hybrid cars, wind power, solar energy and the like. "Going green" just sounds so Earth friendly and responsible. I even have a bumper sticker on my car that reads: "I'm a tree hugging dirt worshipper." Until I thoroughly researched this topic for my speech, however, I never much considered the downside to alternative energy sources. I know arguing against alternative energy sources currently being developed is not a popular idea today, but I hope sharing with you what I have learned from reputable scientific research might change your mind a bit on this subject.

Here, credibility is potentially enhanced by an appeal to trustworthiness—arguing against a previously held position that reveals no bias, just a careful weighing of the relevant evidence. Reference to substantial, credible research also suggests competence on the subject. The research, of course, has to be provided and it must be truly credible and persuasive, or credibility will quickly swirl down the toilet.

Preview the Main Points: The Coming Attractions

A **preview** presents the coming attractions of your speech. *A speech will normally have two to four main points that flow directly from the purpose statement.* For example: "I want to explain how you can save money when purchasing a new car. There are three ways: First, you can save money by comparison shopping, second by lowering your interest payments, and third by purchasing at the end of the year." Here the speaker very specifically enumerates the main points of the speech (i.e., first, second, third) that will be covered in that order in the body of the speech. A preview does not necessarily require such formulaic specificity. For example, this is how student Britton Ody (2018) more casually previews his speech: "To become a part of the cure for Hepatitis C, we must first understand the problem of state prisons not treating Hepatitis C; then we'll consider the causes, and finally formulate solutions."

Although presenting the purpose statement, explaining significance, and establishing credibility can be reversed, attention is always the first objective and the preview is typically last. Consider this *illustration of all five requirements*:

[Attention] On March 26, 2003, Colby Navarro was using his computer when without warning a meteorite 4 inches in diameter crashed through the roof of his home, struck the printer, bounced off a wall, and landed near a filing cabinet. It left a foot-wide hole in the ceiling. On January 2, 2007, Srinivasan Nageswaran walked into his bathroom and noticed a hole in the ceiling and debris on the floor. A small meteorite had crashed through the roof of his New Jersey home. Are these close calls merely freak events, or do we all have something to fear from rocks falling from the sky? **[Purpose Statement]** I want to convince you that a space-based shield from meteorites is critical to human survival.

[Credibility] I've researched this topic extensively and I completed an astronomy class last term, so let me share some insights I learned about the peril of meteorites and the necessity of this proposed space-based shield. Meteorites are fragments of meteoroids that reach Earth before burning up in the Earth's atmosphere. Meteoroids streaking through the Earth's atmosphere are commonly referred to as shooting stars. **[Significance]** Earth has already had many significant direct encounters with meteorites. In 1908 the famous Tunguska meteorite scorched a 20-mile area of Siberian forest and flattened trees. In 1947, a meteorite exploded into fragments in eastern Siberia, leaving more than 200 craters. Even more recently, on February 15, 2013, a meteorite the size of a bus, and estimated by NASA to be traveling at 40,000 miles per hour, exploded in Russia's Ural Mountains close to the city of Chelyabinsk with the force of an atomic bomb. More than a thousand people were injured by the blast. Fortunately, there was no direct impact on a populated area. The need to create a shield against meteorites is real and urgent.

   [Preview] I will explore three points to convince you that this is true. First, the probability of Earth experiencing a catastrophic collision with a meteoroid is very high. Second, current efforts to address this problem are woefully inadequate. Third, a space-based shield is the only sensible alternative.

This introduction provides the five elements of an effective introduction. It presents a novel attention strategy, the purpose statement is clear and concise, credibility is briefly addressed, significance is clearly developed by making the entire audience feel imperiled, and the preview is direct and concise and sets up the body of the speech. These are the makings of an effective introduction, but competent conclusions to your speech have their own requirements.

OBJECTIVES FOR COMPETENT CONCLUSIONS

You want your introduction to be impressive, and you want your conclusion to end with a bang, not a whimper. Your conclusion should create a sense of unity, like completing a circle. Be as organized about your conclusion as you are with your introduction. Consider three ways to finish your speech effectively.

Summarize the Main Points: Connecting the Dots

In your introduction, you preview your main points as a final step. In your conclusion, you summarize those main points, usually as a first step. For example, Student Shayla Cabalan (2018) began the conclusion to her speech with this brief summary: "Today, we discussed the causes, effects, and solutions to underage marriage in the United States" (p. 33). If your speech is lengthy and complex, you may want a slightly more elaborate summary, such as this one by student Nathan Hill (2018): "Today, we have looked at nuisance ordinances, their historical context and weak construction, their negative effects on society, and some simple solutions" (p. 84). Summarizing your main points during your conclusion reminds the audience of the most important points in your speech.

Refer to the Introduction: Bookending Your Speech

If you used a dramatic story or example to begin your speech, referring to that story or example in your conclusion provides closure. Student Vanessa Hickman (2018) bookends her speech: "Alison, Kaitlyn, Patrick, Michelle—their stories barely scratch the surface of the drug treatment crisis that threatens to expand the horrific losses of America's ongoing opioid tragedy." This is how student Rebecca Brown (2015), in lengthier and more personal fashion, bookended her speech:

> Today we have examined the problems, causes, and solutions to the way in which the education system currently handles mental illness. Remember your class from earlier? If you had been in a class with Luke, you would probably only know that he was smart, funny, and had a laugh that filled the room. You would never guess how hard he fought the system, or how devastated he was when he lost. Luke is more than just a classmate to me. He's my younger brother. Mental illness is something that Luke comes face to face with every single day. For him, and for my family, it's impossible to ignore. . . . and it is time to give Luke, and everyone like him, a fighting chance at success. *(p. 43)*

Bookending your speech by referring to an opening story or dramatic example is not always a requirement of an effective conclusion, especially if you did not use either in your introduction. If you have the opportunity to bookend, however, it can prove to be a very strong finish to your speech.

Make a Memorable Finish: Sizzle Don't Fizzle

Surely one of the most powerful speech conclusions ended Martin Luther King's "I Have a Dream" speech delivered in 1963. He concluded:

> When we allow freedom to ring, when we let it ring from every village and every hamlet, from every state and every city, we will be able to speed up that day when all of God's children, black men and white men, Jews and Gentiles, Protestants and Catholics, will be able to join hands and sing in the words of that old Negro spiritual, "Free at last! Free at last! Thank God Almighty, we are free at last!"

You begin your speech with an attention strategy, and you should end your speech in similar fashion. A strong quotation, a powerful rhetorical question,

PHOTO 7.2: Martin Luther King's "I Have a Dream" speech had a powerful finish.

an intense statement, a moving example or story, or a humorous statement is an effective attention grabber for introductions. They serve the same purpose for effective conclusions. For example:

> G. K. Chesterton once remarked, "Going to church doesn't make you a Christian any more than standing in a garage makes you a car." History is replete with examples of bigots who faithfully attended church and called themselves Christians but performed atrocities on their fellow human beings. Do not defile the teachings of Jesus with these ravings about White supremacy. How can anyone claim to be a Christian without practicing kindness and love for all? How can haters look at their reflection in the mirror and not see wickedness and blatant hypocrisy?

This conclusion uses a clever quotation and rhetorical questions for a memorable finish.

One final note about conclusions: *do not end abruptly, or apologize for running short on time, or ramble until you fizzle like a balloon deflating.* Be concise and to the point when finishing your speech. Do not diminish the effect of a great speech with a bloated, aimless conclusion. Student Tunette Powell (2012), winner of the 2012 Interstate Oratorical Association contest, effectively concluded her oration this way:

> Now is the time to separate the war on drugs from the war on addiction. Today you've heard the problems, impacts, and solutions of criminalizing addictions. Bruce Callis is 50 years old now. And he is still struggling with his addiction. While you all are sitting out there listening to this, I'm living it. Bruce Callis is my father and for my entire life, I have watched our misguided system destroy him. The irony here is that we live in a society where we are told to recycle. We recycle paper, aluminum, and old electronics. But why don't we ever consider recycling the most precious thing on Earth—the human life?

She summarizes her main points, refers to her opening anecdote about Bruce Callis, and closes with a memorable revelation and apt rhetorical question. Her conclusion was a forceful finish.

SUMMARY

There are five objectives of a competent speech introduction: gain attention, provide a clear purpose statement, make the topic and purpose relevant to your audience, establish your credibility, and preview the main points of your speech. A competent conclusion typically summarizes your main points, refers to your introduction if relevant, and finishes memorably. No matter how well you have prepared the body of your presentation, giving little preparation to your introduction and conclusion can significantly diminish the impact and effectiveness of your speech.

TED TALKS AND YOUTUBE VIDEOS

Effective Introductions: Conor Neill: "How to Start a Speech"

Pros and Cons of Oliver's Introduction: Jamie Oliver: "Teach Every Child about Food!"

Five Objectives of an Introduction; Anything Missing? Pamela Meyer: "How to Spot a Liar!"

Startling Introduction: "Isaac Lidsky: "What Reality Are You Creating for Yourself"

Introductions and Conclusions: "How to Open and Close Presentations"

For relevant links to these TED Talks and YouTube videos, see the *Practically Speaking* Companion Website: www.oup.com/he/rothwell-ps3e. You can also gain access by typing the title of the speech reference into a Google search window or by doing the same on the TED Talks or YouTube sites.

CHECKLIST

Purpose Statements

☐ Is your purpose statement concise and precise?

☐ Is your purpose statement phrased as a declarative statement?

☐ Is your purpose statement free of colorful language?

☐ Is your purpose statement more than simply a topic?

☐ Is your purpose statement practical?

Introduction Objectives

☐ Have you developed an effective attention strategy?

☐ Is your purpose statement clear?

☐ Have you developed the significance of your topic and purpose?

☐ Have you prepared a rationale that enhances your credibility?

☐ Have you prepared the preview of your main points?

Conclusion Objectives

☐ Do you summarize your main points?

☐ Do you refer to your opening?

☐ Do you finish with strong attention strategies?

CRITICAL THINKING QUESTIONS

1. Is it ever appropriate for your conclusion to be longer than your introduction?

2. When might telling stories not work in an introduction?

3. Should the length of your introduction and conclusion vary with your audience and occasion?

NOTE: Online **student resources**, such as practice tests, flashcards, and other activities, can be accessed at www.oup.com/he/rothwell-ps3e

Outlining and Organizing Speeches

Actress Jodie Foster gave an aimless speech at the 2013 Golden Globes awards ceremony (*see access to link at end of chapter*). Eric Sasson reporting for *The Wall Street Journal* made this assessment: "Watching the show at a friend's apartment, many of us, some gay, some straight, had a strikingly similar reaction: the speech confused us. It disappointed us. It felt confrontational, defensive, disjointed" (Sasson, 2014). Christy Lemure of the Associated Press gave this assessment: "Jodie Foster came out without really coming out, and suggested she was retiring from acting without exactly saying so, in a long, breathless and rambling speech" (quoted in Miller, 2013). Moments after her speech, Foster's *Wikipedia* page was "updated" to announce her retirement. *Los Angeles Times* reporter Amy Kaufman, however, asked Foster whether she had in fact announced her retirement as an actress in her speech. Foster replied, "Oh, no, I could never stop acting. You'd have to drag me behind a team of horses" ("Jodie Foster Speech," 2013). Parts of her speech were impressive, but the organization was not one of them.

The quality of speech organization directly influences how well your listeners understand your key points (Langeslag, 2018). Speakers who are well organized impress listeners as more credible than speakers who are disorganized. A speaker who does not seem able to connect two thoughts together and continually circles before finally landing on a point does not inspire confidence. Recall how frustrating it is to listen to an instructor present a rambling lecture. Note-taking becomes chaotic. Learning is impaired. Impressive research on a topic is mostly wasted effort if the speech is an incomprehensible verbal stew. A disorganized speech creates confusion and misunderstanding, as the Jodie Foster speech did.

PHOTO 8.1: A disorganized speech can be as confusing as this mess of road signs, providing no clear direction.

The purpose of this chapter is to explain effective ways to outline and organize your speeches. Toward that end, this chapter addresses (1) criteria for effective outlining and (2) patterns of competent organization.

EFFECTIVE OUTLINING

The organizational process begins with an understanding of how to outline your thoughts and the underlying logic that guides outlining. The rudiments of effective outlining involve standard formatting, division, coherence, completeness, and balance.

Standard Formatting: Using Correct Symbols

Microsoft Word offers many outlining formats. The bulleted format is one of the most popular, especially for PowerPoint slides, but not necessarily the most effective. The bulleted format, however, can easily become PowerPoint*less* when every point has a bullet in front of it (Mitchell, 2018). Thus, the standard outlining form is required in most speech classes because it is clear, precise, and logical, and it uses a specific set of symbols that more obviously demarcate main points from subpoints. Briefly, these symbols are the following:

I. Roman numerals for main points
   A. Capital letters for primary subpoints
   B. Another primary subpoint
      1. Standard numbers for secondary subpoints
      2. Another secondary subpoint
         a. Lowercase letters for tertiary subpoints
         b. Another tertiary subpoint
II. Roman numeral for second main point, and so forth

Each successive set of subpoints is indented to separate the main points visually from the primary, secondary, and tertiary subpoints. Thus, *you would **not** format an outline as follows*:

I. Main point
A. Primary subpoint
B. Primary subpoint
1. Secondary subpoint
2. Secondary subpoint
a. Tertiary subpoint
b. Tertiary subpoint
II. Main point

You can see that lack of indentation merges all of your points and can easily lead to confusion.

Division: Dividing the Pie

A purpose statement divides into a *minimum of two* main points, and main points divide into at least two subpoints. Logically, you do not divide something into just one. For example, "dividing" a pie into one means someone gets the whole pie, and you get squat.

INCORRECT VERSION

I. Main point
   A. Primary subpoint
II. Main point
   A. Primary subpoint
      1. Secondary subpoint
   B. Primary subpoint
      1. Secondary subpoint

CORRECT VERSION

I. Main point
   A. Primary subpoint
   B. Primary subpoint
II. Main point
   A. Primary subpoint
   B. Primary subpoint
      1. Secondary subpoint
      2. Secondary subpoint

If you cannot divide a point into at least two subpoints, your point probably does not need division, or the point is not substantial enough. It is time to rethink the development of your speech. *The following example shows proper division*:

> PURPOSE STATEMENT: To inform you that obesity has become both a global and a national problem.
> I. Obesity is a serious global problem.
>   A. An estimated 700 million adults are obese worldwide.
>   B. An estimated 155 million children are also obese.
>   C. Worldwide, obesity has nearly doubled since 1980.
>   D. Almost 3 million adults die annually from obesity-related illnesses.
> II. The United States has an especially serious obesity problem.
>   A. Almost one-third of adult Americans are obese.
>   B. Of the top 22 industrialized countries, the United States has the highest rate of obesity.
>   C. Obesity has serious consequences.
>   1. Almost $240 billion annually is added to the annual health care costs in the United States because of obesity.
>   2. Obesity is linked to increases in diabetes, heart disease, stroke, and a host of other preventable diseases.

Even when you have only a single example to illustrate a point, the principle of division still applies, as illustrated in this example:

> I. Professional baseball players' salaries are astronomical.
>   A. Average player salaries are more than $4.5 million per year.
>   B. Example: Mike Trout makes $33.25 million *per year*, more than 10 times what the average person earns in a *lifetime*.

You cannot generalize from a single example, so do not let it dangle as a subpoint all on its own.

Coherence: Logical Consistency and Clarity

Logical consistency and clarity are qualities of an effective outline. Your outline should flow from your purpose statement. When developing your outline, think of your speech as an inverted pyramid with the base on top and the apex on the bottom (see Figure 8.1).

Begin with your topic, narrow the topic to your specific purpose statement, and develop main points from that purpose statement, which break down

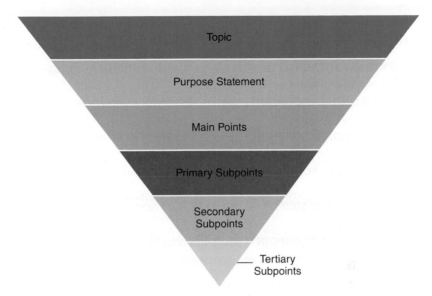

FIGURE 8.1: The organizational logic for developing an outline.

further into subpoints. Work from the most general to the most specific. For example:

[**TOPIC**] The aging U.S. population
[**PURPOSE STATEMENT**] To explain ways longer life spans pose new challenges for America.
  I. [**MAIN POINT**] Americans are living longer than ever before.
  II. [**MAIN POINT**] Longer life spans stress fragile support systems for the elderly in three significant ways.

Coherence requires that main points flow directly from the purpose statement. Subpoints, however, should also flow from main points. For example, look at the development of Main Point I:

  I. [**MAIN POINT**] Americans are living longer than ever before.
    A. [**PRIMARY SUBPOINT**] Average life span of an American is at its highest level in history.
    B. [**PRIMARY SUBPOINT**] Americans are living increasingly to 100 years old and beyond.
Each primary subpoint flows from the main point on "living longer."

Each primary subpoint can be further divided into secondary subpoints that flow from primary subpoints. Note the following example:

A. **[PRIMARY SUBPOINT]** The average life span of an American is at its highest level in history.
   1. **[SECONDARY SUBPOINT]** Average life span of an American is a record 78.8 years old.
   2. **[SECONDARY SUBPOINT]** Average life span of an American has increased from 69 years old just two decades ago.
B. **[PRIMARY SUBPOINT]** Americans are living increasingly to 100 years old and beyond.
   1. **[SECONDARY SUBPOINT]** A record 86,000 Americans are 100 years old or older.
   2. **[SECONDARY SUBPOINT]** The U.S. Census Bureau projects that more than 800,000 Americans will be at least 100 years old in the year 2050.

Working from the most general to the increasingly specific will assure coherence.

Completeness: Using Full Sentences

Your first attempt to outline your speech will prove to be more successful if you use complete sentences. Complete sentences communicate complete thoughts. A word or phrase may suggest a thought without communicating it completely or clearly. For example:

PURPOSE STATEMENT: To explain hazing (initiation rituals).
   I. Hazing
      A. Campus hazing
      B. Military hazing
      C. Corporate hazing
   II. Solutions
      A. Laws
      B. Policies
      C. Penalties
      D. Education

This word and phrase outline creates informational gaps and questions that cannot be answered by merely referring to the outline. The purpose statement provides no direction. What will be explained? Will you explain what hazing is? Why it is a problem? How it can be controlled?

The main points and subpoints are no clearer. Main point I is about hazing, and subpoints indicate three types: campus, military, and corporate. Still, no direction or complete thought is communicated. Are these three types of hazing serious problems? Should they be prevented? Should we find them amusing? Should we encourage hazing on campus, in the military, and in the corporate world? Main point II suffers from the same problem. Solutions are suggested, but solutions imply a problem has been described when no problem is indicated in the previous main point or in the purpose statement. If a problem exists, what type of legal, policy, and educational solutions are offered? The point of the speech remains unclear.

Consider how much more complete a full-sentence outline is when compared to the incomplete and confusing word and phrase outline:

PURPOSE STATEMENT: To explain specific ways to prevent the significant problem of hazing.
  I. Hazing is a growing problem in the United States.
    A. More than 50 deaths and numerous injuries have occurred from hazing in just the last decade.
    B. The number of hazing incidents requiring intervention by authorities has doubled in the last decade.
  II. There are several ways to prevent hazing.
    A. Hazing could be outlawed in all states.
    B. College, corporate, and military policies could specifically ban hazing rituals.
    C. Penalties for violations of laws and policies could be increased.
    D. Students, employees, and soldiers could receive instruction on the dangers of hazing and the consequences of violating laws and policies banning the practice.

Balance: No Lopsided Time Allotment

Each main point deserves substantial development. This does not mean that you have to allot an equal amount of time during your speech to each main point. Nevertheless, you want a relatively balanced presentation. If you have three main points in the body of your speech, do not devote four minutes to the first main point, for example, and only a minute or less to your two remaining main points. Such a lopsided time allotment means either that your second and third main points are not really main points at all or that you have not developed your last two main points sufficiently. Increase the development of main points given insufficient treatment, combine points insufficiently developed into a single point and give the point some beef, or drop the two underdeveloped points and replace them with more substantial points.

Competent outlining requires proper use of symbols, appropriate division of points, coherence, completeness, and balance. An outline maps the flow of a speaker's ideas.

A Student Outline: Rough Draft and Revision

Constructing a competent outline can be a struggle, especially if appropriate outlining form and criteria are not well understood. Initial attempts to outline a speech may prove difficult, and your first attempts may produce seriously flawed results. Do not despair. Outlining is a process that trains your mind to think in an orderly fashion. It takes time to learn such a sophisticated skill.

Compare this seriously flawed rough draft of a student outline to the much improved revised outline constructed by the same student (my comments appear in *italics*):

ROUGH DRAFT OUTLINE

PURPOSE STATEMENT: To eliminate the drug problem by making drug testing mandatory. (*Where is your attention getter? Where is your central idea? You overstate the potential outcomes of mandatory drug testing. Try significantly reducing drug use, not "eliminating the drug problem." General purpose is only implied—will you try to convince us? Also, you are missing significance, credibility, and preview of main points.*)

I. The drugs among society. (*Needs clear direction. What do you want to say about "the drugs among society?" Use a complete sentence.*)
   A. The effects of drugs are serious.
      1. The immediate effects of drugs.
      2. The permanent effects of drugs. (*1 and 2 are not complete sentences.*)
   B. The effects of using drugs are dangerous. (*Unclear how this is different from A above*)
      1. Memory loss.
      2. Addicted babies.
      3. Brain damage.
      4. Physical harm. (*1–4 are not complete sentences.*)
II. Ways to solve drug abuse. (*Your purpose statement indicates only one solution: mandatory drug testing. Stay focused on your purpose statement. Also, not a complete sentence.*)
   A. The first step is to be aware of the problem. (*"Awareness" does not seem related to mandatory drug testing. Let your purpose statement guide your entire outline.*)
      1. Establish drug testing in all companies.
      2. Establish stricter laws against drug users.

3. Start more drug clinics. (*Good use of complete sentences. Subpoints 1–3 do not relate directly to A—they are not kinds of awareness. Subpoints 2 and 3 also seem unrelated to mandatory drug testing. These are coherence problems.*)
(*You have an A point without a B point—problem of division. Also, main point II is less developed than main point I—problem of balance. Where is your conclusion? One final note: You have not included your references.*)

REVISED VERSION

Introduction

ATTENTION STRATEGY: I tell my personal story of battling drug abuse. (*Without the actual personal story written here, it is difficult to judge its effectiveness. Potentially powerful; are you comfortable with such a revelation?*)

CENTRAL IDEA: Drug use in the workplace is a serious problem requiring a new approach to solving this problem. (*Is mandatory drug testing really a "new approach"?*)

PURPOSE STATEMENT: To convince my audience that every place of employment should start a mandatory drug testing program. (*This is a much improved purpose statement. "Every place of employment," however, seems a bit drastic. Are there a lot of drugged-out teachers? Try narrowing the application of your proposal to workers who might jeopardize the health and safety of others if drugs were used—airline pilots, bus drivers.*)

SIGNIFICANCE: Drug use in the workplace potentially affects all workers. (*Vague*)

CREDIBILITY: My experience using drugs in the workplace gives me a special perspective.

PREVIEW: I offer two main points:

I. Drug use in the workplace is a serious problem.

II. Mandatory drug testing in the workplace will reduce drug abuse. (*Good, concise preview that flows nicely from your purpose statement*)

Body

TRANSITIONAL STATEMENT: Let me begin with my first main point:

I. Drug use in the workplace is a serious problem. (*Good, clear main point*)
  A. Drug use in the workplace is widespread.
    1. Many employees in large companies use drugs.
    2. Many employees in factories use drugs.
  B. Drug use in the workplace is dangerous.
    1. Workers injure, even kill themselves.
    2. Customers have been injured and killed. (*Does not the risk go far beyond customers? If a plane crashes on a neighborhood because the pilot was loaded on drugs, dead and injured include far more than customers.*)
(*This entire main point with its subpoints is much improved.*)

(*continued*)

TRANSITIONAL STATEMENT: Clearly, drug use in the workplace is a serious problem. This brings me to my second main point: (*Nice transition with a signpost*)

II. Mandatory drug testing in the workplace will reduce drug abuse.
(*This is a solid second main point that flows nicely from your purpose statement.*)
   A. Drug testing will catch drug users.
      1. Testing is very accurate.
      2. Drug testing will provide absolute proof of drug use by workers.
         (*"Absolute proof" seems overstated. Try "solid proof."*)
   B. Drug testing will prevent drug use in the workplace.
      1. Workers will worry about getting caught using drugs.
      2. Drug testing can prevent drug users from being hired.
   (*The second main point is coherent, balanced, and divided appropriately, and complete sentences were used throughout. One final question: What do you propose should happen to employees who use drugs? Rehabilitation? Immediate job termination?*)

CONCLUSION

I. In summary, drug use in the workplace is a serious problem, and mandatory drug testing in the workplace will significantly reduce this problem. (*Good, concise summary*)

II. I opened with a personal story of my own battle with drug abuse and what it did to my ability to remain gainfully employed. (*Good reference to opening attention strategy*)

III. I am proud to say that I have won my personal war with drugs; I have a great job with lots of responsibility; my future looks bright; and, as a nation, we must forcefully address this scourge of drug abuse in the workplace. (*Pretty good, memorable finish*)

REFERENCES

National Conference of State Legislatures. (2009). *Statutes on drug testing in the workplace.* Retrieved from http://www.ncsl .org/default.aspx?tabid=13395

Reisner, R. (2008, September 16). Issue: Drug abuse in the workplace. *Business Week.* Retrieved from http://www.businessweek.com/ managing/content/sep2008/ ca20080916_40029

U.S. Department of Health and Human Services, Office of Applied Studies. (June 16, 2008). *An analysis of worker drug use and workplace policies and programs.* Retrieved from http://www.oas.samhsa.gov/ wkplace/toc.htm

U.S. Department of Labor, Occupational Safety & Health Administration. (2009, May 26). *Workplace substance abuse.* Retrieved from http://www.osha.gov/SLTC/ substanceabuse/index.html

U.S. Department of Transportation, Office of Drug and Alcohol

Policy and Compliance. (2009). *Best practices for DOT random drug and alcohol testing.* Retrieved from http://www.gov/ost/dapc/testingpubs/final_

random_brochure.pdf (*Solid references; credible and recent sources [speech presented in 2010]; APA style used correctly—good.*)

NOTE: The APA style for source citation in an outline references section is one of the popular choices. There are others, such as the MLA style. Your instructor will direct you regarding which style to use with your outline.

EFFECTIVE ORGANIZATION: CREATING PATTERNS

There are several patterns for organizing the body of your speech into an outline. The most common ones are topical, chronological, spatial, causal, problem–solution, problem–cause–solution, comparative advantages, the motivated sequence, and the narrative pattern.

Topical Pattern: By the Subjects

A topical pattern is appropriate when your information falls nicely into types, classifications, or parts of a whole. A topical pattern is often used for informative speeches but could be used for special occasion speeches (see Chapter 17). Your main topic divides easily into significant subtopics. You are not exploring a problem or looking for a solution. You are not explaining a step-by-step process or a spatial relationship. For example:

GENERAL PURPOSE: To inform
SPECIFIC PURPOSE STATEMENT: To identify different types of humor
  I. **Humor by mistake** is unintentional humor usually resulting from error.
     A. Card: "Your the Best Teacher Ever"
     B. Protest sign: "Get a Brain Morans"
  II. **Ironic humor** is the use of words to imply that the literal meaning is opposite the intended meaning.
     A. "I'd kill for a Nobel Peace Prize."
     B. "They all laughed when I said I'd become a comedian. Well, they're not laughing now" (Bob Monkhouse).

III. **Self-deprecation** is humor that makes fun of yourself.
   A. "Look, people have differing opinions on many issues. Take my (baseball) career. Half the people thought I was the worst player they've ever seen, and the other half thought I was a disgrace to the uniform" (Bob Uecker).
   B. "Every day before I walk out here I have to remind myself to just turn down the sexy" (Ellen DeGeneres).
IV. **Sarcasm** is harsh derision or irony.
   A. "I pretend to work; they pretend to pay me."
   B. "I'm trying to imagine you with a personality."
V. **Pun** is a play on words in which a humorous effect is produced by using a word that suggests two meanings.
   A. "I used to be a banker but I lost interest."
   B. "Did you hear about the guy whose whole left side was cut off? He's all right now."

A topical pattern does not necessarily suggest a particular order of presentation for each main point, as does a chronological pattern.

Chronological Pattern: According to Time

Some speeches follow a time pattern. A chronological pattern suggests a specific sequence of events. When speeches provide a biographical sketch of an individual, explain a step-by-step process, or recount a historical event, chronological order is an appropriate pattern of organization. For example:

GENERAL PURPOSE: To inform
SPECIFIC PURPOSE STATEMENT: To explain the renovation plan for our local downtown city center.

   I. The old Cooper House and Del Rio Theatre will be demolished.
   II. Main Street will be widened.
   III. A Cinemax theatre complex will replace the Del Rio Theatre.
   IV. A new, twice-as-large Cooper House will replace the old Cooper House.

Each main point follows a logical sequence. You do not replace buildings on the same sites until the old buildings are demolished. There is a temporal sequence that must be followed.

Spatial Pattern: Visualization

Some speeches provide information based on a spatial pattern. This spatial pattern may be front to back, left to right, north to south, top to bottom, bottom to top, and so forth. Explaining directions to a particular place requires a spatial order, a visualization of where things are spatially. Directions from your college campus to the local mall, for example, would begin from campus and move spatially ever closer until your destination is reached. You would not begin at the mall and work backward, because that would be difficult to visualize clearly and logically. Consider this example:

GENERAL PURPOSE: To inform
SPECIFIC PURPOSE STATEMENT: To explain space allocation in the new communication building.
  I. There are four main, average-size classrooms on the ground floor.
  II. There are two large lecture halls on the second floor.
  III. Faculty offices are mostly adjacent to the large lecture halls.
  IV. A student study and meeting facility is also located on the second floor at the north end.

The outline helps listeners visualize specific locations spatially in relation to each other. A visual aid showing a diagram of the floor plan of the entire building as you explain each section of the building would be especially informative.

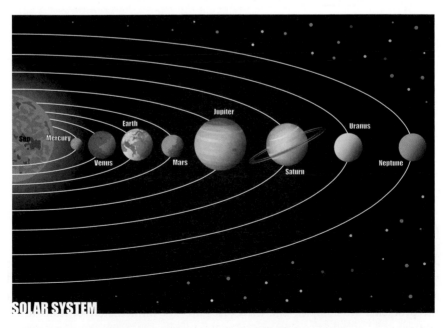

PHOTO 8.2 A spatial organizational pattern can be assisted by a visual aid.

Causal Pattern: Who or What Is Responsible

Humans look for causes of events. A standard organizational pattern is causes–effects or effects–causes. The *causes–effects pattern* is most appropriate when you are discussing why things happen and their consequences. The following is an example:

GENERAL PURPOSE: To inform
SPECIFIC PURPOSE STATEMENT: To explain the causes and effects of the opioid addiction epidemic in the United States.
 I. There are several causes of the opioid epidemic in the United States.
 II. This opioid epidemic has serious consequences for our country.

Your speech can also use the reverse *effects–causes pattern*. For example:

GENERAL PURPOSE: To inform
SPECIFIC PURPOSE STATEMENT: To show that poverty is a devastating global problem.
 I. The effects of global poverty are widespread, many, and severe.
 II. The causes of global poverty are complex.

Problem–Solution Pattern: Meeting Needs

The problem–solution organizational pattern is most appropriate when you explore the nature of a problem and propose a solution or possible solutions for the problem. Consider this example:

GENERAL PURPOSE: To persuade
SPECIFIC PURPOSE STATEMENT: To argue for stricter regulation of the food supply in the United States.
 I. The food supply in the United States is too often contaminated.
 II. More stringent FDA regulation of the US food supply would significantly reduce the problem.

Problem–Cause–Solution Pattern: Knowing Why and How

The problem–cause–solution organizational pattern expands on the problem–solution pattern and the causal pattern by exploring causes of the problem and addressing these causes in the solution. This is especially appropriate when the problems are complex and the causes are not immediately obvious to an audience.

CARTOON 8.1 It makes sense to be logically organized. As you would not put on your shoes before your socks, so also you would not propose a solution before identifying a problem. That is why the organizational pattern is called "problem–solution," not "solution–problem."

GENERAL PURPOSE: To persuade
SPECIFIC PURPOSE STATEMENT: To argue for a government-sponsored program to prevent hearing loss among teens and young adults.

  I. Teenagers and young adults are suffering serious hearing loss.
 II. There are several causes of this hearing loss.
III. A government-sponsored program to prevent hearing loss is critical.

Comparative Advantages Pattern: Who or What Is Better

Sometimes the best organizational pattern is to compare two things and argue that one is significantly better than the other for specific reasons (resulting in advantages). This pattern is especially appropriate for a persuasive speech. It is not that some policy, program, person, or practice is terrible or completely nonfunctional. It may be, however, that significant advantages can be achieved, so why not make the better choice? The following example illustrates the comparative advantages pattern:

PHOTO 8.3 Plastic ocean pollution fits naturally into a problem–solution or problem–cause–solution organizational pattern.

GENERAL PURPOSE: To persuade
SPECIFIC PURPOSE STATEMENT: To argue that women often make better leaders than men in the service industry.
  I. Women typically exhibit greater team leadership skills.
 II. Women offer more social support and are better at it.
III. Women are better suited to the team-oriented business climate in the service industry.

It is not that men are completely terrible team leaders. Many may be very good. You are simply trying to persuade your audience that women may be better suited to the task in the service industry than most men. That is a comparative advantages approach.

Monroe's Motivated Sequence: Five-Step Pattern

Monroe's motivated sequence, not surprisingly, was formulated by a speech professor named Alan Monroe, who synthesized sales techniques and basic principles from motivational psychology into five basic steps (McKerrow et al., 2007). *This organizational pattern is especially appropriate for persuasive speeches because there is a call to act.* The five steps are as follows:

I. *Attention*: Create interest; use attention strategies (see Chapter 6).
(Example: "I have cancer.")

II. *Need*: Present a problem to be solved and relate it to your audience.
(Example: "College students are not immune to the ravages of cancer.")

III. *Satisfaction*: Provide a solution to the problem that will satisfy your audience.
(Example: "Research is providing real cures, but more is needed.")

IV. *Visualization*: Provide an image for your audience of what the world will
look like if your solution is implemented. (Example: "Imagine a world
without cancer.") Asking your listeners to imagine a specific outcome
can be a very effective persuasion technique (Dolinski, 2016).

V. *Action*: Make a call to action; get your audience involved and committed.
(Example: "Donate what you can to the American Cancer Society.")

The motivated sequence is essentially a problem–solution organizational pattern with the added step of helping your audience visualize the benefits of your solution, such as "Increasing the number of student representatives on the College Board will provide a stronger voice for students on this campus. We will have greater influence on decision-making that affects all of us as students." The final step is a call to action on your proposed solution, such as "Sign this petition to be presented to the Board that seeks additional student representation on the College Board." (*See Chapter 15 for another example of Monroe's motivated sequence, and an extensive, much more complex example of this organizational pattern is presented in* **Appendix B**.)

Narrative Pattern: Telling a Story

Speeches are sometimes arranged as a narrative. The speech consists of a story that has a plot, characters, settings, and a theme. Your story, however, may incorporate other organizational patterns as well. You may tell the story chronologically, or you may tell it in an effect–cause pattern (telling first the effect of a crime committed, then telling the cause by digging into the background and experiences of the perpetrator of the crime). The focus is on telling a story to make a point. For example:

GENERAL PURPOSE: To inform
SPECIFIC PURPOSE STATEMENT: To explain how the early life of Mohatma Ghandi transformed him into the world's foremost advocate of nonviolent protest.

I. Ghandi's childhood in India was one of poverty and deprivation.

II. Ghandi's education raised important questions for him.

III. Ghandi's experiences with the British in India had a significant impact on his thinking.

PHOTO 8.4 Telling a story is like a dramatic play.

CONNECTING THE DOTS: ADDITIONAL TIPS

When giving a speech, you have to connect your ideas and create a flow so your listeners can comprehend and remember your message. There are several ways to accomplish these goals.

Provide Definitions

Key terms, especially unfamiliar or technical ones, should be defined clearly and precisely. For example, student Andrew Boge (2018), in his award-winning speech at the Interstate Oratorical Association competition, defined *food desert*, a concept that served as the basis of his entire speech, as "a populated area where a grocery store is not directly accessible" (p. 64). Student Adam Childers (1997) defined a more complicated concept, *endocrine disruptors*, as "human-made chemicals that have an uncanny ability to mimic some of the human body's most powerful hormones" (p. 103). Even though most people have a passing familiarity with the term *hormone*, many may have a difficult time giving a precise definition. Childers anticipates this and defines hormones as "little more than messengers of the endocrine system. They are released by the pituitary gland,

and then they circulate throughout the body, telling different cells what to do. For example, the hormone adrenaline tells our heart when to beat faster" (p. 104). This is a nice definition and explanation of hormones. You can picture what hormones do.

Use Signposts

A **signpost** is an organizational marker that indicates the structure of a speech and notifies listeners that a particular point is about to be addressed. Often signposts are numerical markers. Student Thomas Sullivan (2017) provides an apt example: "First, a fundamental tenet of FC [facilitated communication] practice is that the user must be presumed competent," and "Second, advocates with disabilities exaggerate FC's credibility," and "Finally, FC is constantly rebranded to obscure its true nature" (pp. 93–94). Signposting is a valuable oratorical, organizational tool.

Make Transitions

A **transition** uses words or phrases, even entire sentences, to *connect what was said with what will be said*. It is a bridge between points. Student Dara Quastad (2018) provides this transition: "So how is it that American citizens are denied these most basic rights?" Student Tiana Brownen (2018) offers this sentence as a transition: "Now that we understand the problem and causes, we will propose effective solutions on the legislative and individual levels" (p. 62). Both of these transitions connect the point you are leaving to prepare the audience for what you are about to explore. Table 8.1 offers examples of typical signposts and transitional words and phrases that are *part of complete signposts and transitional statements*.

Use Internal Previews

An **internal preview** is just like a preview in your introduction, except it appears in the body of your speech. Student Stephanie Stovall (2012) provides this transition (*italicized*) and internal preview (underlined): "*Now that we have explored the extent of the problem with juvenile crime, we can discuss* two of its primary causes: a lack of understanding about juvenile brain development and inadequate responses to juvenile crime" (p. 137). She connects her previous point with her next point. Student Tiana Brownen (2017) similarly provides a transitional statement and an internal preview: "*Now that we understand the problem*, we must explore its two main causes—a lack of training for childcare providers and a lack of oversight for faith-based daycares" (p. 102).

TABLE 8.1

Signposts and Transitional Words and Phrases

SIGNPOSTS	
My first point is	The key points are
My second point is	There are two ways to view this
Next	Finally
There are three points to explore	My final point is
TRANSITIONS	
So what does this mean?	However
For example	Why should we care?
Nevertheless	Along the same lines
In summary	Therefore
Consequently	Granted
Conversely	But

Give Internal Summaries

When you say "summary," most people think of a final wrap-up to a speech or essay. There is another type, however, called an internal summary, which is useful for especially informative and persuasive speeches. An **internal summary** is the reverse of an internal preview. Instead of indicating what is about to be addressed, an internal summary reminds listeners of the points already made. *It occurs in the body of the speech, not in the conclusion.* Internal summaries help listeners follow the sequence of ideas, connecting the dots so the picture drawn by the speaker comes into focus. "To review, wildfires cause serious damage to homes, they result in deaths and injuries, and they require huge resources to combat. So let me offer some ways to protect homes from wildfires" is an internal summary followed by a transitional statement. Here, main points already discussed are summarized as a preparation for proposed solutions that follow.

PREPARATION VERSUS PRESENTATION OUTLINES

Typically, you prepare a speech by constructing an outline composed of full sentences. You deliver the speech, however, from an abbreviated version of the full-sentence outline because it is far easier to glance at a word or phrase outline and trigger points to be made than to try to read entire sentences under pressure of speaking. A *presentation outline* is composed of simple words or phrases that trigger complete thoughts and ideas. Keep your presentation outline as brief as possible, highlighting key words and phrases. Use full sentences only for exact wording of your purpose statement and main points, or if you are quoting someone verbatim. Statistics and their sources, especially if there are a substantial number, may be included as well.

Here is a brief sample comparing preparation and presentation outlines:

PREPARATION OUTLINE

   I. Texting while driving is extremely dangerous.
     A. Texting while driving is distracting.
     B. Severe accidents, injuries, and even deaths result from texting while driving.

PRESENTATION OUTLINE

   I. Texting dangerous
     A. Distracting
     B. Accidents, injuries, deaths

Here is a presentation outline, including parenthetical references to sources:

INTRODUCTION

   A. **Attention**: Personal story of student debt
   B. **Significance**: 40 million Americans affected so far; most of you
   C. **Credibility**: Extensive research; father president of major bank
   D. **Purpose Statement**: Student debt in the United States is a serious and rising problem.

BODY

   A. **Student debt serious** (Zach Friedman, *Fortune*, June 13, 2018)
     1. $1.5 trillion
     2. Average debt: $37,172
     3. 2 million students owe $100,000+

    B. **Student debt crushing borrowers** (*Forbes*, November 5, 2018)
       1. 20 years, on average, to pay off student loans
       2. 40% of borrowers may default by 2023

CONCLUSION

    A. Summary of main points
       1. Student debt serious
       2. Student debt crushing borrowers
    B. Connect to personal story
    C. Student debt second only to home mortgage

SUMMARY

Effective and appropriate outlining and organization are important elements of successful public speaking. The criteria for effective outlining include proper use of a standard symbol system, coherence, completeness, balance, and division. The primary organizational patterns include topical, chronological, spatial, causal, problem–solution, problem–cause–solution, comparative advantages, motivated sequence, and narrative. Satisfy the criteria for effective outlining and choose the appropriate organizational pattern and you will be on the road toward a successful public speech.

TED TALKS AND YOUTUBE VIDEOS

Mind Mapping: "Mind Maps for Speeches and Presentations"

Problem–Solution Organizational Speech: Haydn Parry TED Talk: "Re-engineering Mosquitos to Fight Disease"

Well-Organized Speech: Matt Abraham: "No Freaking Speaking: Managing Public Speaking Anxiety"

Problem–Solution Speech: Sheryl Sandberg: "Why We Have Too Few Women Leaders"

Jodie Foster Disorganized Speech: "Jodie Foster: Full 2013 Golden Globes Speech"

For relevant links to these TED Talks and YouTube videos, see the *Practically Speaking* Companion Website: www.oup.com/he/rothwell-ps3e. You can also

gain access by typing the title of the speech reference into a Google search window or by doing the same on the TED Talks or YouTube sites.

CHECKLIST

☐ Are you using standard formatting for your outline?

☐ Are all of your main points divided into a minimum of two subpoints?

☐ Have you checked your outline for coherence—logical consistency and clarity?

☐ Have you used full sentences for your preparation outline?

☐ Have you transposed your preparation outline into a presentation, abbreviated outline?

☐ Are your main points balanced?

CRITICAL THINKING QUESTIONS

1. Is there ever an instance when a disorganized speech might be more effective than an organized speech?

2. Are there times when a bulleted outline works better than a standard outline format?

NOTE: Online **student resources**, such as practice tests, flashcards, and other activities, can be accessed at www.oup.com/he/rothwell-ps3e

Speaking Style: Using Language

When Speaker of the House John Boehner announced his resignation from Congress on September 25, 2015, California congressman Kevin McCarthy seemed a sure bet to assume the prestigious and powerful speakership. Then he opened his mouth and gobbledygook came pouring out, not once, but often. He referred to "an effective politically strategy," said "a safe zone would create a stem a flow of refugees," referred to Hillary Clinton as "untrustable," called Russia's hybrid warfare "high-bred warfare," claimed "we have isolated Israel while bolding places like Iran," offered this mishmash, "We don't have the same as difficult decision that this White House is managing the decline and putting us in tough decisions for the future," and criticized the Department of Veterans Affairs for providing little assistance to *returning* servicemen "who fought to the death in Ramadi" (quoted by Milbank, 2015a).

Comedian Stephen Colbert targeted McCarthy's stylistic stumbles by asserting that he used "strong, English-like words" when speaking. Lampooning McCarthy for calling Hungary "Hungria," Colbert said, "Hopefully his experience in Hungria will allow him to finally broker a peace treaty with Narnia" (quoted by Hensch, 2015). McCarthy withdrew his name from consideration for the House speakership, but in 2018, showing no permanent damage from his stylistic bloopers after cleaning up his linguistic act, he was voted Minority Leader of his party.

British author Oscar Wilde once remarked, "One's style is one's signature always." Kevin McCarthy's signature was, fairly or not, that of an inarticulate, clumsy politician who lacked credibility and gravitas because of his careless use of language (Cesca, 2015). Your speaking style reveals an identity and makes your speech memorable. It is achieved primarily by the way you use words to express your thoughts and bring them to life for an audience. A verbose style may tag you as boring or confused; a clear and detail-oriented style as knowledgeable and instructive; a vivid style as exciting, even inspiring; and a personal, conversational style as approachable and belonging to the group. Take your style seriously. It may leave a more lasting impression than any specific points made in your speech.

The purpose of this chapter is to explain the elements of a competent speech style. Toward that end, this chapter addresses (1) distinctions between oral and written style, (2) style in the electronic age, and (3) standards of competent style.

ORAL VERSUS WRITTEN STYLE

There are distinct differences between oral and written style. First, *oral style usually uses simpler sentences than written style*. Simpler sentences allow an audience to catch your meaning immediately. In contrast, when you read, you can review a sentence several times, if necessary, to discern the correct meaning. You may even consult a dictionary if you do not know the meaning of unfamiliar words. This is not the case while listening to a speech. Audience members cannot rewind a speech as they listen unless they are watching it on YouTube. Very complex sentence structure can confuse your listeners. Unfamiliar words remain meaningless.

Second, *oral style is highly interactive; written style is not*. When speaking, you can look directly into the faces of your listeners. If you sense that they do not understand your point, you can adjust by rephrasing your idea, adding an example, or even asking your listeners if they are confused. Feedback, especially nonverbal, is immediate from listeners, but feedback from readers is delayed and often nonexistent. The speaker and the audience influence each other directly. For example, if you offer an amusing play on words but no one laughs, you may decide to dump other such attempts at humor. The exception to this difference between oral and written style is when speakers look at a camera and post their speeches online without an immediate audience present with which to interact.

Third, *oral style is usually less formal than written style*. Effective writing style adheres to the appropriate use of grammar, includes well-constructed sentences, and uses proper punctuation and spelling. Even highly educated individuals diminish their credibility when they send written messages with obvious grammatical and spelling mistakes. If spoken, not written, a speaker's misspellings would not be an issue. Similarly, oral style tends to be more conversational, including shorter sentences, even sentence fragments. Grammatical errors may be less noticeable and thus less damaging to a speaker's credibility.

Being generally less formal compared to written style, however, does not mean that oral style should never exhibit formality. Some occasions are formal by nature (e.g., trials, some ceremonies) and require a more formal oral style than is typical of most speaking situations. Using slang or obscenities and being too casual and familiar in addressing certain individuals (e.g., referring to a court judge during trial by his or her first name, as in "Hey Pat") represent inappropriate style. Match your style to the occasion.

STYLE IN THE ELECTRONIC AGE

With the rise of the electronic age characterized by the influence of television and more recently YouTube, social networking sites, and text messaging and tweets, the traditional model of eloquent speaking style clashes with newer expectations from audiences. The traditional model is factual, analytic, formal, organized, and impersonal. The newer model is more narrative, personal, informal, conversational, self-disclosive, dramatic, and vivid (Kalnis, 2018; Morgan, 2013). Electronic media, especially television and YouTube, thrive on vivid pictures, terse, compelling storytelling, and clever sound bites (Cyphert, 2009). The data-driven, impersonal, traditional speaking style can come across on visual media as bland, even robotic (e.g., an uninteresting, detailed policy discussion drenched in academic jargon).

Any discussion of style in the electronic age cannot avoid at least passing reference to Donald Trump, regardless of political leanings. During the 2016 presidential campaign, Donald Trump's "telling it like it is" style that attacked "political correctness" seemed more authentic to many voters turned off by perceived prepackaged candidates (Arrigo, 2018). His style was conversational, unscripted, and notable for almost daily, stunning sound bites (Golshan, 2017). He ran the risk, however, of appearing scattered and divisive. As president, his style, without doubt polarizing, controversial, and at times linguistically inept, remained combative, vivid, and dramatic, but unmistakably effective in attracting the news media drawn to the sensational (Lakoff & Duran, 2018).

By contrast, 2016 Democratic presidential candidate Martin O'Malley projected a professional, fact-based, scripted style that, according to Democratic consultant Garry South, sounded "like one of the audio-animatronic robots at Disneyland—programmed and stilted" (quoted by Richman, 2015). O'Malley's candidacy never caught fire partly because his use of language was mostly dull and unmemorable. Many American voters are probably surprised to learn even now that O'Malley was ever a presidential candidate. He dropped out of the race after the Iowa caucus.

Does this mean that your speaking style should pander to the requirements of visual media such as television and YouTube, and bend to the necessarily abbreviated messages of our Twitter environment? Hardly! The challenge for you as a speaker is to blend the traditional with the more contemporary styles, merging the best of both. Ultimately, *blending the two styles, the factual/analytic and the narrative/dramatic, is best suited for most speaking situations that you will face in the electronic age.* Advice offered throughout this text instructs you on how to blend these styles.

STANDARDS OF COMPETENT ORAL STYLE

Style is your signature, but learning how to make that signature is your challenge. Oral style is effective and appropriate when it fulfills certain criteria. In this section, criteria and some examples of competent oral style are discussed.

Clarity: Saying What You Mean

Oral style works most effectively when language is clear and understandable. *Clarity comes from a simple, concise style.* John F. Kennedy asked his speechwriter, Ted Sorensen, to discover the secret of Lincoln's Gettysburg Address. Sorensen noted this: "Lincoln never used a two- or three-syllable word where a one-syllable word would do, and never used two or three words where one word would do" (quoted in National Archives, 1987, p. 1). There are 701 words in Lincoln's Second Inaugural Address, of which 505 are one syllable and 122 are merely two syllables (Zinsser, 1985). Inexperienced speakers may think that big ideas require big words. When listeners start noticing the big words, however, the big ideas shrink into the dark shadows of obscurity. Do not try to impress your audience with a vocabulary that sounds as though you consulted a thesaurus repeatedly. Remember, oral style requires greater simplicity than written style.

A clear style is simple but not simplistic. Although Lincoln used a simple, clear style, his sentence structure and phrasing were not always simple. In his Gettysburg Address, he included several lengthy, complex sentences. He also included this sentence: "We cannot dedicate, we cannot consecrate, we cannot hallow this ground." He could have said, "We cannot set aside for the special purpose of honoring, we cannot make holy this ground." Sometimes more challenging vocabulary provides an economical use of language. By occasionally using more sophisticated vocabulary, Lincoln spoke more concisely, clearly, and eloquently. If in doubt, however, default to simple sentence structure and vocabulary.

This often means avoiding **jargon**—the specialized language of a profession, trade, or group. Jargon is a kind of verbal shorthand. When lawyers use terms such as *prima facie case* and *habeas corpus*, they communicate appropriately to other attorneys and officers of the court very specific information without tedious, verbose explanation. "To the initiated, jargon is efficient, economical, and even crucial in that it can capture distinctions not made in the ordinary language" (Allan & Burridge, 1991, p. 201). Jargon used orally, however, can be inappropriate for those who do not understand the verbal shorthand. Jurors may not fully understand legal jargon when lawyers address them in opening and closing statements. Parents, for example, can be forgiven if they are confused by jargon used by educators, such as *instructional scaffolding, metacognition, growth mindset, flipped classroom, backward design, MOOCs,* and *makerspaces* ("Your Guide to Educational Lingo," 2018). To most parents, this bushel basket of buzzwords probably sounds closer to Klingon than any language they speak. Use jargon only when necessary, and then explain terminology that is likely to be unfamiliar to your listeners. If you use the medical term *tinnitus,* for example, explain immediately to a lay audience that this means "ear ringing."

Euphemisms can also confuse listeners. A **euphemism** is an indirect or vague word or phrase used to numb us to or conceal unpleasant or offensive realities. Substituting a euphemism such as passed away for "dead" when giving a eulogy at a funeral may cushion a painful reality for grieving relatives and friends. This is probably harmless, even compassionate. Nevertheless, euphemisms can create unnecessary, even purposeful, confusion. Rolls-Royce informed customers that their cars don't break down, but sometimes they *fail to proceed*. Repeatedly, the mass media refer to *wardrobe malfunctions* when celebrities have difficulty keeping their clothes from falling off their bodies. The military has often euphemized civilian casualties in war as *collateral damage* and torture as *enhanced interrogation*. The nuclear power industry for years objected to claims that their power plants could explode. The worst-case scenario, we were told, was *spontaneous energetic disassembly* (Rakeshaw, 2014). Student Nick Phephan (2011) notes the problem of euphemism in his speech about hospital overcharges. For example, hospitals refer to a "fog reduction elimination device," which is a small "piece of gauze used to wipe condensation off of stethoscopes." This euphemism that no patient is likely to understand is used to camouflage an exorbitant charge for a commonplace procedure. Generally, avoid using euphemisms in your speeches.

Finally, use slang sparingly. **Slang**, the highly informal speech not in conventional usage, can be employed when you are confident that your listeners will comprehend and identify with such casual speech, the speech occasion is meant to be relatively informal, and using slang will not brand you as ridiculously out of touch. Slang (see UrbanDictionary.com for latest additions) typically works more effectively in oral than in written presentations because you are speaking directly to a specific audience whose members you already know may actually be familiar with the slang. If you are unfamiliar with your audience, stick to more standard colorful language use. Using terms such as *minesweeping, facepalm,*

CARTOON 9.1 Euphemisms blunt unpleasant realities, but they can also confuse listeners. Would you ever guess that "preparation for success" refers to failing a test?

slapchat, and *nomoji* when speaking to an unfamiliar audience may leave your listeners in a state of confusion. Slang also can become dated quickly, as these terms have likely become, although the slang term "cool" has endured for more than a century (Berger, 2015). Using dated slang terms can make you sound hopelessly uncool. If in doubt, skip slang.

Precision: Picking the Apt Words

Baseball great Yogi Berra once observed this about the game that made him a household name: "Ninety percent of this game is half-mental." Yogi also said, "When you get to a fork in the road, take it," and "Our similarities are different."

Yogi was not renowned for his precise use of the English language (or his mastery of arithmetic). Everyone occasionally misuses a word. Nevertheless, you should strive to be as precise in your use of language as possible. *Choose your words carefully and know their exact meaning.* Using words imprecisely or inaccurately diminishes your credibility and can make you appear foolish.

Lack of language precision is one strong reason sexist language should be avoided (see also Chapter 3 discussion). Aside from the bias, sexist language is imprecise and often inaccurate language usage. Terms such as *businessman, policeman, fireman,* and *postman* were once mostly accurate depictions of a society with few female executives, police officers, firefighters, and letter carriers. This is no longer accurate, so such terms are sexist and imprecise. *Eliminate sexist language.*

Words that are vague and abstract need concrete **referents**—the objects, events, ideas, and relationships referred to by words. Terms such as *patriotism, freedom, border security,* and *comprehensive medical care* can be meaningless noise without concrete explanations and definitions provided. Our minds instantly form images of concrete words but can struggle to form images of abstract terms, making understanding a speaker's message difficult. Try this exercise on your friends to prove the point: quickly recite a list of concrete words, such as *comb, hair, house, clown,* and *baseball.* Instruct each person to signal the instant that a clear image comes to mind. Then read a list of more abstract words such as *brotherhood, truth, justice, responsibility,* and *philosophy.* Again, instruct each person to signal the instant that a clear image comes to mind. You'll find that the second list produces a more delayed response, even in some cases no response

PHOTO 9.1: Use language precisely. This sign is amusingly ambiguous.

at all, because the referent is too gauzy and imprecise. The first list will produce instantaneous responses because the words have concrete referents. *It isn't that abstract words should always be avoided.* Instead, when using abstract words, clarify them with concrete explanations or words. "Comprehensive medical coverage" could mean the equally vague "really great coverage for everyone," or a more concrete use of language such as "Medicare for every American citizen." Even this more concrete referent would require further elaboration.

Sometimes our attempt to be precise leads to redundant phrases such as "twelve noon," "true fact," "circle around," "close proximity," "end result," "revert back," and "the future to come." Also be careful when using acronyms that you do not add pointless words such as "ATM machine" (**A**utomatic **T**eller **M**achine machine), "HIV virus" (**H**uman **I**mmunodeficiency **V**irus virus), and "AIDS syndrome" (**A**cquired **I**mmune **D**eficiency **S**yndrome syndrome). *Eliminate redundant words and phrases.*

Vividness: Painting a Picture

Simple, concise, and precise use of language does not mean using words in a boring fashion. A vivid, visual style paints a picture in the minds of listeners and makes a speaker's ideas attention-getting and memorable (Dingemanse, 2014). Award-winning screenwriter Aaron Sorkin once described the Internet as

PHOTO 9.2 Clever wording shows style. This sign is a play on the oft-repeated "separation of church and state."

"a bronchial infection on the First Amendment," vividly highlighting how, through the facility to remain anonymous, users can easily spread misinformation and hatred. Student Melody Carlisle (2011) used vivid language in her speech on bed bugs when she remarked that "bed bugs might be the world's greatest hitchhikers" and sarcastically referred to these "creepy crawlies" as "enchanting houseguests" (p. 138). Each of these examples leaves a visual impression in the listener's mind, grabbing attention and remaining memorable.

There are many ways to make your speech style vivid. Here are a few suggestions for you to consider.

Metaphor and Simile: Figures of Speech   Two main figures of speech that can add vividness to your speeches and help listeners understand a concept are metaphors and similes. A **metaphor** is an implied comparison of two seemingly dissimilar things. Groucho Marx once remarked, "A hospital bed is a parked taxi with the meter running." Author Truman Capote commented, "Life is a moderately good play with a badly written third act."

Be careful not to mix your metaphors, otherwise your vivid imagery may sound laughable. A **mixed metaphor** is the use of two or more vastly different metaphors in a single expression. Famous movie producer Samuel Goldwyn once remarked, "That's the way with these directors. They're always biting the hand that lays the golden egg." Boyle Roche, in his speech before the Irish Parliament, offered this example: "Mr. Speaker, I smell a rat. I see him floating in the air. But mark me, sir, I will nip him in the bud."

A **simile** is an explicit comparison of two seemingly dissimilar things using the words *like* or *as*. For example, "He was as enraged as a raccoon trapped in a garbage can." Author Rita Mae Brown said, "Language exerts hidden power, like the moon on the tides." Curt Simmons described what it was like pitching to baseball great Hank Aaron: "Trying to get a fastball past Hank Aaron is like trying to get the sun past a rooster." "She was as sharp as a box cutter and twice as deadly" is also a simile. Student Melody Carlisle (2011) uses a nice simile in her speech on bed bugs: "Sherri and her little girl were sick of being treated like human buffets" (p. 138).

Vivid phrases can enhance a speech, but not if they become clichés. A **cliché** is a once-vivid expression that has been overused to the point of seeming commonplace. "It's not rocket science," "It's an emotional roller coaster," "He got thrown under the bus," and "I'm between a rock and a hard place" have become shopworn from massive overuse. A survey of 5,000 individuals in 70 countries conducted by the British-based Plain English Campaign showed that "at the end of the day" is the most annoying cliché in the English language across all cultures ("Cliches," 2009). Other clichés vying for most annoying, especially in the business arena, are "giving 110%," "thinking outside the box," and "pushing the envelope" (Pesce, 2018). Be creative and concoct your own vivid metaphors and similes to enliven your speeches.

Alliteration: Several of the Same Sounds   The repetition of the same sound, usually a consonant sound, starting each word is called **alliteration**. It can create a very vivid and effective cadence and make your speech more memorable. Classic examples of alliteration were spoken by the wizard in the movie *Wizard of Oz*. He called the Tin Man a "clinking, clanking, clattering collection of caliginous junk." He referred to the Scarecrow as a "billowing bale of bovine fodder." Student Aaron Klein (2018) used the alliterative phrase "death and devastation for the developing world" (p. 13). Student Daniel Arthur (2017) used the phrase "sleeve the sneeze" (p. 33) as a way of preventing the spread of flu germs, preferable to sneezing into one's hands.

Alliteration can create a captivating cadence, especially when delivered orally. Do not overuse alliteration, however. A little alliteration is appropriate. Frequent alliteration could become laughable.

Repetition: Rhythmic Cadence   Reiterating the same word, phrase, or sentence, usually with parallel structure, is called **repetition**. Martin Luther King's "I have a dream" is perhaps the most memorable example. Barack Obama's "Yes, we can" theme repeated in almost every campaign speech he gave in 2008 was another strong example. It provided a rhythmic cadence for his speeches, unified a series of ideas, and created a powerful, vivid, emotional effect with his audience. His listeners would often shout, without prompting, "Yes, we can," during his speech (*see link at end of chapter*). Such repetition in a written essay to be read would lose some of its rhythmic cadence, and no opportunity for an audience response is available.

Here are two other examples of effective oral repetition:

(Pink re-enacting conversation with her daughter about body image) "Do you see me growing my hair?" She said, 'No, mama.' I said, 'Do you see me changing my body?' 'No, mama' 'Do you see me changing the way I present myself to the world?' 'No, mama.' 'Do you see me selling out arenas all over the world?' 'Yes, mama.' "OK! So baby girl. We don't change. We take the gravel and the shell and we make a pearl. And we help other people to change so they can see more kinds of beauty." *(Pink's VMA speech August 2017)*

"I speak so those without a voice can be heard. Those who have fought for their rights: Their right to live in peace. Their right to be treated with dignity. Their right to equality of opportunity." *(Malala Yousafzai, Pakistani activist and youngest Nobel Prize laureate)*

PHOTO 9.3 Pink delivering acceptance speech at the 2017 VMA awards.

PHOTO 9.4 Malala Yousafzai, youngest Nobel laureate, gives a speech using repetition.

As is true of any stylistic device, a little goes a long way. *Be careful not to overuse repetition and become boringly redundant.*

Antithesis: Using Opposites   Charles Dickens began his famous novel *A Tale of Two Cities* with one of the most memorable lines in literature: "It was the best of times, it was the worst of times, it was the age of wisdom, it was the age of foolishness . . . " This is an example of the stylistic device called **antithesis**—a sentence composed of two parts with parallel structure but opposite meanings to create impact. Former Acting Solicitor General of the United States Neal Katyal offered this use of antithesis upon the release of the 2018 Mueller report on Russian interference in the 2016 presidential election: "This is the end of the beginning, not the beginning of the end." Perhaps the most famous example of antithesis in public speaking is from John F. Kennedy's inaugural address in 1961: "Ask not what your country can do for you, ask what you can do for your country." He also used this example of antithesis: "Let us never negotiate out of fear, but let us never fear to negotiate."

The effectiveness of antithesis is in the rhythmic phrasing. The Reverend Jesse Jackson, in his famous "Rainbow Coalition" speech, provides this example: "I challenge them to put hope in their brains and not dope in their veins." Four months before his inaugural address, Kennedy made this statement: "The new frontier is not what I promise I am going to do for you. The new frontier is what I ask you to do for your country." This also used antithesis, but it was not memorable. It seems more verbose and bland. Be concise when using antitheses.

SUMMARY

Style is the distinctive quality that makes your speech memorable. The principal standards of stylistic effectiveness are clarity, precision, and vividness. You can learn much about style by examining competent speakers who follow these standards. Ultimately, however, your style must be your own. Work on clarity, precision, and vividness by listening to successful speakers, but explore what fits you well. Metaphors and similes may come easily to you, but antithesis may seem artificial and awkward. Develop your own style by experimenting. Try including metaphors in your conversations with others. Play with language informally before incorporating stylistic devices in your formal speeches. Remember, style is your signature.

TED TALKS AND YOUTUBE VIDEOS

The Power of Repetition: Barack Obama: "Yes, We Can" Full Speech

The Power of Language: "The Greatest Movie Speeches: *Malcolm X*"

Cliché and Jargon Overload (See #5): "5 Incredibly Bad Speeches"

The Power of Repetition: "Pink Accepts the 'Michael Jackson Video Vanguard Award'"

Written Versus Spoken Language: "Txting Is Killing Language. JK"

For relevant links to these TED Talks and YouTube videos, see the *Practically Speaking* Companion Website: www.oup.com/he/rothwell-ps3e. You can also gain access by typing the title of the speech reference into a Google search window or by doing the same on the TED Talks or YouTube sites.

CHECKLIST

- ☐ Is your use of language clear?
- ☐ Is your use of language precise?
- ☐ Is your use of language vivid?

CRITICAL THINKING QUESTIONS

1. Is it ever inappropriate to use similes and metaphors in your speeches?

2. When might slang be offensive? Which audiences might be a slang danger zone?

NOTE: Online **student resources**, such as practice tests, flashcards, and other activities, can be accessed at www.oup.com/he/rothwell-ps3e

Delivering Your Speech

She crawled on her hands and knees across the courtroom floor. She kicked the jury box, cried, flailed her arms, and screamed. Her marathon two-and-a-half-hour opening statement was verbose and rambling. Defense attorney Nedra Ruiz's delivery, exhibited before the jury in the trial of Marjorie Knoller and Robert Noel in the highly publicized dog-mauling murder case in San Francisco, became a subject of considerable comment. Loyola University law professor Laurie Levenson remarked during the trial, "There's a pretty decent defense here, but it's getting lost in her [Ruiz's] mannerisms and her theatrics. She's not smooth. She's not polished. She crosses the line from what I think is effective advocacy to cheap theatrics" (quoted in Curtis, 2002, p. A4). Ruiz lost the case.

This is an instance of delivery subverting substance. It illustrates the importance of a competent public speaking delivery. An inappropriate, over-the-top delivery can undermine your effectiveness. Does delivery make a difference in less dramatic and consequential contexts? Unquestionably it does, as this chapter discussion will demonstrate.

At its most basic, a competent delivery seems natural, is intelligible, establishes connection with an audience, is lively, and avoids distractions. These and many other features of competent delivery are explored in this chapter. Thus, *the purpose of this chapter is to explain how you can develop a competent speech delivery.* Toward that end, this chapter addresses (1) methods of delivery and their pros and cons and (2) overcoming delivery challenges with effective strategies.

PHOTO 10.1 Attorney Nedra Ruiz's delivery was highly animated and memorable during her dramatic defense in a California dog mauling trial. Nevertheless, her delivery was more distracting than effective.

METHODS OF COMPETENT DELIVERY

There are several methods of delivery, each with its own pros and cons, depending on the purpose of your speech and the difficulty of each method. The four methods discussed here are manuscript, memorized, impromptu, and extemporaneous speaking.

Manuscript Speaking: Looking for Precision

Speakers often refer to "writing their speeches." It is very difficult to write a speech for oral presentation that would not sound like an essay read to an audience. A read manuscript has a distinct rhythm, and it can sound stilted and overly formal. If the use of a manuscript becomes obvious, it can be a distraction, even in a fairly strong speech.

   A manuscript speech may be an appropriate method of delivery in certain situations. If you must be scrupulously precise in your phrasing for fear of being legally encumbered or causing offense, then a manuscript with all your precise thoughts in black and white may be necessary. Political candidates spend millions of dollars for television and radio ads. They cannot tolerate mistakes in phrasing. Their speeches are precisely written and often delivered from a teleprompter. The teleprompter is an electronic device that scrolls a manuscript speech, line by line, for the speaker to read while looking right at the audience or the television camera. A television audience does not see the manuscript scrolling in front of the speaker.

A manuscript can be useful, but it takes extensive practice to present a manuscript speech in such a way that an audience is not aware that the speaker is reading, even if a teleprompter is available. *A chief drawback of manuscript speaking is that the speaker will appear too scripted, and ownership of his or her ideas becomes suspect.* On February 19, 2010, Tiger Woods read a carefully scripted apology to his fans, colleagues, sponsors, employees, and family members for cheating on his wife with multiple sex partners. One columnist called it "an infomercial" and a "weirdly scripted and strangely robotic appearance" that "had all the soul of one of his prepared releases" and "looked like a bad Saturday Night Live skit" (Dahlberg, 2010, p. C3). Another said that Woods "stayed too on script" and that "it was as awkward to watch as it must have been painfully uncomfortable for him to deliver" (Inman, 2010, p. 1D).

Another drawback is that digressions from the prepared manuscript are difficult to make smoothly, yet such changes may be critical if your audience does not respond well to a portion of the speech. I once witnessed a speaker at a union meeting get interrupted in mid-speech by a heckler who shouted, "Why should we trust anything you say? You're licking the boots of management." The speaker hesitated, then continued with her prepared speech that was wholly unresponsive to the heckler's allegation. The audience subsequently joined the heckler and began chanting "Sit down!" The speaker became discombobulated and, finally, she sat down to the cheers of the audience. She failed to adapt to the unfolding circumstances because she was wedded to her script.

A final drawback of manuscript speaking is that the speaker easily gets buried in the manuscript and fails to establish eye contact with an audience. Reading to your audience can disconnect you from your listeners. (See *"Highlights from the Best Commencement Speeches of 2018"* listed at the end of this chapter to assess the drawbacks of manuscript speaking compared to non-manuscript deliveries in otherwise competent speeches.)

A few basic guidelines should be uppermost in your mind when faced with delivering a manuscript speech. First, *do not use a manuscript as a crutch* because you experience speech anxiety. Use a manuscript because message precision is critical in a specific context. Second, *remember the differences between oral and written style* delineated in the previous chapter. Strive for a more oral style when constructing your speech. Third, *practice repeatedly* so you can frequently look at your audience for longer than occasional glimpses. Fourth, *use vocal variety and some body movement* (see later discussion) so your speech doesn't sound dull and appear stilted. Fifth, *be flexible.* If an ad lib seems appropriate, break from your manuscript. For example, during his 2015 State of the Union address to Congress, President Obama stated as part of his prepared remarks, "I have no more campaigns to run." This ignited a sarcastic round of applause from Republicans in the audience. Obama quickly ad libbed with a wry smile on his face, "I know because I won both of them," which engendered even louder applause from Democrats. Generally, manuscript speaking can be effective with plenty of practice, but it is often best suited to professional speakers who have substantial experience using this difficult delivery method.

Memorized Speaking: Memory Do Not Fail Me Now

Some speakers attempt to memorize their speeches. A short toast at a wedding, a brief acceptance speech at an awards ceremony, or a few key lines in a lengthy speech may benefit from memorization, especially if what you memorize is emotionally touching or humorous (no one wants the punch line of a joke to be read). Memorizing a speech of five minutes or more, however, is a bit like stapling

CARTOON 10.1 Memorizing a speech, especially one longer than a few minutes, is a risky undertaking. If you are a novice speaker, it is best to choose another method of delivery.

oatmeal to a ceiling—it takes lots of energy, it is usually pointless, and it probably would not stick anyway. It is too likely that you will forget portions of your speech; your script will not stick in your mind.

Have you ever grown frustrated or felt uncomfortable when someone tries to remember a joke or funny story and keeps forgetting important details, then, following an agonizing oral search for the correct version ("Oh wait, that's not the way it goes"), he or she finally flubs the punch line? Forgetting can be painful for listeners and speaker alike. Awkward silences while you desperately attempt to remember the next sentence in your speech can be embarrassing. Also, making a memorized speech sound natural, not artificial and robotic, requires considerable experience. Those who have acted on stage know this well.

Generally, do not memorize your speech (Fruciano, 2016). If you do decide that it is necessary, follow a few simple suggestions. First, *practice your speech repeatedly* so it becomes almost second nature to you. Second, *look at your audience*, not the ceiling, while you try to remember each sentence. Third, *if you forget exact phrasing, put the point in other words* until you remember the next scripted sentence of your speech. Fourth, *do not apologize if you momentarily go blank*. Just pause, maybe move toward your audience as if purposely being a bit dramatic, and then begin when you remember.

Impromptu Speaking: Off-the-Cuff Presentations

An **impromptu speech** is an address delivered without preparation, or so it seems. You are asked to respond to a previous speaker without warning or to say a few words on a subject without advance notice. One advantage of impromptu speeches is that audience expectations are likely to be lower than for speakers given adequate time to prepare. If you give a strong impromptu speech, audiences will be impressed. Although impromptu speeches can be challenging, a few simple guidelines can help.

First, *anticipate impromptu speaking*. As Mark Twain once remarked: "It usually takes me more than three weeks to prepare for a good impromptu speech." If you have any inkling that you might be called on to give a short speech, begin preparing your remarks. Do not wait until you are put on the spot. You will deliver it off-the-cuff without notes, but your main points are at the ready.

Second, *draw on your life experience and knowledge for the substance of your remarks*. F. E. Smith once observed that "Winston Churchill has devoted the best years of his life to preparing his impromptu speeches." Churchill had clarified his ideas and points of view in his mind. When called on to speak in an impromptu fashion, he was already prepared. Life experience is preparation for impromptu speaking. Draw from that experience.

Third, *formulate a simple outline for an impromptu speech*. Begin with a short opening attention strategy—a relevant story, a humorous quip you have used successfully on other occasions, or a clever quotation you have memorized. State your point of view or the theme for your remarks. Then quickly identify two or three short points that you will address. Finally, *summarize briefly what you said*. You are not expected to provide substantial supporting material for your points during an impromptu speech, but if you have some facts and figures memorized, you will impress your audience with your ready knowledge. Impromptu speaking is usually more informal than a standard speech, so be conversational in tone and presentation.

Extemporaneous Speaking: The Virtues of an Outline

Most public speaking classes stress extemporaneous speaking, often called "extemp" speaking for short. An **extemporaneous speech** is delivered from a prepared outline or notes. There are several advantages to this method of delivering a speech. First, even though fully prepared in advance, *an extemporaneous speech sounds spontaneous* because you do not read from a manuscript, but instead you glance at an outline or notes, then you put your thoughts into words on the spot. In this sense, extemporaneous speaking falls between impromptu and manuscript speaking. It sounds impromptu and has the detail and substance of a manuscript speech without being either. (See Table 10.1 for comparison of all four delivery types.)

Second, *extemporaneous speaking permits greater eye contact with the audience*. You are not buried in a manuscript with your head down. Of course, an outline can take on the form of a manuscript if it is too detailed. It is possible to write an entire speech, word for word, on a 3 × 5 index card. In such cases, the manuscript is merely tiny and not very useful.

Third, *extemporaneous speaking allows the speaker to respond to audience feedback as it occurs*. You can adjust to the moment-by-moment changes in audience reactions much more so than with manuscript or memorized speeches.

The chief drawback to this method of delivering a speech is that learning to speak from notes or an outline takes practice. Inexperienced speakers tend to worry that they will forget important elements if every word is not written down.

There are several basic guidelines for delivering a speech extemporaneously. First, *use a presentation outline not a preparation outline* (see Chapter 8). Second, *be extremely familiar with your material*. Try explaining key points to friends or relatives in casual conversations. Third, *repeatedly practice delivering your speech from your presentational outline*.

TABLE 10.1

Delivery Methods

METHOD	DESCRIPTION	PROS	CONS
Manuscript	Read the pages of a fully written speech	• Ensures one speaks precisely	• Difficult to sound natural • Difficult to deliver a speech with sensitivity to audience response • Difficult to keep eye contact with audience • Requires practice to be able to speak from teleprompter; not generally available
Memorized	Memorize a fully written speech	• Feasible for speeches shorter than five minutes	• Difficult to sound natural without considerable experience • Easy to forget parts of speech
Impromptu	Formulate a general outline and anticipate particular topics	• Audience expectations are lower • Sounds conversational	• Less formal than a standard speech • Difficult to provide substantial evidence in support of arguments
Extemporaneous	Refer to presentation outline, but do not read	• Sounds natural and spontaneous • Permits greater eye contact with audience • Allows speaker to modulate delivery with sensitivity to audience • Can respond to audience feedback	• Requires practice to be able to speak effectively from an outline

DEVELOPING COMPETENT DELIVERY

The method of delivery does not resolve many of the delivery challenges you face when presenting a speech and specific ways to address these challenges. This section discusses these challenges with numerous tips on how to improve your delivery.

Eye Contact: Connecting with Your Audience

Eye contact is an important element of a speaker's credibility (Neal & Brodsky, 2008). Even across cultures a fair amount of eye contact during speaking is important to enhance credibility and to connect with listeners (Johnson & Miller, 2002). Direct, penetrating eye contact can be quite intense, even intimidating (Anderson, 2016). If you doubt this, try staring at someone for a prolonged period of time. Good luck with that. Research shows that prolonged eye contact can seem threatening (Moyer, 2016). When you zero in on listeners, it is difficult for them to ignore you, sometimes to the point of annoyance if prolonged. Research shows that the typical preferred duration of direct eye contact is three seconds (Binetti et al., 2016). This means that we can handle about three seconds of direct eye contact and then we become twitchy and want to avert our gaze to break connection. You don't want to break connection with your audience, so vary your gaze.

PHOTO 10.2 Strong eye contact is critical to connecting with your audience, but vary your gaze. Don't lock onto a single person in your audience. That is too intense, even intimidating.

Conversely, when you do not look directly at your audience, listeners' minds can easily wander. This also creates a disconnection between you and your audience (Jarrett, 2016). This is often the case when speakers make PowerPoint presentations. They look at the slides, not the audience. Inexperienced speakers tend to look at the ground, above the heads of their listeners, at one side of their audience or the other but not both, or they bury their head in a manuscript.

Strive for balance. First, *be very familiar with your speech so you avoid getting pinned to your notes or manuscript*. Second, *practice looking at your entire audience*, beginning with the middle of your audience, then looking left, then right, and then to the middle again. Do not ignore a section of your audience by looking only left or right. Also, do not focus on a single listener (e.g., instructor grading your speech). Gradually sweep across your audience as you speak. Don't dart your eyes quickly back and forth. With practice, your eye contact will become automatic.

Voice: Developing Vocal Variety

Using your voice effectively is an important aspect of speech delivery. A study of 120 executives' speeches found that the speakers' voice quality can affect an audience's evaluation more than the content of the speech. "People who hear recordings of rough, weak, strained or breathy voices tend to label the speakers as negative, weak, passive or tense. People with normal voices are seen as successful, sexy, sociable and smart . . ." (Zandan, 2018b).

Strive for vocal variety called **inflection**. Raise and lower the pitch of your voice. **Pitch** is the range of your voice from high to low sounds. The singing voice has a range of pitch from soprano to bass. Similarly, you can vary your speaking voice by moving up and down the vocal range from high sounds to lower sounds and back. Of course, you are not trying to hit the extreme highs and lows. Guys do not want to switch into a falsetto or sound like a three-year-old on helium, and women do not want to sound like they are digging for the deep bass sound. Just vary your voice enough to avoid a monotonous sameness to your pitch. Research shows that "variance in pitch may reveal the presence of an active and lively mind. Pitch variance can convey enthusiasm, interest, and active deliberation, whereas a monotone voice sounds dull and mindless" (Schroeder & Epley, 2015, p. 889). The same research also shows that pitch variance influences employers' view of job candidates' competence and intelligence.

Monotony can also be avoided by varying the **volume** of your voice from loud to soft. A loud voice signals intense, passionate feeling. It will punctuate portions of your presentation much as an exclamation point punctuates a written sentence. Do not be excessive, however. As Mark Twain noted, "Noise proves nothing. Often a hen who has merely laid an egg cackles as if she laid an asteroid."

Incessant, unrelenting, bombastic delivery of a message can irritate and alienate your audience. Speak loudly only when you have an especially important point to make. All points in your speech do not deserve equal attention.

Speaking softly can also induce interest. When you lower the pitch and loudness of your voice, the audience must strain to hear. This can be a nice dramatic twist to use in a speech, if used infrequently. Vocal variety signals a shift in mood and does not permit an audience to drift into the hypnotic, trance-like state produced by the white noise of the monotone voice. Practice vocal variety on your friends during casual conversations. Experiment with different voice inflections and volume.

Fluency: Avoiding Excessive Vocal Fillers

A common delivery challenge is to exclude **vocal fillers**—the insertion of *um, uh, like, you know, know what I mean, whatever*, and other variants that substitute for pauses and often draw attention to themselves. Such dysfluencies are common in normal conversations.

Despite how common they are, vocal fillers when giving a speech are not always problematic (Sedivy, 2015). They often go unnoticed by listeners. Actually, error-free speaking may strike some audiences as too slick and insincere (Erard, 2008).

CARTOON 10.2 Occasional dysfluencies are normally not a problem. Frequent dysfluencies, however, can destroy an otherwise quality speech.

Research reveals that an optimum frequency of vocal fillers is about one per minute, but the average speaker uses about five per minute when they are not nervous, but even more often when they are anxious (Zandan, 2019).

When your audience begins to notice these "vocal hiccups" because of overuse, it can divert attention and reduce your credibility (Zandan, 2019). In a brief interview with George Stephanopoulos in March 2013, Barack Obama used "you know" 43 times, and he used "uh" 236 times during one of the 2016 debates with Mitt Romney (*see link at end of chapter*). Caroline Kennedy, daughter of President John F. Kennedy, used "you know" an astounding 142 times during a brief interview when she was contemplating running for the U.S. Senate (Ghosh, 2014). If you slip into a habit of using vocal fillers frequently in your conversations, you will very likely suffer the same problem when giving a speech. It can be a tough habit to break.

The fluency of your delivery suffers mightily when vocal fillers are used more than occasionally. Almost all speakers use vocal fillers once in a while. When they become frequent, however, it may be the only part of your speech that is memorable (Zandan, 2018a). Practice not using vocal fillers during casual conversation with friends and family. Appreciate the power of the pause without interjecting a vocal filler. "Great public speakers often pause for two to three seconds or even longer," which, when done occasionally, can help you collect your thoughts, calm your nerves, and build suspense (Zandan, 2019). Focus on noticing how often other people use vocal fillers. Practice your speech in front of a friend, or video record it. Have your friend tap a pencil on a table every time you use a vocal filler during your speech. When you review the video-recorded practice speech, count the number of vocal fillers. Even quicker and easier, try using the free UmLikeYknow app (http://www.umlikeyknow.com/) that automatically counts your vocal fillers. With time, you will eliminate the habit.

Speaking Rate: Finding the Right Pace

Sean Shannon, a Canadian residing in Oxford, England, recited the famous soliloquy "To be or not to be . . ." from Shakespeare's Hamlet at 650 words per minute (wpm) (*see access to link at end of chapter*). Talking at 650 wpm is clearly possible, but how fast should you speak to an audience? Moderately fast and rapid speaking rates (180–210 wpm) increase the audience's perception of you as intelligent, confident, and effective compared to slower paced speakers (Smith & Shaffer, 1995). Speaking rapidly shows that you are quick on your feet and can handle ideas swiftly. Conversely, linguist Deborah Tannen (2003) notes that a very slow speaking rate (fewer than 100 wpm) is stereotyped as slow-witted and unintelligent in every culture studied. Nevertheless, you may begin your speech slowly and increase the pace as you build momentum and audience enthusiasm.

Speaking rate does not have to be uniform throughout. Martin Luther King's "I Have a Dream" speech began at 92 wpm but ended at 145 wpm (*see access to link at end of chapter*).

Some listeners, however, may not be able to keep pace with you if you are attempting to speak at the pace of someone who has downed three hyper-caffeinated energy drinks. Listeners' comprehension of speech declines rapidly once the speaking rate exceeds 250 wpm (Foulke, 2006). Auctioneers typically reach 250 wpm or higher (Barnard, 2018), but do you really want to blitz your audience like you're taking bids on cows or rare paintings? Normal conversational speaking pace ranges between 140 and 180 wpm (McCoy et al., 2005). Because people generally are accustomed to a fairly standard conversational pace, speaking at a normal conversational rate is appropriate for most speaking situations. Audience members will find such a pace comfortable and easy to comprehend, and they will be unlikely to notice your pace, which avoids distraction. One analysis of TED Talks determined that the average speaking rate was 173 wpm (Barnard, 2018). Without actually measuring, *you can get a rough idea of your speaking pace by enunciating your words carefully and pausing to take breaths without gasping for air.* Proceed as you would in normal conversation. You can actually determine your rate by speaking into a recorder for exactly one minute, then counting the words.

Articulation and Pronunciation: Striving for Clarity of Speech

Sloppy speech patterns can make comprehending what you are saying tough for listeners. When you mumble your words, who can tell what you said? Mispronouncing words and poor articulation are also common issues for speakers. Proper **articulation** (speaking words clearly and distinctly) and **pronunciation** (saying words correctly as indicated in any dictionary based on Standard English rules) can become a credibility issue.

Mispronunciations can make a speaker an object of ridicule. The *YourDictionary* website identifies the 100 most often mispronounced words and phrases in English, and many are comical. Imagine an audience's reaction if a speaker said, "it's a doggy-dog world" instead of the correct "dog-eat-dog world." It is not the male "prostrate" gland; it is the "prostate" gland, although the gland can make you want to lie flat at times. You do not "take for granite" unless you are into geology; you "take for granted." Another common mispronunciation is "prevent*a*tive" instead of "preventive." It is "card*sharp*" not "cardshark." It is not "revelant" but "relevant," it is not "orientate" but "orient," and it is not "mispro*noun*ciation" but "mispro*nun*ciation." If in doubt, practice your speech in front of several people who know proper pronunciation and can listen for precise articulation.

CARTOON 10.3 Precise articulation and pronunciation are important, especially when using idioms while speaking to an audience composed partly of members whose native language is not English. For example, "curling up in the fetal position" could be mistaken for "curling up in the feeble position." Likewise, "statute of limitations" could be heard as "statue of limitations," and "nip it in the bud" might become "nip it in the butt."

Body Movements: Finding the Right Balance Nonverbally

Standing rigidly before your audience or moving around wildly can be very distracting. A straight upright posture exudes confidence and enhances credibility. It can also positively influence audience attitudes (Brinol et al., 2009). You do not want to appear statue-like, however. You should move some, or your physical form will meld into the scenery. You want to work the room. Sometimes moving away from a podium and toward your audience creates greater attention. Strive for a balance between excessive and insufficient body movement. The general guideline is "everything in moderation." An animated, lively delivery can excite an audience to pay attention, but you do not want to seem out of control. Posture should be erect without looking like a soldier standing at attention. Slumping your shoulders, crossing and uncrossing your legs, and lurching to one side with one leg higher than the other call attention to awkward movements. Practice speaking in front of a mirror or record your practice speech to determine whether you have any of these awkward movements.

Gestures can enhance perceptions by listeners of a speaker's composure and confidence, and can increase speaker persuasiveness (Maricchiolo et al., 2009). *There is no need to plan gestures.* As Motley (1995) explains, gestures "are supposed to be non-conscious. That is to say, in natural conversation we use gestures every day without thinking about them. And when we do consciously think about gestures, they become uncomfortable and inhibited" (p. 99). Choreographing your gestures will make them appear awkward and artificial, thereby distracting audience attention. For example, consider Andrew Dlugan (2008), a self-described "award-winning speaker" and author of the "Six Minutes" website on "speaking and presentational skills." Delivering his "model" of how to choreograph gestures, there is an artificial and obviously staged quality to his gestures that is distracting. (*See access to link at end of chapter.*) Choreographing speech gestures is reminiscent of the old elocution movement of previous centuries that produced textbooks with graphics illustrating precisely coded poses and gestures for specific emotions. Elocution mostly disappeared because of its association with mere recitation of poems and readings and the mechanistic and unnatural appearance of bodily movements and gestures while speaking (Kirkpatrick, 2007).

Focus on your message and your audience, and the gestures will follow. When you are genuinely enthusiastic about your topic, for example, your gestures will naturally be enthusiastic. It is when you have to fake excitement that gestures become mismatched and look staged (Fruciano, 2014).

If, however, you realize that you have hyper hands that wildly gesticulate when you experience anxiety, concentrate on relaxing (see Chapter 2). If this does not calm the hand and arm flailing, try purposely not gesturing at all when practicing your speech to calm the wandering appendages. This can train you for your actual speech.

Podium Usage: Avoiding the Lectern Lean

A lectern, or podium, is useful for placing your notes within easy view so you can avoid holding them for all to see. Rustling a stack of notes or sheets of paper distracts an audience. Teachers usually use a lectern for their lengthy lectures so their hands are free to write on the board, advance PowerPoint slides, access Internet sites, or present demonstrations to the class. The lectern, however, can easily become a crutch for inexperienced speakers, seeming to prop them up before they fall over. Student speakers often have to be advised not to lean on the lectern. There is no need to embrace the lectern. It looks awkward. Just rest your notes on the podium, stand back slightly, and occasionally move beside it or toward your audience. Moving away from the podium entirely, perhaps occasionally glancing at notes to refresh your memory, has the distinct advantage of permitting a closer connection with your audience and seeming more conversational than stiffly formal.

CARTOON 10.4 A lectern is not a crutch to lean on but a convenient place to set notes for your speech.

Microphone Usage: Amplifying Your Delivery

Microphones amplify your voice and are essential if you are addressing a large audience in a big room, but that amplification can produce some tricky issues. A clip-on wireless microphone (called a lavaliere) must be placed just right on your clothing. If it is too close to your voice, it will be too loud for listeners, and if it is too far away, it will not amplify your voice sufficiently. You also have to be careful that your clothing does not rub against the microphone, creating a scraping sound. A stationary microphone, typically mounted on a stand or onto a podium, is also tricky to use. If you move away from the microphone, your voice fades, but if you speak too closely to it, you will blast your voice and distortion will occur. If you move toward and away from the microphone as you speak, your voice will fade in and out like a bad cellphone connection, becoming quite annoying for your listeners. Audition with the microphone if possible. Work with the technician on producing a nice, even sound. Find the optimum distance from the microphone that produces the least distortion and the most natural sounding voice. Remember that microphones amplify all sounds, so shuffling papers, coughing, clearing your throat, and clicking a pen become more audible to listeners.

PHOTO 10.3 Practice using a microphone. It isn't as easy as it might look, and it can become a huge distraction.

Distracting Behaviors: Avoiding Interference

This is a catch-all category. There are numerous quirky behaviors that speakers can exhibit, often without realizing it (see "28 Distracting Mannerisms," 2011). Playing with your pen or pencil while speaking is one example. I once had a student who tapped a pencil loudly on the podium nonstop. For her sake and for the mental well-being of her audience, I had to stop her in mid-speech and tell her to put away the makeshift drumstick. Fiddling with change in your pocket, tapping fingers on the podium, and shifting your weight from right to left and back like a ship being tossed on the high seas are other distracters.

Distracting behaviors can easily be eliminated. If you do not hold a pen or pencil in your hand, you cannot click it, tap the podium with it, or wave it around while speaking. Take change out of your pocket before speaking if you tend to jiggle coins when you put your hand in your pocket. Move away from the podium so you cannot tap your fingers. Practice standing erect, balanced on both feet, when rehearsing your speech, and you will eliminate the shifting weight problem. Distracting behaviors will not destroy a quality speech unless the behavior is beyond weird. Nevertheless, eliminating them makes your presentation more effective.

Online Speeches: Clean Up Your Room

Online speeches are becoming more common. Speaking to a camera, sometimes with a view of your audience and sometimes not, depending on the software, requires some adaptations to the online environment ("7 Tips," 2017). First, when using a webcam, stay two to three feet from the camera. If you move closer, your face will be magnified and your eye movements will be more noticeable. Second, look directly at the camera not your computer screen. Unlike in-person presentations where your eye contact can sweep the room, eye contact during webcam speeches must be more narrowly focused. You don't want your eyes darting back and forth or up and down. This can make you look frenetic. Third, unless you are merely video recording your speech to post on YouTube, which allows for a full-body view (such as TED Talks), using a webcam significantly limits your ability to gesture. You don't want to be waving your hands across the screen. Small natural gestures used occasionally work best. Fourth, if you cannot see your audience while presenting your online speech, the lack of feedback is severely constraining. Using humor can be more challenging because you don't know whether audience members are laughing or rolling their collective eyes. Use humor, but recognize that the lack of audible laughter can seem awkward. If this is too difficult for you, skip attempting humor until you become more practiced giving online speeches. Fifth, set the stage. For a webcam speech (e.g., presentation for a job interview; speech for online class), be aware of your background. Dark colors and dark lighting can interfere with the video image of you giving your speech. Video recording your speech for posting on YouTube can also present problems. I've viewed student online speeches delivered from their dorm rooms. Invariably, you can see unmade beds, piles of dirty clothes, messy desks, and other distracting environmental displays. Clean up your mess. This includes dressing appropriately and not looking like you just rolled out of bed. Zoom in so background distractions are not visible. Your audience wants to see you, not your apartment environment. If you have a dog who loves to beg for a biscuit, remove your canine companion. Typically, you want your upper torso and face to show, not much more. Sixth, use rhetorical questions to create the appearance of interacting with your audience. Show props or interesting visual aids held up to the camera for easy viewing. Seventh, practice with the technology before giving your speech "for real." Glitchy interruptions can be beyond annoying (*see access to link of student disasters at end of chapter*). Finally, do a sound test before giving your speech. Make certain that you are not too close or far away from the microphone. You don't want your speech to appear to be a silent movie requiring captioning. You also don't want it to blast your audience.

PHOTO 10.4 Webcam speeches require careful preparation. Here this speaker follows several guidelines for presenting an effective online speech. Which ones are apparent?

Audience-Centered Delivery: Matching the Context

Finally, *delivery should match the context for your speech*. Like every other aspect of public speaking, delivery is audience centered. The appropriateness of your delivery is dependent on certain expectations inherent to the occasion and purpose of your speech. A eulogy calls for a dignified, formal delivery. The speaker usually limits body movements and keeps his or her voice toned down as a sign of respect. A motivational speech, however, requires a lively, enthusiastic delivery, especially if you are speaking to a large audience. Your voice may be loud, pace fairly rapid, body movements dramatic, eye contact intense and direct, and facial movements expressive. During a motivational speech, the podium is usually moved aside or ignored and the speaker moves back and forth across a stage, sometimes even moving into the audience. An after-dinner speech or "roast" calls for a lively, comic delivery. Facial expressions consist mostly of smiles or gestures; they may be gross or exaggerated, and a speaker's voice may be loud, even abrasive, for effect. There is no one correct way to deliver a speech but many effective ways. Match your delivery to the speech context and audience expectations.

SUMMARY

The general guidelines for effective delivery are these: use direct eye contact, vocal variety, and few if any vocal fillers; moderate pace and body movement; and eliminate distracting mannerisms. Defer using manuscript and memorized speeches until you become an experienced public speaker. Extemporaneous speaking is the type of delivery to master for most occasions.

TED TALKS AND YOUTUBE VIDEOS

Manuscript Versus Extemporaneous Commencement Speeches: "Highlights from the Best Commencement Speeches of 2018"

Stilted, Unnatural Delivery: Andrew Dlugan: "Speech Preparation #7: Choreograph Your Speech with Staging, Gestures, and Vocal Variety"

Stilted, Unnatural, Choreographed Delivery: "2012 World Championship of Public Speaking: Trust Is a Must"

Speed Speaking: "Sean Shannon: The Fastest Talker in the World"

Martin Luther King, Jr.: "I Have a Dream," August 28, 1963, Full Speech

Pronunciation Errors: "25 Common Phrases That You're Saying Wrong"

Perils of Winging It: "Clint Eastwood: 2012 Republican National Convention"

Potential Hazards of Online Speeches: "Warning: Do Not Take a Public Speaking Class, Online"

Extemporaneous Speaking: "How to Deliver an Extemporaneous Presentation or Speech"

Vocal Fillers: "Obama "UH" Counter in Presidential Debate. Wow!!"

For relevant links to these TED Talks and YouTube videos, see the *Practically Speaking* Companion Website: www.oup.com/he/rothwell-ps3e. You can also gain access by typing the title of the speech reference into a Google search window or by doing the same on the TED Talks or YouTube sites.

CHECKLIST

Manuscript Speech

☐ Do not use a manuscript as a crutch.

☐ Remember the differences between oral and written style.

☐ Practice repeatedly.

☐ Use vocal variety and some body movements.

☐ Be flexible; ad lib if appropriate.

Memorized Speech

☐ Practice your speech often.

☐ Look at your audience, not at the ceiling as if you are trying to remember.

☐ If you forget exact phrasing, put the point in other, non-scripted words.

☐ Do not apologize if you momentarily go blank.

☐ Pause if you forget; move as if deliberately being dramatic until you remember (hopefully soon).

Impromptu Speech

☐ Anticipate impromptu speaking.

☐ Draw on your life experience and knowledge.

☐ Formulate a simple outline.

☐ Summarize briefly.

Extemporaneous Speech

☐ Use a presentation outline not a preparation outline.

☐ Be extremely familiar with your material.

☐ Practice often using your presentation outline.

CRITICAL THINKING QUESTIONS

1. In what ways is an online speech different than an in-person presentation?

2. Can a strong delivery compensate for a poorly organized speech?

3. How do you know when your delivery is "over the top" (too animated)?

4. Is it ever appropriate to pace across a stage while delivering your speech?

NOTE: Online **student resources**, such as practice tests, flashcards, and other activities, can be accessed at www.oup.com/he/rothwell-ps3e

11

Visual Aids

I once had a student who realized five minutes before his speech that a visual aid was required for the speaking assignment. I actually saw him take his lunch bag, pour out the contents, take a black marker pen, and quickly sketch a drawing for his visual aid. When he gave his speech and showed his lunch bag drawing, audience members had to stifle their laughter. When discussing visual aids, it is important that you recognize both words in that term. The visual part is necessary, but so is the aid part. You do not choose just anything visual to show during your speech. You choose that which actually aids your presentation and does not invite ridicule or serve as a distraction.

Thus, there is little reason to use visual aids if the choice of aids serves no useful purpose. A speech on apple farming, for example, does not require a picture of an apple split in half unless the speaker plans to present information at a much deeper level than merely identifying readily apparent parts of this common fruit. Visual aids can be exceedingly helpful, however. *The purpose of this chapter is to explain how to use visual aids appropriately and effectively.* The benefits and types of visual aids available, presentational media, and the guidelines for competent use of visual aids are discussed.

BENEFITS OF VISUAL AIDS: REASONS TO USE THEM

Effective visual aids provide several benefits for a speaker (Gutierrez, 2014). First, they *clarify difficult points* or descriptions of complex objects. Actually showing an object to an audience helps listeners understand. Showing different styles of sunglasses is better than simply describing differences. Second, effective visual aids *gain and maintain audience attention*. A dramatic photograph of an anorexic teenager can capture attention during the opening of a speech on eating

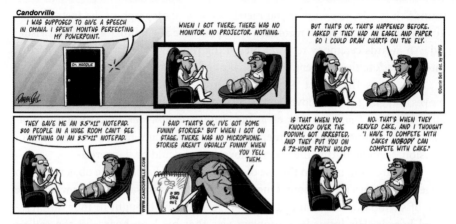

CARTOON 11.1: A visual aid must achieve specific purposes and be an appropriate choice. You do not want to use a visual aid that detracts from the effectiveness of your speech. Some visual aids just do not work well depending on the context.

disorders. Third, visual aids *enhance speaker credibility*. Presenting impressive statistics in a graph, chart, or table drives home an important point in your speech. You appear knowledgeable. Fourth, visual aids can *improve your delivery*. Novice speakers find it difficult to stray from notes or a manuscript. When you are showing a visual aid, however, you can move away from reading your speech, and you assume a more natural delivery when you explain your visual aid to your listeners. Finally, effective visual aids can be *memorable*. Demonstration speeches rely heavily on visual aids. You can remember a magic trick or the proper way to arrange flowers when you have actually seen them demonstrated.

TYPES OF VISUAL AIDS: MAKING APPROPRIATE CHOICES

There are several types of visual aids. Each must be considered for how it either contributes to or detracts from the purpose of your speech. This section discusses making appropriate visual aids choices and identifies both strengths and limitations of each type.

Objects: Show and Tell

Sometimes there is no substitute for the actual object of your speech. For example, giving a speech on playing different types of recorders really requires demonstrating with the actual musical instruments. "Bass and tenor recorders have very different sounds" just does not work if you merely show a photograph of the instruments. You must actually play the recorders. Here you have an auditory as well as a visual aid. An awards ceremony requires presenting the physical trophy, plaque, certificate, or check to the recipient. A handshake and a promise do not work as well.

Sometimes the object is you. Exhibiting martial arts techniques, dance moves, juggling, yoga movements, and myriad other demonstrations can be quite effective. *Don't use yourself as the visual aid, however, unless you are proficient.* Demonstrating juggling ineptly, for example, might make you the object of derision. Demonstrating the use of a hoverboard could be dangerous.

There are limitations to the use of objects as visual aids. Some objects are too large to haul into a classroom. One student in my class wanted to show how the size of surfboards has changed over the years, so he brought in four different-sized boards. His immediate problem was that his long board hit the ceiling when it was placed on its end, punching a hole in the ceiling tiles. Some objects are also impractical to bring to most speaking venues. A speech on building a bullet train in the United States may benefit from a visual aid, but you surely cannot drive a real train into a classroom or auditorium.

Some objects are illegal, dangerous, or potentially objectionable to at least some audience members. Firearms, poisons, or combustible liquids are dangerous. Simply *exercise responsible judgment.* Check for rules or laws that could invite trouble before using any visual aid that seems questionable.

PHOTO 11.1 Showing an oversized object can be a very effective visual aid. Here US surfer Carissa Moore holds a replica of an oversized check over her head while on the winner's podium.

Inanimate objects are usually preferable to living, squirming objects. Puppies are unfailingly cute and great attention grabbers, but they are also very difficult to control. A student of mine brought a puppy to class for her speech. The puppy whined, barked, and howled throughout her presentation. At first it was cute. After five minutes the audience was thoroughly annoyed. My student ended her speech as the puppy urinated on the classroom carpet.

Some living objects can frighten audience members. A live snake, especially one not in a cage, will make some audience members extremely uneasy, even agitated. One student brought a live tarantula to class for her presentation. She let the spider walk across a table as she presented her informative speech. Audience members were transfixed—not by what she was saying but by the hairy creature moving slowly in front of them.

Models: Practical Representations

When objects relevant to your speech are too large, too small, expensive, fragile, rare, or unavailable, models can often act as effective substitutes. A speech on dental hygiene requires a larger-than-normal plastic model of a human mouth full of teeth. You want to avoid asking for a volunteer from the audience to open wide so the speaker can show the volunteer's teeth. The teeth will be too small to see well, and such a demonstration will also be extremely awkward. You may have to point out tooth decay, gum disease, and fillings in the volunteer's mouth—not something most people want others to notice, much less have spotlighted.

Demonstration speeches on cardiopulmonary resuscitation (CPR) require a model of a person. You cannot ask for an audience member to serve as a victim for the demonstration. Pushing forcefully on a person's chest could be dangerous and potentially embarrassing.

Graphs: Making Statistics Clear and Interesting

When your speech includes several statistics, merely listing those statistics can be tedious and confusing for your audience. A graph can clarify and enliven statistics. A **graph** is a visual representation of statistics in an easily understood format. There are several kinds. Figure 11.1 is a *bar graph,* which compares and contrasts two or more items or shows variation over a period of time. Bar graphs can make a dramatic visual impact. Figure 11.2 is a line graph. A *line graph* is useful for showing a trend or change over a period of time. A *pie graph,* as shown in Figure 11.3, depicts a proportion or percentage for each part of a whole. A pie graph should depict from two to six "pie pieces." Much more than this will make the pie graph difficult for your audience to decipher.

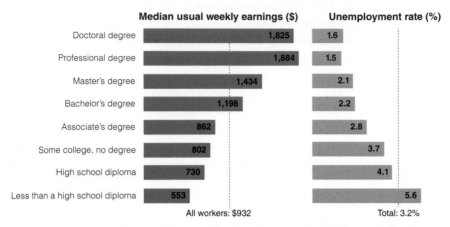

Unemployment rates and earnings by educational attainment, 2018

	Median usual weekly earnings ($)	Unemployment rate (%)
Doctoral degree	1,825	1.6
Professional degree	1,884	1.5
Master's degree	1,434	2.1
Bachelor's degree	1,198	2.2
Associate's degree	862	2.8
Some college, no degree	802	3.7
High school diploma	730	4.1
Less than a high school diploma	553	5.6
	All workers: $932	Total: 3.2%

Note: Data are for persons age 25 and over. Earnings are for full-time wage and salary workers.

FIGURE 11.1 A bar graph illustrating the monetary advantage of education. Trends (unemployment rates and median weekly earnings) are visually apparent. (Source: U.S. Bureau of Labor Statistics, March 2019)

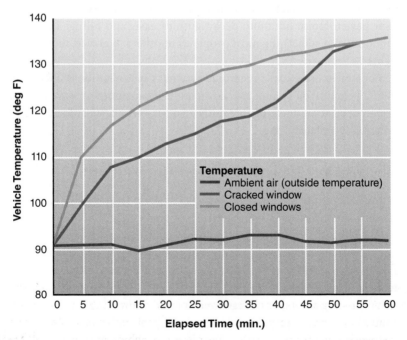

FIGURE 11.2 A line graph comparing interior temperatures over time in cars with closed or "cracked" windows. (Source: McLaren et al., 2005)

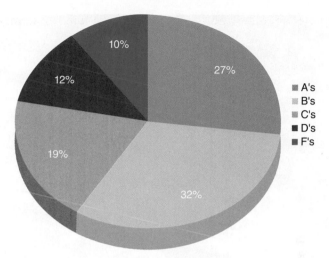

FIGURE 11.3: This is a pie graph depicting breakdown of grades in a public speaking class.

Graphs are effective if they are uncluttered. Too much information in a graph makes it difficult for an audience to understand. More detailed graphs published in print media can be effective because readers can examine the graphs carefully. During a speech, however, this is neither possible nor desirable.

Maps: Making a Point Geographically

When geography is central to your speech or a key point, there is no good substitute for a map. Imagine teaching a geography class without showing maps. "Picture the Arabian Peninsula" does not work for a geography-challenged audience. Commercial maps are often too detailed to be useful as a visual aid. The most effective maps are large, clear, and directly relevant to the speaker's purpose. Some speakers attempt to draw their own maps, but the proportions and scale of continents, countries, or bodies of water are often badly represented. A map should be exact to be effective. You do not want the United States to look three times bigger than Asia.

Tables: Factual and Statistical Comparisons

Tables are effective for depicting blocks of information. A **table** is an orderly depiction of statistics, words, or symbols in columns or rows. Table 11.1 is an example. A table can provide easy-to-understand comparisons of facts and statistics. Tables, however, are not as visually interesting as graphics, and they can become easily cluttered with too much information.

PHOTO 11.2: Maps can provide visual perspective on the magnitude of natural disasters such as hurricanes and tropical storms.

Tables will be a visual distraction if the headings are too small to read, the columns or rows are crooked, and the overall impression is that the table was hastily drawn. With readily available computer technology, there is little excuse for amateurish-looking tables.

Photographs: Very Visual Aids

The many photographs included in this textbook underline the effectiveness of this visual aid to make a point, clarify a concept, and draw attention. When objects are too big, fragile, unwieldy, or unavailable to use as visual aids, photographs may serve as effective substitutes. Instead of bringing the wiggling, fussing, barking, urinating puppy to class, try showing several photographs of the cute pet.

Photographs have some drawbacks. They may need to be enlarged for all to see. Technological advances with digital photography and Photoshop have made enlarging relatively easy if you have access to the technology and know how to use it. Also, document cameras, such as ELMO, can be used to enlarge small photographs. Postage-stamp-size photographs are worthless as visual aids. When a speaker says, "As you can see in this photograph," and no one can, the photo becomes not an aid but a cause for snickering.

TABLE 11.1

World's Deadliest Earthquakes in the Last 100 Years

	LOCATION	MAGNITUDE	DEATHS
1.	Haiti Region (2010)	7.0	316,000
2.	Tangshan, China (1976)	7.5	255,000
3.	Sumatra, Indonesia (2004)	9.1	228,000
4.	Haiyuan, China (1920)	7.8	200,000
5.	Kanto, Japan (1923)	7.9	143,000
6.	Turkmenistan (1948)	7.3	110,000
7.	Eastern Sichuan, China (2008)	7.9	88,000
8.	Northern Pakistan (2005)	7.6	86,000
9.	Chimbote, Peru (1970)	7.9	70,000
10.	Western Iran (1990)	7.4	50,000

SOURCE: U.S. Geological Survey. (2016). Note: Statistics are rounded off for easier reading.

Drawings: Photo Substitutes

When photographs are unavailable, a careful drawing might be an effective substitute (see Figure 11.4). Drawings of figures performing ballet moves or an athlete pole vaulting could be instructive for an audience. If the drawings are sloppy, distorted, small, or appear to have been drawn by a five-year-old with no artistic talent, find a different visual aid.

VISUAL AIDS MEDIA: SIMPLE TO TECHNOLOGICALLY ADVANCED

There are many media, or means of communicating, with visual aids. Tables or graphs, for example, can appear on chalkboards, posters, PowerPoint slides, or other media. Choosing the appropriate visual medium should take into consideration what you are comfortable using, whether your speech really requires a

CURRY'S KNEE INJURY

Warriors' guard Stephen Curry sprained his medial collateral
ligament in his right knee.

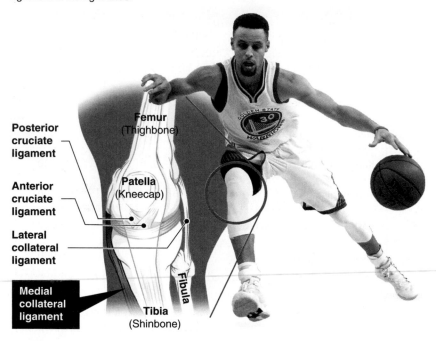

FIGURE 11.4: The San Francisco Bay Area almost had a collective nervous breakdown when
most valuable player Steph Curry injured his knee in the 2016 NBA playoffs. This drawing
simulates ones appearing in several sports pages of major newspapers. In 2018, Curry injured his
other knee in the same manner, but recovered for the playoffs.

visual aid, and what best suits your audience. A multimedia presentation may be
too complicated for you to master in time for your speech, or the proper equipment may not be available. Showing very simple visual aids to an audience of
experts may be viewed as condescending. *Ask yourself, "Do I need a visual aid
and, if so, which medium works best to accomplish my purpose?"*

Chalkboard and Whiteboard: All Dinosaurs Are Not Extinct

Every student is familiar with the chalkboard or whiteboard. Despite its "dino-
saur" reputation of late, chalkboards and whiteboards are appropriate when time
and resources do not permit the use of more sophisticated media. Chalkboards
and whiteboards are widely available and allow great flexibility. Tables, drawings, and graphs all can be drawn on them. Lecture material can be outlined.
Mistakes can be immediately, and easily, erased. The evolving flow of an idea or

process can be drawn in an as-you-go technique. This can allow for nice interaction with your audience. If you have real artistic ability, this art-in-progress can be quite impressive.

Words written on either a chalkboard or whiteboard should be printed if your cursive handwriting is difficult to decipher. Always write or draw images large enough for audience members sitting in the back rows to see easily. It is usually best to use proper outlining form (see Chapter 8) when listing main ideas and their subpoints. You do not want topics and ideas to appear unconnected.

Chalkboards and whiteboards do have several serious drawbacks. The quality of the table, drawing, or graph is usually inferior. Students sometimes draw on a chalkboard or whiteboard during their speech, consuming huge portions of their allotted speaking time. If a student uses the chalkboard or whiteboard prior to his or her speech, the class waits impatiently while the speaker creates the visual aid. It is too time-consuming. Turning to write or draw on the board also breaks eye contact with your audience. *Most instructors discourage or even forbid the use of both for student speakers*, but if you become a teacher, the chalkboard and whiteboard, unlike the dinosaurs, likely will have avoided extinction because they are cheap and easy to use.

SMART boards are computer-assisted versions of interactive whiteboards with a variety of accessories. They are expensive, and your classroom or speech venue may not have access to one, but if you do have access, there are a number of tutorials online to help you learn to use this option (*see link at end of chapter*).

Poster Board: Simplicity Itself

A poster board is a very simple medium for visual aids. You can draw, stencil, and make graphs or tables using poster board. They are a staple of recent political protests. Making the poster appear professional, however, is a primary challenge. Several guidelines can help. First, all lettering and numbering should be large enough for anyone in the back of the room to see easily. Second, your poster should be neat and symmetrical. Headings, lettering, and numbering should be even, not sloping downward, upward, or any combination that looks like a roller coaster. Use a ruler to keep lines straight. Letters and numbers should be of the same size or font. Third, strive for simplicity. Avoid cluttering the poster with a collage of pictures that meld into a blob of images, unless the assignment requires a collage. Glitter, feathers, and other "accessories" are distracting and rarely beneficial.

Posters are usually attached to an easel for display. A tri-fold poster board, however, can usually stand on its own without easily falling over. Simply standing a poster on a chalk tray, however, will usually result in the poster curling at the top and flopping onto the ground, unless the poster is made of very stiff, sturdy material. Watching a speaker repeatedly fuss with a poster trying desperately to keep it upright is awkward for everyone. Tape it to a wall if necessary.

Handouts: An Old Standby

Distributing a handout is a popular form of visual aid. Tables, maps, drawings, PowerPoint slides, or even photographs can be copied onto a handout. One significant advantage of a handout is that the listeners can keep it long after the speech has been presented. It can serve as a useful reminder of the information presented. A handout can also include a great quantity of information to be studied carefully as a presentation unfolds (e.g., college budget details).

Handouts have potential disadvantages, however. Passing out a handout in the middle of your speech wastes time and breaks the flow of the speech. If your listeners are busy reading your handout while you are speaking, they will not be attending to your message.

Distribute a handout just prior to your speech if the handout will be an integral part of your presentation. The handout will not distract but will assist audience members to maintain focus and increase understanding of your message. If the audience is large and your speech is short, do not distribute a handout—it is too time-consuming. A handout with names, email addresses, Internet links, and phone numbers of organizations or agencies that can provide additional information on your subject can be made available after your speech.

Video Excerpts: DVDs, YouTube, and Visual Power

An excerpt from a movie, YouTube, or a video segment you shot yourself can be a valuable visual aid. Videos can be dramatic, informative, and moving. They often are great attention grabbers. Videos used during a speech, however, have several limitations. First, the sound on a video will compete with the speaker for attention. Shut off the sound when you are trying to explain a point while the video is playing, unless the video excerpt is very short, such as 30 seconds or less, and sound is essential. Longer video excerpts with sound may be effective in lengthy presentations. Second, a video with its dramatic action can make your speech seem tame, even dull, by comparison. Also, be careful that the dramatic action depicted in a video excerpt is not overly graphic and offensive. For example, showing a video clip of dolphins or harp seals being slaughtered should come with a warning before showing the scene, if the scene is deemed absolutely necessary to make the point. The warning allows audience members to choose whether to view the scene. Third, *a video is not a speech*. There is a real temptation to show a video as a major portion of a speech without any narration or direct reference to it while it is playing. Remember that short video clips should support your speech, not be the main message. This is a public speech, not a movie presentation.

If you use a video excerpt during your speech, cue it properly so you will not have to interrupt the flow of your presentation by looking for the right place to start the excerpt. Downloading several short excerpts onto a blank DVD is preferable to loading several separate DVDs. Also, downloading any YouTube excerpts onto a blank DVD is less cumbersome and time-consuming to set up and use than accessing the YouTube site or connecting to your thumb drive. Most laptops can be connected directly to flat-screen TVs by an HDMI cable, so links to YouTube or other video excerpts can be placed in a file or directory in advance and accessed easily from your computer. YouTube video excerpts should also be embedded into any PowerPoint presentation to avoid interrupting the flow of your presentation by accessing YouTube sites (see *D'Angelo, 2017*). Typically, use only a few very short video excerpts (30 seconds) when your speech is short.

Tim Berners-Lee, credited with inventing the World Wide Web, delivered a TED (Technology, Education, Design) lecture titled "The Year Open Data Went Worldwide." During his 20-minute lecture, he used slides and brief video excerpts effectively. Since the video excerpts required no sound, he narrated the excerpts, always talking directly to his audience and not at the large video screen behind him. (*See access to link at end of chapter.*)

Projection Equipment: Blowing It Up

There are several options for projecting images onto a large screen. Slide projectors used to be very common, but they have neared extinction as a visual aid medium, mostly replaced by PowerPoint slide presentations. Kodak stopped manufacturing slide projectors in 2004.

Overhead projectors, despite being an aging technology, continue to be used in some circumstances. Overhead projectors can be used to display enlarged images. They are still around because they are easy to use, mostly problem-free, relatively inexpensive, and a flexible piece of equipment. Transparencies are placed on the overhead projector, enlarging a table, map, picture, graph, or drawing. Transparencies are very simple to prepare. Whatever can be photocopied can be made into a transparency. The relative ease with which this equipment can be used tempts speakers to overdo the number of transparencies used during a speech. Be careful not to substitute transparencies for an actual speech.

Document cameras, such as the ELMO series, offer similar advantages of overhead projectors, but they do not require creating transparencies. Almost any image from a magazine, book, or pamphlet or a simple object can be projected onto a large screen. They also can magnify very small images a hundredfold, and they allow you to zoom in and out on images. Some versions of this technology have wireless remote control, split-screen, masking, and highlighting capabilities. Becoming familiar with this equipment is essential to using it effectively.

Finally, there are computer projectors. Pictures taken directly from computer software presentations can be shown on a large screen. The time needed to prepare the computer presentation and possible technical breakdowns in the middle of the presentation are potential drawbacks.

Computer-Assisted Presentations

By now you should be familiar with the many options available for computer-assisted presentations. PowerPoint is probably the most widely available and utilized example of this visual aid medium, although other computer-assisted presentational software options such as Prezi and SlideRocket have emerged more recently (see Guay, 2018). There are also several additional user-friendly presentation tools such as Canva, Emaze, and Vizia (Rabidoux & Rottman, 2017). Harvard researchers compared PowerPoint to "zoomable user interfaces" (ZUIs) such as Prezi and found that Prezi presentations were perceived by audience participants to be more organized (13%), engaging (16%), persuasive (22%), and effective (25%) than PowerPoint. Prezi, however, gets complaints about being confusing and challenging to use (Armstrong, 2017). PowerPoint continues to dominate as a computer-assisted visual aid tool. Space does not allow a "how-to" explanation for preparing PowerPoint slides or Prezi presentations. There are several excellent sites on the Internet that provide step-by-step instructions (*see access to link at end of chapter*).

The biggest drawbacks of PowerPoint presentations are the time it takes to prepare the slides, the potential for glitches to occur during the actual speech, and the tendency to become so enamored with the software capability that it detracts from the actual speech (see p. 211, PowerPoint: Lots of Power, Little Point?). "PowerPoint presentations are often so poorly executed that they actually obstruct the brain's cognition of the material being presented" (Hoffeld, 2015). You might want to check out award-winning comedian Don McMillan's amusing YouTube presentation "Life after Death by PowerPoint" to see what not to do in this regard (*see access to link at end of chapter*).

Consultant Cliff Atkinson (2008), author of *Beyond Bullet Points*, offers several research-based suggestions for improving PowerPoint presentations (see also Paradi, 2018). Unlike some conventional suggestions, such as the "rule of seven" (no more than seven bulleted lines on a slide or seven words per line), Atkinson translates theory and research on communication into solid advice for improving PowerPoint presentations.

1. **Do not overwhelm listeners with complicated slides.** Text-heavy slides with numerous bullet points, what Atkinson calls the "grocery list approach," that require listeners to read for 10 to 15 seconds or more distract from your speech and are not visually interesting. Using several different fonts also can be confusing.

2. **Do not read the slides to your audience, and do not wait for your listeners to read lengthy slides.** This interrupts the flow of your presentation. Research also shows that reading a list of bulleted points diminishes learning the information (Bayston, 2016; Mitchell, 2009). Attention fades.

3. **Narrate your PowerPoint slides.** You tell the story that focuses listeners on your main points as you advance your slides (Reynolds, 2012).

4. **Most slides should have a full-sentence headline at the top with a descriptive graphic (picture) underneath.** Exceptions would be some photographs or cartoons that need no explanation, or slides that convey easy-to-grasp points. Research shows that full-sentence headlines improve listeners' knowledge and comprehension when compared to sentence fragments or phrase headings (Alley, 2005).

5. **Remember that PowerPoint is a visual aid, so *the slides should be visually interesting* (Reynolds, 2012).** Seven bulleted points are a snooze; a simple but interesting graphic for each slide is not. The **Picture Superiority Effect** based on brain research indicates that when text alone is presented, audience members usually remember only about 10% of the information three days later. If you combine brief text with relevant, interesting images, however, audience members typically remember about 65% of the information three days later (Medina, 2014).

6. **Don't get graphic crazy.** As Atkinson (2008) notes, "When you finish the presentation, you want the audience to talk about your special ideas, not your special effects" (p. 323). Heavy use of animation and clever graphics can make the razzle-dazzle memorable but the main points of your speech opaque and unmemorable. Animation to create humor may be appealing if used infrequently.

7. **Use a remote to advance slides.** Having to press a key on the keyboard chains you to the computer. Either you must stay located at the computer keyboard throughout your presentation, which makes your presentation stilted, or you must keep running back to the keyboard to advance the slides, which can look comical, not professional.

IT IS VERY IMPORTANT TO SPEND TIME OUTDOORS BEING *ACTIVE AND DOING SOMETHING* YOU ENJOY. THIS CAN EITHER BE A HOBBY, A SPORT, OR JUST RECREATIONAL FUN. THE POINT IS TO BREATH FRESH AIR AND ENJOY YOURSELF AND THOSE AROUND YOU. IT WILL MAKE YOU A HAPPIER, HEALTHIER PERSON. EXAMPLES OF OUTDOOR ACTIVITIES ARE: ATTENDING A SPORTING EVENT, GOING TO THE BEACH, ROCK CLIMBING, GOING FOR A DRIVE, OR PLAYING ON A TRAMPOLINE OR WHATEVER YOU LIKE.

PHOTO 11.3: Although this slide avoids the bullet point "grocery list" problem, it is a collage, not a simple PowerPoint slide. To exaggerate all that can go wrong with PowerPoint slides, this example has no header; different font sizes, colors, and typefaces are confusing; there are too many pictures to be useful; far too much text is provided and the extensive text bleeds into images; tight spacing makes text difficult to read; and italics and underlining are not useful because too much is highlighted. "Breath" also should be "breathe." This slide is a mess.

Being Outdoors Provides 5 Benefits

1. Fresh air
2. Exercise
3. Vitamin D
4. Stress relief
5. Mood elevation

PHOTO 11.4: This is a good slide. It is simple, visually interesting, and relevant. The full-sentence header is not mandatory because the point is very basic, but it is included as a preferred sample. Numbers are used instead of bullet points for clarity. Typically, each "benefit" would be selected separately from this first slide during your explanation, with a new slide and visual image for each benefit point.

PowerPoint: Lots of Power, Little Point?

The year 2017 marked the thirtieth anniversary of PowerPoint, "one of the most elegant, most influential and most groaned-about pieces of software in the history of computers" ("PowerPoint Turns 20," 2007, p. B1). Edward Tufte (2003), Yale political scientist and specialist in graphic display of information, wrote an editorial in *Wired* magazine in 2003 titled "PowerPoint Is Evil: Power Corrupts, PowerPoint Corrupts Absolutely." Tufte claimed that PowerPoint "elevates format over content, betraying an attitude of commercialism that turns everything into a sales pitch." Tufte even suggested that PowerPoint might have played a role in the *Columbia* shuttle disaster because vital technical information was swamped in the glitzy PowerPoint slides and endless bullet points. The report by the Columbia Accident Investigation Board (2003) seemed to agree: "It is easy to understand how a senior manager might read this PowerPoint slide and not realize that it addresses a life-threatening situation." The report then went on to criticize "the endemic use of PowerPoint briefing slides" as a substitute for quality technical analysis. Inventors of the software, Robert Gaskin and Dennis Austin, agree with Tufte's criticisms. "All the things Tufte says are absolutely true. People often make very bad use of PowerPoint" (quoted in "PowerPoint Turns 20," 2007, p. B1).

The heavy reliance on PowerPoint during speeches should be discouraged. As Brig. Gen. H. R. McMaster, who banned PowerPoint presentations when he led forces in Iraq, notes, "Some problems in the world are not bulletizable" (quoted by Bumiller, 2010). Imagine a bullet-point presentation of Martin Luther King's inspiring "I Have a Dream" speech.

"I HAVE A DREAM" (SEVERAL DREAMS, ACTUALLY) —M. L. KING

- Dream #1: Nation live true meaning of "all men created equal"
- Dream #2: Sit down at table of brotherhood
- Dream #3: Mississippi: transformed into oasis of freedom/justice
- Dream #4: My four children—judged by content of character not color of skin
- Dream #5: Alabama: Black and White boys/girls become sisters/brothers

This PowerPoint slide drains the vitality from a powerful, beautifully composed speech. No one is likely to feel moved to march for freedom from reading this lifeless laundry list of longed for "dreams."

PowerPoint also can place too much focus on the bells and whistles—the surface "gee whiz" computer capabilities—and too little on the content. Consider carefully whether multimedia presentations are appropriate and whether they really enhance the content of your presentation. Too often, speakers obsess about font size and animation instead of concentrating on developing a quality speech.

(continued)

If you do choose to use PowerPoint, avoid listing every point in your outline. This is tedious and uninteresting. Remember that the power of PowerPoint is in its ability to make presentations far more interesting than your standard chalkboard or whiteboard listing of main points. When PowerPoint becomes little more than a computer version of a chalkboard or overhead transparencies, little is gained by using this technology. PowerPoint slides should meet the same criteria as visual aids in general (see next section).

There are exceptions to every rule. A list of bulleted points may be necessary in some circumstances, and a single word or phrase header may work well in some situations, but Atkinson's suggestions are excellent guidelines for using PowerPoint effectively. PowerPoint can be a wonderful *visual* aid.

GUIDELINES FOR COMPETENT USE: AIDS NOT DISTRACTIONS

Poorly designed and clumsily presented visual aids will detract, not aid, your speech. Here are some general guidelines for the competent use of visual aids.

Keep Aids Simple

Complex tables, maps, and graphics can work well in print media such as magazines and newspapers. Readers can closely examine a visual aid. Listeners do not have the same option. Complex visual aids do not work well for speeches, especially short ones, where the information needs to be communicated clearly and quickly. Your audience will be intent on figuring out a complex visual aid, not listening to you speak. Keep visual aids simple.

Make Aids Visible

The general rule for visual aids is that people in the back of the room or auditorium should be able to see your visual aid easily. If they cannot, it is not large enough to be effective. Effective font size depends on the size of the screen and the room. A huge screen in a large auditorium requires a larger font size for PowerPoint presentations than for a regular-sized classroom: typically 44 points for

PHOTO 11.5: Name the mistakes this speaker makes using this visual aid.

headlines, 32 points for main points, and 24 points for subpoints (Paradi, 2018). Font size of 16–20 points usually works well in standard-sized classrooms.

Make Aids Neat, Attractive, and Accurate

Do not embarrass yourself by showing a visual aid of poor quality. Make visual aids neat and attractive. Especially proofread your aids before showing them. Misspelled words or grammatical mistakes on PowerPoint slides, posters, charts, or tables scream "CARELESSNESS!" Tea Party protesters at 2010 rallies carried signs reading: "No Pubic Option," "Politians Are Like Dipers: They Need to be Changed Often," and "Crisis of Competnce." Carelessness kills credibility.

Do Not Block the Audience's View

A very common mistake made even by professional speakers is that they block the audience's view of the visual aid. Standing in front of your poster, graph, drawing, table, or PowerPoint slide while you talk to the visual aid, not to your audience, is awkward and self-defeating. Audience members should not have to stand and move across the room to see a visual aid, crane their necks, or give up in frustration because a speaker's big pumpkin head is blocking their view. Simply stand beside your poster, drawing, graph, or video excerpt while you

CARTOON 11.2 Standing in front of a visual aid and talking to it, not to your audience, are two common mistakes. Speakers need to get their planet-size heads out of the way, stand beside their visual aid, and speak directly to their audience.

explain it to the audience. Point the toes of your shoes toward the audience and imagine that your feet are nailed to the ground. If you do not move your feet, you will continue to stand beside, not in front of, your visual aid. *Talk to your audience, not to your visual aid.*

Keep Aids Close to You

Placing a visual aid across the room from where you speak is awkward. This is particularly problematic when using PowerPoint (Atkinson, 2008). You do not want to split the listeners' attention and create the look of a crowd at a tennis match shifting eye contact back and forth from projection screen to you speaking across the room.

Put the Aid Out of Sight When Not in Use

Cover your poster or drawing, graph, or photo when not actually referring to it. Simply leaving it open to view when you no longer make reference to it or showing it before you actually use it distracts an audience. Atkinson (2008) suggests including blank slides between images on PowerPoint slides when you are not referring to them for a while (a minute or more). Shut off the overhead projector, document camera, or video player when you are finished using it.

Practice with Aids

Using visual aids competently requires practice. At first, using a visual aid may seem awkward, even unnatural. Once you have practiced your speech using a visual aid, however, it will seem more natural and less awkward. Practice will also help you work out any problems that might occur before actually giving your speech for real.

Do Not Circulate Your Aids

Do not pass around photos, cartoons, drawings, objects, or anything that can distract your audience from paying attention to you while you are speaking. If audience members want to see your visual aid again, let them approach you after the speech for a second viewing.

Do Not Talk in the Dark

I have had to advise student speakers not to turn off the classroom lights when they are showing video clips during their presentations. When lights are off, the room becomes so dark that the student speaker becomes a disembodied voice. The audience cannot see nonverbal elements of the presentation, and it all comes off as just weird. Some professional speakers do the same thing. With a huge screen and PowerPoint slides flashing one after the other, speakers become "little more than well-educated projectionists whose major role is to control the PowerPoint and video displays projected on the screen" (Nevid, 2011, p. 54). If possible, dim the lights so slides or video excerpts show more effectively without putting everyone in darkness. If there is no dimmer switch, try bringing in a lamp with a low-wattage bulb and lighten the room that way with the main lights switched off. If the room is very large and there is no way to raise the lights slightly, try focusing a light on you at a podium so the audience can see you as you speak.

Anticipate Problems

The more complicated your technology, the greater the likelihood that problems will occur before or during your presentation. Projection bulbs burn out unexpectedly, computers crash, programs will not load. Have a backup plan. If the audience is small (30 or fewer), a hard copy of PowerPoint slides, for example, can be prepared just in case your computer fails. Overhead transparencies of slides

PHOTO 11.6: You cannot see the speaker's face in the darkness, making this speech little more than a voice-over for PowerPoint slides.

PHOTO 11.7: Do not speak in the dark. Use indirect lighting if room lighting cannot be dimmed.

also can be prepared if the audience is large. Show up early and do a quick test to verify that all systems are GO! If your easel falls over during your presentation, be prepared with a casual remark to lighten the moment ("Just checking to see if everyone is alert; obviously I wasn't"). Think about what might go wrong and anticipate ways to respond.

SUMMARY

Visual aids must be both visually interesting and an actual aid to your speech. Sloppy, poorly prepared, and poorly selected visual aids can bring you ridicule and embarrassment. Always choose and prepare your visual aids carefully. Visual aids can clarify complicated points, gain and maintain audience attention, enhance your credibility, improve your delivery, and make your information memorable. You have many types of visual aids to choose from, but make sure that you do not become enamored with the technologically sophisticated and glitzy aids when you are not well versed in their use, and your speech would be diminished by too much flash and not enough substance. Follow the guidelines for using visual aids appropriately and effectively.

TED TALKS AND YOUTUBE VIDEOS

Embedding Video: D'Angelo, M.: "How to Embed a Video on PowerPoint"; tutorial

Using Visual Aids Well: Tim Berners-Lee: "The Year Open Data Went Worldwide"

Smartboard Tutorial: "How to Use a Smartboard"; and "Get to Know Your SMART Board 800 Series"; tutorial

Powerpoint Slides Tutorial: "PowerPoint 2013: Slide Basics"

Amusing Critique Of Powerpoint: Don McMillan: "Life after Death by PowerPoint 2012"

Terrible Use of Powerpoint: Hal Varian at RSS 2012 Conference: "Statistics at Google"

For relevant links to these TED Talks and YouTube videos, see the *Practically Speaking* Companion Website: www.oup.com/he/rothwell-ps3e. You can also gain access by typing the title of the speech reference into a Google search window or by doing the same on the TED Talks or YouTube sites.

CHECKLIST

☐ Are you familiar with the venue for your speech so you know how to display your visual aids most effectively?

☐ Have you chosen to use a visual aid only when your message requires a visual illustration?

☐ Have you chosen the most appropriate visual aids to make your points?

☐ Have you practiced using your visual aids while you give your speech?

☐ Are you talking to your audience, not your visual aid, when practicing your speech?

☐ Do your visual aids blend seamlessly with your speech content—have you briefly introduced the point of the visual aid and then briefly summarized what point the visual aid illustrated?

☐ Have you carefully checked all equipment that you plan to use to make sure everything works properly?

☐ Do you have a backup if your PowerPoint slides do not work?

☐ Have you planned for any potential problems that might occur while using your visual aids?

☐ Have you considered all of the guidelines for using visual aids effectively?

CRITICAL THINKING QUESTIONS

1. How do you know when you have used too many PowerPoint slides?

2. When might a speech not require a visual aid?

3. When are simple visual aids preferable to complex, tech-dependent aids?

NOTE: Online **student resources**, such as practice tests, flashcards, and other activities, can be accessed at www.oup.com/he/rothwell-ps3e

CHAPTER 12

Skepticism: Becoming Critical Thinking Speakers and Listeners

The communication of our beliefs is often a central function of public speaking, but all beliefs are not created equal. People used to think that the Earth was flat, that pus healed wounds, that ground-up mummies had curative powers, and that bloodletting cured diseases. A 1902 publication authored by a group of "the best physicians and surgeons of modern practice" titled *The Cottage Physician* claimed that cataracts on the eye could be removed by generous doses of laxatives. These physicians claimed that problems urinating could be relieved by marshmallow enemas, and tetanus could be treated effectively by "pouring cold water on the head from a considerable height" (quoted by Weingarten, 1994, p. B7).

We hear a dizzying array of claims every day that beg to be questioned. For example, 65% of people surveyed believe that people use only 10% of their brains ("New Survey," 2013). "There is no reason to suspect evolution—or even an intelligent designer—would give us an organ that is 90 percent inefficient" (Chabris & Simons, 2010, p. 199). Then there are the deeply troubling claims made by a host of individuals that the 9/11 terrorist attacks, the Sandy Hook massacre of 20 elementary school children and 6 teachers, the Marjory Stoneman Douglas High School shootings of 17 students and staff in Parkland, Florida, the Pittsburgh synagogue shootings of 11 Jewish worshippers, and other horrifying massacres were all hoaxes (Criss, 2018; Kingkade, 2015). These were all intensely covered events by highly diverse media. If these events were faked, thousands of people would have to be involved in their execution and subsequent cover-up. Such claims are simply implausible.

Critical thinking as a centerpiece of much public speaking has never been more important or challenging given the eruption of fake news, fabricated studies, "alternative facts," and conspiracies disseminated on social media (Chan et al., 2017; Debies-Carl, 2017). A Rand Report dubs this deterioration of critical thinking practices as "truth decay" (Kavanagh & Rich, 2018). Jonathan Swift long ago noted, "Falsehood flies, and the truth comes limping after it." Researchers at the Massachusetts Institute of Technology confirmed this by conducting a study on lies and false information spread on Twitter. Their results are troubling: fake news is 70% more likely to be retweeted than real, substantiated news, and it takes the truth six times as long as misinformation to reach 1,500 people. Truthful information rarely spreads to more than 1,000 people, but the top 1% of false news routinely spreads to between 1,000 and 100,000 people on Twitter. The researchers found that "bots" were not the culprits in spreading misinformation, but instead it is people who are more drawn to the novel, surprising, and emotional nature of most false claims (Vosoughi et al., 2018).

You don't build a competent speech by asserting an unsupportable claim. A **claim** is a generalization that remains to be proven with reasoning and evidence. You should aim to present claims that are well researched and well supported. Thus, *the primary purpose of this chapter is to explain and promote the process of skepticism in the service of competent public speaking*. Toward that end, this chapter (1) defines true belief, cynicism, and skepticism; (2) examines the dangers of true belief; and (3) provides a comparative analysis of the process of true belief as wholly different from the process of skepticism.

Please note that both knowledge and skills are the first two elements of the communication competence model detailed in Chapter 1. *This chapter provides the essential knowledge base, the rationale and justification that underpin the skills discussed in the next chapter.* Practical public speaking doesn't mean merely learning to be a glib, smooth talker capable of galvanizing an audience. As a speaker and listener, you should strive to be a critical thinker capable of distinguishing fact from fiction. *There is a process for being a critical thinking public speaker, and it is called skepticism.*

SKEPTICISM, TRUE BELIEF, AND CYNICISM

Skepticism is the critical thinking *process of inquiry* whereby claims are evaluated by engaging in a rigorous examination of evidence and reasoning used to support those claims (Shermer, 2013). Skepticism is a kind of "rigorous curiosity"

(Torres, 2016). The term "skeptic" is derived from the Greek *skeptikos*, which means *thoughtful or inquiring*, not *doubtful and dismissive*. Skepticism is a process for acquiring beliefs and changing them when warranted. *Skeptics are not of one mind on controversial issues.* They can be politically liberal, moderate, or conservative. They can be devoutly religious or atheistic. (See Dowd, 2008, for an excellent discussion of the compatibility of religious faith and skepticism.)

Conversely, **true belief** is a willingness to accept claims without solid reasoning or valid evidence and to hold these beliefs tenaciously even if a mountain of contradictory evidence proves them wrong. As Winston Churchill commented, a true believer is "one who can't change his mind and won't change the subject." True belief is a closed-minded system of thought.

Cynicism is nay-saying, fault-finding, and ridiculing. H. L. Mencken once described a cynic as someone who "smells flowers and looks around for a coffin." They are quick to mock human frailties and imperfections and to deride the beliefs of others. *Cynics do not seek truth; they seek their next target.* Skepticism, unfortunately, is often confused with cynicism. The two are significantly different. In some instances, skeptics have exhibited condescension and arrogance when commenting on questionable beliefs, acting more like cynics, and justly deserving criticism. Gentle teasing and some sarcasm have their place in public speaking, but vicious, unwarranted personal attacks so often witnessed in political speeches are inappropriate. Skepticism requires humility because no one's ideas and beliefs are immune to challenge (Hare, 2009).

Finally, true belief does not simply mean "strong belief." Skepticism also does not mean "no belief" (Shermer, 2013). Advocates for truth and justice in all spheres of life are often passionate in their beliefs, and rightly so. This does not make them true believers. *The key distinction between a true believer and a skeptic is the process used to arrive at and maintain a belief.* "It is not the embracing of an idea that causes problems—it is the refusal to relax that embrace when good sense dictates doing so" (Ruggeiro, 1988). Skepticism is a profoundly positive intellectual journey that seeks knowledge and understanding in the preparation and presentation of your speeches while avoiding the dangers of oratorically promoting true belief.

DANGERS OF TRUE BELIEF

The dangers of true belief are real and extensive (Lewandowsky et al., 2012). There are at least three serious harms: the danger to individual well-being including death; significant monetary losses; and a serious threat to the maintenance and well-being of our democratic society (Sidky, 2018). Consider just one example. Measles, one of the most contagious and serious diseases, was virtually eradicated from the United States for years. It re-emerged, however, in 2014 because many Americans refused to vaccinate their children and themselves based on inflated fears of vaccine side effects often asserted in speeches and talk show interviews by celebrities with no professional expertise on the subject ("Measles Cases and Outbreaks," 2018). Before widespread U.S. vaccination programs, 3 to 4 million people contracted the disease annually. Of these, 400 to 500 died, about 48,000 were hospitalized, and 4,000 suffered encephalitis (brain swelling). According to the Centers for Disease Control and Prevention, fears of serious and rampant side effects from the vaccine are simply unfounded ("Measles History," 2018).

True believers, however, are unmoved by even vast amounts of documentation contradicting their beliefs (Hambrick & Marquardt, 2018). Research at the University of Michigan, for example, found that when strong political partisans, both left and right, were presented with facts that corrected their misinformed beliefs, the political partisans didn't correct their views, but instead they clung to their erroneous beliefs even more steadfastly (Keohane, 2010). Measles vaccine critics typically cling to their beliefs regardless of the voluminous evidence that contradicts their claims (Byrne, 2013; Kristof, 2015).

Practitioners of true belief are not always hucksters looking to con a gullible public, or fanatical speakers raving about conspiracies to audiences of rabid supporters. Many true believers are well-meaning, caring individuals who firmly believe they can help others, but good intentions and the strength and tenacity of one's beliefs do not negate the serious harm they can do. True belief is a poor pattern of thinking when listening to a speaker, and it is a deeply flawed basis upon which to build a speech.

THE PROCESS OF TRUE BELIEVING

True beliefs vary widely. They can even be contradictory. Nevertheless, despite the differences in the details, true believers all operate in essentially the same way, as discussed in this section.

Confirmation Bias: Searching for Support

Confirmation bias is the tendency to seek information that supports one's beliefs and to ignore information that contradicts those beliefs (*see access to Eli Pariser link at end of chapter*). One of the hallmarks of true belief is confirmation bias (Lilienfeld et al., 2009). *True believers are belief-driven, not evidence-driven.* Their beliefs are formed first, and then they look for confirming evidence. Studies show that confirmation bias is pervasive (Palminteri et al., 2017). Individuals generally do not give themselves a chance to spot faulty claims from speakers because they search for and listen to assertions and information that support their beliefs, and they ignore contrary information.

When researching your speeches, you want to seek information reflecting various points of view, then weigh the evidence and decide which point of view has the most credible support. Defending the indefensible because of a biased search for confirming information is public speaking in service to true belief, not an admirable desire to search for what is true and accurate. It is admittedly difficult to change a belief, especially one strongly held. Nevertheless, a one-sided search for only confirming support to bolster a belief has practical risks. Confirmation bias can leave you unprepared for strong counterarguments and research that might be used against you in a debate or an exchange with audience members after your speech.

Rationalization of Disconfirmation: Clinging to Falsehoods

True believers hold firmly to unwarranted beliefs by using **rationalization of disconfirmation**—inventing superficial, even glib, alternative explanations for contradictory evidence. For example, a preacher named Harold Camping adamantly predicted that the Rapture—Judgment Day—would occur on May 21, 2011. He posted 5,000 billboards around the country that cost more than

PHOTO 12.1: Harold Camping predicted the end of the world and posted 5,000 billboards to announce it. When his prediction proved to be wrong, he "revised" the date of doom, but not the essential claim, thus using rationalization of disconfirmation, the hallmark of a true believer.

$5 million to advertise his prediction, and he gave numerous speeches warning of the impending Rapture (Gafni, 2013). The popular media gave Camping's prediction wide coverage. As you know, his prediction did not come true. Did he admit his mistake and accept that his prediction was based on no credible evidence? He did not. Instead, he "revised" the date to October 21, 2011, claiming that May 21 was the "spiritual" Rapture and that October 21 would be the "physical" Rapture. Again, you know he was wrong. To his credit, however, this time Camping apologized to his followers for his mistake, but then he said it was God's will, which is unprovable, that the predicted Rapture did not occur ("Harold Camping Apologizes," 2011). The tenacity with which true believers cling to false beliefs by rationalizing indisputable contradictory information is noteworthy.

Burden of Proof: Whose Obligation Is It?

As a speaker, whenever you make a claim to an audience, you assume the **burden of proof**, that is, your obligation to present compelling reasoning and evidence to support your claim (Freeley & Steinberg, 2013). You are not being reasonable if you challenge your audience to disprove your claims that you have not sufficiently defended with logic and evidence. This is **shifting the burden of proof**— inappropriately assuming the validity of a claim unless it is shown to be false by another person who never made the original claim (Verlinden, 2005).

Shifting the burden of proof is common among true believers (e.g., "Prove I'm not a psychic"). This approach is inappropriate because skeptics would have to disprove all manner of absurd, unsupported claims. I once had a student who gave a speech in which he challenged his audience to disprove his claim that life is merely a dream and nothing is real. It was an amusing speech that consisted mostly of raising funny questions and speculating, but I had to remind him afterwards of that annoying burden of proof, which he clearly shifted inappropriately to his audience. *Those who make the claim have the burden to prove the claim.*

An important additional element of burden of proof is that *extraordinary claims require extraordinary proof* (Shermer, 2013). If your claim requires rewriting the laws of physics, for example, no ordinary evidence will do. Mega-inspirational speaker Tony Robbins, who built a financial empire on his super-charged motivational speeches and self-help advice, regularly uses fire-walking in his huge workshops as a final "proof" that "people change their physiology by changing their beliefs" (quoted by Anderson, 2012). If participants can walk barefoot over burning coals without injury, so goes the argument, surely they can accomplish anything by willing it with their minds.

The mind-over-matter explanation, however, is contradicted by hard evidence. "The very idea that brain activity could alter the physical properties of burning carbon compounds or the reactivity of skin cells to extreme heat contradicts volumes of well-established scientific data" (McDonald, 1998, p. 46). Wood coals are poor thermal conductors, unlike metal rods (Carroll, 2016). If you decided to walk on hot metal rods, the moment your feet hit the metal you would hear the same sound a steak makes when it first hits the barbecue grill—SIZZLE. Note that fire-walking is not called fire-*standing*, but if minds truly can control matter, why do participants have to move at all? In fact, dozens of attendees at a June 23, 2016, Tony Robbins oratorical extravaganza in Dallas, Texas, got burned when they didn't move quickly enough across the red-hot coals, reminiscent of a similar incident in San Jose, California, in 2012 where 21 participants at Robbins's motivational event suffered burns to their feet. One participant rationalized his burns by stating that he "didn't get into the right state of mind" (Anderson, 2012). Remember: Extraordinary claims require extraordinary proof. Fire-standing without injury would be extraordinary; fire-walking without injury is not.

PHOTO 12.2: It is called fire-walking, not fire-standing, for a reason. Fire-standing would result in horrible burns; fire-walking is simple physics—keep moving and you won't be burned. The extraordinary claim of "mind over matter" exhibited by fire-walking enthusiasts requires extraordinary proof far beyond this simple demonstration.

THE PROCESS OF SKEPTICISM: INQUIRING MINDS WANT TO KNOW

Skepticism can be taught in public speaking courses, and it should be. Such instruction corresponds nicely with results from a study of more than 7,000 undergraduates at more than 120 four-year colleges and universities. It found that the total college experience in which students necessarily mix with students of diverse backgrounds has a modifying effect on political attitudes about those with differing political viewpoints. Almost half of respondents after a single year of college came to view liberals and conservatives more favorably than when they initially arrived on campus. As the researchers note, "One central aim of higher education is to encourage contact, debate, discussion and exposure to persuasion from different kinds of people" (Mayhew et al., 2018). In other words, the aim is to produce skeptics and to combat true belief. *Critical thinking is an essential component of competent public speaking.* Thus, this section discusses the skepticism process and encourages its practical speech application.

Probability Model: Likely But Not Certain

The process of skepticism begins with the probability model. Claims speakers assert can vary in degrees of likelihood from *possibility* to *plausibility*, to *probability* and all the way to *certainty* (Freeley & Steinberg, 2013). Any informative or persuasive speech you present requires your immediate determination of how strong a claim—what degree of likelihood—you want to defend. Remember: *The stronger the claim, the greater your burden of proof.*

Few things in this world are certain. Death and that your dryer will eat your socks are two that come to mind, but these are rare exceptions. Decision-making and problem-solving are best based on probabilities (Silver, 2012). Skeptics do not claim certainty because skepticism is an open system of thought and inquiry. Skeptics seek the highest degree of probability attainable. Thus, *skepticism is based on a probability, not a certainty model.*

Possibility: Could Happen, But Do Not Bet on It   If you flunked all your speeches, failed all your tests, and missed most class sessions in your public speaking course, you could possibly receive an A grade. There could be a clerical error by the instructor or a computer glitch. You would be foolish, however, to risk failing your class based on such an unlikely possibility. True belief often rests on the "anything is possible" rationale. This allows for no distinctions to be drawn between fact and fiction. Thus, claims based on possibility require no diligent research in preparing a speech or use of compelling evidence during a speech.

Suppose, for example, a stranger offers you $1,000 to walk blindfolded across a busy highway. Would you do it? Hey, it is possible you could succeed! What if you saw someone else do it without getting hit by a car? Now would you do it? One successful crossing proves that it is possible to cross a busy highway blindfolded and not get catapulted into the next county by a speeding automobile. It is possible, but not likely. "Anything is possible" is insufficient justification for gambling with your life or with your educational future. It is also a woefully inadequate basis for any speech you might present.

Plausibility: Making a Logical Case   The next step up from possibility is plausibility. For a claim to be plausible, it must at least seem to be logical. When the cause of AIDS was first determined to be a virus, only the most plausible theories

CARTOON 12.1: Basing your decisions on only a possibility is silly in the extreme. It makes the weakest "possible" argument for a speech.

on how to attack it were likely to gain federal grants to conduct research. Implausible theories (drink lots of orange juice) provide no logical basis for distributing scarce resources for research.

Plausibility alone is a basis for inquiry when substantial evidence is lacking, but it is an insufficient basis for acceptance of a claim. In the wake of the horrendous, incomprehensible massacre of 20 young children and 6 adults at the Sandy Hook Elementary School in Newtown, Connecticut, in December 2012, the executive vice-president and chief spokesman for the National Rifle Association, Wayne LaPierre, gave a much anticipated, nationally televised speech (*see access to link at end of chapter*). He asserted, "The only thing that stops a bad guy with a gun is a good guy with a gun" (quoted by Castillo, 2012). He called for an armed security guard in every school in America. LaPierre's proposal was based on plausibility. "Gun-free school zones," as LaPierre asserted in his speech, simply announce to deranged individuals that "schools are their safest place to inflict maximum mayhem with minimum risk." He continued his plausibility argument by noting, "We protect our banks with armed guards. American airports, office buildings, power plants, courthouses—even sports stadiums—are all protected by armed security" (quoted in "Full Text," 2013). Plausible arguments such as LaPierre's can be convincing. A *Washington Post*/ABC poll showed that 55% of those surveyed supported LaPierre's proposal ("Post–ABC Poll," 2013).

LaPierre's plausible case did not go unchallenged. Many media sources and numerous legislators offered a plausible case of their own, countering LaPierre's speech (*see access to Jim Jefferies link at end of chapter*). They noted that there were two armed police officers at Columbine High School when a massacre of 12 students and a teacher occurred in 1998. Virginia Tech University had its own police force on campus composed of more than four dozen armed officers at the time of the 2007 massacre in which 32 people died and 17 more were injured. With approximately 100,000 public schools in the United States, providing even a single armed guard for every school would cost billions of dollars annually. What would prevent the guard, armed only with a handgun, from becoming the first target of a mass murderer armed with assault weapons intent on causing mayhem (Burke & Chapman, 2012; Klein, 2018)?

The point here is not to resolve who is right in this most contentious, complex debate based only on plausibility. In the absence of careful research and bountiful evidence beyond a few selective examples to support claims, *plausibility alone on this or any other controversial topic serves as an insufficient basis for drawing any useful conclusions.* Plausibility may rightly provoke a dialogue and debate on controversial issues, but just because a claim seems plausible should not end the dialogue and the search for truth.

Probability: What Are the Odds? *Your strongest speech arguments are both plausible and highly probable.* This means offering claims that are both logical and supported with abundant, high-quality evidence. If your claim cannot even pass the plausibility test, if it is demonstrably implausible, further consideration and evidence gathering seem unwarranted.

Consider, for example, the persistent claim that the Moon landing was a hoax perpetrated by the American government for all sorts of asserted reasons. A Chapman University survey found that 24% of respondents believed the Moon landing never happened (Poppy, 2017). An earlier survey of British respondents found a similar 25% believed the Moon landing was not real (Bizony, 2009). The Internet is replete with sites alleging the Moon landing never occurred.

The Moon hoax conspiracy is a nice, practical example of how to exercise your critical thinking abilities by employing a healthy skepticism. A Moon hoax conspiracy is *highly implausible* because it would have involved about 411,000 NASA employees as collaborators (Berezow, 2016), none of whom has ever blown

PHOTO 12.3: The "Moon landing hoax" is one of those persistent conspiracy theories that defies logic and is contradicted by massive mountains of evidence. True believers, however, are impervious to such overwhelming support. The hoax claim is implausible; the Moon landing claim is extremely probable.

the whistle in more than four decades. If Soviet scientists who were monitoring the Apollo Moon flights had discovered any credible evidence of fakery, they surely would have announced it to the world. The Soviet Union was our Cold War nemesis and was racing us to the Moon. Thus, the Moon hoax conspiracy does not even pass the plausibility test.

Assuming your argument passes the plausibility test, you then move to probability to make a strong argument. Probability is a concept not well understood by most people (Silver, 2012). There is high probability that unusual events will occur, but that is no reason to give them special significance. For example, Ethem Sahin was playing dominoes with his friends in a coffee house in Ankara, Turkey, when a cow fell on him, breaking his leg and gashing his forehead. The coffee house was built on the side of a hill and the cow wandered onto the roof, which caved in from the cow's weight ("Falling Cow Injures Coffee House Customer," 2001). It is doubtful that you will agonize about suffering a similar incident in a coffee house, but it did happen. With almost 8 billion people in the world, weird things will occur to some of them. This demonstrates the **Law of Truly Large Numbers**—with large enough numbers, almost anything is likely to happen to *somebody, somewhere, somehow, sometime* (Carroll, 2014). On June 8, 2009, a small meteorite hit a boy in Germany ("14-year-old

Hit," 2009). The odds of this specific little boy being hit by a meteorite were astronomical. The odds of someone at some time being struck by a meteorite, however, are high, considering that thousands of meteorites hit the ground each year (Mathewson, 2016).

Recognizing the Law of Truly Large Numbers, you should avoid making a speech that rests primarily on a handful of vivid, extraordinary examples. Remember, the unusual is likely to happen to someone, but that is poor justification for generalizing to a much broader population from "news of the weird." It is weird because it is improbable but not impossible.

Base your speech claims not on the improbable but on the highest degree of probability attainable. Scientists from around the world documented the Moon landing. The whole world was watching. It was one of the most thoroughly documented events in human history, thus establishing extremely *high probability* of its occurrence. In a more down-to-Earth example, polio vaccinations have a 99% probability of preventing the disease ("Polio Vaccine Effectiveness," 2018). The vaccine is so effective that polio has been nearly wiped out across the globe (Beaubien, 2017). Thus, the effectiveness of a polio vaccine is both plausible, based on previous experience with vaccines used against diseases in general, and highly probable, based on extensive studies on polio vaccines in particular. Do careful research to discover strong evidence that bolsters the probability of your claims. *Chapter 13 discusses in detail how to determine the strength of your evidence.*

Certainty: Without Exception   Claims of true believers are frequently stated as absolute certainties. A true believer by definition exhibits no doubt. *Skeptics, however, can aspire to no stronger claim than very high probability.* As a speaker, you do not want to make a claim that is absolute (e.g., "Higher education can *never* be free"; "Every politician lies"). Practically speaking, a claim asserting certainty requires only a single exception to disprove it. Why set such an argumentative trap for yourself? "Highly likely" avoids the trap of certainty because exceptions do not disprove strong probability.

Skepticism discourages claims that any phenomenon is "impossible," although some skeptics have intemperately done so. What first appears to be impossible may prove to be disastrously incorrect. For example, the Fukushima nuclear reactor was designed to withstand an earthquake up to 8.6 in magnitude, in part because some seismologists thought it impossible that any earthquake larger than this could occur at this location (Silver, 2012). In addition, the plant was built on the expectation that no tsunami wave from a major earthquake could rise higher than 5.7 meters. On March 11, 2011, Japan experienced the "impossible," suffering a 9.0 magnitude quake that resulted in a 15-meter-high tsunami wave that claimed almost 20,000 lives and engulfed the reactor, which produced a meltdown and a severe radiation leak (Aldhous, 2012).

Skepticism and Open-Mindedness: Inquiring Minds, Not Empty Minds

Although skeptics avoid claims of certainty, this does not open the door to the everything-is-possible "open-mindedness" justification for true belief (Petrovic, 2013). Open-mindedness does not require us to entertain obviously false claims made by speakers or to give them a forum for expression. Do you really want to listen to a speaker argue that the world is flat or that gravity does not exist? As the bumper sticker says: "Gravity: Not just a good idea; it's the law!" "What truly marks an open-minded person is the willingness to follow where evidence leads" (Adler, 1998, p. 44). This requires *self-correction of erroneous beliefs*. Self-correction should be embraced, not resisted. Defending a belief you know to be untrue before an audience inclined to embrace the error raises an ethical red flag. It is pandering. Ethical public speaking requires honesty (see Chapter 1), and honesty demands self-correction of mistaken ideas. Skepticism mandates tough choices and the courage to correct error.

PHOTO 12.4: Open-mindedness does not mean that you have to listen to hateful bigotry spouted, for example, by Westboro Baptist Church members at funerals for dead soldiers.

Becoming a Skeptic: Steps to Be Taken

Now that the differences between skeptics and true believers have been detailed, what steps should you take to become a skeptic, both as a speaker and as an audience member? Developing a healthy skepticism effectively combats misinformation and "fake news" (Chan et al., 2017). This section enumerates those steps.

What Speakers as Skeptics Do   It isn't enough to be able to differentiate true belief from skepticism. You need to be able to put skepticism into practice. Here's how to do that; first as a speaker:

1. Choose and build a claim based on high probability.
2. Avoid claims based on possibility alone. Possibility provides no basis for determining the quality of an argument.
3. Avoid claims of certainty. Claims that use words such as "always," "never," "impossible," "absolutely," and "undoubtedly" place you in an untenable position of having to be perfect—accounting for every conceivable possibility or unanticipated event.
4. Be open-minded—follow where the reasoning and evidence lead you; avoid preconceived conclusions that may be contradicted by proof. Be evidence-driven, not belief-driven.
5. Avoid confirmation bias when researching your speech. Seek information that reflects various points of view, then weigh the evidence and decide what claim is best to defend.
6. Remember that when you make any claim, it is your burden to support that claim, not someone else's to disprove your claim. Also remember that extraordinary claims require extraordinary proof.

What Listeners as Skeptics Do   Public speaking isn't just about speaking. You want to be a skeptic as an audience member as well. To do that, take the following steps:

1. Beware of confirmation bias. Don't listen only to speeches that reinforce your preconceived beliefs.
2. Avoid rationalization of disconfirmation. Lame excuses and reasons to reject a speaker's claims because they are uncomfortable are the refuge of a true believer.
3. Recognize that the Law of Truly Large Numbers accounts for unusual events and such events should not be given special significance.

4. Understand that being open-minded does not mean listening to bigotry or nonsense. Being open-minded means basing your beliefs on reasoning and evidence—follow where it leads you.

5. Engage in self-correction—when reasoning and evidence presented by speakers clearly disprove a belief, change your belief. Correcting erroneous beliefs advances knowledge. Failing to correct erroneous beliefs perpetuates ignorance.

SUMMARY

Skepticism is a critical thinking process of inquiry whereby claims are evaluated by engaging in a rigorous examination of the evidence and reasoning used to support those claims. Skeptics seek to present plausible arguments that are also highly probable based on substantial, high-quality evidence. They recognize that those making claims have the burden of proof. They must engage in self-correction when beliefs are contradicted by compelling logic and evidence. Possibility or surface plausibility, however, is sufficient for true believers to accept claims. True believers engage in confirmation bias, rationalization of disconfirmation, and shifting the burden of proof inappropriately to skeptics. As a practical public speaker, embrace skepticism in both the preparation and the presentation of your speeches. The practical public speaker strives to do much more than simply speak fluently and present points with impact. You want to communicate substantial, well-supported ideas. Skepticism should guide your search and construction of these substantial ideas.

TED TALKS AND YOUTUBE VIDEOS

Plausibility Argument: "Jim Jefferies: Gun Control (Part 1) from *BARE* Netflix Special"—Warning: rough language but hilarious

Plausibility Argument: "Wayne LaPierre: NRA Response to Sandy Hook, December 21, 2012"

Confirmation Bias Online: "Eli Pariser: Beware Online 'Filter Bubbles'"

Tenacity of True Belief: "The Daily Show—Putting Donald Trump Supporters Through an Ideology Test"

Truth Decay: "Truth Decay: A Primer"

For relevant links to TED Talks and YouTube videos, see the *Practically Speaking* Companion Website: www.oup.com/he/rothwell-ps3e. You can also gain access by typing the title of the speech reference into a Google search window or by doing the same on the TED Talks or YouTube sites.

CHECKLIST

☐ Did you follow the steps for what speakers as skeptics do?

☐ Did you follow the steps for what listeners as skeptics do? Remember that in public speaking situations you will be both a speaker and a listener depending on the circumstances. Skepticism is critical in both capacities.

CRITICAL THINKING QUESTIONS

1. Can you be a true believer on some issues and a skeptic on others?

2. Can true belief ever have positive consequences? Does a "righteous cause" excuse true belief?

3. Are there any situations in which skepticism might be counterproductive, even harmful?

4. Provide arguments that explain why ridiculing true believers might backfire and strengthen the erroneous belief.

NOTE: Online **student resources**, such as practice tests, flashcards, and other activities, can be accessed at www.oup.com/he/rothwell-ps3e

CHAPTER 13

Argument, Reasoning, and Evidence

You live in a world of claims. Hyper-caffeinated pitchmeisters on infomercials proclaim the wonders of cordless vacuums with the sucking power of a tick. Products are advertised as medical breakthroughs, yet suspiciously, these breakthroughs are announced on TV or print advertisements instead of in professional medical journals. Weight-loss diets and pills promising a thin body without effort emerge almost daily. Hard-to-believe, get-rich-quick real estate programs and business schemes are exuberantly promoted. You hear political candidates slander each other with negative ads on various media. What is a person to believe? That is where skepticism serves you well.

In the previous chapter, differences between true believers and skeptics were identified. The justification for carefully reasoned and well-supported claims was extensively developed. This chapter expands on the practical ways you can implement skepticism as a public speaker or as someone listening to those who give speeches. This is skepticism in action. *Although all of the material in this chapter is relevant to persuasive speaking, much of it also relates directly to informative speaking as well.* For example, clarifying the seriousness of the potential threat of a new virus is informative, but the evidence used to support claims of a specific threat should meet the criteria for competence discussed in this chapter. Similarly, lectures in biology, chemistry, history, communication, and a host of other college courses are informative, but all should be based on the best available evidence.

CARTOON 13.1: Credible arguments, reasoning, and evidence are necessary in informative as well as persuasive presentations. You don't want to misinform.

Thus, *the purpose of this chapter is to explain ways to distinguish degrees of strength or weakness in reasoning and evidence used to support informative or persuasive claims*. In Chapter 5, how to use supporting materials competently was discussed. This chapter goes deeper and explores (1) how to construct an argument and (2) how to apply criteria for determining fact from fallacy in reasoning and evidence.

AN ARGUMENT: STAKING YOUR CLAIM

Remember that skepticism is the critical thinking process of inquiry that scrutinizes arguments based on reasoning and evidence. Aristotle used the term *logos* when referring to persuasive appeals that rest on reasoning and arguments. An **argument** "implicitly or explicitly presents a claim and provides support for that claim with reasoning and evidence" (Verlinden, 2005, p. 5). **Reasoning** is the thought process of drawing conclusions from evidence. **Evidence** consists of statistics, testimony of experts and credible sources, and verifiable facts. Developing a sound argument begins with understanding how reasoning and evidence mesh logically.

Syllogism: Formal Logic

In formal logic, the basic structure of an argument is called a **syllogism**. A syllogism contains three parts: a major premise (an absolutely certain general statement), a minor premise (a specific statement related to the major premise), and a conclusion (a logical result of the major and minor premises). A standard example of a categorical syllogism is:

> Major premise: All humans are mortal.
> Minor premise: Bridgett is human.
> Conclusion: Bridgett is mortal.

Not all categorical syllogisms make sense. Consider this bumper sticker syllogism:

> Major premise: Nobody's perfect.
> Minor premise: I'm nobody.
> Conclusion: I'm perfect.

It almost seems logical. The meaning of terms used twice in a syllogism, however, must be identical. Here "nobody" in the major premise means "no one at all," but in the minor premise it means "a person of no consequence." The syllogism should actually be written this way to see its illogic clearly:

> Major premise: All people are imperfect.
> Minor premise: I'm a person of no consequence.
> Conclusion: I'm perfect.

In the formal logic of categorical syllogisms, you can reach certainty because premises are stated categorically, and conclusions logically follow from those absolutes. Consider this example:

> Major premise: All individuals who kill another human being deliberately and with malice aforethought are guilty of first-degree murder.
> Minor premise: Tom Higgins killed Alfonso Carbonati deliberately and with malice aforethought.
> Conclusion: Tom Higgins is guilty of first-degree murder.

As discussed in the previous chapter, however, human decision making and problem solving navigate in a sea of varying uncertainty. High probability, not certainty, should be your goal. In the previous example, a jury must determine that Tom Higgins is guilty of first-degree murder "beyond a reasonable doubt" but not with certainty. Thus, informal logic described by British philosopher

Stephen Toulmin more aptly depicts how people usually conduct argumentation and decision making based on probabilities (Freeley & Steinberg, 2013; Verlinden, 2005).

Toulmin Structure of Argument: Informal Logic

Toulmin's (1958) description of informal logic identifies and explains the six elements of an argument:

1. **Claim**—A generalization that remains to be proven with reasoning and evidence.
2. **Grounds** (Reasons/Evidence)—Reasons to accept a claim and the evidence used to support those reasons. Reasons justify the claim, and evidence provides firm ground for these reasons.
3. **Warrant**—The reasoning that links the grounds to the claim. It is often implied, not stated explicitly.
4. **Backing**—The reasons and relevant evidence that support the warrant.
5. **Rebuttal**—Exceptions or refutations that diminish the force of the claim.
6. **Qualifier**—Degree of truth to the claim (possible, plausible, probable, highly probable).

Everyday reasoning follows this pattern known as the Toulmin structure of argument. Figure 13.1 provides an example. The **claim** is that no final exam should be given. The reason or **grounds** provided is that five exams have already been completed by students in the class. At this point, the logical question that a skeptic should ask is: "Why does taking five exams justify skipping a final?" The answer serves as your **warrant**, namely, that the purpose of a final has already been accomplished. This should raise questions in your mind: "What is the purpose of a final exam, and how has taking five previous exams satisfied this purpose?" **Backing** provides the answers: the professor's stated purpose of a final exam is to test the comprehensive knowledge of students on all subject matter presented in class. The five exams already completed tested every section of the course and thus accomplish the stated purpose of a final, so the final is irrelevant. Controversial claims inevitably invite rebuttals. The **rebuttal** tries to weaken or demolish the claim by attacking its underlying logic and supporting evidence. For example, without a final exam, students will not see the connections between different segments of the class material. Furthermore, material covered in the first part of the course may be forgotten if there's no final exam. The **qualifier** weighs both sides of the argument and attaches a degree of likelihood that the claim is true or warranted. Although the reasoning provided for this claim is decent, the evidence provided is sparse (one statistic and one source citation). The rebuttal, however, consists of unsupported assertions. Neither side offers a

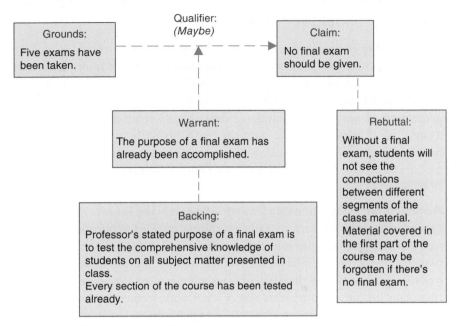

FIGURE 13.1: Toulmin structure of argument.

strong case, but the original claim is somewhat better supported than the rebuttal, so the qualifier is a mildly affirmative "maybe."

CRITERIA FOR REASONING AND EVIDENCE: IS IT FACT OR FALLACY?

The Toulmin structure of an argument blends well with the skepticism perspective. For a skeptic, the more probable the claim, the more valuable it is as a basis for decision making, provided that the speaker making the claim meets his or her burden of proof. You determine whether the burden of proof has been met by evaluating the evidence (grounds, backing) and the reasoning (warrants) that supports the claim. Then you assign a qualifier to the claim based on how well the burden of proof has been met. Any fallacies diminish the warrant for the claim.

The term "fallacy" is derived from the Latin *fallere*, which means *to deceive*. A **fallacy** is any error in reasoning and evidence that may deceive your audience, whether the speech is informative or persuasive. This section explains the *three principal criteria for evaluating evidence and reasoning*: credibility, relevance, and sufficiency. Fallacies that commonly occur when these criteria are unmet are discussed.

Credibility: Should We Believe You?

The **credibility** of evidence refers to its believability as determined by consistency and accuracy. *Consistency* means that what a source of information says and does agree. A source of information should not be quoted as support for claims if that source says one thing but does another or has not been truthful in the past. *Accuracy* means that the evidence has no error; it is free of fallacies. If cited "facts" prove to be inaccurate, the credibility of the source of those inaccuracies should suffer. As a speaker, you want to build a speech with strong reasoning and evidence, not weaken it by using fallacious reasoning and evidence.

Manufactured or Questionable Statistics: Does It Make Sense?   When giving a speech, you will likely include statistics while attempting to inform or persuade your audience. For example, student Tennisha Sonsalla (2017) cites this disturbing statistic: "The Avon Foundation for Women released a breast-cancer-mortality study in October of 2016 that showed black women were 43% more likely to die after being diagnosed with breast cancer [than white women]" (p. 186). This is a plausible statistic cited by a reputable, current publication.

Some statistics, however, are fake (manufactured), and others are highly questionable (make no sense). Be careful that the statistics you use to support your claims make sense. Do not fall victim to confirmation bias by grabbing the first statistic that supports your claim without analyzing its credibility.

Consider the manufactured statistic that became a source of controversy during the 2016 presidential campaign. The claim was that according to the Crime Statistics Bureau in San Francisco, *81%* of white victims of homicide are "killed by blacks." First, the statistic should immediately seem dubious since African Americans comprise slightly less than 14% of the total population of the United States, according to the U.S. Census Bureau ("Quick Facts," 2017). Second, the source cited does not exist. There is no Crime Statistics Bureau in San Francisco. Third, according to the FBI, the actual statistic is *14%* of white victims are killed by African Americans (Fang, 2015). The manufactured statistic came from a neo-Nazi Twitter account that was retweeted widely (Sarlin, 2016).

Then there is the highly questionable statistic asserted every year by the Academy of Motion Picture Arts and Sciences, and repeated in opening remarks by the hosts, that a billion people worldwide watch the Academy Awards. The implausibility of this oft-repeated statistic is easily deduced given that most nominated movies are American, the awards show is aired on American television in English, which is not the language of most other countries, and only 29.6 million Americans viewed the 2019 show (Patten, 2019). *The Hollywood Reporter*, which compiles data and estimates for key market viewership, puts the likely total worldwide viewership at 65 million (Szalai & Roxborough, 2016).

CARTOON 13.2: This is an implausible statistic. Check snopes.com for an explanation. Even usually credible newspapers and other media have repeated this bogus statistic.

Biased Sources: Grinding an Ax   Biased sources are an increasingly serious problem with the easy access to false information. A Stanford University study showed that more than half of the college students participating thought the American College of Pediatricians was a reliable source after accessing the group's website and given the opportunity to do a wider search online to check on this group. The Southern Poverty Law Center, however, identifies the American College of Pediatricians as a hate group because of its "history of propagating damaging falsehoods about LGBT people, including linking homosexuality to pedophilia, and claiming that LGBT people are more promiscuous than heterosexuals, and . . . a danger to children" ("Meet the Anti-LGBT Hate Group," 2015). A quick Google search easily reveals these details. Also, almost two-thirds of

PHOTO 13.1: Beware biased sources of information. The car salesman stands to gain financially, so information he provides must be viewed skeptically.

the same college student participants failed to recognize the political bias of a negative tweet about the National Rifle Association made by the liberal group MoveOn.org (Wineberg et al., 2016).

Don't accept just any source that might sound credible. This is important. Research shows that ideologically leaning Internet news sources (e.g., Daily Kos; Drudge Report), for example, have a strong biasing effect that produces "a distorted understanding of evidence, potentially promoting inaccurate beliefs" (Garrett et al., 2016). (*See Chapter 4 discussion on evaluating Internet sites and information.*) Also, any website providing nutritional information while pushing vitamins, minerals, and other "health" products is biased (e.g., GNC, Vitacost, Vitamin World, etc.). Although these sites may provide reputable sources for medical and health claims, they are unlikely to include studies that debunk the value of certain supplements and products sold on the website.

Look for sources to bolster your claims that have no personal stake in the outcome—a source that seeks the truth, not personal benefit or political advantage. *Recognize that special-interest groups or individuals who stand to gain money, prestige, power, or influence if they advocate a certain position on an issue are biased sources of information.*

Expert Quoted Out of Field: No Generic Experts Allowed   In Chapter 5, the value of citing experts as supporting materials for your speeches was explored.

Quoting experts outside their field of expertise, however, runs the substantial risk of promoting inaccurate claims supported by invalid and unreliable evidence (Nichols, 2017). For example, Iben Browning, the chief scientist for Summa Medical Corporation, had a doctorate in physiology and a bachelor's degree in physics and math. He predicted a major earthquake for December 3 and 4, 1990, along the New Madrid Fault in the Midwest. Schools in several states dismissed students for these two days as a result of Browning's prediction. Browning had some scientific expertise, but not in the area of earthquake prediction. In fact, earthquake experts, with geotechnical engineering degrees and experience in seismology, denounced Browning's predictions because those who study earthquakes cannot accurately predict them ("Can You Predict Earthquakes," 2019). The 7.0 magnitude earthquake that shook Anchorage, Alaska, on November 30, 2018, for example, was not predicted. No earthquake, large or small, occurred on the dates Browning predicted, and no major earthquake on the New Madrid Fault has occurred in three decades since his prediction. The first sizable earthquake on the New Madrid Fault since Browning's prediction occurred on April 17, 2008, and it was considered "moderate" by quake experts and caused little damage.

Relevance: Does It Follow?

Evidence used to support claims must have relevance—it must relate directly to those claims, or the claims are unwarranted. A classic type of fallacy is called a **non sequitur**, which is Latin for "it does not follow." A conclusion that does not follow from its premises is a non sequitur fallacy. The non sequitur is a kind of general fallacy that encompasses many more specific fallacies in which claims do not follow (are unwarranted) from evidence and reasoning (Norquist, 2019a). Consider two common non sequiturs: ad hominem and ad populum fallacies.

Ad Hominem Fallacy: Diversionary Tactic   During the Republican presidential campaign in 2016, Marco Rubio and Donald Trump traded personal insults repeatedly (*see access to links at end of chapter*). Trump accused Rubio of having a "meltdown" backstage during a commercial break at the CNN debate on February 25, 2016. Trump in campaign speeches repeatedly called Rubio a "lightweight," a "choke artist," and a "liar." He mocked Rubio for sweating during the debates, splashing water in all directions to indicate Rubio flop sweating. He claimed that Rubio applied makeup "with a trowel" to cover his perspiration problem. Rubio responded at one of his rally speeches by claiming that Trump feared that he had "wet his pants" and tried to apply makeup to cover a "sweat mustache" at one of the debates. He lacerated Trump as a "con artist" and ridiculed Trump's "worst spray tan in America" (Fang, 2016; Kopan, 2016).

The **ad hominem fallacy** is a personal attack on the messenger to avoid the message. It is a *diversionary tactic* that is irrelevant to the primary message. In the Rubio–Trump verbal food fight, none of the personal attacks could reasonably be tied directly to issues of presidential leadership or positions either candidate espoused. They were irrelevant, ad hominem fallacies.

Not all personal attacks, however, are ad hominem fallacies. If a claim raises the issue of a person's credibility, character, or trustworthiness, the attack is not irrelevant to the claim being made. For example, student Ashanti Holland (2018) in her speech at The Interstate Oratorical Association contest, identifies Levy Rosenbaum as an unsavory character, "nicknamed the Kidney Broker, who was sentenced to two-and-a half years in prison" for illegal human organ trafficking. Attacking Rosenbaum's character hardly qualifies as a fallacy. It isn't a diversionary tactic; character is a central issue. Consider another example. Criticisms that led to the impeachment and removal from office of Democratic Illinois governor Rod Blagojevich in 2009 for trying to "sell" Barack Obama's vacant U.S. Senate seat to the highest bidder when Obama became president involved legitimate questions about Blagojevich's character and credibility. The Illinois state senate apparently felt the charges were credible and relevant; it voted 59–0 to remove Blagojevich from office. On December 7, 2011, Blagojevich, following a high-profile trial, was sentenced to 14 years in prison for corruption.

Ad Populum Fallacy: Arguing from Public Opinion   Psychologist David Myer (2016) shows that preponderant scientific evidence on issues such as climate change, nuclear energy, genetically modified foods, and gun safety can strongly contradict popular opinion held by both liberals and conservatives, depending on the issue. Should we base our views on science or popular opinion on issues of great significance? If views are based primarily on popular opinion, this is called the **ad populum fallacy**.

Be it a majority or a vocal minority, public opinion can be fickle and unsound. At one time in our history, majorities favored slavery and segregation for African Americans in restaurants, schools, housing, and public transportation; they opposed voting rights for women and minorities as well as women serving on juries or owning property or receiving credit cards in their own names. Recognizing that popular opinion often can be grossly wrong, the number of people supporting a claim is therefore irrelevant to its validity. Speech claims should be weighed on the basis of sound reasoning and substantial high-quality evidence, not merely on majority opinion or even that of a vocal minority.

PHOTO 13.2: Segregation in the South was supported by the majority White population in the pre–civil rights era. Popular opinion can be a weak, even an inhumane, basis for a claim.

Sufficiency: Got Enough?

As explained in Chapter 12, the person who makes a claim has the burden to prove that claim. Insufficient evidence in a court trial, for example, warrants either a "not guilty" verdict for the defendant or dismissal of the charges. Sufficiency requires judgment. There is no precise formula for determining sufficiency. Generally, strong, plentiful evidence and solid reasoning meet the sufficiency criterion. More than three decades ago, 40,000 studies had already been conducted that showed cigarettes are a serious health hazard ("Advertising Is Hazardous," 1986). Thousands more have since been added to the list. Now that is sufficient proof. Combating false beliefs based on misinformation and "fake news" requires more than a casual correction. Abundant, credible evidence is often necessary to shake a person's false beliefs, and even then such wrong beliefs may change only for those who are not true believers (Shermer, 2018). Several fallacies, however, clearly exhibit insufficiency.

Self-Selected Sample: Partisan Power   To achieve sufficiency, any poll or survey must use a random sample. A **random sample** is a portion of the target *population*, the entire set of individuals of interest, chosen in such a manner that every member of the entire population has an equal chance of being selected. Any poll or survey that depends on respondents selecting themselves to participate provides results that are insufficient to generalize beyond the sample. This **self-selected sample** attracts the most committed or motivated individuals to fill out surveys on their own and answer polling questions (Smith, 2015). Printing a survey in a magazine and collecting those that have been returned is an example of a self-selected sample. Calling an 800 number to answer questions about politics or social issues is another example.

Results of surveys and polls conducted with a self-selected sample can significantly distort the facts. For example, the California Public Interest Research Group contacted almost 80,000 students 18–24 years old to complete an online survey on voter participation. A mere 1,057 students responded. When asked, "Do you plan to vote in the June primaries?" a surprising 75% said yes. Historically, a primary in a non-presidential election year has low voter turnout (2018 being a notable exception). Only 25.2% of 18–24-year-olds, however, ultimately voted (Manjikian & Rusch, 2014). Good intentions explain part of the discrepant statistics, but the self-selected sample represented mostly motivated young voters.

Surveys using self-selected samples are insufficient to support general claims, not because the sample size is inadequate but because it represents only a narrow, biased population. Self-selected samples often involve huge numbers of respondents. Increasing the number of respondents does not improve the results, unless you survey everyone in the population, because the sample comes from the most motivated, committed individuals. The indifferent or nonpartisan, which may be a majority, are less likely to participate in the survey or poll.

Inadequate Sample: Large Margin of Error   Almost every day you read in the newspaper or hear on radio or television about some new study that "proves" coffee is dangerous, certain pesticides sprayed on vegetables are harmful, power lines cause cancer, or massive doses of vitamin C prevent colds. A consistent problem in this regard is the tendency of the mass media to sensationalize each new study that gets published. *A single study, however, proves very little and is insufficient to draw any general conclusion.* In science, studies are replicated before results are given credence because mistakes can be made that may distort the results. The greater the number of carefully controlled studies that show similar or identical results, the more sufficient is the proof.

So what is an adequate sample size for a survey? In general, the **margin of error**—a measure of the degree of sampling error accounted for by imperfections in sample selection—goes down as the number of people surveyed goes up. For example, a sample of 100 survey respondents has a ±10% margin of error; a 500 sample size yields a ±4.5% margin of error; a 1,000 sample size yields a ±3.2% margin of error; and a 2,000 sample size produces a ±2.2% margin of error ("Sample Size," 2019). Thus, if you sampled only 100 people on federal legalization of marijuana and 50% of these respondents favor it the actual result if every adult American were surveyed, would be between 40% and 60%. With such a whopping margin of error, this survey could mean that Americans either favor or oppose marijuana legalization. That is why an adequate sample size will have a margin of error no greater than plus or minus 3% to 4%. No poll is without some margin of error. It is usually impractically expensive and time consuming to survey every person in a population, but increasing the sample size improves the chances that the poll is accurate if the sample is random, not self-selected. Margin of error applies only to random samples, not self-selected samples that are inherently biased.

Hasty Generalization: Arguing from Example We often use **inductive reasoning**—drawing conclusions from specific instances. Such reasoning, however, can pose problems. When individuals jump to a conclusion based on a single or a handful of examples, especially vivid ones, they have made a **hasty generalization** (Nordquist, 2019b).

How many times have you avoided a class based solely on the claim of another student that the professor was "incredibly boring" or "sexist" or "terribly unfair"? Perhaps the student told a startling tale of poor behavior from the teacher. A sample of one is hardly conclusive evidence to warrant such choices, yet such choices are made. If you seek out other students' opinions of the same professor, many may actually have very positive things to say, completely countering the single student with the negative opinion. There are exceptions, however, in which you may need to take seriously a vivid tale, even if told by only one person. If you hear that someone is dangerous and potentially violent, even if it proves to be erroneous, it deserves to be considered seriously until proven wrong.

CARTOON 13.3: Generalizing from anecdotes is a hasty generalization fallacy.

In general, however, avoid hasty generalizations, especially those based on vivid examples and anecdotes.

Correlation Mistaken for Causation: *X* Does Not Necessarily Cause *Y*   Humans are intensely interested in discovering causes of events that remain unexplained. **Causal reasoning** occurs when we see events and infer what caused these events. For example, scientists, journalists, and health seekers have visited Vilcabamba, Ecuador, for a half-century to discover the causes of their unusual longevity. Manuel Picoita, when 102 years old, thought getting along with his neighbors was the cause of his reaching centenarian status. Josefa Ocampa, when 104, believed the secret to her long life was that each morning she drank a glass of goat's milk with a bit of her own urine added (Kraul, 2006). Pinning down exact causes of phenomena can often be elusive.

Everyone is prone to draw causation (*x* causes *y*) from mere correlation (*x* occurs and *y* also occurs either sequentially or simultaneously). "The invalid assumption that correlation implies cause is probably among the two or three most serious and common errors of human reasoning" (Gould, 1981, p. 242). A **correlation** is a consistent relationship between two variables. A **variable** is anything that can change. Finding a strong correlation between two variables does not prove causation. A research team, for example, found that the number of electric appliances (ovens, irons, toasters) found in Taiwanese homes correlated most strongly with birth control use (Li, 1975). As the number of appliances increased, use of contraceptives also increased. So, based on this study, do you think distributing free toasters would likely reduce teen pregnancies? Most likely, this correlation merely reflects socioeconomic status that is also strongly correlated with contraceptive use and is a better candidate for causation. A more recent study found a strong correlation between teenage acne and higher overall grade point averages (Wong, 2018). Despite the correlation, acne hardly qualifies as a causal reason for good grades. Plenty of teens who are not afflicted with acne get good grades. Reasons for the correlation are entirely speculative and dubious (e.g., social inhibition from acne leads to greater concentration on one's studies).

Correlations suggest *possible* causation, and that can be an important starting point for further investigations, but correlations alone are insufficient reasons to claim *probable* causation (Sherman, 2009; Silver, 2012). "The vast majority of correlations in our world are, without doubt, noncausal" (Gould, 1981, p. 242). Tyler Vigen (2015), in his book *Spurious Correlations*, cites numerous amusing correlations that no one would suggest are meaningful causal relations. For example, there is a strong correlation between per capita consumption of cheese and the number of people who died by becoming tangled in their bedsheets. The divorce rate correlates with the per capita consumption of margarine. The marriage rate in Kentucky correlates strongly with the number of people who drowned after falling out of a fishing boat.

Even a perfect correlation does not mean there is causation. For instance, what if you surveyed 100 college students and found that none of the 55 who regularly eat breakfast dumped their girlfriend or boyfriend in the past two years but all of the 45 students who regularly skip breakfast did? Here is a perfect correlation—no exceptions. Eat breakfast—keep your girlfriend/boyfriend; avoid breakfast—dump your girlfriend/boyfriend. Would you assert in a speech that this perfect correlation was sufficient proof that skipping breakfast causes a person to dump his or her girlfriend or boyfriend? Only a cereal manufacturer might try this to boost sales.

False Analogy: Mixing Apples and Oranges   Analogical reasoning alleges that because two things closely resemble each other, both should logically be viewed in similar ways. Historically, marriage recognized by the state exempted husbands from any criminal charge of rape against their wives, even if sex was obtained by force. These laws began to change in the United States in 1975, primarily based on analogical reasoning. Those who supported marital rape laws argued: Is there any essential difference between rape by a stranger and rape by a spouse? Both acts involve nonconsensual sexual penetration achieved by force and violence. This should be viewed as rape in either instance. The analogy was a good one, and marital rape laws have been passed in all 50 states.

Johnny Smith (2016), assistant professor of history at Georgia Tech, uses analogical reasoning to argue that student-athletes should be compensated. "Student-athletes are the only group of students on campus who are told that they cannot be students and employees. Athletic departments regularly hire students as assistant trainers, equipment managers, marketers, ticket sellers, and video producers. Yet no one argues that they should not get paid since they are receiving an education, too." Smith continues, "No one tells a student on a music scholarship that she can't sign a recording contract or that an English major can't sign a publishing contract." The proposal to pay college athletes steps into a hornet's nest of controversy and counterarguments, but the analogical reasoning that undergirds the basic premise of Smith's argument is certainly debatable. Anne Marie Lofaso (2017) of the West Virginia University College of Law argues as much, claiming that college football players, for example, meet the "statutory definition of employee" that "disrupts the student-athlete myth."

False analogies occur when a significant point or points of difference exist despite some superficial similarities between the two things being compared (Govier, 2010). Presidents George W. Bush, Barack Obama, and Donald Trump have all been characterized by opponents in numerous fiery speeches as the new Hitler. Protesters have prominently displayed posters showing each with

DILBERT   **BY SCOTT ADAMS**

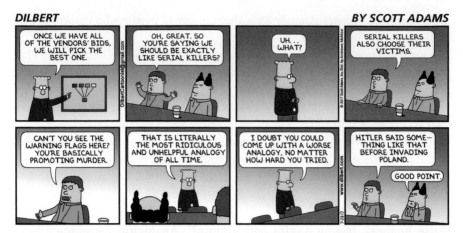

CARTOON 13.4: Analogies to Hitler are almost always ludicrously misapplied and therefore false.

Hitlerian mustaches and swastikas. "If you hate Hitler, you should hate these individuals because they are so similar" goes the strained analogy.

The analogy to Hitler and to "Gestapo tactics" and "big government" enforced by the "jack-booted Nazis" is false. The comparison in each case should be rejected by any reasonable person. Hitler was a mass murderer of unparalleled infamy. He systematically exterminated whole populations and instituted a worldwide reign of terror. Even ugly and polarizing language and behavior from Donald Trump does not justify the comparison to Hitler.

Disagree passionately with their policies, or the policies of any other person you dislike—even warn of potential dangers in their ideologies, practices, prevarications, and rhetorical excesses when speaking to audiences—but do not accept or use the analogy to Hitler. Pulitzer Prize–winning historian Jon Meacham (2009) said it well: "We are in danger of turning evil itself into a triviality when we draw on the images of Hitler's Germany to make political points in debates that are in no way comparable to the terrors of Nazism" (p. 9). The analogy to Hitler is grossly misapplied in speech after speech and is false because the dissimilarities are enormous.

This concludes the discussion of specific fallacies. Only the most common fallacies among the hundreds that could be identified have been examined. These examples should serve you well, however, in constructing speeches and discussing and debating controversial issues.

SUMMARY

The previous chapter laid out the fundamental justification for skepticism, for why you need to think critically as a public speaker and listener and how to do it generally. This chapter specifically illustrates skepticism in action. The formal logic of syllogisms is not as applicable to constructing speeches as Toulmin's structure of arguments model. The six elements of the model—claim, grounds, warrant, backing, rebuttal, and qualifier—can be applied to a single argument or to an entire debate on an issue. Understanding the connections between each element clarifies the importance of reasoning and evidence to the validity and probability of a claim. There are three main criteria for evaluating reasoning and evidence: credibility, relevance, and sufficiency. Fallacies, those errors in reasoning and evidence, violate these three criteria.

TED TALKS AND YOUTUBE VIDEOS

Ad Hominem Fallacies: "Marco Rubio Mocks Donald Trump in Dallas"; ad hominem fallacies

Ad Hominem Fallacies: "Trump Strikes Back at Rubio, Cruz's Attacks"; ad hominem fallacies

Statistical Fallacies: "Emily Dressler: Don't Be Fooled by Bad Statistics"

Hasty Generalizations: "Chimamanda Ngozi Adichie: The Danger of a Single Story"

Even Experts Cite Credible Evidence: "Simon Sinek: Why Good Leaders Make You Feel Safe"

For relevant links to these TED Talks and YouTube videos, see the *Practically Speaking* Companion Website: www.oup.com/he/rothwell-ps3e. You can also gain access by typing the title of the speech reference into a Google search window or by doing the same on the TED Talks or YouTube sites.

CHECKLIST

☐ **Are your sources used as evidence to support your claims consistent and accurate?**

☐ **Do your statistics make sense, or are they questionable or even manufactured?**

☐ **Are any sources biased? If so, find different sources that do not stand to gain money, prestige, power, or influence from taking a particular point of view.**

☐ Are your experts quoted within their field of expertise? If not, find those that are.

☐ If you attack someone's character or trustworthiness, is it backed by credible evidence, or is it an ad hominem fallacy of diversion from real issues?

☐ Does your claim rest on popular opinion only? Remember that majorities have historically taken positions that sometimes were shockingly bigoted or wrong.

☐ If you cite a poll or survey, is the sample random or self-selected? Is the sample size sufficient (margin of error should not exceed about 3%)?

☐ Are any claims supported only by a single example? Beware of committing a hasty generalization.

☐ Are you claiming a causal relationship based only on a correlation? Remember that a correlation is not a causation.

☐ If arguing from analogy, are there significant points of difference between the two things compared, making it a false analogy?

CRITICAL THINKING QUESTIONS

1. Is it ever ethical to use fallacies to achieve a righteous goal?

2. Are some fallacies more serious and dangerous than others? If so, which ones are the most dangerous and why?

NOTE: Online **student resources**, such as practice tests, flashcards, and other activities, can be accessed at www.oup.com/he/rothwell-ps3e

Informative Speaking

Two theorists speak metaphorically of surfing, swimming, and drowning in information to underline the need to manage it effectively (Crawford & Gorman, 1996). Although discussing information in the context of electronic technology, their metaphors seem applicable to informative speaking. An informative speech with too little information presented is unsatisfying to an audience. This is analogous to surfing, merely skimming the top of a subject without delving deeply. Presenting too much information is analogous to drowning, swamping an audience in a tidal wave of information too voluminous to appreciate or comprehend. An informative speech works best when the speaker swims in the information, finding the right balance between too little and too much information for the audience. In this chapter, the focus is on constructing and presenting a specific type of speech—the informative speech—that must find that right balance between too much and too little information.

Everywhere you look, informative speaking occurs. YouTube and other Internet sites provide access to all manner of informative speeches from education and industry, some great (see especially www.ted.com) and some not so great. Teachers spend the bulk of their time in the classroom speaking informatively. Managers present information at meetings. Religious leaders speak informatively when interpreting religious doctrines and organizing fund drives, charitable activities, and special events. Students give informative presentations in a wide variety of courses and disciplines. Competent informative speaking is a valuable skill.

The principal purpose of this chapter is to explain how you construct and present a competent informative speech. Toward that end, this chapter discusses (1) the differences between informative and persuasive speeches, (2) the types of informative speeches, and (3) guidelines and strategies for delivering competent informative speeches.

DISTINGUISHING INFORMATIVE FROM PERSUASIVE SPEAKING

The overriding difference between an informative and persuasive speech is your general purpose. *The general purpose of an informative speech is to **teach** your audience something new, interesting, and useful.* You want your listeners to learn. *The general purpose of a persuasive speech is to **convince** your listeners to change their viewpoint and behavior.* You want your listeners to think and act differently.

Do not think of informative and persuasive speeches as opposites. They differ more by degree than in kind. A teacher, for example, is primarily interested in informing students, but controversial issues arise, and advocacy of a particular theory or perspective may occur. So teaching is not purely informative. Persuasive speeches also inform. You often have to teach your audience about the magnitude of a problem that listeners may not have been aware of before advocating solutions. For example, have you heard of light pollution—the biological and ecological disrupting influence of bright artificial lights at night, especially the result of newer LEDs? Nighttime across the globe is becoming increasingly

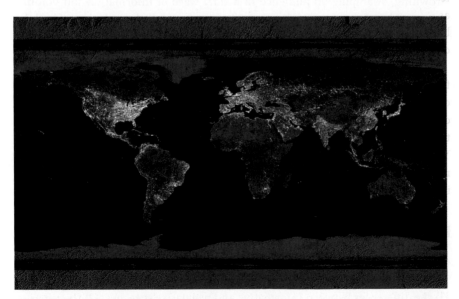

PHOTO 14.1: Light pollution, the disrupting influence of bright artificial lights at night, makes an interesting informative topic. Audiences sometimes have to be taught first about a subject as a prelude to possible persuasion later.

lighter, and this disrupts human sleep patterns, migration, and reproduction patterns of birds, fish, and other life forms, including plant life (Dunn, 2017). You may have to explain a problem before advocating solutions.

There are two specific distinctions between informative and persuasive speeches. They can help you understand where a speech falls on the informative–persuasive continuum.

Noncontroversial Information: Staying Neutral

Informative speeches do not usually stir disagreement and dissension. It is hard to imagine any audience getting worked into a froth if you offered study tips to improve students' test scores or ways to avoid the common cold, as long as the information is accurate. Teachers provide a cornucopia of information to advance students' understanding of subject matter without controversy arising. Some information, however, can ignite dissension even if presented as purely informational. Teaching evolution in schools is such an example. Explaining cultural differences, especially when they touch on gender roles and expectations, can be controversial no matter how neutrally presented, as any teacher of anthropology has likely confronted. Rutgers University Professor of Marine Science Jennifer Francis (2018) offers this unsettling information: "The last time the Arctic was only slightly warmer than today—about 125,000 years ago—oceans were 13 to 20 feet higher. Goodbye Miami, New Orleans . . . New York City and Silicon Valley, as well as Venice, London and Shanghai" (p. 50). Those are the "neutral" facts, but they cry out for "what must we do to stop this calamity?" and that's when controversy typically emerges.

Nevertheless, presenting all relevant, credible sides on an issue in a neutral fashion focuses on teaching something new, interesting, or useful, not on advocating a specific point of view. For example: "I've explained three ways that you can build your finances for the future. Whichever one you choose, know that there is a strong financial future awaiting you" does not advocate; it informs. You are not being told which choice to make. If, however, conclusions are drawn regarding which side is correct after weighing the evidence and a specific choice is advocated, then you are trying to persuade.

Precursor to Persuasion: No Call to Action

An informative speech may arouse your listeners' concern on a subject. This concern may trigger a desire to correct a problem. Your informative speech may act as a precursor, or stepping stone, to a subsequent persuasive speech advocating strong action. If you hear a speech informing you of the pros and cons of hybrid cars, you might be encouraged without any prompting from the speaker to investigate such cars further or even to buy one. If a speaker relates a personal story about the rewards he or she experiences teaching young children, you might begin to consider teaching as a profession, even though the speaker never makes such an appeal.

In some cases, you may be presenting interesting information to your audience without connecting it to any particular issue, but someone in the audience might. For example, do you know who Otis Blackwell was? He died May 6, 2002, at the age of 70. He was credited with writing more than 1,000 songs that were recorded by such international stars as Elvis Presley, Ray Charles, Billy Joel, The Who, Otis Redding, James Taylor, Peggy Lee, and Jerry Lee Lewis ("Otis Blackwell," 2018). His songs sold more than 185 million copies. Providing further details about the life of this remarkable African American talent would be an interesting informative speech. Someone listening to such a speech, however, might wonder why mainstream America is mostly oblivious that Blackwell ever lived. A persuasive speech that advocates teaching more African American history to American college students might be triggered by an informative speech on Otis Blackwell.

PHOTO 14.2: Otis Blackwell wrote songs for Elvis and numerous other famous singers, but he is largely unknown to most Americans.

If you are given an assignment by your teacher to present an informative speech to the class, or are told by your boss to make a report to a committee or group, or are asked to explain a new software package to novice computer users, remember that your focus will be on teaching, not convincing your listeners. The more neutral and even-handed your presentation, the more essentially informative it is. When you take a firm stand, present only one side without critique, or advocate a change in behavior from your listeners, you have moved into persuasive territory.

The competent public speaker recognizes when persuasion is appropriate and when the specific context calls for a presentation more informative in nature. When teachers use the classroom as a platform for personal advocacy, they may step over the not always clear line between informative and persuasive speaking. Advocacy on issues directly relevant to the teaching role, such as advocating the scientific method as a means of critical thinking, is appropriate. Advocating "correct" political points of view, however, such as who to vote for in an election, can run dangerously close to proselytizing, or converting the "unbelievers," not teaching. Again, *it can be a blurry line that separates informative from persuasive speeches.*

TYPES OF INFORMATIVE SPEECHES

The issue of what constitutes an informative speech becomes clearer by looking at different types. *Informative speeches are about ideas, objects, events, procedures, concepts, and people.* How you approach each of these subjects determines the type of informative speech you present. There is some overlap, but each type has its own unique qualities.

Reports: Facts in Brief

A **report** is usually a brief, concise, informative presentation that fulfills a class assignment, updates a committee about work performed by a subcommittee, reveals the results of a study, provides recent findings, or identifies the latest developments in a current situation of interest. Students give reports in classes and during meetings of student government. Scientists give reports on research results. Press secretaries give reports, or briefings, to members of the mass media. Military officers give reports to fellow officers and to the press.

Reports need to be clearly presented. *Make sure that you have your facts straight and that all information presented is accurate.* Complex, detailed information should be summarized succinctly. Present the main points and the most significant specifics. Avoid getting lost in minutia. Use clear, interesting visual aids if necessary.

Explanations: Deeper Understanding

Unlike a simple report, which merely states the facts to an audience that often is already familiar with the topic, *speeches that seek to explain are concerned with advancing deep understanding of complex concepts, processes, events, objects, and issues for listeners who are typically unfamiliar with the material presented.*

The lecture is a common example of informative speeches that explain. Students are most familiar with this type of informative speech, having heard

PHOTO 14.3: Daily press briefings are a standard form of presenting reports.

hundreds of lectures from numerous instructors. Unlike reports that typically run about 15 minutes or fewer, lectures often last an hour or more. Also unlike most reports, lectures work best when they are highly entertaining. Attention strategies discussed extensively in Chapter 6 are extremely important to the success of a lecture. Maintaining the attention of listeners for long periods of time is a huge challenge. Teachers, celebrities, famous authors, politicians, consultants, and experts of all types use the lecture platform to share ideas.

Demonstrations: Acting Out

A **demonstration** is an informative speech that shows the audience how to use an object or perform a specific activity. Dance teachers demonstrate dance steps while explaining how best to perform the steps. Cooking and home-improvement television programs are essentially demonstration speeches. Demonstration speeches require the speaker to show the physical object or to display the activity for the audience. *A demonstration is not a mere description of objects or activities.* If you are going to give a speech on martial arts, do not ask your audience to imagine specific movements and techniques. Show them. A speech on how card tricks and magic are performed must actually demonstrate the trick slowly and clearly so the audience can understand (*see access to James Randi link at end of chapter*).

PHOTO 14.4: Lectures that explain difficult concepts need to be not just clear, but entertaining as well.

Narratives: Storytelling

One morning, a blood vessel burst in neuroanatomist Jill Bolte Taylor's brain. She was 37 years old. As a brain scientist, she realized that she had a rare opportunity to witness her own stroke and understand what was happening while it occurred: movement, speech, memory, and self-awareness all became impaired. As she observed, "How many brain scientists have been able to study the brain from the inside out? I've gotten as much out of this experience of losing my left mind as I have in my entire academic career" (quoted in "Jill Bolte Taylor: Neuroanatomist," 2008). She spent eight years recovering her ability to walk, talk, and think. She tells her amazing story of what it was like experiencing a stroke and what it took to recover from it in a bestselling book titled *My Stroke of Insight: A Brain Scientist's Personal Journey*. She also gave an 18-minute narrative presentation at the TED conference in Monterey, California, on February 27, 2008, explaining what her stroke was like and what insights she learned. Her story is intensely moving. By the conclusion, she is in tears, as are many in the audience. It became one of the top 10 presentations for the TED organization (*see access to link at end of chapter*).

A story well told, such as Dr. Taylor's fascinating journey, can be thoroughly engaging (Zak, 2014). Our brains respond "with more focus and engagement when we hear stories than facts" (Werk, 2017). Why do we watch movies if not

PHOTO 14.5: Neuroanatomist Dr. Jill Bolte Taylor suffered a severe stroke and told her story at a TED lecture titled "My Stroke of Insight" (also the title of her book).

to enjoy storytelling? Why do we attend speeches delivered by individuals with an interesting story to tell? Our brains are wired to enjoy storytelling (Hsu, 2008).

Narratives may be about you or about other people. Instructors may give a short presentation at the beginning of a course informing students about number of years spent teaching, where teaching occurred, the joys and challenges of teaching, and prospects for teaching in the future. Also relating really dumb things tried in the classroom that went embarrassingly wrong can make a professor seem more human and approachable. Narratives may be historical ("The Struggles of Rosa Parks"), personal ("My Life as a Surgeon"), self-disclosive ("I once lived a life of drug addiction"), or merely amusing ("What It's Like Being a Technophobe"). Narratives are most effective when they entertain an audience.

Speeches That Compare: Balancing the Pros and Cons

Some informative speeches explain serious problems that exist and then compare a variety of potential solutions without taking a stand on any of the remedies offered. For example, increasing prices of college textbooks is a recognized national problem. There are several possible solutions: increasing the availability of used books, using open-source public domain materials available for e-readers, establishing textbook rental programs, urging professors to adopt only textbooks that have minimal ancillaries (websites, CDs, etc.), discouraging publishers from producing new editions sooner than every three to four years, encouraging customized versions of textbooks, and offering more "stripped down" versions of standard textbooks that can be priced more cheaply than more elaborate versions. Each of these solutions has pros and cons. For instance, expanding the availability of used books means more students can purchase textbooks at three-quarters the cost of a new textbook ($75 used compared to $100 new), but as the availability of used books increases, textbook publishers are pressured to increase the cost of new versions of textbooks to counter losses engendered by used books. Presenting the positives and negatives of various solutions without taking a stand on any of them is structured as an informative speech. You leave it to the audience to make choices based on a balanced presentation of possible remedies for a problem.

These five types of informative speeches can overlap. A report may occasionally veer into a demonstration when listeners appear confused about what is reported. A teacher typically lectures for a majority of a class period, but the teacher may do demonstrations to add variety and make a point more memorable and meaningful. I have used a fairly lengthy demonstration of a polygraph, or lie-detector machine, using student volunteers, to drive home several points related to nonverbal communication and connotative meaning related to words. It never fails to engender interest, even fascination, from the class. Years later, students tell me they still remember that particular demonstration and what it showed.

GUIDELINES FOR COMPETENT INFORMATIVE SPEAKING

In general, informative speeches work best when the information presented is clear, accurate, and interesting instead of opaque, wrong, and boring. Thus, *review Chapter 6 on attention, Chapter 8 on outlining and organizing your informative speech, Chapter 11 on visual aids, and Chapter 13 on reasoning and use of evidence.* This section provides additional tips for presenting effective informative speeches.

Be Informative: Tell Us What We Do Not Know

Your first guideline for an effective informative speech, and seemingly most obvious, is to provide new information to your listeners. I say seemingly obvious because I have sat through far too many "informative" presentations that never told me a thing I did not know previously, and in some cases the speaker should have known that the points made were trivial and lacked any insight. If your listeners say after your presentation, "I didn't learn a thing," then you have been ineffective. This does not mean that everything you present must be new information, but the emphasis should be on providing information that is not widely known.

PHOTO 14.6: To be informative, tell us what we do not know already, or isn't obvious.

Adapt to Your Audience: Topic Choice and Knowledge Base

How do you know whether your informative speech goes beyond what your listeners already know? That requires an analysis of your audience (see Chapter 3). If the topic choice is at your discretion, then choose what will likely interest your listeners and is well suited to their knowledge, concerns, and expectations. If the subject of your speech is too high level, complex, and abstract for the educational level of your audience, then you have chosen poorly. Presenting information on systems theory or thermodynamics will not resonate with very young audiences because the information is well over their heads. Set theory in mathematics will probably baffle a lot of adult audiences.

If the choice is not up to you and the topic is very high level, complex, and abstract (a professor teaching quantum physics to students), your challenge is to explain clearly each facet of your subject. *Use multiple examples, personal stories, visual aids, metaphors, analogies, and demonstrations to clarify difficult material.* Albert Einstein, when faced with explaining his immensely complex theory of relativity to laypeople, offered this as a starting point: "When you sit with a nice girl for 2 hours you think it's only a minute. But when you sit on a hot stove for a minute you think it's 2 hours. That's relativity" (quoted in "Famous Quotes and Authors," 2009). Remember that oral style requires simpler language than written style. Strive for language simplicity as discussed in Chapter 9, and avoid highly complex language that may confuse even a well-educated audience.

If your subject is fairly simple and you are addressing an educated audience, be careful not to condescend to your listeners. Acting as though they are third graders is patronizing and will insult them. If your audience is already knowledgeable about your subject, more difficult material can be included earlier and with less need to elaborate extensively.

Avoid Information Overload: Beware the Data Dump

A chief challenge you face when constructing an informative speech is typically not too little information available on your subject but too much (Silver, 2012). Separating the useless from the useful information takes effort. The ready availability of huge quantities of information because of computer technologies also can tempt a speaker to provide way too much detail and complexity in a speech. Avoid the tedious "data dump." Know when to quit. Preparation and practice are essential. Prepare a well-organized informative speech, then practice the speech and *time it precisely* while giving it beforehand. Timing your speech will immediately indicate whether you have provided way too much information for the time allotted. Be careful not to offer needless detail. *Ask yourself, "Do they really need to know this?"*

Tell Your Story Well: Narrative Tips

Stories can be short vignettes or lengthy detailed narratives. Randy Pausch, a 47-year-old Carnegie Mellon University computer science professor who contracted pancreatic cancer, gave a lecture at his university on September 18, 2007, to a crowd of 500 students, faculty, and friends. In a 75-minute presentation, Pausch told many stories about his life, each relating to his central idea about achieving his childhood dreams. His stories were humorous, poignant, and very entertaining. Although he knew he was dying, he conducted himself as though he were perfectly healthy, at one moment dropping to the floor and doing push-ups both one- and two-handed. When he finished his final lecture, his audience gave him a prolonged, standing ovation. The video of his lecture was seen by millions on YouTube (*see access to link at end of chapter*), and it became a book titled *The Last Lecture*.

How do you tell an effective story when giving an informative speech (see Friend, 2013; Karia, 2015)?

1. *Choose a story that fits your audience.* A story about the challenge and strategies of online poker playing will not likely resonate with an audience that abhors gambling.

2. *Make sure that the story fits your purpose and illustrates a key point.* You should not tell stories just to entertain if they have no relevance.

3. *Keep the stories concise.* Do not get bogged down in details that can become confusing or tedious for your listeners or lose sight of the key theme. If a detail does not advance the story but sidetracks it, cut it.

4. Remember that the typical structure of a narrative has *three main components: challenge, struggle, and resolution.* Jill Bolte Taylor's speech is a perfect example.

5. *Practice telling your story.* Tell it to friends, family members, or anyone who will listen.

6. *Do not read your story to your listeners.* You want to sound natural, not artificial.

7. *Be animated, even visual, when telling a story.* If you are not interested in telling the story, why should your listeners care? Pausch was very engaging because he was unafraid to do push-ups, wear a crazy-looking Jabberwocky hat, and walk around with fake arrows in his back while lecturing.

Terry Hershey is a Protestant minister who for more than three decades has presented enormously popular lectures at the annual Religious Education Congress in Anaheim, California. He tells this story often at this conference to make the point that we learn very early in life to fear making mistakes:

PHOTO 14.7: Remember that most stories told effectively have three main components: challenge, struggle, and resolution.

There's a terrific story about a first-grade Sunday school class. The children were restless and fussy. The teacher, in an attempt to get their attention, said, "Okay kids, let's play a game. I'll describe something to you. And you tell me what it is."

The kids quieted down. "Listen. It's a furry little animal with a big bushy tail, that climbs up trees and stores nuts in the winter. Who can tell me what it is?" No one said anything. The teacher went on. "You are a good Sunday school class. You know the right answer to this question. It's a furry little animal with a big bushy tail, that climbs up trees and stores nuts in the winter." One little girl raised her hand. "Emily?" "Well, teacher," Emily declared, "it sounds like a squirrel to me, but I'll say Jesus." *(Hershey, 2000, pp. 100–101)*

Unfailingly, when Hershey tells this story, the audience roars with laughter. The story is brief, humorous, has a challenge (guess the right answer), a struggle (kids trying to figure out what the teacher wants), and a resolution that fits the audience perfectly because it has religious overtones; it also has a moral to the story that is delivered in an animated style (you had to be there) and is told fluently as though Hershey has told this story many times.

Terry Hershey is a great storyteller because he has clearly practiced the art of telling a narrative (*see access to link at end of chapter*). Each of you has stories to tell, whether they be personal experiences, stories told to you by parents, relatives, or friends, or perhaps stories you have seen and heard presented on television, on the Internet, or at Sunday sermons. When you are researching your topic, notice clever, amusing, poignant, and powerful stories told by others. You can retell many of these to make a point. "Let me tell you a story" immediately perks up an audience.

For a lengthy example of an informative speech, consult **Appendix A** *at the end of this text.* A written text is provided with application of material relevant to making effective informative speeches.

SUMMARY

A key difference between informative and persuasive speaking is that informative speeches attempt to teach listeners something new, and persuasive speeches, although oftentimes informative, move beyond and attempt to change attitudes and behavior. There are five types of informative speeches that sometimes overlap during the same presentation: those that report, explain, demonstrate, tell a story, or compare pros and cons of a proposal without taking a position. Competent informative speaking is achieved by providing new information, considering your audience when choosing a topic, organizing carefully, avoiding information overload, keeping your audience interested, using supporting materials competently, and telling stories well.

TED TALKS AND YOUTUBE VIDEOS

Narrative and Explanation: "Your Brain Hallucinates Your Conscious Reality"

Informative or Persuasive Speech? "Dalia Mogahed: What Do You Think When You Look at Me?"

Powerful Informative Speech: "Randy Pausch's Last Lecture: Achieving Your Childhood Dreams"

Powerful Informative Speech: "Jill Bolte Taylor: Stroke of Insight"

Effective Narrative: "REC2015, Period 4: Rev. Terry Hershey"

Demonstration: "James Randi Demonstrates How 'Psychic' Uri Geller Bends Spoons and Other Magic Tricks"

Narrative Speech: "Dananjaya Hettiarachchi World Champion of Public Speaking 2014—Full Speech"

For relevant links to these TED Talks and YouTube videos, see the *Practically Speaking* Companion Website: www.oup.com/he/rothwell-ps3e. You can also gain access by typing the title of the speech reference into a Google search window or by doing the same on the TED Talks or YouTube sites.

CHECKLIST

☐ Know the differences between informative and persuasive speaking.

☐ Tell your audience what it likely does not know already.

☐ Choose a topic, if it is an option, that would appeal to your particular audience.

☐ Be sure that the amount of information fits the time limit for your speech.

☐ Follow the tips for telling stories effectively.

☐ Don't forget to use attention strategies to keep interest (Chapter 6).

☐ Carefully outline and organize your speech, following guidelines discussed in detail in Chapter 8.

☐ Use visual aids when appropriate, and follow the guidelines provided in Chapter 11.

☐ Strive for accuracy: consult Chapter 5 on supporting materials and Chapter 13 on fallacies.

CRITICAL THINKING QUESTIONS

1. When might an informative speech become dangerous?

2. Is "stretching the truth" ever ethical and permissible in an informative speech?

NOTE: Online **student resources**, such as practice tests, flashcards, and other activities, can be accessed at www.oup.com/he/rothwell-ps3e

Foundations of Persuasive Speaking

t was the sixtieth annual convention of the California Federation of Teachers (CFT). Keynote speaker Charles Kernaghan, director of the National
Labor Committee, was addressing an audience of California teachers. His
central idea (theme) was that extreme poverty of much of the world's workforce accrues from economic globalization and the exploitation of workers. His
speech was a rousing anti-sweatshop call to arms. Kernaghan held up garments
produced overseas, and he told stories of the exploitation of workers who made
these garments, most of whom are between the ages of 6 and 16. He argued
that young people "have a right to ask, how do the people live who produce
the clothes they wear?" ("Anti-Sweatshop Activist," 2002, p. 4). Kernaghan discussed the Students Against Sweatshops movement in the United States and
its hundreds of chapters on college campuses. The audience cheered when he
thundered, "These kids are on fire!" Kernaghan brought his listeners to their
feet when he concluded, "There can never be peace without social justice, or in
a world with child labor" (p. 4).

Kernaghan's speech was masterful and an enormous success. "Of all the
speakers at the 60th annual convention, none stirred delegates as deeply
as Charles Kernaghan," reported the article in *California Teacher* ("Anti-
Sweatshop Activist," 2002, p. 4). His speech was successful for several reasons. First, the CFT convention had social justice as one of its primary
themes. As members of a powerful teachers' union, listeners were receptive

to Kernaghan's message that non-union workers can be and are exploited as "cheap labor." Second, he evidently researched his topic very carefully. He had the facts to support his claims. Third, he used very effective attention strategies. His speech was not a dry recitation of facts and figures; it was a passionate presentation that was at times intense, startling, and vital in its depiction of the plight of garment workers in countries around the world. It aroused anger at injustice. He told stories about young women he interviewed who worked in deplorable sweatshop conditions for $1.38 a day after expenses. Fourth, he ended with a rousing appeal to stamp out exploitation of workers worldwide.

Possessing the persuasive knowledge and skills demonstrated by Kernaghan has practical significance. Although the anti-sweatshop student movement continues because the problem remains a global tragedy (Rathe, 2017), persuasion is central to making important change occur in a variety of other arenas. Persuasion is an integral part of being a lawyer, manager, administrator, salesperson, public relations specialist, political office holder, consultant, religious leader, or an abundance of other career choices. What is a job interview if not an exercise in public speaking persuasion? News networks interview individuals every day who engage in persuasive speaking before the cameras. Most talk shows display

PHOTO 15.1: Think of all the professions and careers that depend on persuasive public speaking, a courtroom lawyer being just one example.

persuasive speaking from panelists and audience members, although many of these persuasive attempts are dismal efforts by unskilled and untrained speakers. Individuals often are required to speak persuasively in courtrooms, classrooms, cultural events, and other venues.

Almost 2,500 years ago, Aristotle systematically discussed persuasion in his influential book *Rhetoric*. The scientific study of persuasion, however, began less than a century ago in the United States. Much has been learned from this research on persuasion, providing many insights for you to learn that go well beyond the useful observations provided by Aristotle. Capitalizing on this research and insight, ***the primary purpose of this chapter is to explain the foundations of persuasive speaking***. Toward that end, this chapter discusses (1) the goals of persuasion, (2) the relationship between attitude change and behavior change, (3) the elaboration likelihood model that explains how persuasion works generally, (4) the types of propositional claims that characterize specific persuasive messages, and (5) the influence of culture on persuasion. *Specific persuasive strategies for public speaking based on an understanding of these foundations of persuasion are discussed in the next chapter.*

DEFINING PERSUASION

Persuasion is a communication process of converting, modifying, or maintaining the attitudes and/or behavior of others. In Chapter 3, an **attitude** was defined as "a learned predisposition to respond favorably or unfavorably toward some attitude object" (Gass & Seiter, 2014). "The iPhone is better than the Droid phone" is an attitude and so is "Consistency requires you to be as ignorant today as you were a year ago" (Bernard Berenson) or "All I know is one of us is right and the other one is you" (poster). An attitude sets our mind to draw certain judgments.

Although much effort to persuade audiences is aimed at attitude change, behavior of others can change without attitude change. Threats of violence may produce behavioral change without changing attitudes. Forced compliance from threats of physical harm, damage to one's reputation, financial ruin, and the like, however, are usually seen as coercion, not persuasion.

The perception of free choice is the essential difference between coercion and persuasion (O'Keefe, 2016; Perloff, 2017). Those who coerce seek to eliminate choice by force, threats of force, or intimidation. Those who seek to persuade do so with logic, evidence, and psychological appeals that leave listeners free to choose whether to change their attitudes and/or their behavior.

PHOTO 15.2: Where on the persuasion–coercion continuum does this demonstration lie? Explain.

GOALS OF PERSUASION

Persuasive speaking can have several goals. Choosing the appropriate goal for the situation will largely determine your degree of success or failure.

Conversion: Radical Persuasion

Psychologist Muzafer Sherif and his associates (1965) developed the **social judgment theory** of persuasion to explain attitude change (see also Littlejohn & Foss, 2017). Their theory states that when listeners hear a persuasive message, they compare it with attitudes they already hold. The core preexisting attitude on an issue serves as an **anchor**, or reference point. Surrounding this anchor is a range of possible attitudes an individual may hold. Positions a person finds tolerable form his or her **latitude of acceptance**. Positions that produce only a neutral or ambivalent response form the **latitude of noncommitment**. Those positions the person would find objectionable because they are too far from the anchor attitude form the **latitude of rejection**. Figure 15.1 depicts this range of possible opinions on an issue. Persuasive messages that fall within a person's latitude of rejection almost never produce a change in attitude (Sherif et al., 1965). *The further away a position is from the anchor attitude, the less likely persuasion will be successful* (Sherif et al., 1973; Littlejohn & Foss, 2017).

Strongly Agree	Agree	Indifferent	Disagree	Strongly Disagree
Anchor	**Latitude of Acceptance**	**Latitude of Noncommitment**		**Lat. of Rejection**
College should be free	Minimal tuition & fees can be charged	Public colleges should be supported by taxes		Students should pay entire cost or students should pay at least 75% of cost

FIGURE 15.1: Social Judgment Theory and Persuasion.

Social judgment theory strongly suggests that setting conversion as your goal for persuasive speaking is usually unrealistic. Conversion asks your listeners to move from their anchor position, such as generous tax cuts for corporations, to a completely contradictory position that falls within their latitude of rejection, such as significant corporate tax increases. If your message seeks conversion from your audience, it will likely meet with quick resistance, especially if your listeners have strongly formed attitudes on the subject. Hearing a 10-minute persuasive speech, no matter how eloquent, rarely converts anyone holding strong views.

Conversion usually occurs over time and often requires a significant emotional event to motivate such radical attitude change. For example, if you have been a strong gun control advocate, but experience a home invasion that threatened your life and the lives of family members, you may think seriously about purchasing a handgun for protection. Even a significant emotional event, however, doesn't necessarily alter strongly held attitudes. The massacre of innocent school children certainly qualifies as a significant emotional event. Even after repeated mass school shootings, however, and powerful speeches by student survivors of the Marjory Stoneman Douglas High School massacre at the huge March 24, 2018 demonstration in Washington, DC, attitudes have changed little. An October 2018 Pew Research study found that attitudes favoring stricter gun laws increased only marginally from 52% in 2017 to 57% in 2018 ("Gun Policy Remains Divisive," 2018). Conversion, then, is an unrealistic goal for most persuasive speeches, especially short classroom presentations.

Modification: Do Not Ask for the Moon

Incremental change, not abrupt, major change is far more likely to be persuasive (Rhodes, 2015). For example, just for the sake of illustration, let's suppose that Medicare for all U.S. citizens is a person's anchor position. Recognizing that this requires major attitude adjustment from her audience, this speaker instead advocates only a modification, namely, expanding Medicare to include 50–64-year-old U.S. citizens. This modified position likely falls within the speaker's latitude of acceptance—it is not objectionable—and it is more likely to persuade her audience

CARTOON 15.1: Conversion from one strong belief to a contradictory belief is highly unlikely to occur, especially from a single speech. Would this speaker's appearance pose an issue of identification with his audience?

than a Medicare-for-everyone advocacy. On a national level, this moderate expansion of Medicare could be a stepping stone for further expansion to all citizens who have no employer provided health insurance and are below the age of 50. Subsequent persuasive efforts may even move incrementally until Medicare for all U.S. citizens becomes a reality. The change in attitude occurs bit by bit. It is rarely a one-time effort to move audiences toward major change. *Modification of attitudes and behavior incrementally is an appropriate, realistic goal for a persuasive speech.*

Maintenance: Keep 'Em Coming Back

When most people think of persuasion, changing attitudes and behavior immediately comes to mind. Much persuasion, however, does not aim to produce change. Few in that audience of active labor organizers and CFT members for Charles Kernaghan's speech would have disagreed with much of what Kernaghan said in his rousing oration. This same speech, however, would likely trigger a much less favorable reaction from an audience composed of Chamber of Commerce members or small business owners who depend on selling inexpensive clothing to stay competitive in a tough business climate.

PHOTO 15.3: The goal of persuasive speaking is sometimes just maintaining current attitudes and motivating corresponding behavior such as occur at political conventions.

Most advertising of well-established products, such as Coke or the Toyota Camry, aims to maintain buying habits of the public. The goal is to keep consumers purchasing their products over and over and preventing purchases of competing products. In political campaigns, initial persuasion is usually aimed at "securing the base." This means motivating Democrats to keep voting for Democratic candidates and to keep Republicans voting for Republican candidates. The message is "do what you've been doing." Sunday sermons usually change few minds because most people who attend a church service require no such change. They already believe the religious dogmas articulated by the religious leader. "Preaching to the choir," however, can inspire the faithful, energize believers, and reinforce preexisting attitudes.

ATTITUDE–BEHAVIOR CONSISTENCY

Very often, changing attitudes is not sufficient. It is behavior we seek to change, and behavior does not always correspond to attitudes. Consider the abstinence-only programs to prevent premarital sex among teenagers. Despite a vigorous campaign, and speeches galore at high school assemblies to convince teenagers to take a public pledge to abstain from premarital sex, a careful analysis of data reveals that those who took the "virginity pledge" were just as likely as non-pledgers within a five-year period to have had premarital sex. They also were less likely to use birth control, and pregnancy was more likely (Lehmiller, 2017). If a principal purpose of abstinence-only programs is to prevent teen pregnancy and all the problems associated with it, then the evidence on virginity pledges is quite disheartening. The pledge (stated attitude) does not produce the desired behavior (abstinence). There are other ways to strengthen abstinence-only persuasive efforts (see Jemmott et al., 2010), but inducing teens to make public pledges of abstinence is, by itself, unlikely to produce actual abstinence. So, asking your audience to make a verbal pledge (e.g., abstaining from drugs; getting better grades) may be an exercise in futility. You'll need more effective persuasive public speaking strategies.

Why are there inconsistencies in our attitudes and behaviors that directly affect our choice of persuasive speaking strategies? Several variables affect how consistent our attitudes and behaviors are likely to be.

Direct Experience: No Secondhand Attitudes

Attitudes that are formed from direct experience usually conform more closely to actual behavior than those formed more indirectly (Perloff, 2017). When you have encountered a problem in your life, thought about it, felt its implications, and considered appropriate responses, your relevant attitude has been formed through direct experience. Have you ever been unemployed or experienced poverty or had to solicit money from strangers? Have you ever been a small business owner who has worried about high taxes jeopardizing your ability to thrive or even survive? That is direct experience. Your attitudes about food stamps for the poor, unemployment benefits, and business taxation are likely influenced strongly by these directly related experiences. Your behavior toward those similarly disadvantaged is more apt to coincide with these attitudes than if you have only indirect experience of such things.

Even forming relationships with individuals who have experienced problems of discrimination, for example, brings you closer to direct experience of that problem than if you have no such relationships. In a Pew Research Center poll, about a third of respondents cited a personal relationship with a gay or lesbian person as the reason they now support same-sex marriage ("Gay Marriage," 2013). Robb Willer, professor of sociology at Stanford University, explains why this occurs: "When people have the opportunity to hear a person's story and feel empathy for that person, they're more willing to consider a new political view" (quoted by DeCourcey, 2016).

Those attitudes that are shaped more indirectly by media images or by your participation in discussion with strangers on blogging sites tend to be inconsistently related to actual behavior. These *"secondhand attitudes"* (Gass & Seiter, 2014) derived from indirect experience usually serve as weak predictors of behavior because, when faced with actual situations, the attitudes are more borrowed than personal. For example, it is far easier to ignore panhandlers begging for money when you have never had the desperate, frightening experience of joblessness and homelessness. Directly formed attitudes derived from personal experience are also likely to be more strongly held than secondhand attitudes.

So, how is this information tied to your public speaking? *The more directly you can make your audience feel that they are affected by the problem you describe or empathize with those afflicted, the greater is the chance that listeners' behavior will move in the direction you advocate in your speech.* For example, state budget cuts may seem abstract and even a dull "wonkish" issue, but if you can directly tie such cuts to your student audience's ability to get access to higher education, then you improve your chances of gaining listeners' votes on a state proposition to increase taxes. For example:

> If you don't vote for Proposition X on Tuesday, your annual tuition to attend this college will increase by 25% next year and 35% the following year. Financial aid will not cover such a huge increase. The Legislative Analyst's Office estimated last month on its website that at least 400,000 students in this state will be forced to drop out of college because of these massive tuition hikes. Can you really afford to continue your college education if Proposition X is defeated?

Make your audience "feel the pain."

Social Pressure: Getting Heat from Others

Social pressure has been shown to be a very strong influence on human behavior (Brewer et al., 2017), and it is a significant reason why your attitudes and behavior may be inconsistent at times (Wallace at al., 2005). You may want to speak up when someone makes a bigoted remark, but you may remain quiet if you fear social disapproval from others for being a "troublemaker." You may not particularly enjoy drinking alcohol, but maybe you drink to excess at parties because it is the social expectation of your peer group. In 2015, the drought emergency in California prompted the governor at the time, Jerry Brown, to set a statewide water conservation target of 25%. California consumers met this goal in 2016 when El Niño rain storms provided some much-needed relief (Smith, 2016). A principal reason for the significant drop in water usage was social pressure (Krieger & Mattson, 2015). If your lawn is green when your neighbors have let theirs go brown from lack of water, you become a social pariah for not joining others in the conservation effort.

Social pressure and fear of disapproval make standing before an audience and giving a speech that you know will incite a negative reaction very challenging. You want your peers to like and accept you, so you may be tempted to say what your audience is comfortable hearing but conflicts with your true attitude. Sometimes, however, you have to take a public stand that will likely invite disapproval. Otherwise, your attitude and behavior are inconsistent.

Effort Required: Degree of Difficulty

Despite the best intentions, attitudes and behavior will often be inconsistent because consistency may require too great an effort to perform the behavior (Wallace et al., 2005). For example, you know that regular exercise is good for your health (attitude), but it also can require great effort to start and stay with an exercise program (behavior). It can be time consuming, uncomfortable, and difficult. It requires substantial effort. Reducing that perceived effort by making it fun (e.g., dance routines; walks on the beach), readily accessible (e.g., exercise equipment available at home), or a series of short exercise events (e.g., going up and down stairs several times a day instead of a half-hour workout on an exercycle) can increase daily exercise (Itkowitz, 2016).

CARTOON 15.2: Attitudes and behavior are not always consistent. Here the attitude is "smoking is bad for me and I should quit," but the behavior persists because the effort required to quit is difficult due to addiction. Thus, changing an attitude will not necessarily change a behavior. Just because you want to quit smoking doesn't necessarily mean that you will.

When trying to persuade an audience to act on a problem, find the easiest ways for listeners to express their support. Signing a petition or donating a dollar on the spot after your speech is an easy way to show support. Asking listeners to canvass neighborhoods, to call strangers on the phone to solicit support for a cause or a candidate, or to raise money for a program is hampered by the effort required to perform the behavior. Far less participation in such activities should be expected as a result.

Consider how student Sean McLaughlin (1996) offers simple, yet effective, solutions for the problem of food poisoning:

> First, wash hands well and wash them often. . . . If you prefer to use sponges and dishcloths, be sure to throw them in the dishwasher two or three times a week. Also, try color coding your sponges—the red one for washing dishes and a blue one for wiping up countertops. . . . Experts also suggest using both sides of a cutting board—one side for meats and the other side for vegetables. And those who wash dishes by hand, be careful. Scrub dishes vigorously with an antibacterial soap and rinse with hot water. Air drying is preferred to drying with a towel. . . . Finally, and perhaps the best advice—don't become lax when it comes to food safety in your home. Don't write your congressperson, write your mom. As we have seen today, re-educating yourself and spreading the word on kitchen safety can significantly reduce chances of food poisoning. *(p. 75)*

This speaker provides several easy steps that will protect you from food poisoning. One step, air drying dishes, actually reduces labor. Towel drying requires effort; air drying requires merely waiting.

Solutions to serious problems offered in your speech cannot always be simple and easy to implement. Nevertheless, try to suggest ways that even complex solutions can be implemented in relatively simple, straightforward steps.

ELABORATION LIKELIHOOD MODEL

The **elaboration likelihood model** (ELM) of persuasion is an overarching explanation for how listeners cope with the bombardment of persuasive messages by sorting them into those that are important, or central, and those that are less relevant, or peripheral (Petty & Cacioppo, 1986a, 1986b). The *central route* is mindful—the content of the message is scrutinized for careful reasoning and substantial, credible evidence. Counterarguments are considered and weighed. Questions come to mind, and a desire for more information (elaboration) emerges. This is skepticism in action. The *peripheral route* is relatively mindless—little attention is given to processing a persuasive message. The listener looks for mental shortcuts to make quick decisions. Credibility, likability, and attractiveness of a persuader, how other people react to the message, and the consequences that might result from agreeing or disagreeing with the persuader are some of the shortcuts used in the peripheral route (Shadel et al., 2001).

Mainstream and social media are quick to latch on to peripheral cues of persuasion that work for or against an individual or group. For example, the Twitterverse went into hyperdrive during the 2012 Joe Biden–Paul Ryan vice-presidential debate, excessively focusing on Biden's flamboyant style of presentation and Ryan's seeming need to drain a reservoir of water during the debate. Biden's "smiles of contempt" and exaggerated facial expressions became a focus. A video was released on the Internet afterward showing Ryan drinking substantial quantities of water 22 times during the 90-minute exchange, suggesting that he was extremely nervous. Peripheral cues that an audience views as positive or negative may render carefully prepared arguments (central processing) relatively inconsequential. Our attention becomes distracted by the noise of peripheral cues.

To illustrate the two routes to persuasion working in tandem, consider an example offered by Gass and Seiter (2014). Michael and Maria are on a date and about to order dinner at a nice restaurant. The waiter suggests several specials, all of them meat or fish. He even volunteers which one is his favorite. Maria orders first. She is very careful to choose only vegetarian dishes from the menu. She asks the waiter whether an entrée is cooked in animal fat, if there is butter in the pasta, and if the sauce contains any dairy products. Maria turns to Michael and says with an animated delivery that he should eat vegetarian because scientific evidence shows that it is healthier, and it reduces animal deaths. Michael has

PHOTO 15.4: Joe Biden's "facial calisthenics" in his 2012 debate against Paul Ryan were peripheral cues that, at times, comically distracted from his central arguments (Bruni, 2012).

no strong opinion on the subject, but he is very attracted to Maria. He tells the waiter, "I'll have what she ordered." Maria used the central route to decide her order. She was very mindful of her decision. She considered her decision very carefully because it was important to her. Michael, on the other hand, used the peripheral route. The decision was relatively unimportant to him so he based his order on a cue unrelated to the menu, the waiter's preference, or the arguments offered by Maria. He ordered vegetarian because he wanted Maria to like him.

Listeners are more motivated to use the central route when the issues affect them personally. They are more likely to use the peripheral route when issues seem tangential to their interests and are largely inconsequential to their lives, their knowledge of a subject is limited, and they are distracted or preoccupied (Petty et al., 2004). If you were Michael in the earlier situation, you are motivated to please your date (peripheral processing), not to learn about vegetarianism, which would require careful thought (central processing). Your knowledge of issues related to vegetarianism is superficial at best, and you are distracted by your attraction to your date. It's a wonder you can think at all.

Attitude change produced by the central route tends to be more persistent, resistant to change, and predictive of behavior than attitude change produced by the peripheral route (Cooper et al., 2016). If Michael never again went on another outing with Maria, he probably would eat dead cow flesh with relish because his flirtation with vegetarianism was arrived at by peripheral influences.

PHOTO 15.5: Identify positive peripheral cues depicted in this photo. Note that both central and peripheral processing can, and often do influence listeners together to greater or lesser degree. It is called **parallel processing**.

Clearly, *central processing of persuasive messages should be encouraged because it is what skeptics do* when presented with a persuasive message (see Chapter 12). You can increase central processing when giving speeches by making issues relevant to listeners' lives. Complex, technical issues can be simplified for lay audiences. If listeners understand the basic concepts, they can analyze arguments and evidence presented. They can't if their minds are in a fog of confusion.

Because of time constraints and information overload, however, you sometimes have no choice but to use peripheral processing. That is why dressing appropriately for the speaking engagement, using language that doesn't offend and is vivid and fluid, exhibiting a poised delivery, and handling visual aids adroitly all serve an important purpose—enhancing positive peripheral cues. *The ideal, of course, is combining strong arguments (central processing) with positive peripheral cues.* This is called **parallel processing**.

PROPOSITIONS: FACT, VALUE, AND POLICY CLAIMS

Once you have decided the goal of your persuasive speech, recognized the challenge of changing both attitudes and behavior, and understand how persuasion works in general through central and peripheral routes, the next foundational decision is determining the type of persuasive claim that you want to advocate. The primary, overriding claim for a persuasive speech is called a **proposition**. A proposition presents a controversial claim, limits issues to what is relevant to that claim, and states a desired point of view (Freeley & Steinberg, 2013).

The type of proposition depends on your persuasive goal. Do you want to argue factual accuracy, suggest the worth of something, or propose change? *There are three types of propositions relevant to these three goals: fact, value, and policy.* A **proposition of fact** alleges a truth, such as *Open carry gun laws would provide significant protection against criminals.* Here you would argue factual accuracy. Each main point provides a reason supporting factual accuracy, such as

I.   Open carry gun laws provide a deterrent to serious violent crime.
II. Citizens with open carry permits can reduce bloodshed from individuals engaged in massacring innocent civilians.

Note that a proposition of fact is an assertion of fact, not a description of what is true. Propositions are controversial and debatable.

A **proposition of value** calls for a judgment that assesses the worth or merit of an idea, object, or practice. For example, twice the American Film Institute ranked the movie *Citizen Kane* as the "best American movie" ever ("*Citizen Kane*," 2007). For most college students who may never have heard of this film, or the few who have seen it, this must seem like a perplexing choice. *Citizen Kane*, released in 1941, is a black-and-white film, it has limited body count, the action is plodding by today's standards, and the special effects must seem goofy compared to CGI extravaganzas of today's blockbusters.

You attempt to justify your proposition of value by providing standards, or criteria, for assessing the value or worth of what you are claiming. Such standards can be debatable. If, for example, American movies are assigned value based on such criteria as buckets of blood and number of sex scenes, then your criteria are certainly debatable, bordering on ludicrous. Degree of cinematic experimentation and influence on American film making, however, more substantial and defensible criteria, were used to rank *Citizen Kane* as the top choice.

A proposition of value typically is organized into two main points: (1) criteria for assessing your value judgment and (2) applying those criteria to the subject of your speech. Consider speaking on this controversial proposition of value: *In general, America's best colleges are private, not public universities.* Your speech outline might be organized as follows:

I. The best American colleges should meet three criteria.
   A. Student retention rates should be at least 75%.
   B. Student graduation rates within six years should be above 75%.
   C. Quality of faculty as measured by academic publications and student evaluations should be in the top 10%.
II. Private colleges in the United States meet these criteria better than public colleges.
   A. Student retention rates are higher at most private colleges.
   B. Student graduation rates are also higher at most private colleges.
   C. Private colleges tend to attract higher quality faculty.

(Please note that claims made on this proposition of value are for illustration only. The claims are not necessarily based in fact.)

A **proposition of policy** calls for a significant change from how problems are currently handled, such as *Public higher education in the United States should be free for all American residents. The basic elements of a policy proposition are need, plan, and workability.* You want to show that a current policy is harmful (need), provide a plan (solution) to significantly reduce or eliminate the need, and show that your plan is practical (workability). These three elements can be developed in a variety of organizational patterns. The problem–solution, problem–cause–solution, and Monroe's motivated sequence discussed in Chapter 8 are three such options. **Monroe's motivated sequence**, however, is a popular choice. Consider this approach using the free higher education proposition:

I. **Attention**: Tell short stories of students who have had to drop out of college because of the staggering cost of higher education.

II. **Need**: Public higher education has become unaffordable for a significant and increasing number of students.

III. **Satisfaction**: By altering the tax code and using the billions of dollars spent on scholarships and grants, public higher education could be free.

IV. **Visualization**: California used to provide tuition-free public higher education for its residents, and its colleges and universities were the envy of the world. Imagine returning to those halcyon days again.

V. **Action**: We can make this happen by signing this petition to place an initiative on the California ballot, starting a nationwide movement to make public higher education in the United States free for all Americans.

(See **Appendix B** for a much more in-depth example of the Monroe motivated sequence organizational pattern of persuasion.)

CULTURE AND PERSUASION

The scientific investigation of persuasive speaking is a peculiarly Western interest. In Asian countries, for instance, spirited debates to influence decision making have been viewed as relatively pointless. Debates create friction and disharmony and usually end inconclusively. The idea of participating in persuasive jury deliberations and deciding court cases after hearing testimony from witnesses and closing arguments from attorneys does not immediately appeal to Japanese citizens (Johnson, 2016). There is a deep cultural reticence to express opinions in public discourse, to argue different points of view, and to question authority (Tabuchi & McDonald, 2009; Onishi, 2007). Japan began implementing a jury-style system in its criminal courts in 2009 (Vanoverbeke, 2015). To acclimate a hesitant populace to the new system, 500 mock trials were held. Nevertheless, 80% of Japanese surveyed about the new jury system expressed dread at the prospect of participating. Absence of a jury system is not unusual in Asian countries. South Korea, for example, did not institute a jury system until 2008 (Young, 2008).

Persuasive speaking works best when it is adapted to the cultural composition of your audience (see Figure 15.2). Persuasive strategies that may successfully change attitudes and behavior in an individualistic country such as the United States may not be so successful in collectivist countries (Murray-Johnson et al., 2001). **Individualist cultures** emphasize personal autonomy and competitiveness, privacy, individual liberties, and toleration of nonconformity. **Collectivist cultures** emphasize group harmony, intragroup cooperation and conformity, and individual sacrifice for the sake of the group (Hofstede & Hofstede, 2010). Appeals to order should be more persuasive in collectivist cultures, and appeals to individual rights should be more persuasive in individualist cultures.

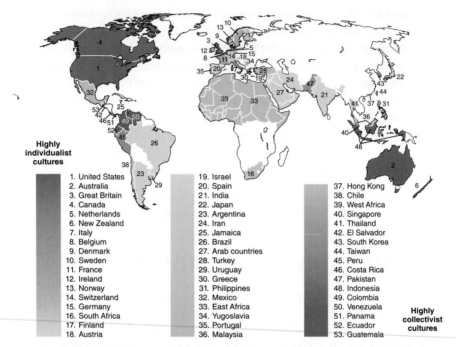

FIGURE 15.2: Map of individualist and collectivist cultures (see Hofstede & Hofstede, 2010).

For example, an American ad shows a young man at the wheel of a Cadillac CTS and presents a choice between "The nail that sits up gets hammered down" or "You can be the hammer." The first is an aphorism well known in Japan that expresses a collectivist viewpoint. The second is a clearly individualist viewpoint. Cadillac is obviously appealing to individualist values of American culture to sell cars when the ad implies being the hammer is the preferred position. Such an ad would likely backfire in Japan.

Clearly, your choice of persuasive strategies when giving speeches should be influenced by the diversity of your audience. Not everyone from either individualist or collectivist countries, however, embraces the predominant cultural values. Recognize that a variety of persuasive strategies that appeal to diverse audiences, the subject of the next chapter, is important.

SUMMARY

When you attempt to persuade an audience, you try to convert, modify, or maintain your listeners' attitudes and/or behavior. Conversion is the least likely achievable goal when giving a speech. Attitudes do not always predict specific behavior. Reasons for possible inconsistency include whether the attitudes are derived from direct or indirect experience, the degree of effort required to perform the behavior, and the amount of social pressure applied to behave differently from your attitudes. The elaboration likelihood model explains persuasion in general by noting that there are two paths to persuasion. These are the peripheral route that includes likeability, attractiveness, and emotional appeals of the speaker, and the central route that embraces skepticism and its emphasis on reasoning and evidence. Choosing which type of persuasive claim—fact, value, or policy—provides the foundation for your entire persuasive speech. Persuasion that works well in American culture may be ineffective in other cultures, especially those that are collectivist.

TED TALKS AND YOUTUBE VIDEOS

Central Route Used Effectively: "Nick Hanauer: Rich People Don't Create Jobs"

Student Speech Using Mostly Central Route: "TS149: Excellent Persuasive Speech Example"

Student Speech and Effort Required: "Persuasive Presentation: Blood Donation"

Peripheral Cues in Excess: "The Ultimate Biden Laugh and Smirk Compilation"

Offering Easy Solution: "Jane Chen: A Warm Embrace That Saves Lives"

Social Judgment Theory and March for Our Lives Speeches: "The 6 Most Memorable Speeches at March for Our Lives in D.C."

For relevant links to these TED Talks and YouTube videos, see the *Practically Speaking* Companion Website: www.oup.com/he/rothwell-ps3e. You can also gain access by typing the title of the speech reference into a Google search window, or by doing the same on the TED Talks or YouTube sites.

CHECKLIST

☐ Do you have a clear persuasion goal? Are you trying to convert, modify, or merely maintain an audience's attitudes and behavior? Remember that conversion is unlikely to result from a single speech.

☐ Are you presenting a proposition of fact, value, or policy?

☐ Are you making a strong effort to make your audience members feel that they are directly affected by the problem that you describe?

☐ Is your solution to a problem relatively easy for audience members to perform?

☐ Have you based your message mostly on the central route (skepticism) to persuasion?

CRITICAL THINKING QUESTIONS

1. Is coercion ever an appropriate strategy to change attitudes and behavior? Is it ethical?

2. Are there certain events or circumstances in which basing your attitude and behavior on peripheral cues entirely is ever appropriate?

3. Despite numerous mass shootings in the United States, there has been little movement in attitudes and behavior regarding gun legislation. Why do you think that is?

NOTE: Online **student resources**, such as practice tests, flashcards, and other activities, can be accessed at www.oup.com/he/rothwell-ps3e

Persuasive Speaking Strategies

Suppose you plan to give a speech convincing your listeners that poor signage is a serious problem warranting a strong solution. You might begin this way:

> "Drop Your Pants Here and You Will Receive Prompt Attention" says the sign outside a laundry. "Kids With Gas Eat Here Free" says another. "Hidden Entrance" reads a third sign. They can be funny, but signs are a critical element of our everyday transit from place to place. Signs such as "Soft Shoulder, Blind Curves, Steep Grade, Big Trucks, Good Luck!" warn us of impending dangers with a touch of humor, but poor signage is no laughing matter. A report by the Department of Transport in the United Kingdom, cited in a March 9, 2018 article in *The Sunday Times,* concludes that "signage clutter" can cause deadly accidents. Unfortunately, as I will show, the danger of traffic and business signage clutter is taken more seriously in the UK than in the U.S., and that needs to change. Therefore, Congress should mandate that all local and state highway authorities significantly improve their regulation of public signs for proven safety.

This opening tries to persuade an audience by using humor, appealing to fear, and using evidence. The effectiveness of these or any persuasive strategies is not sure-fire, however, because they must be used under the right conditions.

Consideration of all possible persuasive speaking strategies would require a lengthy book. *The purpose of this chapter is to explore a few of the most prominent and effective persuasive strategies for public speakers.* Toward that end, this chapter addresses (1) the power of specific persuasion strategies and (2) the conditions that determine their potential persuasive effectiveness.

ENHANCE THE SPEAKER: IDENTIFICATION AND CREDIBILITY

Persuasive speaking begins with enhancing the speaker, or developing **ethos** as Aristotle termed it. Crafty, carefully planned persuasive strategies will not matter if your audience has a problem with you, the speaker. Enhancing your ethos can be accomplished in two primary ways: establishing identification with your audience and bolstering your credibility. *Both were discussed extensively in Chapter 3* for a variety of purposes and audiences beyond just the persuasive arena. Both are especially critical when your purpose is to persuade.

Regarding identification, Kenneth Burke (1950) wrote, "You persuade a man [or woman] only insofar as you can talk his language by speech, gesture, tonality, order, image, attitude, idea, identifying your ways with his" (p. 55). Burke considered identification, the affiliation and connection between you and your audience, to be the essence of persuasion (see also Nordquist, 2017). Enhancing

PHOTO 16.1: How does Greta Thunberg, at the time of this photo a Swedish 16-year-old activist on climate change, enhance her credibility with an adult audience? (*See access to links of her speeches at end of chapter.*)

your likability, developing stylistic similarities, and noting substantive similarities with your audience are ways to create identification (*see access to Reagan link at end of chapter*), as previously discussed.

You enhance your credibility by appearing competent, trustworthy, and dynamic, yet composed. Your credibility has more influence, however, on listeners with weak or nonexistent views on issues than it does on listeners with strong views (Kumkale et al., 2010). Listeners with weak or nonexistent views typically are influenced by peripheral cues such as source credibility. Listeners with strong viewpoints typically require powerful evidence and arguments to influence them via the central route to persuasion.

Humor has been discussed as a superior attention-getting strategy, but it can also enhance identification and credibility (*see access to Obama and McCain links at end of chapter*). It can influence perceptions of your communication competence (Banas et al., 2011). Humor can also increase your likability and help establish rapport with your audience (Weisinger, 2015). Self-deprecating humor, poking fun at yourself, is especially effective in this regard. Be cautious, however. Excessive self-deprecation can weaken credibility (see Chapter 3). Inappropriate humor can also do the same (Banas et al., 2011).

USE LOGIC AND EVIDENCE: A PERSUASIVE FOCUS

Much has already been said in Chapters 5, 12, and 13 about the structure of arguments, the importance of effective use of supporting materials, the essential use of strong logic and evidence, and the imperative avoidance of common fallacies. In this section, however, building arguments based on logic and evidence, what Aristotle called **logos**, is addressed with a specific focus on persuasion.

Persuasive Arguments: Quality and Quantity

The quality and number of arguments advanced for a proposition can be factors in persuasive speaking. One study tested to what degree students could be persuaded that completing comprehensive examinations as a condition for graduating from college is an effective proposal (Petty & Cacioppo, 1984). How do you feel about this proposal? Students *directly affected* by the proposal (they'd have to take the test) were not persuaded by nine weak arguments. In fact, the greater the number of weak arguments they heard, the more they disliked the proposal. They were persuaded only when strong arguments were used, especially when many strong arguments were used. For students *unaffected* by the proposal (they wouldn't need to take the test), however, the quality of the arguments was relatively unimportant. They were more persuaded that the proposal was a good idea when nine arguments were presented than when only three were offered, no matter how strong or weak the arguments.

When constructing your persuasive speech, do not be satisfied when you find one or two strong arguments to support your proposition. *If several strong arguments emerge when you research your proposition, and time permits, present them all.* Several strong arguments can be persuasive to listeners who process your message either peripherally by noting the quantity of supporting arguments, or centrally by considering the quality of arguments.

Persuasive Evidence: Statistics Versus Narratives

Using evidence can change minds. To be persuasive, however, your evidence must be attributed to a highly credible source, be seen by audience members as free of fallacies (see Chapter 13), gain the attention of your audience and not put your listeners to sleep (see Chapter 5), and not overwhelm your audience with an excessive abundance (Perloff, 2017).

What about types of evidence? Vivid narratives and examples can be more persuasive than statistics, partly because they typically are more interesting and memorable (Friend, 2013). Narratives with strong arguments are more persuasive than narratives with weak arguments (Schreiner at al., 2018), but statistics can enhance the perception of the strength of arguments. Research is mixed on which is more persuasive, narratives or statistics (Feeley et al., 2006), but why separate the two? *Use both narratives and statistics as your optimum strategy, thereby capitalizing on the strengths of both forms of evidence* (Allen et al., 2000).

TRY EMOTIONAL APPEALS: BEYOND LOGIC

Although logic and evidence can be very persuasive, especially for highly involved listeners, emotional appeals—what Aristotle partially meant by **pathos**—are also powerful motivators. As social psychologist Drew Westen (2007) observes, "We do not pay attention to arguments unless they engender our interest, enthusiasm, fear, anger, or contempt. . . . 'Reasonable' actions almost always require the integration of thought and emotion . . ." (p. 16). In this section, emotional appeals with special emphasis on fear and anger are discussed.

General Emotional Appeals: Motivating Change

Appeals to sadness, pride, honor, hope, joy, guilt, envy, and shame all have their place as persuasion strategies that ignite emotional reactions and change behavior (Gass & Seiter, 2014). Climate change activist Greta Thunberg, for example, used a combination of shame and guilt in her address at the House of Parliament in London on April 24, 2019. For example, in her usual blunt style, she claimed, "You lied to us. You gave us false hope. You told us that the future was something to look forward to" (quoted by Silberman, 2019). Research, however, on the persuasiveness of these particular emotional appeals is sparse. Nevertheless, there is some evidence that they have persuasive potential (Dillard & Nabi, 2006; Panagopoulos, 2010).

PHOTO 16.2: Using emotional appeals can be a very powerful persuasion strategy.

Hope, for example, is sometimes a cornerstone of an entire political campaign. Barack Obama's 2008 presidential campaign revolved around a strong appeal to hope, typified in a victory speech the night of the 2008 Iowa caucus (*see access to link at end of chapter*):

> We are choosing hope over fear. . . . Hope is what led me here today—with a father from Kenya, a mother from Kansas, and a story that could only happen in the United States of America. Hope is the bedrock of this nation, the belief that our destiny will not be written for us, but by us, by all those men and women who are not content to settle for the world as it is; who have the courage to remake the world as it should be. (*"Remarks of Senator Barack Obama," 2008*)

Appeals to hope and other emotions can be persuasive. This next section, however, concentrates on fear appeals, a very common persuasive strategy.

Fear Appeals: Are You Scared Yet?

"Don't put that in your mouth. It's full of germs." "You'll poke your eye out if you run with those scissors." "Never cross the street before looking both ways. You could be killed." From childhood you are undoubtedly familiar with fear appeals. Your parents probably gave you a heavy dose to keep you safe and out of trouble. Fear appeals are used on adults as well. In 2001, Canada began using the most shocking, fear-inducing warnings on cigarette packages ever used anywhere in the world (Bor, 2001). Photos of blackened, bleeding gums, a diseased heart, a lung tumor, or a gangrenous foot appeared on a rotating basis on all cigarette packs along with information on the hazards of smoking.

Student Karin Nordin (2015) used fear appeals in her award-winning oration on the flaws in our 9-1-1 emergency system presented at the Interstate Oratorical Association contest:

> We are helpless in the case of a 9-1-1 blackout. The Huffington Post of April 14th, 2014 tells the story of Alicia Cappola, a single mother forced to fight an intruder with a kitchen knife after her 37 9-1-1 calls went completely unanswered. Cappola's crisis struck during a six-hour, multi-state 9-1-1 outage, the largest in American history. If our system was nationally connected, one of the other 6000 dispatch centers across the nation could have taken the calls, dispatched emergency services, and saved lives. Instead, 770 emergencies were unheard, and 11 million citizens were at risk. *(p. 58)*

Do fear appeals work? The quick answer is yes. *In general, the more fear that is aroused in listeners, the more vulnerable they feel, and the more likely they will be convinced* (Tannenbaum et al., 2015). This is particularly true when a threat is initially perceived by listeners to be low (e.g., flaws in our 9-1-1 system that most people are probably unaware exist), so your fear appeal must be strong, and the threat must be shown to have a personal impact on your audience to arouse concern.

A study of graphic images of warning on cigarette packages found that they "have the most pronounced short-term impacts on adult smokers, including smokers from groups that have in the past been hard to reach" (Thrasher et al., 2012). In Montana, a state plagued by methamphetamine use, young people were targeted for a barrage of extremely graphic, terrifying video ads of teens hooked on the drug (Montana Meth Project, 2019). Studies showed that a dramatic shift occurred in attitudes about meth use among teens as a result. Teens' perceptions of great risk from trying meth even one time increased substantially to 93% of respondents, and 87% of young adults believed their friends would give them a hard time for using meth. Behavioral changes also occurred. Teen meth use declined 73% in Montana and adult meth use declined 72% since the beginning of the campaign. Meth-related crime also decreased by 62%. Other states subsequently followed the Montana Meth persuasive model with similar results (Montana Meth Project, 2019).

Fear appeals, however, do not always work. *Five conditions determine whether high fear appeals used in your speeches will likely produce constructive action* (Gass & Seiter, 2014).

1. *Your audience must feel vulnerable* (Tannenbaum et al., 2015). People do not all fear the same things. Some fear heights, while others relish jumping out of planes and skydiving. Teens feel more threatened by social rejection than physical harm caused by drug use ("Principles of Adolescent Substance Use," 2014). Recognizing this, the anti-meth campaign in Montana tried to create strong social disapproval for meth use (*see access to link at end of chapter*) in addition to fear appeals about physical harm (Montana Meth Project, 2019).

2. *A clear, specific recommendation for avoiding or lessening the fear is important* (Tannenbaum et al., 2015). A vague recommendation, such as "Get financial aid," is not as effective as a specific recommendation, such as "Fill out this application for a Pell grant," to assuage the fear of having to drop out of school and be left with an uncertain future.

3. *The recommendation must be perceived as effective* (Tannenbaum et al., 2015). Encouraging your audience to get a flu shot is an effective recommended behavior. Wearing a mask to avoid infection is not nearly as effective and is often impractical. Imagine yourself delivering a speech to a class while everyone wears a mask. When the personal threat is perceived to be high but the solution is viewed as ineffective by listeners, a denial such as "We can't do anything anyway, so why worry?" or a rationalization such as "You've got to die of something" typically neutralizes fear-arousing messages (Goldstein et al., 2008).

4. *Listeners must perceive that they can perform the actions recommended* (Lennon & Rentfro, 2010). Again, the effort required to perform the behavior is a key variable. Asking members of your audience

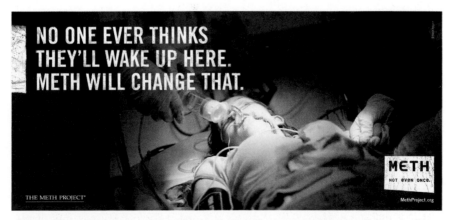

PHOTO 16.3: Strong fear appeals can be highly persuasive, but can fear appeals become too extreme and backfire?

to give up sugary sodas entirely for the rest of their lives to avoid dental and health problems may not be possible for most people. The effort is too great. Encouraging your listeners to cut their soda consumption in half, however, may be seen as realistic.

5. *Fear appeals are more persuasive when combined with high-quality arguments.* The fear appeal becomes more believable when it is bolstered by arguments supported by credible evidence.

Strong fear appeals may backfire if these five conditions are not met (Leshner et al., 2011). This is particularly true when the fear appeal combines with disgusting images. We may just avoid the images (Sreenivasan & Weinberger, 2018).

Anger Appeals: Moderately Upset

Arousing anger is often used to persuade listeners. Mounting political anger has been an issue for several years, culminating in the volcanic eruption conventionally called the 2016 presidential election campaign (Mason, 2016). Anger permeated both Democratic and Republican campaigns, except over different issues. Attempting to ignite anger in an audience is a common persuasive appeal because anger can provide a strong motivation to act. Anger drove markedly higher turnout among Democratic voters in the 2018 election that culminated in flipping the U.S. House of Representatives from Republican to Democrat ("Emotions Stir Engagement," 2018). Double student tuition and watch the student response. Anger was a prime motivator of teen survivors of the Marjory Stoneman Douglas High School massacre in 2018 to organize a mass protest. In fact, notable instances of teens acting to address critical world problems (e.g., climate change, diversity in the media, education for refugee children, and gun violence) have been motivated by palpable anger, especially as a result of the inaction of adults (Pires, 2018).

Anger, however, does not always provoke constructive behavior. People sometimes become verbally and/or physically violent when angry. The intensity of the anger is key. Intense anger can short-circuit an individual's ability to think clearly and act responsibly. Intensely angry individuals may lash out at any perceived source of their anger, real or imagined. Ethically, you would not want to inflame anger in your audience if you suspected a destructive reaction might ensue. As a speaker, you want to keep calm, be unconditionally constructive in your comments even when others are losing their heads, and avoid taunting a heckler in your audience, especially if your audience is predominantly hostile. You could provoke a physical confrontation or even a riot. *Arousing anger in your audience can be persuasive, but it can also backfire.* You want to arouse moderate anger, not rage. Moderate anger can be channeled toward constructive action. Rage can provoke a mob scene.

The **Anger Activism Model** helps explain the relationship between anger and persuasion (Turner, 2014; Turner et al., 2013). This model posits that anger provokes desired constructive behavior change when (1) the target audience initially agrees with your persuasion message, (2) the anger produced by your message is fairly strong but not to the point of rage, and (3) your audience members perceive that they can act effectively and constructively to address their anger (Ilakkuvan, et al., 2017). Two studies show that if all three of these conditions are met, arousing anger has the potential to motivate appropriate action, even if the action required to quell or satiate the anger is very difficult to perform (Turner et al., 2013; Turner et al., 2007).

PHOTO 16.4 Expressing anger can be an effective persuasive strategy, but the challenge is to channel audience anger in a positive direction.

How can you use moderate anger arousal in a speech? Consider this account based on Boone (2009):

Abdullah al-Kidd, a United States citizen and former University of Idaho student and running back for the football team, was detained for more than two weeks as a witness in a federal terrorism case in 2003. He was handcuffed, strip-searched, and repeatedly interrogated. There was no evidence of wrongdoing by al-Kidd. He was jailed and then investigated, not the other way around, as required by the U.S. system of justice. A three-judge panel from the 9th Circuit Court ruled in September 2009 that his incarceration was "repugnant to the Constitution and a painful reminder of some of the most ignominious chapters of our national history." As a result of the illegal detention, al-Kidd lost a scholarship to graduate school, lost security clearance and subsequently lost a job with a government contractor, lost his passport, and was ordered to live with in-laws in Las Vegas. We should all be angry that our government so blatantly abused one of our citizens.

This story likely arouses appropriate anger on behalf of social justice. That is a first step toward producing constructive change.

PHOTO 16.5: Speeches that appeal to anger can provoke violence.

Ethics and Persuasion: Emotional Appeals Revisited

Emotional appeals can be very persuasive, but are they ethical? It depends. Surely, you should be angry about racism, sexism, homophobia, and all manner of injustice, right? Likewise, you should fear terrorism, drunk drivers, food poisoning, plastic pollution in our oceans, and flu pandemics. Emotional appeals are not inherently unethical just because they are not a logical appeal. Emotion in the service of logic and truth can equal constructive action to do good. Emotional appeals motivate action. They also create attention so we might listen more intently to a clearly reasoned and supported argument.

Emotional appeals are ethical as long as they complement the central route to persuasion (skepticism). Emotional appeals in the service of fabrications, distortions, and rumors are unethical. Unfortunately, politicians are noted for their casual relationship with the truth. The "all politicians lie" excuse, however, should not lend them a free pass to inflame passions of audiences by being dishonest. Politicians lie to get elected to office and to pass or oppose legislation that can affect millions of people, even the country or the world. That's significant.

Emotional appeals should not be a substitute for logic and evidence. If an individual knowingly uses emotional appeals that contradict facts, sound logic, and solid evidence, then it becomes the tool of the True Believer (see Chapter 12). This violates ethical standards detailed in Chapter 1.

FRAMING: USING LANGUAGE TO SHAPE ATTITUDES AND BEHAVIOR

Should you call it *political correctness* or *showing respect*? *Estate tax* or *death tax*? *Undocumented immigrants* or *illegal aliens*? *Income inequality* or *class warfare*? *Playing the woman's card* or *sexism*? *Fake news* or *truthful journalism*? Framing matters. **Framing** is the influence descriptive wording has on our perception. Our "frames determine whether people notice problems, how they understand and remember problems, and how they evaluate and act upon them" (Fairhurst & Sarr, 1996, p. 4). Much like a photographer frames a picture to communicate a point of view, language frames communicate points of view. When a photographer changes the frame from a person as the center of interest to a mere bystander, our thoughts and perception of the picture change.

When I ran successfully for the Cabrillo College Board of Trustees in 2018, garnering 71% of the vote, I framed my campaign with the slogan, "Restore *Community* to Our Community College." I wanted voters to focus on the diminishment of lifelong learning opportunities at the college and the unfortunate movement to change California community colleges to more narrowly focused junior colleges. My opponent used the slogan, "Experience Counts" to frame his campaign. In my judgment, that was a mistake. He spotlighted his more general business experience while unwittingly highlighting my much more direct experience at Cabrillo College. Thus, my specific experience likely "counted" more than his indirect experience. Effective framing can be a critical persuasive strategy.

Studies abound showing the power of framing (Feinberg & Willer, 2015). When subjects were presented with the option of treating lung cancer with surgery, 84% chose surgery when it was framed in terms of the odds of *living*, but 56% chose surgery when it was framed in terms of the chances of *dying* (McNeil et al., 1982). Most subjects thought condoms were an effective method of preventing AIDS when they were told that condoms have a "95% success rate," but a majority did not view condoms as effective prevention when told that they had a "5% failure rate" (Linville et al., 1992). In these instances, the two choices compared have identical outcomes, but they are perceived differently because of how the wording frames them. When participants were presented brief passages that either described crime as a "beast preying" on a city or as a "virus infecting" a city, those presented with the "beast" framing were likely to choose punishment as the solution, but those presented with the "virus" framing were likely to choose reform measures (Thibodeau & Boroditsky, 2011).

Reframing—altering perception by changing how issues and problems are descriptively phrased—can change how we perceive those issues and problems (Deggans, 2012). Student Vanessa Hickman (2018) reframes her speech on *sober homes*, officially defined as "halfway houses intended to integrate recovering drug and alcohol users back into community life," by calling them *flophouses* "where crimes like rape, theft, human trafficking, prostitution, and illegal drug use are rampant" because these facilities are mostly unregulated (p. 29). The *sober homes* frame conjures a positive image of drug treatment facilities; the *flophouses* frame produces a negative image of toxic, drug- and crime-ridden facilities.

Clearly, framing or reframing significantly influences our attitudes and behavior. As a persuasive strategy that centralizes the essence of your speech, *it is especially powerful with those who initially view the issue being promoted as one of low importance* (Lecheler et al., 2009). Framing alone as a peripheral route to persuasion will likely resonate more with those less informed and less interested initially in an issue. Framing supported by strong evidence and reasoning, however, can crystallize your viewpoint favorably and your opponents' viewpoint unfavorably and enhance your persuasive impact enormously.

INDUCE COGNITIVE DISSONANCE: CREATING TENSION

When we want to persuade, one of the most common strategies is to point out inconsistencies between two attitudes or between attitudes and behavior. This is because such inconsistencies make a person appear hypocritical, and research shows that we strongly dislike hypocrites (Jordan et al., 2017). A student asks her professor for more time on an assignment. The professor says no. The student retorts, "But you gave extra time to Tyrene. Why won't you give me the same extension?" The professor sees herself as a very fair-minded person. Faced with this apparent inconsistency in the treatment of two students, the professor feels tense and uncomfortable. Festinger (1957) called this unpleasant feeling produced by apparent inconsistency **cognitive dissonance**.

Whenever a person holds two inconsistent ideas, beliefs, or opinions at the same time, or when an attitude and a behavior are inconsistent, dissonance likely occurs (Cooper et al., 2016; Tavris & Aronson, 2016). Parents often confront this persuasive strategy from their children. "Why do I have a curfew? You never gave a curfew to Marianna." We want to be perceived as consistent, not hypocritical or nonsensical, so dissonance emerges when inconsistencies are pointed out to us (Brannon & Gawronski, 2018). Cognitive dissonance appears to be common, appearing in a variety of cultures studied (Hoshino-Browne et al., 2005).

PHOTO 16.6: These opposing protests are both attempts to arouse cognitive dissonance.

"Cognitive dissonance is a motivating state of affairs. Just as hunger impels a person to eat, so does dissonance impel a person to change his [her] opinions or his [her] behavior" (Festinger, 1977, p. 111). *According to this theory, you have to awaken dissonance in listeners for persuasion to occur.* Without dissonance, there is little motivation to change attitudes or behavior. Here is how the strategy works:

> The [persuader] intentionally arouses feelings of dissonance by threatening self-esteem—for example, by making the person feel guilty about something, by arousing feelings of shame or inadequacy, or by making the person look like a hypocrite or someone who does not honor his or her word. Next, the [persuader] offers one solution, one way of reducing this dissonance—by complying with whatever request the [persuader] has in mind. The way to reduce that guilt, eliminate that shame, honor that commitment, and restore your feelings of adequacy is to give to that charity, buy that car, hate that enemy, or vote for that leader. *(Pratkanis and Aronson, 2001, p. 44)*

Does inducing dissonance change behavior? It is unlikely to be successful with true believers (Walker, 2013), but with others it certainly can be (Czopp et al., 2006; McLeod, 2018). Important decisions arouse more dissonance than less important ones. Pointing out to a teacher, for example, that he or she was not consistent when grading a test could elicit varying degrees of dissonance. If the inconsistency involves a single point on a 100-point exam, the teacher can easily downplay the inconsistency as minor and inherent to any subjective grading system. If the inconsistency involves an entire grade difference and seems based on gender bias, however, the dissonance could be quite large.

Notice how student Gary Allen (1996) uses cognitive dissonance in a speech on drug testing in the military:

> The final problem is caused by a double standard, because a program is only as good as the goal it achieves. While alcohol is universally recognized as the most commonly abused drug, the military does not test for alcohol as regularly as for other drugs . . . Soldiers caught drunk on the job are given 45 days extra duty, that is work that must be performed after the regular duty day, they have a letter put into their permanent file, and they are returned to light duty. Yet the soldier who receives a positive [drug] test result is, currently, kicked out of the military with a dishonorable discharge. Let me say that again. Every day soldiers are required to undergo a test of their innocence without suspicion of guilt. The soldier who is found guilty is kicked out and marked for life with a dishonorable discharge, while soldiers drunk on the job, endangering everyone's life, are returned to duty with a slap on the hand. *(p. 82)*

The speaker points out a glaring inconsistency to induce dissonance in the audience. Supporting such a "double standard" is hypocritical and unjust, so the speaker implies. One could argue that there is a big difference between alcohol and other drugs, namely, legality. Nevertheless, concerning possible dangerous effects of use, an inconsistency does seem apparent. Cognitive dissonance can be an effective persuasive strategy, but as is true with fear and anger appeals, an effective solution to a problem that engenders dissonance is required. The dissonance must be assuaged. If audience members are made to feel hypocritical, they can alleviate that dissonance by changing their behavior as you propose.

USE THE CONTRAST EFFECT: MINIMIZE THE MAGNITUDE

You are a salesperson. Most of your pay is based on commission, so you want to sell as much merchandise as you can at the highest prices possible. Do you show the customer the inexpensive product first, then gradually show the more expensive version, or do you begin with the expensive product? Which will net you the biggest commission? According to research on the contrast effect, you would make a better choice if you began expensive and moved to less expensive (Cialdini, 1993). The **contrast effect** says listeners are more likely to accept a bigger second request or offer when contrasted with a much bigger initial request or offer. If shown a really nice leather coat that costs $450, most shoppers will balk at purchasing it because it is "so expensive." If shown a $650 leather coat first, however, then shown the $450 version, the second coat just seems less expensive by contrast with the first.

CARTOON 16.1: The contrast effect can make it appear that you are getting a bargain instead of a costly trinket.

The contrast effect, sometimes referred to as the **door-in-the-face strategy**, is used successfully in a wide variety of persuasion attempts (Feeley et al., 2012), and in all types of sales (Dolinski, 2016). For example, I once purchased a recliner for $250. It was not "on sale." About two months later I was browsing through a furniture store and spotted the identical recliner advertised as part of a "giant blowout sale." The price tag showed $800 marked out, then $600 marked out, then $475 marked out, and finally the "sale price" of $400. A casual customer who had not shopped around might see this recliner as a super bargain. The price had been cut in half. Yet this store was asking $150 more than I paid for the same recliner at the regular price from another store.

Cialdini (1993) provides a stellar, amusing example of the contrast effect in action in parent–child persuasion. Although this example is a letter, you can easily see how this strategy could apply in a persuasive speech.

Dear Mother and Dad:

Since I left for college I have been remiss in writing and I am sorry for my thoughtlessness in not having written before. I will bring you up to date now, but before you read on, please sit down. . . . Well, then, I am getting along pretty well now. The skull fracture and the concussion I got when I jumped out the window of my dormitory when it caught on fire shortly after my arrival here is pretty well healed now. I only spent two weeks in the hospital and now I can see almost normally and only get those sick headaches once a day. Fortunately, the fire in the dormitory, and my jump, was witnessed by an attendant at the gas station near the dorm, and he was the one who called the Fire Department and the ambulance. He also visited me in the hospital and since I had nowhere to live because of the burnt-out dormitory, he was kind enough to invite me to share his apartment with him. It's really a basement room, but it's kind of cute. He is a very fine boy, and we have fallen deeply in love and are planning to get married. We haven't set the date yet, but it will be before my pregnancy begins to show.

Yes, Mother and Dad, I am pregnant. I know how much you are looking forward to being grandparents and I know you will welcome the baby and give it the same love and devotion and tender care you gave me when I was a child. The reason for the delay in our marriage is that my boyfriend has a minor infection which prevents us from passing our premarital blood tests and I carelessly caught it from him. I know that you will welcome him into our family with open arms. He is kind and, although not well educated, he is ambitious.

Now that I have brought you up to date, I want to tell you that there was no dormitory fire, I did not have a concussion or skull fracture, I was not in the hospital. I am not pregnant, I am not engaged, I am not infected, and there is no boyfriend. However, I am getting a "D" in American History and an "F" in Chemistry, and I want you to see those marks in their proper perspective.

Your loving daughter,

Sharon

As a strategy to use in a persuasive speech, *the contrast effect works well when presenting your solution to a problem*. For example, say you have argued that taxpayer dollars do not begin to cover the costs of educating college students. You could begin the solution portion of your speech this way:

Clearly, we cannot expect taxpayers to continue shouldering almost the entire burden of higher education expenses. I think it would be entirely justified if our state legislature immediately doubled tuition for every student in the state. This would provide some tax relief for already overburdened taxpayers while still covering less than half the cost of educating each student.

Although doubling student tuition is justified, fair, and beneficial, I can see that such a proposal probably isn't entirely practical for a number of reasons, not the least of which is the stunned looks on your faces and the suddenness of such a large tuition increase. Having weighed the potential merits and demerits of such a proposal, let me propose instead that the state phase in a much smaller tuition increase over the next decade to ease the burden on students and still provide taxpayer relief in the long run.

Peruse the *sample persuasive speech* in **Appendix B** for another example of the contrast effect.

USE A TWO-SIDED ORGANIZATIONAL PATTERN: REFUTATION

Is it better to present arguments in favor of your proposition and ignore opposing arguments (one-sided message), or should you make your case, then refute opposing arguments (two-sided message)? *Two-sided persuasive messages are more effective than one-sided messages in convincing listeners to change attitudes* (Allen, 1991, 1993, 1998). This is true, however, only if you provide effective refutation of opposing arguments. Two-sided but ineffectual refutation actually is less persuasive than one-sided presentations (see also Perloff, 2017).

A two-sided organizational pattern begins with a presentation of main arguments supporting your proposition. After you have laid out your case, you then answer common objections, or opposing arguments, against your case (see **Appendix B**). Answering opposing arguments is called **refutation**. Recall that this is an element of the Toulmin structure of an argument discussed in Chapter 13. Effective refutation, of course, means that you need to anticipate what an audience might question about your position. There are four steps to refutation.

1. **State the opposing argument.** "A common objection to colleges shifting from a semester to a quarter system is that not as much subject matter will be covered each term" is a statement of an opposing argument.

2. **State your reaction to the opposing argument.** "This isn't true. Courses that meet three hours per week could meet five hours per week under the shorter quarter system" is a statement of response to an opposing argument.

3. **Support your response with reasoning and evidence.** Failure to present strong arguments backed by solid reasoning and evidence may backfire and actually promote more entrenched attitudes instead of changing attitudes (Rucker & Petty, 2004). Weak refutation can be worse than no refutation at all because listeners may deduce that poorly supported counterarguments mean that currently held attitudes are meritorious.

4. **Indicate what effect, if any, opposing arguments have had on the strength of your case.** This is a damage assessment. If some disadvantage will occur from your proposal, admit it, but weigh the damage against the claimed advantages of your proposal. "No quarter system is perfect. Students will be pressured in some instances to work more intensely in a condensed period of time. Overall, however, the advantages of a quarter system—greater number and variety of courses, more diversity of instructors, better vacation schedules, and greater retention and success rates—far outweigh this minor objection."

The two-sided approach to persuasion can be very effective (*see access to Jim Jefferies link at end of chapter*).

SUMMARY

There are many persuasive strategies a speaker can use. Among these are establishing identification, building credibility, building strong arguments, inducing cognitive dissonance, making emotional appeals, framing, using the contrast effect, and using a two-sided organizational pattern. Competent public speakers will find success if they utilize some or all of these strategies to persuade others. There are conditions that determine the likelihood of success using each strategy, so make sure that you are cognizant of these conditions and that you adapt your persuasive strategy to meet those conditions.

TED TALKS AND YOUTUBE VIDEOS

Ethos, Pathos, & Logos: "Mr. Rogers and the Power of Persuasion"

Cognitive Dissonance, Fear Appeals, & Credibility: "You Are Stealing Our Future: Greta Thunberg, 15, Condemns the World's Inaction on Climate Change"; see also "School Strike for Climate—Save the World by Changing the Rules/Greta Thunberg/TEDxStockholm"

Use of Evidence to Persuade: "Aaron Sorkin's *The Newsroom*: America Is Not the Greatest Country—Anymore"

Powerful Use of Emotion: "Mary Fisher: A Whisper of AIDS 1992" (at the Republican National Convention); #50 on "American Rhetoric: Top 100 Speeches"

Fantastic Example of Power of Framing: "Climate Name Change"

Power of Framing; Great AD: "Purple Feather: Blind Man Help"

Two-Sided Persuasion: "Jim Jefferies: Gun Control (Part 1) from BARE" (Warning: Rough language)

Fear Appeals: "Montana Meth Project" (Warning: Graphic video)

Hope as Emotional Appeal: "Barack Obama: Iowa Caucus Victory Speech"

Emotional Appeals: "Michelle Obama's Speech Moves Many to Tears in Charlotte"

Humor and Identification: "McCain Roasts Obama at Alfred E. Smith"

Humor and Identification: "Obama at the Alfred E. Smith Memorial Dinner 10/16/08"

Several Strategies: "Ronald Reagan: Peace Through Strength"

Identification: "Ronald Reagan: The Great Communicator"

True Believers Unaffected by Cognitive Dissonance: "The Daily Show: Putting Donald Trump Supporters Through an Ideology Test"

For relevant links to these TED Talks and YouTube videos, see the *Practically Speaking* Companion Website: www.oup.com/he/rothwell-ps3e. You can also gain access by typing the title of the speech reference into a Google search window or by doing the same on the TED Talks or YouTube sites.

CHECKLIST

☐ Learn when to use specific persuasive strategies

☐ Remember the importance of using identification strategies to bond with your audience, especially if your audience is initially hostile to your point of view.

☐ Build your credibility, especially if your audience does not initially see you as particularly credible (e.g., not an expert).

☐ Combine strong arguments supported by credible reasoning and evidence with emotional appeals.

☐ Choose fear appeals if your audience is likely to be afraid, but not otherwise; choose anger appeals if your audience is likely to get angry, but not otherwise.

☐ If using fear or anger appeals, make sure to meet all of the conditions for their effective use.

☐ If you can induce cognitive dissonance among your audience members, be sure to provide an effective alternative that can assuage the dissonance.

☐ Remember that a two-sided strategy works best with an informed audience that may already anticipate objections to your proposal. The refutation, however, must be strong to be effective. When "preaching to the choir," however, a one-sided approach is probably sufficient.

CRITICAL THINKING QUESTIONS

1. Is name-calling, as we see so often in these polarized political times, ever ethical?

2. Do the ends (e.g., restoring civil rights; reducing violence) ever justify lying to your audience?

3. Which emotional appeal is more likely to change a person's political attitude and behavior: fear or anger?

4. Can you provide an example of when a speaker was not liked and did not identify well with his or her audience yet changed listeners' attitudes and behavior?

NOTE: Online **student resources**, such as practice tests, flashcards, and other activities, can be accessed at www.oup.com/he/rothwell-ps3e

Speeches for Special Occasions

Speeches for special occasions should be special. They are different from informative and persuasive speeches. Although a special occasion speech may impart knowledge and information or briefly persuade, that is not its main purpose. Audience expectations are critical to the effectiveness of a special occasion speech. The occasion sets the expectation for the audience, and your primary goal is to meet your audience's expectations. An inspirational occasion requires an inspirational speech. Listeners want to be moved, not merely informed. Listeners at a roast expect to laugh heartily and often. Little effort should be made to offer deep insights or persuade anyone to action. Eulogies are not opportunities to score political points. Special occasion speeches of praise or celebration should capitalize on similes, metaphors, and other compelling uses of vivid language, which are detailed in Chapter 9 on style.

The primary purpose of this chapter is to explore ways to give effective and appropriate special occasion speeches. Toward that end, this chapter (1) addresses a variety of special occasion speeches and (2) provides advice on presenting these speeches competently.

TRIBUTE ADDRESSES

Tribute speeches praise or celebrate a person. They honor the person. You hear tribute speeches at retirement parties, birthdays, anniversaries, going-away parties, award ceremonies, and funerals. Principal tribute speeches include toasts, roasts, tributes for colleagues, and eulogies.

Toasts: Raising a Glass in Tribute

A **toast** is a brief tribute to a person or couple. Sometimes a new spouse or partner is welcomed into the larger family with a toast at a Thanksgiving dinner, for example. We make toasts at college graduation parties, employment promotion ceremonies, and anniversaries of important life events. Weddings usually have several toasts offered by the best man and maid of honor, and sometimes by bridesmaids and friends and family members of the bride and groom. *Keep them brief.* Avoid reading your toast. This is a short speech, so memorize key passages that aren't simple stories easily delivered extemporaneously. A well-known, oft-quoted Irish toast goes:

> May the road rise to meet you.
>
> May the wind be always at your back.
>
> May the sun shine warm upon your face.
>
> And rains fall soft upon your fields.
>
> And God hold you in the hollow of His hand.

If so inclined, you could play off this well-known toast and give it your own unique linguistic twist, such as:

> May the road rise to meet you, and may you avoid the potholes of life.
>
> May the wind be always at your back, unless a cool breeze in the face offers refreshment.
>
> May the sun shine warm on your face, but never burn you.
>
> And may rain fall softly, washing away any sadness you may feel.

Because a toast is often accompanied by a drink of wine or other alcoholic beverage, be cautious about the effect alcohol can have on your ability to offer a coherent and effective toast. Your toast may follow many others. You do not want to make a fool of yourself and make others uncomfortable. Always be appropriate. Remember, weddings almost always have young children present. *Your humor should be playful but G-rated*: "To keep your marriage brimming, with love in the wedding cup, whenever you're wrong, admit it; whenever you're right, shut up" (Ogden Nash) or "If I'm the best man, why is she marrying him?" (Jerry Seinfeld) or "Love is an electric blanket with someone else in control of the switch" (Cathy Arlyle). Your toast should also be addressed to the couple. You stand and deliver the toast while everyone else remains seated, unless everyone is already standing and milling about. In either case, tap your glass, ask for attention from the assembled group, and make a simple statement to begin, such as: "May I have your attention, please. I'd like to propose a toast." At the finish you raise your glass and salute the couple.

PHOTO 17.1 Wedding toasts are a common tribute speech.

Roasts: Poking Fun with Admiration

A **roast** is a purposely humorous tribute to a person. Although the humor can be sarcastic, insulting, ribald, even wildly exaggerated, everyone in attendance knows and expects that the entire affair is meant to praise the honoree. You poke fun at the honoree as a way of expressing your admiration and affection for the person. A roast carries the message that you're important enough to be roasted. Here are some guidelines:

1. **Humor is the key ingredient of any roast.** This is not meant to be a serious event. It is supposed to be light-hearted and amusing. Follow the guidelines in Chapter 6 on using humor appropriately and effectively.

2. **Keep the tone positive.** A roast is meant to be a good-natured kidding of the honoree, not an opportunity to embarrass the person in front of friends and relatives. Some celebrity roasts get way too personal, even vicious.

3. **Be brief.** This is not your audition for stand-up comedian of the year. Usually, each speaker at a roast addresses the audience for about three to five minutes. Stick to the time limit.

4. **Finish on a heartfelt, serious note.** Playfully making fun of the honoree should be amusing, but do not forget that a roast is meant to express admiration and affection for the person roasted. "All kidding aside, you know how much I respect and admire my dear friend. He is a beacon of light in a sometimes dark world" is one way to close your roast on a serious note.

Tribute to Colleagues: Honoring the Departing

A tribute to someone leaving due to retirement or simply moving to another place of employment is a *commemorative speech* that has its own expectations and requirements. Your revered athletic coach is leaving and you want to give him or her a great send-off, so you hold a tribute dinner. A highly popular teacher retires and students and faculty want to pay tribute. These and other situations provide opportunities for tribute speeches. The audience may not welcome the departure, but it should be a cause for a happy send-off of the person paid tribute. This type of speech, given while the honored person is present, *should be light-hearted and should emphasize the contributions and notable qualities that everyone will miss.*

Recently, I was asked to give a tribute speech for a friend and long-time colleague who was retiring. I began this way:

I'd like to begin this tribute to Jack with a short poem I've written for this occasion. I apologize in advance.

There is a professor named Jack.

Who deserved a most elegant plaque.

With flattering comments and turn of phrase.

Abundant awards and plentiful praise.

But instead he must settle for this sorry rhyme.

Knowing full well that he'll be teaching part-time.

Because try as he might; no matter what he may say

Old teachers never die; they just grade away.

The point of this opening was to create a light-hearted tone, and to be a bit playful. The last line is a glancing reference to the famous line from General Douglas MacArthur in his April 19, 1951, address to the U.S. Congress, "Old soldiers never die, they just fade away." I continued by reflecting on some of my friend's accomplishments during his long career as a teacher and administrator. I finished lightheartedly, as I began, with a "bit of doggerel" or bad poetry:

The power of one is so often unclear.

But let voices be raised and perhaps a dark beer.

To proclaim across campus for all to hear.

There's one special man whose impact is felt.

And although his physique is no longer so svelte.

Our dear friend and colleague will surely be missed.

> But let's all make a vow to steadfastly resist.
>
> Dwelling long on Jack's parting, no need for redundance.
>
> And instead wish he and Diane joy in abundance.

No one in the audience expected great poetry from me, and none was evident, but listeners were amused and attentive to hear something a bit different than the previous tribute speeches. *Do not be afraid to take a small risk and produce a speech that tries something different.* My attempt was greatly appreciated by my friend, who recognized immediately that I had put some effort into constructing the tribute. It is the apparent effort that you put into a tribute speech that sends the message, "I care about you and you will be missed."

Eulogies: Praising the Departed

A **eulogy** is a tribute delivered in praise of a deceased friend or family member. Unlike other tributes where the honored person is present to hear the speech, eulogies pay tribute to someone who has died. Given the sadness that typically surrounds a funeral, your challenge is to show respect for those grieving and provide a sense of closure for those feeling the profound loss of a loved one. The word *eulogy* originates from the Greek word that means "to praise." You want to capture the essence of the person eulogized. For years I required my speech students to deliver their own eulogy, to play the role of someone paying tribute to them after their death. It offered a way of getting in touch with how my students saw themselves, who they wanted to become, and what they would want others to say about them after they died. The assignment was always instructive and often quite moving and insightful.

Eulogies do not have to be somber speeches; as newscaster Tom Brokaw said at the funeral of his colleague Tim Russert, there would be "some tears, some laughs and the occasional truth" (quoted in Wilson, 2008, p. 2D). Capturing the essence of the person may mean paying tribute to his or her uniqueness as a human being. My father was just such a person, and when he died, I delivered his eulogy. I not only described my father's many acts of kindness, but I also tried to transform his legendary impatience into moments of gentle humor that all could appreciate. Here is an example:

> Dad hated to get behind slow drivers (which was anyone obeying the speed limit). When Dad was in his 70s, he barely slowed down. I remember Mom and Dad picking me up at the airport one time. Dad was driving his Thunderbird. The freeways were jammed, so Dad took a back route home. At one point he was flying down the boulevard. From the back seat I gently inquired: "Dad, when exactly will our flight be leaving the ground?" He reduced his speed only slightly.

PHOTO 17.2 Kate Edwards, daughter of former presidential candidate John Edwards, delivers the eulogy for her mother, Elizabeth. The word *eulogy* is derived from Greek and means "to praise."

Using humor in a eulogy can be tricky. You want to show the utmost respect for the deceased, and you certainly do not want to cause offense for the grieving. Listeners typically welcome gentle humor that humanizes and explores the principal personal characteristics of the deceased.

In constructing an effective and appropriate eulogy, follow these guidelines:

1. **Your opening should capture attention and set the theme.** A relevant quotation, a short story that reflects the core characteristics of the deceased, or a novel example from the life of the lost loved one are a few possibilities. "There's a Jewish saying, 'The only truly dead are those who have been forgotten.'" This quotation makes a nice introduction about how unforgettable the deceased individual is.

2. **Your organizational pattern is typically narrative.** You are briefly telling a story of the person's life, capturing the important plot lines about this character. This is not a mere biography of the person. Do not simply list the person's resume of awards, degrees, professional publications, and the like. Tell a story about what this person was like. Personal attributes are more important and heartfelt than personal accomplishments unless the accomplishments illustrate important and personal laudatory attributes.

3. **Strive for emotional control.** Your audience already feels grief. A eulogy is a tribute. It should offer uplifting praise. You want the audience to feel a little better, not worse, after your speech.

4. **Be balanced and realistic in your praise.** Senator Ted Kennedy, in his eulogy of his brother Robert who was assassinated during his California campaign for president in 1968, chose the perfect line to make this point: "My brother need not be idealized, or enlarged in death beyond what he was in life; to be remembered simply as a good and decent man, who saw

wrong and tried to right it, saw suffering and tried to heal it, saw war and tried to stop it" (quoted in "Ted Kennedy's Eulogy," 1968).

5. **Relate what you will most remember and miss about the person.** Here are a few things I related about my father:

> I will miss his puns—most of them real groaners. I will remember Dad getting up in restaurants, grabbing the coffee pot and serving himself and other customers because the service was too slow. Most of all, I will remember Dad's unconditional love, unfailing support, and boundless generosity.

6. **Finish strong.** Ted Kennedy finished his eulogy for his brother Robert this way: "As he [Robert] said many times, in many parts of this nation, to those he touched and who sought to touch him: 'Some men see things as they are and say why. I dream things that never were and say why not'" (quoted in "Ted Kennedy's Eulogy," 1968). George W. Bush finished his eulogy to his father, who passed away in 2018 at the age of 94, this way: "So through our tears, let us know the blessings of knowing and loving you, a great and noble man, the best father a son or daughter can have. And in our grief, let us smile, knowing that Dad is hugging Robin and holding Mom's hand again" (quoted by Carlisle & Paschal, 2018).

When the space shuttle *Challenger* exploded in 1986 with the loss of the entire crew, Ronald Reagan delivered a nationally televised eulogy commemorating our fallen heroes who risked their lives to explore space. Ranked eighth on the Top 100 American Speeches of the twentieth century (Lucas & Medhurst, 2008; *see access to link at end of chapter*), Reagan captured the essence of the moment with these final few sentences: "The crew of the space shuttle *Challenger* honored us by the manner in which they lived their lives. We will never forget them, nor the last time we saw them, this morning, as they prepared for their journey and waved goodbye and 'slipped the surly bonds of earth' to 'touch the face of God.'" Using the words from a sonnet titled "High Flight," a poem many pilots know well and some keep on their person, Reagan gave nobility to the deaths of our astronauts in his moving, eloquent finish to his eulogy.

INTRODUCTIONS OF FEATURED SPEAKERS

A **speech of introduction** prepares an audience for a speech to be given by a featured speaker. Sometimes an audience is very familiar with the speaker, requiring a very brief introduction. *You want to create enthusiasm for the* *speaker, but remember that you are not the main focus.* Identify who you are if the audience is unfamiliar with you, but place the focus on the speaker being introduced.

If I were introducing American humorist Dave Barry, a well-known personality in many circles, I would keep the introduction very brief because the audience is not excited to hear me speak. They have gathered to hear the featured speaker. I would mostly quote his own self-description taken from his website because it is so amusing, places the focus squarely on him, and sets the mood for his speech. Consider this example:

> Thank you for attending this anxiously anticipated event. It is my great honor to introduce to you a man who describes himself in these words: Dave Barry has been a professional humorist ever since he discovered that professional humor was a lot easier than working. He won the Pulitzer Prize for Commentary. Many people are still trying to figure out how this happened. For many years he wrote a newspaper column that appeared in more than 500 newspapers and generated thousands of letters from readers who thought he should be fired. Dave has also written more than 30 books, although virtually none of them contain useful information. In his spare time, Dave is a candidate for president of the United States. If elected, his highest priority will be to seek the death penalty for whoever is responsible for making Americans install low-flow toilets. Anything else I might add about Dave Barry would pale in comparison to his own self-description, so without further ado, please welcome Dave Barry.

Notice that the last statement asks the audience to welcome the speaker. This cues the audience to applaud the speaker as a welcoming gesture.

Less familiar speakers require a bit more information for an audience. As student body president or spokesperson for a campus club, for example, you may introduce a speaker at a college presentation. Build the speaker's credibility by briefly listing awards, titles, accomplishments, and the like: "Carmen Jimenez has advanced degrees in geotechnical engineering and has investigated some of the worst natural disasters in our recent history, including our own all-too-familiar and tragic collapse of the county's earthen dam. She is a recognized geological expert internationally, and she has won numerous awards for her service to our country." Remember, the audience does not assemble to hear you speak, so keep the credential building short. Also, make sure that you pronounce the speaker's name correctly. If you are unsure, ask the speaker before introducing him or her. Finally, never provide any potentially embarrassing details about the speaker. Making a speaker and the audience uncomfortable at the outset sets an awful tone for the ensuing speech.

As a featured speaker, responding well to an introduction, especially an effusively positive one, can ingratiate you to your audience. Henry Shelton, when General Chairman of the Joint Chiefs of Staff, responded to just such an effusive introduction this way: "Thank you, Mr. Secretary, for that incredible introduction. If I had known you were going to eulogize me, I would have done the only decent thing and died" ("Victory, Honor, Sacrifice," 2001). *For more standard introductions, simply offer a gracious thanks, express enthusiasm for appearing before this audience, and then begin your speech.*

SPEECHES OF PRESENTATION

Awards ceremonies have become commonplace. It is difficult to find a week on television in which there is a total absence of some award program. As a student, you may find occasions on campus and off in which you are responsible for giving a presentation speech. A **speech of presentation** must communicate to the audience assembled the meaning and importance of the award. "The Floyd Younger award for excellence in teaching is offered each year to the one instructor on our campus, chosen by committee from nominations made by his or her colleagues, who has exhibited outstanding effectiveness as a teacher" is an example. Also, a presentation speech should identify why the recipient has earned the award. The following is an example:

> This year's award recipient has taught creative writing on this campus for 15 years. Her students adore her. One student remarked, "I've never had a teacher who was so enthusiastic, so encouraging, so downright fun in class." Another student said this: "She's simply the best instructor in the universe." It is my great pleasure to present the Floyd Younger award for excellence in teaching to Karen Follett.

Present the award to the recipient with your left hand so you are free to shake the recipient's right hand.

SPEECHES OF ACCEPTANCE

How many times have you watched the Academy Awards presentations and heard a winner begin an acceptance speech, "I didn't think I would win, so I didn't prepare a speech"? It is false humility, and it is lame. Actors especially should have a prepared script. It is the essence of their business. Some of the worst, most cringe-inducing acceptance speeches have occurred at the Oscars (*see access to link at end of chapter*).

PHOTO 17.3 Arike Ogunbowale of the 2018 Notre Dame women's basketball team receives an ESPY award, and she focuses on thanking her coaches and teammates for the honor. When receiving an award, express appreciation without being boastful.

If you have any inkling that you might win an award, large or small, on campus or off, prepare a brief acceptance speech. For example:

Thank you so much for this "Sportsmanship Award." I'm honored to receive it. Mark Twain once quipped, "It's good sportsmanship to not pick up lost golf balls while they are still rolling." Sound advice! Good sportsmanship for me is all about character—showing that, win or lose, you play fair and accept the result with graciousness and modesty. I want to thank my coaches and teammates for helping me to mold my character. I'm a work in progress, but this award validates that I am indeed making progress as a human being. My humble thanks.

Your acceptance speech should be appreciative, genuine, and humble. No one wants to hear the winner gloat. "I knew I would win this" or "Boy, I deserve this" does not endear you to the audience. Show your appreciation with a simple statement: "Thank you so much for this great honor." Thank the most important people who helped you and those who gave you the award. Keep the list short.

COMMENCEMENT ADDRESSES

A **commencement address** is an inspirational speech that occurs at graduation ceremonies. You want to move your listeners to think in new ways, to participate in a cause, or to help your community to solve problems. The primary focus is on engaging your listeners and imparting wisdom. This is no small task. Celebrities, comedians, actors, CEOs of major corporations, politicians, members of the news media, and individuals who have overcome great obstacles in life are invited every year to give commencement addresses at colleges and universities all across the United States. Even presidents of the United States give commencement addresses. As a student, you may be asked to give one type of commencement address, the valedictory speech.

PHOTO 17.4 Valedictory speeches are examples of commencement addresses delivered by students. Blending humor and a serious message is a winning combination for such presentations.

Commencement addresses usually have a serious message to impart to graduates, but the best such addresses blend abundant humor with a serious theme (see access to Brad Delson link at end of chapter). J. K. Rowling, author of the Harry Potter series, in her 2008 Harvard commencement address, began this way: "The first thing I would like to say is 'thank you.' Not only has Harvard given me an extraordinary honor, but the weeks of fear and nausea I have endured at the thought of giving this commencement address have made me lose weight" ("The Fringe Benefits of Failure," 2008). Her amusing opening tapped beautifully into her theme—fear of failure and the fringe benefits of experiencing failure.

Stephen Colbert delivered a commencement address to graduates at Wake Forest University on May 18, 2015 (*see access to link at end of chapter*). Not surprisingly, there was abundant humor sprinkled throughout his presentation. He began with this introduction: "Congratulations to you, the class of 2015. You did it and you look amazing. Although it's a little embarrassing you all showed up in the same outfit. Really, even the accessories are the same." He later launched into his theme: "I hope you find the courage to decide for yourself what is right and what is wrong, and then please, expect as much of the world around you" (quoted by Mosbergen, 2015).

Inspirational commencement addresses should appeal to our better nature. You want to touch deep feelings of your audience, encouraging pure motives and greater effort to achieve a common good. This is a commencement, a new beginning.

AFTER-DINNER SPEECHES

An **after-dinner speech** is a presentation that typically occurs at a formal gathering of some group. After-dinner speeches are not always presented after dinner. Developed in England in the nineteenth century as a formal type of presentation, such speeches were literally delivered right after a dinner, usually to a large gathering for some occasion. More recently, such presentations may occur after a luncheon or even a breakfast gathering of business or civic groups. They probably should be renamed *after-meal speeches*, but after-dinner speech remains the common term still used.

An after-dinner speech is meant to entertain. Although your topic can be a serious one, you need to take an amusing approach to it. For example, a speech on vegetarianism could be informative if you describe the pros and cons of eschewing meat, it could be persuasive if you argue forcefully that we should convert to vegetarianism, and it could be an after-dinner speech if you made light of the vegetarian substitutes for meat (e.g., lentil loaf, soy burgers). The tone should be whimsical, not serious. This makes some topics more appropriate than others. AIDS is not a whimsical topic; neither is child abuse, terminal illness, or torture. "The Most Ridiculous Things People Do with Cellphones" or "My Top Ten List of Irritating Behaviors in Restaurants" or "The World's Most Pointless Signs" all suggest humorous potential. Again, review the guidelines for using humor effectively and appropriately discussed in Chapter 6.

Despite the whimsical nature of after-dinner speeches, this is not stand-up comedy. Refrain from delivering a series of one-liners unrelated to any theme or thoughtful point. *Your after-dinner speech should have a central theme and a serious point relevant to that theme*, even though you accomplish this with humor. Often the topic and theme are your choice, or the group that invites you to speak considers you an authority on certain topics and wants you to speak on one of them. *The occasion and makeup of your audience may also dictate certain topic choices.* If you are speaking before an environmental group, there should be an environmental flavor to your theme (e.g., common mistakes the public makes about the environmental movement in America). Skip the canned jokes. Telling lawyer jokes to a group of attorneys will likely backfire. They probably have heard every lawyer joke ever made. Be original and creative.

SUMMARY

Special occasion speeches are different from informative and persuasive speeches. Each type has its special guidelines for it to be effective and appropriate. In most cases, such speeches work best when they are relatively brief, heartfelt, entertaining, and well-suited to audience expectations. Make your special occasion speeches truly special.

TED TALKS AND YOUTUBE VIDEOS

Simple Tips: "How to Give a Toast"

Eulogy: "George W. Bush Cries Delivering Eulogy for His Father, George H. W. Bush (Full Eulogy)"

Commencement Speech from a Communication Major: "Linkin Park's Brad Delson Speaks at UCLA Graduation/Part 1"

Commencement Speech: "The Most Inspiring Speech: The Wisdom of a Third Grade Dropout Will Change Your Life/Rick Rigsby"

Commencement speech: "Amy Poehler: Amazing Harvard Speech"

Commencement Speeches: "These Great Commencement Speeches Will Change How You Look at Success and Failure"

Acceptance Speech: "Tina Fey: The Mark Twain Prize Speech"

Bad Acceptance Speeches: "The 9 Worst Oscar Speeches Ever"

Classic Eulogy: "*Challenger*: President Reagan's Challenger Disaster Speech, 1/28/86"

Commencement Speech: "Stephen Colbert Offers Spot-on Life Advice in Wake Forest Commencement Speech: Have Your Own Standards"

Excellent Eulogy: Billy Crystal "Muhammad Ali Funeral/Billy Crystal Imitates Ali"

For relevant links to TED Talks and YouTube videos, see the Practically Speaking Companion Website: www.oup.com/he/rothwell-ps3e. You can also gain access by typing the title of the speech reference into a Google search window or by doing the same on the TED Talks or YouTube sites.

CRITICAL THINKING QUESTIONS

1. Should you ever criticize a departed person in a eulogy? What if the deceased was not a very nice person?

2. Is sarcasm appropriate when giving an acceptance speech?

NOTE: Online **student resources**, such as practice tests, flashcards, and other activities, can be accessed at www.oup.com/he/rothwell-ps3e

Text of an Informative Speech

(Problem–Cause–Solution Organizational Format)

THE ANNUAL PLAGUE

(Prepared January 2019; about a **seven-minute** speech)
[Application of text material in brackets]

It infected an estimated half-billion people worldwide, killed an estimated 50 million of them including 675,000 Americans, according to the Centers for Disease Control and Prevention website accessed January 3, 2019. [Use of startling statistics gains attention; credible source] Mortality rates were highest among 20–40-year-olds. City morgues across the United States became overwhelmed with bodies stacked like cords of wood [Use of simile]. Undertakers rapidly ran out of coffins, and graves couldn't be dug fast enough to accommodate the rising death toll, so bodies often lay in homes for days or even weeks. According to highly respected *New York Times* science journalist, Gina Kolata, in a book she wrote on the subject, victims suffered agonizing symptoms that included high fever and violent coughing fits that cracked ribs and spewed blood from victims' mouths. Fluid filled their lungs, causing many to drown in their own juices. [Vivid description keeps attention]

What was this terrifying killer? [Transition] The Black Death of the fourteenth century revisiting the human species? AIDS? Some biological warfare agent? The start of the Zombie Apocalypse? [Rhetorical questions involve audience, create curiosity] The global killer was the flu! The so-called Spanish flu of 1918–1919 caused a pandemic, or worldwide epidemic.

The previously cited Centers for Disease Control and Prevention, commonly referenced as simply the CDC, [abbreviated citation to avoid tedious repetition] notes more recent flu pandemics. A 1957/1958 "Asian flu" killed almost 70,000 Americans and 2 million worldwide. In 1968/1969, the "Hong Kong flu" killed almost 34,000 Americans, and as many as 575,000 people worldwide died from the 2009 H1N1 flu strain. Even more recently, 80,000 Americans died from the 2017/2018 flu. Medical researcher Chris Murray of Harvard University and his associates, in a frightening December 23, 2006, issue of *Lancet*, estimates that the H5N1 "avian flu," still circulating mostly among birds, could kill as many as 81 million people globally if it were to mutate and cross over to humans. No one knows if or when this could happen. [Credible source; more really startling statistics; stacking statistics for effect]

Why should we care about flu pandemics of the past? [Rhetorical question engages audience, makes transition] There are two good reasons [signposting]: (1) a flu pandemic could strike again, and (2) everyone in this room is a potential victim of a deadly flu virus. [Significance of topic] Consequently, you'll want to listen carefully as I inform you about ways to prevent contracting the flu. [Clear purpose statement] My careful and extensive research on this subject [brief reference to credibility] leads me to make three main points. First, even seasonal flu viruses are a serious health hazard; second, flu viruses are difficult to combat; and third, there are several ways to prevent the flu. [Clear, concise preview of main points]

Let's begin by [transition] discussing the serious health hazards produced by a normal flu season. [Signposting first main point] Even ordinary flu viruses that hit the United States every year between the months of October and April are killers. An April 19, 2017, report by the CDC notes that flu-associated deaths in the U.S. vary from a low of 12,000 to a high of 56,000 annually. [Credible, recent source for statistic]

Most of you won't die from a common flu virus, but you may wish you were dead. According to the CDC website previously referenced [abbreviated citation], typical flu symptoms include high fever, sore throat, intense muscle aches, congestion, cough, and severe fatigue. My friend Terry once described how he feels when he gets the flu: "It's like being suddenly hit by a speeding car, catapulted into a concrete wall, roasted in an oven, then forced to participate in the Ironman marathon. Death, by comparison, seems pleasant." [Vivid similes and intensity maintain attention] Symptoms of flu can last from a few days to several weeks. The flu can often lead to severe complications, such as bronchitis and pneumonia, which may require hospitalization.

In addition to the severity of its symptoms [transition], flu is hazardous to humans because it is highly contagious. The CDC website again [abbreviated citation] notes that coughing, sneezing, even talking can spread the flu virus. Long ago, Daniel Haney, science reporter for the Associated Press, in a November 8, 1998, article in the *San Jose Mercury News* [credible source; date is fine since facts haven't changed], called young children "flu incubators." He vividly noted, "In epidemiological terms, children are in the same category as ticks, rats, and mosquitoes: they are vectors of disease." [Vivid description creates attention] Nothing in this regard has changed. Day care centers and classrooms are flu breeding grounds where sick children spew the virus everywhere by coughing, sneezing, and wiping their runny noses and leaving the residue on a wide variety of surfaces. Children also bring the flu home and infect adult parents, who pass it along to coworkers, and so it spreads throughout the population.

Naturally, [transition] we're all interested in why flu is an annual event about as welcome as flies, frogs, and the other plagues God visited upon the ancient Egyptians in the biblical story of the Exodus. [Vividness as attention-getter] This brings me to my second main point, [signposting main point] that flu viruses are difficult to combat.

Over the centuries many theories about the causes of the flu emerged. Influenza, flu being the shortened version of this term, reflects the fifteenth-century astrological belief that the disease was caused by the "influence" of the stars. According to Laurie Garrett, award-winning author of the 1994 book *The Coming Plague*, [credible source; date is fine because these historical facts don't change] prominent American physicians of the time thought the 1918 Spanish flu might have been caused by nakedness, fish contaminated by Germans, dirt, dust, Chinese people, unclean pajamas, open windows, closed windows, old books, or "some cosmic influence." [Historical examples are novel attention getters]

Unlike our predecessors and their wrong-headed prejudices and ignorance, [transition] we know that a virus causes flu, but a flu virus is difficult to combat. There are many strains, not just a single type, and these strains continually change over time. Thus, your immune system's antibodies produced to fight a previous flu will not combat the disease as well when exposed to a slightly altered virus. Occasionally, a flu strain will mutate, altering the genetic structure of the virus so greatly that human antibodies from previous exposures to flu will be useless. Previous flu pandemics were mutated flu strains according to the CDC website [continued use of credible source; abbreviated citation]. The changing structure of flu viruses and their many strains make finding a cure very challenging.

Now that you realize how hazardous flu can be, and understand that its chief cause is a frequently changing virus, [brief internal summary] what can be done about it? [Transition] This brings me to my final main point, [signposting main point] that there are several ways to prevent catching the flu. First, stay generally healthy. [Signposting subpoint] Those in a weakened or vulnerable physical state, such as the very young, the elderly, those with chronic health conditions, and pregnant women, are most likely to catch the flu. All reputable health care professionals encourage a series of preventive steps, including exercise, healthy diet, sufficient rest, frequent hand washing, and avoiding touching your eyes, nose, and mouth. Also, whenever possible avoid large crowds and confined spaces where flu sufferers can infect dozens of individuals. Airplanes, classrooms, dorms, and offices are flu factories [alliteration for vivid style].

Second, [signposting subpoint] a yearly flu shot is an effective preventive. An October 12, 2018, CDC article titled "Vaccine Effectiveness" concludes that annual flu vaccinations typically reduce the risk of contracting the virus from between 40% and 60%, with higher effectiveness among younger individuals. [Credible recent source;

credible statistics] Those who are vaccinated but still get the flu usually experience less severe symptoms. Despite the all-too-common belief that discourages some from getting vaccinated, a flu shot cannot give you the flu because, as the CDC article explains [abbreviated citation], flu shots contain no live virus. If you contract the flu soon after receiving the shot, it is because you were exposed to the flu, and the vaccine does not provide protection [alliteration] until two weeks after being vaccinated. The most frequent side effect is brief soreness at the site of the shot.

For those who get weak in the knees and queasy in the stomach at the very sight of a syringe, there are nasal spray flu vaccines available. These sprays do contain live virus, so there is a small chance of experiencing flu-like symptoms from the spray. Its side effects are minimal, however, especially when compared to some things people shoot up their noses. Pain phobics take note—it doesn't hurt!

None of these options is guaranteed to prevent the flu, so if you do contract this seasonal sickness [alliteration], there are antiviral prescription drugs. A December 10, 2018, CDC article [credible recent source] on antiviral drugs reports that they are effective in reducing flu symptoms and preventing serious complications if taken soon after the onset of the flu. There is also hope on the horizon for a universal flu vaccine, but promising versions still require years of human testing before becoming available to the public.

In review, [transition] I have shown that flu viruses can be hazardous to humans [alliteration], that combating flu can be difficult because flu viruses can easily change, but that catching the flu can be prevented. [Summary of main points] I began with a reference to the 1918 Spanish flu. Author John Barry called the Spanish flu "the deadliest pandemic in history" in his critically acclaimed 2005 book *The Great Influenza*. Nobody knows where the Spanish flu virus went or whether it will surface again. [Bookending introduction and conclusion] The World Health Organization, the National Academy of Sciences, and the CDC all predict that flu pandemics are nearly certain to recur. Until we find a lasting cure for the flu, we'll have to be vigilant in our effort to prevent this annual plague ["annual plague" provides memorable finish].

Text of a Persuasive Speech

(Monroe's Motivated Sequence Organizational Format)

GET BIG MONEY OUT OF COLLEGE SPORTS

(Prepared January 2019)
[Application of text material in brackets]

This text of a model persuasive speech takes about **10 minutes** to present. This is a slightly longer speech than most in-class presentations, but shorter than many public speeches. This somewhat lengthier speech is presented to provide a more comprehensive illustration of several persuasive strategies.

[***ATTENTION***—*1st step, Monroe's Motivated Sequence*] "We want to put our materials on the bodies of your athletes, and the best way to do that is buy your school. Or buy your coach. You sold your souls, and you're going to continue selling them. There's no one of you in this room that's going to turn down any of our money. You're going to take it." So said Sonny Vaccaro in 2001 before shocked members of the Knight Commission on Intercollegiate Athletics. Vaccaro was a slick athletic shoe salesman who worked for various companies such as Nike, Reebok, and Adidas to establish licensing rights with universities for his products. What Vaccaro asserted about the influence of money on collegiate sports was true then, and it is even truer now.

Intercollegiate athletic programs are being corrupted by massive mountains of money [alliteration]. *Time* magazine, November 12, 2018, notes that ESPN paid the National Collegiate Athletic Association (NCAA) $7.3 billion for the rights to air college football's postseason for a dozen years. CBS/Turner television contracted with the NCAA to pay $10 billion from 2011 to 2024 to broadcast the men's college "March Madness" basketball tournament. That contract was extended in 2016 to a gobsmacking $1 billion *annually* until 2032 [Startling statistics]

Let's be honest: [transition] college athletics, especially Division I-A big-time football and basketball programs, have become "a marketing venture rather than an educational venture," as Villanova Professor of Sociology Rick Eckstein claims in his November 9, 2017, article, "Engaging Sports." Student athletes serve as "walking advertisements" [framing] to raise colleges' national profile and serve as a gateway for enticing students to apply for entrance to the university generally, according to a September 28, 2018, *Chronicle of Higher Education* article. [Significance]

Because this is a serious problem, [transition] I will try to convince you that colleges and universities should significantly reduce the scale of their athletic programs. [Proposition of policy]

Every college student listening to me speak today is affected by this commercialization of college [alliteration] sports. As I intend to prove, it is you who partially pay for big-time athletic programs with increased student fees and tuition. [Significance; personal impact]

I can guess what some of you are thinking. [Transition] "He wants to reduce college athletic programs because he hates jocks and was a geek who always lost at sports." Not true! Baseball and basketball were my two favorite sports, and I earned my share of trophies and accolades playing both. I do not propose reducing the scale of college athletics because I hate sports. [Identification; credibility] A college education, however, can open the doors of success for each and every one of you. It is your ticket to a better future [metaphors]. College sports should never serve as a substitute for academic success or impede any student's chance to acquire the best education possible [significance; personal impact], but the commercialization of college athletics threatens to do just that.

So, [transition] I have three arguments that support my proposal to significantly reduce the scale of college athletic programs. First, I will show how big-time athletic programs contradict the educational mission of colleges. Second, I will offer a specific plan to rectify this serious problem. Finally, I will refute primary objections you may have to my proposal, and from the looks on many of your faces, you do have objections. [Preview of main arguments]

[**NEED**–2nd step, Monroe's Motivated Sequence] Returning to my first argument, [transition] that big-time athletic programs contradict the educational mission of colleges, [signposting] let me begin with what I think we all know is true. The principal mission of a college or university is to provide a quality education for all students, including athletes. The NCAA's own Regulation 2.5 states: "Intercollegiate athletics programs shall be maintained as a vital component of the educational program, and student-athletes shall be an integral part of the student body." Excessive emphasis on sports programs, however, contradicts this stated mission in two ways. [Cognitive dissonance]

First, [signposting] athletic prowess, not academic ability, is often given priority. An April 24, 2018, Rice Commission report concluded that there is "a toxic mix of perverse incentives to cheat." This conclusion was based primarily on an FBI investigation into college basketball that resulted in 10 criminal indictments for under-the-table payoffs to high school players and kickbacks to coaches. Schools cheat to attract the best athletes, not the best students [antithesis]. The report, chaired by former Secretary of State Condoleezza Rice, continues: "The levels of corruption and deception are now at a point that they threaten the very survival of the college game as we know it." [Mild fear appeal] An April 16, 2015, report on "Academic Integrity in Collegiate Sport" by The Drake Group concludes: "Institutional admissions standards are routinely waived for academically underprepared athletes whose performances can deliver millions in gate and television revenues." The report cites common practices motivated by the need to win athletic competitions that include "ghost courses" for athletes, awarding them unearned grades, and disproportionate enrollment of athletes in independent studies, online courses, or less demanding courses and majors. The Rice Commission agreed: "There are multiple cases of compromised academic standards and institutional integrity." Clearly, athletic prowess, not academic potential, is what counts. The label "student-athlete," [framing] promoted by the NCAA since the early 1950s, is a myth. More accurately, they are athlete-students [reframing], with only a pro forma, glancing concern aimed at academic competence [continuation of cognitive dissonance]. A study by Ursinus College sociology professor Jasmine Harris, reported in her article in the October 15, 2018, *Houston Chronicle,* notes that, on average, college athletes spend more than three times as many hours per week on sports as they do on their classwork.

Second, [signposting] the primary mission of colleges and universities, to educate students, is often diminished by athletic department deficits. According to a July 7, 2017, article in *Sports Business Daily,* only 10% (23/228) of NCAA Division I university athletic programs are self-sustaining, meaning revenues equal or exceed expenditures. Then there is the added burden of long-term debt resulting from lavish spending on arenas, stadiums, and facilities upgrades. As Thom Patterson of CNN reports, "Many universities in places like Tennessee, Kansas, Arizona and elsewhere are shelling out astronomical funds to build shiny new stadiums, or to make their existing facilities bigger and better." Although private donors pay for some of the expenses, much is left as long-term indebtedness. Economics professors Allen Sanderson and John Siegfried, in a July 31, 2018, article in the *Milken Institute Review,* conclude that "*the vast majority of universities* must redirect funds to cover sports deficits—funds that might otherwise support academic programs." You're paying for the deficits with excessive increases in tuition and fees and shrinking academic offerings. *Forbes* magazine, November 17, 2016, notes that just mandatory student fees alone are increasing 30% faster than tuition, averaging $1,700 per year at four-year colleges with big sports programs. Division I colleges with big football programs spend more than $90,000 per athlete—seven times the average spending per student generally. If you aren't red-faced angry about this state of affairs, you should be. [Continuation of cognitive dissonance; persuasive evidence; anger appeal]

So, what should be done about this problem? [Transition] Clearly, since football and basketball programs are typically the source of all these problems, we should eliminate them from all colleges and universities. If we were to eliminate football and basketball, less visible and far less costly sports such as baseball, golf, gymnastics, and field hockey could provide some athletic opportunities for students. Intramural football and basketball programs could be established for students who prefer those sports at virtually no cost to the college. Let's face facts—getting the money out of college sports is essential if we are going to solve the problems I've outlined. [Contrast effect—door-in-the-face strategy]

Total elimination of football and basketball except for intramural programs solves the problems I've underscored. Perhaps, however, we don't need such a radical solution. As a sports fan and former athlete, I would be disappointed if colleges dumped their football and basketball programs entirely. [Identification] Nevertheless, significant steps must be taken to substantially reduce the corrupting influence of massive expenditures on college sports.

[**SATISFACTION**—3rd step, Monroe's Motivated Sequence] My plan to do this is simple.

1. All athletic programs (including all sports, male and female combined) must be self-supporting. Ticket sales and sports merchandise will be primary sources of funds. This does not mean that every sport must be self-sufficient. Football receipts, for example, could be used to sustain less popular college sports such as golf or field hockey.
2. There will be no scholarships for students based on athletic ability. Scholarships and grants must be based on academic potential and financial need. This is a strong recommendation of the National Alliance for College Athletic Reform. It is also the current practice of Division III NCAA schools.
3. Student athletes must be admitted according to the same standards as all other students. They must maintain a minimum 2.5 GPA to participate in athletic programs.
4. Absolutely no corporate money goes to athletic programs. No corporate logos or names should appear on any sports facilities, equipment, or apparel of any kind. Private donations must go entirely to academic programs and facilities only.
5. Any revenue earned from television or other media programming must be used exclusively for academic programs.
6. My plan will be enforced by the NCAA where legally possible and by all member colleges individually or in concert within each league where antitrust laws prohibit NCAA action; enforcement sanctions include probation, suspension, and/or banishment from league play.

This plan will substantially reduce college athletic programs without eliminating them. I have merely taken the mega-money [alliteration] out of college sports. Leagues, championships, and bowl games can continue, but without the huge financial incentives to distort the academic mission of colleges. Academic programs will no longer be threatened by huge athletic department debts. Without the big money, colleges can return to their primary mission: to provide a quality education for all students.

[**SATISFACTION STEP**, *continued*] In case you're not completely convinced that my plan is a good idea, [transition] let me refute common objections to my proposal. [Two-sided persuasion strategy] First, am I not advocating an implausible proposal that will never occur? Not so! As the Rice Commission already noted, the current trajectory of college athletic spending is unsustainable. A January 4, 2017, *Bloomberg News* article concludes that "College football's top teams are built on crippling debt." The article cites UC Berkeley's half-billion-dollar debt as the worst among dozens of schools, with annual payments just to service the debt at $18 million. It's not a matter of if, but when, the entire collegiate athletic system of commercialization and corruption will collapse [alliteration] from its heedless avarice [vivid language].

The second objection [signposting] might be that disadvantaged student-athletes will lose scholarships and be denied a college education. That's true, but eliminating all athletic scholarships could save money for general scholarships and grants at each college. The net effect on students as a group would be zero. The faces would change, but the same number of students, many financially disadvantaged minorities, could receive financial help. In addition, if student athletes realize that they cannot play college sports unless they qualify academically, this will provide an incentive for them to take their studies seriously or risk ineligibility.

A third objection might be that, [signposting; continuation of two-sided strategy] without athletic scholarships, many student athletes will lose a training ground for a career in professional sports. This may be true, but is it relevant? Should a college be a farm team [framing] for professional sports corporations interested only in profits? Why should a college create false hope for athletes, most of whom will never make it into professional sports? Official NCAA statistics reported on its website and accessed on January 3, 2019, show that fewer than 2% of both male and female football and basketball athletes will become pros. Yet too many student athletes are attending college primarily to play ball as a way of auditioning for professional teams, not to get a quality education. Educational success often gets lost in the hoopla and hubbub [alliteration] over athletic accomplishment. [Cognitive dissonance]

Finally, [signposting; transition] won't sports fans lose a key source of entertainment if my plan is implemented? [Two-sided strategy continued] This is not true. Notre Dame and USC will still remain arch-rivals on the football field. Bowl games will still exist. Championships will still be contested, simply in scaled-down versions as they once were in the 1950s and 1960s before big money began exerting its corrupting influence. The difference will be that academic programs will not be diminished because of huge deficits from athletic programs, and the academic mission of colleges will not be distorted to pay for a bloated athletic program.

[*VISUALIZATION*—4th step; Monroe's Motivated Sequence] Imagine what my plan will accomplish. No longer will colleges be tempted or forced to reduce or eliminate an academic program, perhaps a program in your major, to pay for deficits incurred by out-of-control sports spending. Millions of dollars in scholarships and grants will be available for academically qualified and needy students. Colleges will no longer serve as mere farm teams for profit-motivated corporations [framing]. Colleges will no longer appear hypocritical, espousing an educational mission on one hand while undermining it on the other. [Cognitive dissonance neutralized] Your student fees and tuition will not have to be raised to support a faltering, expensive sports program [assuaging anger].

Picture what will happen if this problem is ignored. Athletic budgets will continue to swell and deficits will rise. Your tuition and fees will increase and academic programs will be cut out of necessity. The quality of your education and your opportunities for academic success will be threatened. [Mild fear appeal]

[*ACTION*—5th step; Monroe's Motivated Sequence] I ask that you support my proposal to significantly reduce college athletic programs. Stop the erosion of academic values and quality. Speak to your Student Senate officers and representatives. Discuss the issues I have raised with the college administration. This college can be a beacon of light signaling the way for other colleges to follow. Change begins with us. Get big money out of college sports! [Effort required is minimal]

Group Oral Presentations

Groups sometimes have public-speaking responsibilities. In some cases, the group has been formed to present information orally before an audience of interested people. This appendix covers some of the basics of oral presentation not already discussed that apply to groups.

PANEL DISCUSSIONS

Panel discussions assemble a small group of participants, usually experts, to engage in a free exchange of information and ideas on a specific issue or problem before an audience. Purposes of a panel discussion include solving a difficult problem, informing an audience on an issue or topic of interest, or stimulating audience members to think about the pros and cons of a controversial issue.

Panel discussions require a moderator. The moderator usually organizes the group presentation by soliciting panel members who represent different points of view on the topic or issue. Panel members should be informed in advance of the topic to be discussed and major issues that should be addressed by panelists. *The moderator should follow several steps to make the panel discussion successful.*

1. Suitable physical arrangements for the panel discussion should be organized in advance. Usually, the number of panelists should be no fewer than three and no more than seven. Panelists should be seated at a long table in front of the audience, normally on a stage overlooking audience members. When group discussions involve more than four or five participants, seating panelists at two tables formed in a slight V-shape to the audience helps panelists address each other during discussions without closing off the audience. Name cards placed on the table in front of each speaker will help the audience become familiar with each panelist. If the room where the panel discussion takes place is relatively large, a microphone at the table should be available for each speaker. If panelists request a DVD player and monitor, computer hook-up, Smartboard, easel, whiteboard, or other means

of presenting visual aids, provide these if possible and place them in a location where access to them is easy and will not block the audience's view.

2. The moderator usually begins by welcoming the audience, providing a brief background on the topic or issue to be discussed, and introducing each panel member, citing specific background and qualifications of each speaker.

3. Panelists should be encouraged to bring notes but discouraged from reading a prepared manuscript.

4. Begin the discussion with a question posed to the panel (e.g., "What is the extent of the problem of binge drinking on college campuses?"). The opening question can be posed to the entire panel, or a specific panelist can be asked to begin the discussion. The moderator identifies who has the floor during the discussion.

5. The moderator acts as a discussion guide. If a panelist has been left out of the discussion, the moderator may direct a question to him or her. If a panelist begins to dominate discussion, the moderator should step in and request participation from other panelists. Controversy should be encouraged, but polite conversation should be the norm. It is the responsibility of the moderator to keep the conversation civil. If it begins to turn ugly, the moderator should remind panelists to disagree without being disagreeable. Move the discussion along so that all major issues are discussed in the allotted time (usually about 45 minutes to an hour).

6. The moderator closes discussion by summarizing main points made by panelists and identifying new issues raised during the discussion to be further explored.

SYMPOSIUMS

A **symposium** is a relatively structured group presentation to an audience. It is composed of several individuals who present uninterrupted speeches with contrasting points of view on a central topic. Unlike a panel discussion, speakers do not engage in a discussion with each other. Each speaker presents a relatively short speech (usually 4–6 minutes apiece) addressing a separate segment of the overall topic. The primary purpose of a symposium is to enlighten an audience on a controversial issue or to inform audience members on a subject of interest.

A symposium also benefits from having a moderator. *The moderator should follow a few important steps to ensure a successful symposium.*

1. Physical arrangements made for a panel discussion, just discussed, should also be used for a symposium.

2. To avoid redundancy, speakers should be chosen who represent different points of view.

3. The moderator should provide a brief background on the subject, introduce the speakers, and identify the speakers' order of presentation.

4. When each speaker is finished, acknowledge who speaks next.
5. When all speakers have presented, thank participants.

FORUM DISCUSSION

A forum discussion allows members of an audience listening to a public speech, panel discussion, symposium, or debate to participate in a discussion of ideas presented. The primary purpose of a forum is to engage the audience in the discussion of issues raised. The moderator's role is critical to the success of a forum discussion. *Some suggestions for the moderator who directs the forum include:*

1. Announce to the audience that an open forum will occur after a panel discussion or symposium has concluded. Audience members can prepare questions or short remarks as they listen to speakers.
2. Rules for forum participation should be clearly articulated before any discussion occurs. Rules may include: raise your hand to be recognized or stand in a line where a microphone has been placed and wait your turn; keep remarks and questions very brief (about 15 to 30 seconds); each person should ask only one follow-up question.
3. Set a time limit for the forum (usually about 30 minutes). Indicate when there is time for only one or two more questions. Accept questions until the deadline has been reached, then conclude the forum by thanking the audience for its participation.
4. Encourage diverse points of view from the audience. A pro and con line might be established. The moderator could move back and forth, recognizing audience members on both sides so a balanced series of questions and comments will be presented.
5. If a question cannot be heard by all members of the audience, the moderator should repeat the question. If a question is confusing, the moderator may ask for a restatement or try to paraphrase the question so panelists or forum speakers can answer.

Glossary

Ad hominem fallacy A personal attack on the messenger to avoid the message; a diversionary tactic that is irrelevant to the primary message.

Ad populum fallacy Erroneously basing a claim on popular opinion.

After-dinner speech A humorous presentation that typically occurs at a formal gathering of some group after a meal that is meant to entertain on some topic of interest to an audience.

Alliteration The repetition of the same sound, usually a consonant sound, starting each word in a phrase or sentence.

Ambushing Looking for weaknesses in a speaker's arguments and preparing to pounce on perceived mistakes without listening for understanding of a speaker's message first.

Analogical reasoning Alleges that because two things closely resemble each other, both should logically be viewed in similar ways.

Anchor In social judgment theory, this is the preexisting attitude on an issue that serves as a reference point.

Anecdote A short, entertaining, real-life story used to illustrate a speaker's point.

Anger activism model Explains the relationship between anger and persuasion.

Antithesis A sentence composed of two parts with parallel structure but opposite meanings to create impact.

Appropriateness Behavior that is perceived to be legitimate and fits the speaking context.

Argument Implicitly or explicitly presents a claim and provides support for that claim with reasoning and evidence.

Articulation Speaking words clearly and distinctly.

Attention The act of focusing on a specific stimulus to the exclusion of competing stimuli.

Attitude A learned predisposition to respond favorably or unfavorably toward some attitude object.

Backing The reasons and relevant evidence that support the warrant in the Toulmin structure of an argument.

Belief What a person thinks is true or probable.

Brief example Short instances used to illustrate points in a speech.

Burden of proof The obligation of those making a claim to present compelling evidence and reasoning to support the claim.

Causal reasoning Occurs when we see events and infer what caused these events.

Central idea Sometimes referred to as the theme, it identifies the main concept, point, issue, or conclusion that you want the audience to understand, believe, feel, or do.

Claim A generalization that remains to be proven with reasoning and evidence.

Cliché A once-vivid expression that has been overused to the point of seeming commonplace.

Cognitive dissonance The unpleasant feeling produced by apparent inconsistency in ideas, beliefs, or opinions; holding two contradictory cognitions simultaneously and feeling uncomfortable when this is pointed out to you.

Coherence Main points of your speech flow directly from the purpose statement, and subpoints likewise flow from main points.

Collectivist culture A culture that emphasizes group harmony, intragroup cooperation and conformity, and individual sacrifice for the sake of the group.

Commencement address An inspirational speech that occurs at graduation ceremonies.

Commitment A passion for excellence; accepting nothing less than the best that you can be and dedicating yourself to achieving that excellence.

Communication A transactional process of sharing meaning with others.

Communication competence Engaging in communication with others that is perceived to be both effective and appropriate in a given context.

Communication orientation A method of addressing speech anxiety by focusing on making your message clear and interesting to your listeners instead of focusing on being evaluated.

Communication skill The ability to perform a communication behavior effectively and repeatedly.

Competence An audience's perception of the speaker's knowledge and experience on a topic.

Composure Exhibiting emotional stability, confidence, and control while speaking.

Confirmation bias The tendency to seek information that supports one's beliefs and to ignore information that contradicts those beliefs.

Context The environment in which communication occurs; the who, what, where, when, why, and how of communication.

Contrast effect A persuasive strategy that begins with a large request that makes a smaller request seem more acceptable.

Correlation A consistent relationship between two variables.

Credibility Judgments made by a perceiver concerning the believability of a communicator.

Credibility of evidence Refers to the believability of evidence as determined by consistency and accuracy.

Cynicism Nay-saying, fault-finding, and ridiculing the beliefs of others; often confused with skepticism.

Demographics Characteristics of an audience such as age, gender, culture, ethnicity, and group affiliations.

Demonstration An informative speech that shows an audience how to use an object or perform a specific activity.

Direct question A question asked by a speaker that seeks an overt response from the audience.

Directory An Internet tool where humans edit indexes of Web pages that match, or link with, keywords typed in a search window.

Door-in-the-face strategy A persuasive strategy that uses the contrast effect.

Dynamism The enthusiasm, energy, and forcefulness exhibited by a speaker.

Dysfunctional speech anxiety Occurs when the intensity of the fight-or-flight response prevents an individual from giving a speech effectively.

Effectiveness The degree to which speakers progress toward the achievement of their goals.

Ego involvement In social judgment theory, it refers to the degree to which an issue is relevant or important to a person.

Elaboration likelihood model An overarching perspective on persuasion that explains how listeners cope with the bombardment of persuasive messages by sorting them into those that are important, or central, and those that are less relevant, or peripheral.

Ethics A system for judging the moral correctness of human behavior by weighing that behavior against an agreed-upon set of standards of right and wrong.

Ethnocentrism The biased belief that customs, practices, and behaviors of your own culture are superior to any other culture.

Ethos Aristotle's ingredients of speaker credibility consisting of good sense, good moral character, and good will.

Eulogy A tribute delivered in praise of a deceased friend or family member.

Euphemism An indirect or vague word or phrase used to numb us to or conceal unpleasant or offensive realities.

Evidence Statistics, testimony of experts and credible sources, and verifiable facts used to support claims.

Examples Specific instances of a general category of objects, ideas, people, places, actions, experiences, or phenomena.

Extemporaneous speech A speech delivered from a prepared outline or notes.

Extended example A detailed, lengthy example to illustrate a point in a speech.

Fallacy Any error in reasoning and evidence that may deceive your audience.

False analogy A fallacy that occurs when erroneously reasoning from two things with superficial similarities that also have a significant point or points of difference.

Fight-or-flight response The physiological defense-alarm process triggered by stress.

Forum discussion Permits members of an audience listening to a public speech, panel discussion, symposium, or debate to participate in a discussion of ideas presented.

Framing The influence wording has on our perception of choices.

Functional speech anxiety Occurs when the fight-or flight response is managed and stimulates an optimum presentation.

General purpose Identifies the overall goal of a speech such as to inform, describe, explain, demonstrate, persuade, celebrate, memorialize, entertain, or eulogize.

Graph A visual representation of statistics in an easily understood format.

Grounds The reason or reasons provided to accept a claim and the evidence used to support those reasons in the Toulmin structure of an argument.

Hasty generalization A fallacy that occurs when individuals jump to conclusions based on a single example or only a handful of examples.

Hypothetical example An example that describes an imaginary situation; one that is created to make a point, illustrate an idea, or identify a general principle.

Identification The affiliation and connection between speaker and audience.

Illusion of transparency The overestimation of the extent to which audience members detect a speaker's nervousness.

Impromptu speech A speech delivered without preparation, or so it seems.

Individualist culture A culture that emphasizes personal autonomy and competitiveness, privacy, individual liberties, and toleration of nonconformity.

Inductive reasoning Drawing conclusions from specific instances.

Inflection Vocal variety used when speaking.

Intensity Concentrated stimuli; an extreme degree of emotion, thought, or activity.

Internal preview Mimics a preview in the introduction of a speech except it appears in the body of your speech.

Internal summary The reverse of an internal preview; it reminds listeners of points already made in a speech but appears in the body, not the conclusion, of a speech.

Jargon The specialized language of a profession, trade, or group.

Latitude of acceptance In social judgment theory, it is the position a person finds tolerable, if not preferable.

Latitude of noncommitment In social judgment theory, it is the position that provokes only a neutral or ambivalent response.

Latitude of rejection In social judgment theory, it is the position a person finds objectionable because it is too distant from the anchor attitude.

Law of Truly Large Numbers With large enough numbers, almost anything is likely to happen to somebody, somewhere, somehow, sometime.

Logos Aristotle's term for building arguments based on logic and evidence to persuade listeners.

Margin of error A measure of the degree of sampling error accounted for by imperfections in sample selection.

Mean The arithmetic average determined by adding the values of all items and dividing the sum by the total number of items.

Measure of central tendency Shows how scores cluster so you can get a sense of what is typically occurring.

Median The middle score in a cluster of numbers.

Metaphor An implied comparison of two seemingly dissimilar things.

Metasearch engine An Internet tool that sends your keyword request to several search engines at once.

Mindfulness Occurs when you think about your communication and concentrate on changing what you do to become more effective.

Mindlessness Occurs when you are not cognizant of your communication with others or simply do not care, so no improvement is likely.

Mixed metaphor The use of two or more vastly different metaphors in a single expression.

Mode The most frequent score in the distribution of all scores considered.

Monroe's motivated sequence A popular persuasive organizational pattern consisting of attention, need, satisfaction, visualization, and action steps.

Non sequitur Classic type of fallacy in which a conclusion does not follow from its premises.

Panel discussion A small group of participants, usually experts, who engage in a free exchange of information and ideas on a specific issue or problem before an audience.

Parallel processing Using both the central and peripheral routes to persuasion.

Pathos Aristotle's term for emotional appeals to persuade audiences.

Performance An attempt to satisfy an audience of critics whose members are focused on evaluating your presentation.

Persuasion A communication process of converting, modifying, or maintaining the attitudes and/or behavior of others.

Picture Superiority Effect Interesting images vastly increase an audience's memory of information in a speech than words alone.

Pitch The range of your voice from high to low sounds.

Plagiarism The dishonest theft of another person's words.

Preview Presents the coming attractions of your speech; identifying the main points of your speech before developing them.

Probability of feared occurrence Likelihood that the feared worst-case scenario while giving a speech would actually happen.

Pronunciation Saying words correctly as indicated in any dictionary based on Standard English rules.

Proposition The primary, overriding claim for a persuasive speech.

Proposition of fact An overriding speech claim that alleges a truth.

Proposition of policy An overriding speech claim that calls for a significant change from how problems are currently handled.

Proposition of value An overriding speech claim that calls for a judgment that assesses the worth or merit of an idea, object, or practice.

Pseudo-paraphrasing Form of plagiarism in which a quotation is changed only slightly by substituting synonyms.

Public speaking An act of communication in which a clearly identified speaker presents a message in a more formal manner than mere conversation to an audience of multiple listeners on an occasion to achieve a specific purpose.

Random sample A portion of a target population chosen in such a manner that every member of the entire population has an equal chance of being selected.

Rationalization of disconfirmation Inventing superficial, even glib, alternative explanations for contradictory evidence that exposes unwarranted beliefs.

Real example Actual occurrences used in a speech to make a point, illustrate an idea, or identify a general principle.

Reasoning The thought process of drawing conclusions from evidence.

Rebuttal Exceptions or refutation that diminish the strength of a claim in the Toulmin structure of an argument.

Referents The objects, events, ideas, and relationships referred to by words.

Reframing Altering perception by changing how issues and problems are descriptively phrased.

Refutation Answering opposing arguments.

Repetition Stylistic use of language that reiterates the same word, phrase, or sentence, usually with parallel structure.

Report A brief, concise, informative presentation that fulfills a class assignment, updates a committee about work performed by a subcommittee, reveals the results of a study, provides recent findings, or identifies the latest developments in a current situation.

Rhetorical question A question asked by a speaker that the audience answers mentally but not out loud.

Roast A purposely humorous tribute to a person typically using sarcasm, exaggeration, even ribald humor.

Rule A prescription that indicates what behavior is obligated, preferred, or prohibited in certain contexts.

Search engine An Internet tool that computer-generates indexes of Web pages that match, or link with, keywords typed in a search window.

Self-deprecation Humor that makes gentle fun of your own failings and limitations.

Self-selected sample Any poll or survey that depends on respondents selecting themselves to participate.

Sensitivity Receptive accuracy whereby one can detect, decode, and comprehend signals in a social environment.

Severity of a feared occurrence Approximated by imagining what would happen if catastrophic failure did occur when giving a speech.

Shared meaning This occurs when both the speaker and receivers have mutual understanding of a message.

Shifting the burden of proof Inappropriately assuming the validity of a claim unless it is proven false by another person who never made the original claim.

Signpost An organizational marker that indicates the structure of a speech and notifies listeners that a particular point is about to be addressed.

Simile An explicit comparison of two seemingly dissimilar things using the words *like* or *as.*

Skepticism A critical thinking process of inquiry whereby claims are evaluated by engaging in a rigorous examination of evidence and reasoning used to support those claims.

Slang The highly informal speech not in conventional usage.

Social cohesion That which binds us together in mutual liking.

Social judgment theory A theory of persuasion that focuses on how close or distant an audience's position on a controversial issue is from its anchor attitude.

Specific purpose A concise, precise statement composed of simple, clear language that both encompasses the general purpose and indicates what the speaker hopes to accomplish with the speech.

Speech anxiety Fear of public speaking and the nervousness that accompanies that fear.

Speech of introduction Prepares an audience for a speech to be given by a featured speaker.

Speech of presentation Communicates to an audience the meaning and importance of an award presented to an individual or group.

Statistics Measures of what is true or factual expressed in numbers.

Stylistic similarity Creating identification with an audience by looking and acting similarly to others.

Substantive similarity Creating identification with an audience by establishing common ground with listeners.

Supporting materials Examples, statistics, and testimony used to bolster a speaker's viewpoint.

Syllogism In formal logic the basic structure of an argument that includes a major premise, minor premise, and conclusion from these two premises.

Symposium A relatively structured group presentation before an audience.

Systematic desensitization A technique used to control anxiety, even phobias, triggered by a wide variety of stimuli that operates on the principle that relaxation and anxiety are incompatible and do not occur simultaneously; incremental exposure to increasingly threatening stimuli coupled with relaxation techniques.

Table An orderly depiction of statistics, words, or symbols in columns and rows.

Testimony A firsthand account of events or the conclusions offered publicly by experts on a topic.

Theme A central idea for a speech that identifies the main concept, point, issue, or conclusion that you want the audience to understand, believe, feel, or do.

Toast A brief tribute to a person or couple.

Transactional communication A process in which each person communicating is both a sender and a receiver simultaneously, not merely a sender or a receiver, and all parties influence each other.

Transitions Use of words or phrases to connect what was said with what will be said in a speech.

Tribute speech Speech that praises or celebrates a person.

True belief A willingness to accept claims without solid reasoning or valid evidence and to hold these beliefs tenaciously even if a mountain of contradictory evidence proves the belief incorrect.

Trustworthiness Refers to how truthful or honest we perceive a speaker to be.

Uncertainty reduction theory As novelty wears off from experience, uncertainty is reduced and anxiety consequently diminishes.

Value The most deeply felt, generally shared view of what is deemed good, right, or worthwhile thinking or behavior.

Variable Anything that can change.

Virtual library A search tool that combines Internet technology and standard library techniques for cataloguing and appraising information.

Visualization Countering negative thoughts of catastrophe when giving a speech with positive images of success.

Vividness effect The outrageous, shocking, controversial, and dramatic events that can distort our perceptions of the facts.

Vocal filler The insertion of *um, uh, like, you know*, and similar variations that substitute for pauses and often draw attention away from a speaker's message.

Volume The range of your voice from loud to soft.

Warrant The reasoning that links the grounds to the claim.

References

Ackrill, C. (2012, October 5). 6 thought patterns of the stressed: No. 3—catastrophizing. *American Institute of Stress.* Retrieved from http://www.cynthiaackrill.com/6-thought-patterns-of-the-stressed-no-3-catastrophizing-lions-and-tigers-and-bears-oh-my/

Adams, T. B. (2016, March 1). Reporters dismayed by Rubio jabs at Trump. *Washington Examiner.* Retrieved from http://www.washingtonexaminer.com/reporters-dismayed-by-rubio-jabs-at-trump/article/2584577

Adler, J. E. (1998, January/February). Open minds and the argument from ignorance. *Skeptical Inquirer,* pp. 41–44.

Advertising is hazardous to your health. (1986, July). *University of California, Berkeley Wellness Letter,* pp. 1–2.

Ahmed, S., & Mendoza, D. (2014, October 20). Ebola hysteria: An epic, epidemic overreaction. *CNN.com.* Retrieved from http://www.cnn.com/2014/10/20/health/ebola-overreaction/

Aldhous, P. (2012, March 9). Fukushima's fate inspires nuclear safety rethink. *New Scientist.* Retrieved from http://www.new scientist.com/article/dn21556-fukushimas-fate-inspires-nuclear-safety-rethink.html

Ali, A. (2016, January 4). UK universities in "plagiarism epidemic" as 50,000 students caught cheating in the last 3 years. *Independent.* Retrieved from https://www.independent.co.uk/student/news/uk-universities-in-plagiarism-epidemic-as-almost-50000-students-caught-cheating-over-last-3-years-a6796021.html

Allan, K., & Burridge, K. (1991). *Euphemism and dysphemism: Language used as shield and weapon.* New York, NY: Oxford University Press.

Allen, G. (1996). Military drug testing. In L. G. Schnoor & B. Wickelgren (Eds.), *Winning orations.* Mankato, MN: Interstate Oratorical Association.

Allen, M. (1991). Comparing the persuasiveness of one-sided and two-sided messages using meta-analysis. *Western Journal of Speech Communication, 55,* 390–404.

Allen, M. (1993). Determining the persuasiveness of one- and two-sided messages. In M. Allen & R. Preiss (Eds.), *Prospects and precautions in the use of meta-analysis.* Dubuque, IA: Brown & Benchmark.

Allen, M. (1998). Comparing the persuasive effectiveness of one- and two-sided messages. In M. Allen & R. W. Preiss (Eds.), *Persuasion: Advances through meta-analysis.* Creskill, NH: Hampton Press.

Allen, M., Bruflat, R., Fucilla, R., Kramer, M., McKellips, S., Ryan, D. J., & Spiegelhoff, M. (2000). Testing the persuasiveness of evidence: Combining narrative and statistical forms. *Communication Research Reports, 17,* 331–336.

Allen, M., Hunter, J. E., & Donohue, W. A. (2009). Meta-analysis of self-report data on the effectiveness of public speaking anxiety treatment techniques. *Communication Education, 38,* 54–76.

Alley, M. (2005). *The craft of scientific presentations: Critical steps to succeed and critical errors to avoid.* New York, NY: Springer.

Anderson, A. (2016, January/February). Your turn to say something: We signal our intention to speak or pause for a response by directing our eyes. *Scientific American Mind,* p. 9.

Anderson, L. V. (2012, July 23). Hot feet: Why don't all firewalkers get burned? *Slate.com.* Retrieved from http://www.slate.com/ articles/ health_and_science/explainer/2012/ 07/ tony_robbins_firewalking_injuries_ why_doesn_t_everyone_who_walks_ on_hot_coals_get_burned_.html

Anderson, M. (2018, May 31). Teens, social media & technology 2018. *Pew Research Center*. Retrieved from https:// www.pewinternet.org/2018/05/31/ teens-social-media-technology-2018/

Anderson, R., & Ross, V. (1994). *Questions of communication: A practical introduction to theory*. New York, NY: St. Martin's Press.

Angier, N. (2002, March 5). One lifetime is not enough for a trip to distant stars. *The New York Times*. Retrieved from http:// www.nytimes.com/learning/teachers/ featured_articles/20020305tuesday.html

Anti-sweatshop activist brings delegates to their feet. (2002, March/April). *California Teacher*, p. 4.

Aretha Franklin's family criticizes reverend's "offensive and distasteful" eulogy during funeral. (2018, September 4). *Variety*. Retrieved from https://variety. com/2018/music/news/aretha-franklins-family-criticizes-reverends-offensive-and-distasteful-eulogy-during-funeral-1202925757/

Armstrong, P. (2017, July 5). Stop using PowerPoint, Harvard University says it's damaging your brand and your company. *Forbes*. Retrieved from https://www.forbes.com/sites/ paularmstrongtech/2017/07/05/stop-using-powerpoint-harvard-university-says-its-damaging-your-brand-and-your-company/#45882d8b3e65

Aronson, E., Fried, C., & Stone, J. (1991). Overcoming denial and increasing the intentions to use condoms through the induction of hypocrisy. *American Journal of Public Health, 81*, 1636–1638.

Arrigo, A. (2018, December 21). What Aristotle can teach us about Trump's rhetoric. *The Conversation*. Retrieved from http://theconversation.com/what-aristotle-can-teach-us-about-trumps-rhetoric-107761

Arthur, D. (2017). Pandemics—an existential threat. In L. G. Schnoor & L. Mayfield (Eds.), *Winning orations*. Mankato, MN: Interstate Oratorical Association.

Atkinson, C. (2008). *Beyond bullet points: Using Microsoft Office PowerPoint 2007 to create presentations that inform, motivate, and inspire*. Redmond, WA: Microsoft Press.

Auerbach, D., Buerhaus, P., Staiger, D., & Skinner, L. (2017, April 8). 2017 data brief update: Current trends of men nurses. *Center for Interdisciplinary Health Workforce Studies*. Retrieved from http:// healthworkforcestudies.com/publications-data/data_brief_update_current_trends_ of_men_in_nursing.html

Ayres, J. (2005). Performance visualization and behavioral disruption: A clarification. *Communication Reports, 18*, 55–63.

Bailey, E. (2008, August 7). Celebrities with anxiety: Harrison Ford: Fear of public speaking. *Healthcentral.com*. Retrieved from http://www.health-central.com/anxiety/c/22705/36519/ celebrities-public

Baker, A. (2018). A just release: Compensating the wrongfully convicted. In L. G. Schnoor & L. Mayfield (Eds.), *Winning orations*. Mankato, MN: Interstate Oratorical Association.

Banaji, M. (2011, February). Harnessing the power of *Wikipedia* for scientific psychology: A call to action. *Observer*, pp. 5–6.

Banas, J. A., Dunbar, N., Rodriguez, D., & Liu, S. (2011). A review of humor in education settings: Four decades of research. *Communication Education, 60*, 115–144.

Baram, M. (2009, June 8). Stephen Colbert Iraq show: Gen. Odierno shaves his head. *Huffington Post*. Retrieved from http:// www.huffingtonpost.com/2009/06/08/ stephen-colbert-iraq-show_n_212388. html

Barnard, D. (2018, January 20). Average speaking rate and words per minute. *Virtual Speech*. Retrieved from https://virtualspeech.com/blog/ average-speaking-rate-words-per-minute

Bauer-Wolf, J. (2018, November 28). Civility at Berkeley. *Inside Higher Ed.* Retrieved from https://www.insidehighered.com/news/2018/11/28/new-policies-student-groups-change-culture-free-speech-berkeley

Baxter, J. (2012). Women of the corporation: A sociolinguistic perspective of senior women's leadership language in the U.K. *Journal of Sociolinguistics, 16,* 81–107.

Bayston, R. (2016, January 6). Bite the bullet: Science says bullet points make presentations fail, so do this instead. *Datanyze.com.* Retrieved from https://resources.datanyze.com/h/i/189700084-bite-the-bullet-science-says-bullet-points-make-presentations-fail-so-do-this-instead

Beard, H., & Cerf, C. (2015). *Spinglish: The definitive dictionary of deliberately deceptive language.* New York, NY: Blue Rider Press.

Beaubien, J. (2017, October 20). Webcast: Can the world finally wipe out polio? *NPR.* Retrieved from https://www.npr.org/sections/goatsandsoda/2017/10/20/558734436/webcast-can-the-world-finally-wipe-out-polio

Beltzer, M. L., Nock, M. K, Peters, B. J., & Jamieson, J. P. (2014). Rethinking butterflies: The affective, physiological, and performance effects of reappraising arousal during social evaluation. *Emotion, 14,* 761–768.

Berezow, A. (2016, January 26). Math's study shows conspiracies "prone to unravelling." *BBC News.* Retrieved from https://www.bbc.com/news/science-environment-35411684

Berger, J. (2015, November 20). Why "cool" is still cool. *The New York Times.* Retrieved from http://www.nytimes.com/2015/11/22/opinion/why-cool-is-still-cool.html

Bernieri, F. J. (2001). Toward a taxonomy of interpersonal sensitivity. In J. A. Hall & F. J. Bernieri (Eds.), *Interpersonal sensitivity: Theory and measurement.* Mahwah, NJ: Lawrence Erlbaum.

Binetti, N., Harrison, C., Coutrot, A., Johnston, A., & Mareschal, I. (2016, July 1). Pupil dilation as an index of preferred mutual gaze duration. *Royal Society Open Science.* Retrieved from https://royalsocietypublishing.org/doi/10.1098/rsos.160086

Bizony, P. (2009, July 6). It was a fake, right? *Engineering and Technology Magazine.* Retrieved from http://eandt.theiet.org/magazine/2009/12/fake-right.cfm#

Bodie, G. D. (2010). A racing heart, rattling knees, and ruminative thoughts: Defining, explaining, and treating public speaking anxiety. *Communication Education, 59,* 70–105.

Boge, A. (2018). "Nothing natural about it": Food apartheid and the colored body. In L. G. Schnoor & L. Mayfield (Eds.), *Winning orations.* Mankato, MN: Interstate Oratorical Association.

Boone, R. (2009, September 5). Court: Ashcroft can be held liable. *San Jose Mercury News,* p. A5.

Bor, J. (2001, January 3). Canadian smokers get stark warning: New labels depict harsh consequences. *San Jose Mercury News,* p. 6A.

Boudreau, J. (2007, August 12). Beijing brushes up on its English skills. *San Jose Mercury News,* p. 17A.

Boyes, A. (2013a, March 13). 6 tips for overcoming anxiety-related procrastination. *Psychology Today.* Retrieved from https://www.psychologytoday.com/blog/in-practice/201303/6-tips-overcoming-anxiety-related-procrastination

Boyes, A. (2013b, January 10). What is catastrophizing? Cognitive distortions. *Psychology Today.* Retrieved from https://www.psychologytoday.com/blog/in-practice/201301/what-is-catastrophizing-cognitive-distortions

Brannon, S. M., & Gawronski, B. (2018, March). Cognitive consistency in social cognition. *Oxford Research Encyclopedias.* Retrieved from http://oxfordre.com/psychology/abstract/10.1093/acrefore/9780190236557.001.0001/acrefore-9780190236557-e-314?rskey=Q4Dybi&result=1

Brewer, N. T., Chapman, G. B., Rothman, A. J., Leask, J., & Kempe, A., (2017). Increasing vaccination: Putting psychological science into action. *Psychological Science in the Public Interest*, 18, 149–207.

Bridges, M. (2018). Zero tolerance for zero tolerance. In L. G. Schnoor & L. Mayfield (Eds.), *Winning orations*. Mankato, MN: Interstate Oratorical Association.

Brinol, P., Petty, R. E., & Wagner, B. (2009). Body posture effects on self-evaluation: A self-validation approach. *European Journal of Social Psychology, 39*, 1053–1064.

Brownen, T. (2018). K12 schools: A "breeding ground" for sexual assault. In L. G. Schnoor & L. Mayfield (Eds.), *Winning orations*. Mankato, MN: Interstate Oratorical Association.

Brown, R. (2015). Mental illness is not a learning disability. In L. G. Schnoor & L. Mayfield (Eds.), *Winning orations*. Mankato, MN: Interstate Oratorical Association.

Bruni, F. (2012, October 11). Big bad Biden. *The New York Times*. Retrieved from http://bruni.blogs.nytimes.com/2012/10/11/big-bad-biden/

Bruskin-Goldring Report. (1993). *America's number 1 fear—Public speaking*. Edison, NJ: Bruskin/Goldring.

Budziszewska, M., Hansen, K., & Bilewicz, M. (2014). Backlash over gender-fair language: The impact of feminine job titles on men's and women's perception of women. *Journal of Language and Social Psychology, 33*, 681–691.

Bumiller, E. (2010, April 26). We have met the enemy and he is PowerPoint. *The New York Times*. Retrieved from http://www.nytimes.com/2010/04/27/world/27powerpoint.html?partner=rss&emc=rss&pagewanted=print

Burke, K. (1950). *A rhetoric of motives.* New York, NY: Prentice Hall.

Burke, K., & Chapman, B. (2012, December 21). NRA's "ludicrous" proposal to have armed guards at every school would cost $3.3 billion. *New York Daily News.* Retrieved from http://www.nydailynews.com/new-york/nra-ludicrous-proposal-cost-3-3b-article-1.1225758

Byrne, J. (2013). Vaccine denialism. *Skeptical Medicine.* Retrieved from https://sites.google.com/site/skepticalmedicine//psuedoskepticism/anti-vaccine-propaganda-and-the-autism-scare

Cabalan, S. (2018). Eleven and engaged: On America's unseen child marriage crisis. In L. G. Schnoor & L. Mayfield (Eds.), *Winning orations*. Mankato, MN: Interstate Oratorical Association.

Campbell, S., & Larson, J. (2012). Public speaking anxiety: Comparing face-to-face and web-based speeches. *Journal of Instructional Pedagogies, 9*, 51. Retrieved from http://www.aabi.com/manuscripts/121343.pdf

Cannon, W. B. (1932). *The wisdom of the body.* New York, NY: Norton.

Can you predict earthquakes? (June, 2019). *USGS.* Retrieved from https://www.usgs.gov/faqs/can-you-predict-earthquakes?qt-news_science_products=0#qt-news_science_products

Carlisle, M. (2011). Bed bugs. In L. G. Schnoor, L. Mayfield, & K. Young (Eds.), *Winning orations*. Mankato, MN: Interstate Oratorical Association.

Carlisle, M., & Paschal, O. (2018, December 5). George W. Bush's eulogy for his father. *The Atlantic*. Retrieved from https://www.theatlantic.com/politics/archive/2018/12/george-w-bushs-eulogy-for-george-h-w-bush/577348/

Carpenter, C. J. (2012). A meta-analysis and an experiment investigating the effects of speaker disfluency on persuasion. *Western Journal of Communication, 76*, 552–569.

Carroll, R. (2016, July 14). Starved, tortured, forgotten: Genie, the feral child who left a mark on researchers. *The Guardian*. Retrieved from https://www.theguardian.com/society/2016/jul/14/genie-feral-child-los-angeles-researchers

Carroll, R. T. (2014, January 14). Law of truly large numbers (coincidence). *The*

Skeptic's Dictionary. Retrieved from http://skepdic.com/lawofnumbers.html

Carroll, R. T. (2016, June 25). Fire walking. *The Skeptic's Dictionary.* Retrieved from http://skepdic.com/firewalk.html

Castillo, M. (2012, December 21). NRA clear on gun debate stance: Arm schools. *CNN.com.* Retrieved from http://www.cnn.com/2012/12/21/us/connecticut-school-shooting/index.html

Ceci, S. J., & Williams, W. M. (2018). Who decides what is acceptable speech on campus? Why restricting free speech is not the answer. *Psychological Science, 13,* 299–323.

Cesca, B. (2015, October 5). Kevin McCarthy is a total dope: This bumbling yahoo is about to be second in line to the presidency. *Salon.com.* Retrieved from http://www.salon.com/2015/10/05/kevin_mccarthy_is_a_total_dope_this_bumbling_yahoo_is_about_to_be_second_in_line_to_the_presidency/

Chabris, C., & Simons, D. (2010). *The invisible gorilla: And other ways our intuitions deceive us.* New York, NY: Crown.

Chan, M. S., Jones, C. R., Jamieson, K. H. (2017). *Psychological Science, 28,* 1531–1546.

Chaplin, T. M. (2015). Gender and emotion expression: A developmental perspective. *Emotion Review, 7,* 14-21.

The Chapman University survey on American fears. (2015, May 17). *Chapman University.* Retrieved from http://www.chapman.edu/wilkinson/_files/fear-2015/codebook.pdf

Charges alleging sexual harassment FY 2010–FY 2019. (2019). *U.S. Equal Employment Opportunity Commission.* Retrieved from https://www.eeoc.gov/eeoc/statistics/enforcement/sexual_harassment_new.cfm

Chasm in the classroom: Campus free speech in a divided America. (2019, April 2). *PEN America.* Retrieved from https://pen.org/wp-content/uploads/2019/04/2019-PEN-Chasm-in-the-Classroom-04.25.pdf

Chemerinsky, E. (2017, December 26). Hate speech is protected speech, even on college campuses. *Vox.* Retrieved from https://www.vox.com/the-big-idea/2017/10/25/16524832/campus-free-speech-first-amendment-protest

Chemerinsky, E. (2018, March 1). The challenge of free speech on campus. *Berkeley Law Scholarship Repository.* Retrieved from https://scholarship.law.berkeley.edu/cgi/viewcontent.cgi?article=4027&context=facpubs

Cheney, G., May, S., & Munshi, D. (2011). *Handbook of communication ethics.* New York, NY: Routledge.

Chen, M. S., Jones, C. R., Jamieson, K. H., & Albarracin, D. (2017). Debunking: A meta-analysis of the psychological efficacy of messages countering misinformation. *Psychological Science, 28,* 1531–1546.

Chen, S. (2015). Chinese intern exploitation. In L. Schnoor & L. Mayfield (Eds.), *Winning orations.* Mankato, MN: Interstate Oratorical Association.

Cherry, K., & Gans, S. (2018a, September 21). How the fight-or-flight response works. *Very Well Mind.* Retrieved from https://www.verywellmind.com/what-is-the-fight-or-flight-response-2795194

Cherry, K., & Gans, S. (2018b, October 28). When and why does habituation occur? *Very Well Mind.* Retrieved from https://www.verywellmind.com/what-is-habituation-2795233

Childers, A. (1997). Hormone hell. In L. G. Schnoor & B. Wickelgren (Eds.), *Winning orations.* Northfield, MN: Interstate Oratorical Association.

Cialdini, R. (1993). *Influence: Science and practice.* New York, NY: HarperCollins.

Citizen Kane holds its spot as AFI's top American film (2007, June 21). *San Jose Mercury News,* p. 2A.

Clay, R. A. (2002). Advertising as science. *Monitor on Psychology, 33,* 38–41.

Clichés. (2009, January 28). *Plain English Campaign.* Retrieved from http://www.plainenglish.co.uk/examples/clich.html

Clinton, H. (2011, December 6). Remarks in recognition of International Human

Rights Day. *U.S. Department of State.* Retrieved from http://www.state.gov/secretary/rm/2011/12/178368.htm

Cole, S. (2015, February 26). New research shows we're all bad listeners who think we work too much. *Fast Company.* Retrieved from https://www.fastcompany.com/3042863/new-research-shows-were-all-bad-listeners-who-think-we-work-too-much

Columbia Accident Investigation Board. (2003, August). *Columbia Accident Investigation report, volume 1.* Retrieved from http://www.nasa.gov/columbia/home/CAIB_Vol1.html

Connors, C. D. (2016, August 26). The formula that leads to wild success—Part 9: Ellen DeGeneres. *Medium.com.* Retrieved from https://medium.com/the-mission/the-formula-that-leads-to-wild-success-part-9-ellen-degeneres-fed4ac228061

Cooper, J., Blackman, S. F., & Keller, K. T. (2016). *The science of attitudes.* New York, NY: Routledge.

Cooper, L. (1960). *The rhetoric of Aristotle: An expanded translation with supplementary examples for students of composition and public speaking.* New York, NY: Appleton–Century–Crofts.

Cotton, G. (2013, August 13). Gestures to avoid in cross-cultural business: In other words, "Keep your fingers to yourself." *Huffington Post.* Retrieved from http://www.huffingtonpost.com/gayle-cotton/cross-cultural-gestures_b_3437653.html

Covin, R. (2011, September 18). What makes a person likeable? *Huffington Post.* Retrieved from http://www.huffingtonpost.ca/roger-covin/likeable_b_901191.html

Crawford, J. T., Malinas, S. R., & Furman, B. F. (2015). The balanced ideological antipathy model: Explaining the effects of ideological attitudes on inter-group antipathy across the political spectrum. *Personality and Social Psychology Bulletin, 41,* 1607–1622.

Crawford, M., & Kaufman, M. R. (2006). Sex differences versus social processes in the construction of gender. In K. Dindia & D. J. Canary (Eds.), *Sex differences and similarities in communication.* Mahwah, NJ: Lawrence Erlbaum.

Crawford, W., & Gorman, M. (1996). Coping with electronic information. In J. Dock (Ed.), *The press of ideas: Readings for writers on print culture and the information age.* Boston, MA: St. Martin's Press.

Crescenzo, S. (2005). It's time to admit the hard truth: We're not photographers. *Communication World, 22,* 12–14.

Criss, D. (2018, February 21). The mass shooting conspiracy theories that just won't go away (and why they should). *CNN.* Retrieved from https://www.cnn.com/2018/02/21/us/mass-shootings-conspiracy-theories-trnd/index.html

Cuncic, A. (2018a, May 31). What is the spotlight effect? Not everyone is staring at you. *Very Well Mind.* Retrieved from https://www.verywellmind.com/what-is-the-spotlight-effect-3024470fear of public speaking.

Cuncic, A. (2018b, September 11). How do I get over my fear of public speaking. *Very Well Mind.* Retrieved from https://www.verywellmind.com/how-do-i-get-over-my-fear-of-public-speaking-3024827

Curtis, K. (2002, March 8). Critics nip at attorney's trial tactics. *Santa Cruz Sentinel,* pp. A1, A4.

Cyphert, D. (2009). PowerPoint and the evolution of electronic eloquence: Evidence from the contemporary business presentation. *American Communication Journal, 11,* 1–20.

Czopp, A. M., Monteith, M. J., & Mark, A. Y. (2006). Standing up for change: Reducing bias through interpersonal confrontation. *Journal of Personality and Social Psychology, 90,* 784–803.

Dacey, T. (2008). Water is not free: Think outside the bottle. In L. G. Schnoor & D. Cronin-Mills (Eds.), *Winning orations.* Mankato, MN: Interstate Oratorical Association.

Dahlberg, T. (2010, February 20). Contrived script lacks soul. *Santa Cruz Sentinel*, p. C3.

D'Angelo, M. (2017, October 9). How to embed a video on PowerPoint. *Business News Daily*. Retrieved from https://www.businessnewsdaily.com/10264-embed-video-powerpoint.html

Davies, J. W. (2011, September 25). Is there any real evidence that people are more afraid of public speaking than dying? *Quora.com*. Retrieved from http://www.quora.com/Is-there-any-real-evidence-that-people-are-more-afraid-of-public-speaking-than-dying

Dean, J. (2012, October 10). The illusion of transparency. *PsyBlog*. Retrieved from http://www.spring.org.uk/2012/10/the-illusion-of-transparency.php

Debies-Carl, J. S. (2017, November/December). Pizzagate and beyond: Using social research to understand conspiracy legends. *Skeptical Inquirer*, pp. 34–37.

DeCourcey, D. (2016, May 22). How to actually change someone's political opinion. *ATTN.com*. Retrieved from https://archive.attn.com/stories/7868/how-change-someones-political-opinion

Deggans, E. (2012). *Race-baiter: How the media wields dangerous words to divide a nation.* New York, NY: Palgrave Macmillan.

De Luna, R. (2018). The chemical restraint of the elderly. In L. G. Schnoor & L. Mayfield (Eds.), *Winning orations.* Mankato, MN: Interstate Oratorical Association.

Democrats introduce Americans with No Abilities Act. (2017, June 2). *Truth or Fiction.* Retrieved from https://www.truthorfiction.com/americans-no-abilities-act-anna/

Dershowitz: Knock-knock joke told by Zimmerman's attorney grounds for mistrial. (2013, June 25). *Fox News*. Retrieved from http://www.foxnews.com/us/2013/06/25/dershowitz-knock-knock-joke-told-by-zimmerman-attorney-was-inappropriate/

Digest of education statistics. (2018). *National Center for Education Statistics.* Retrieved from https://nces.ed.gov/programs/digest/d17/tables/dt17_211.60.asp

Dillard, J. P., & Nabi, R. L. (2006). The persuasive influence of emotion in cancer prevention and detection messages. *Journal of Communication, 56,* 123–139.

Dimock, M. (2018, March 1). Defining generations: Where Millennials end and post-Millennials begin. *Pew Research Center.* Retrieved from http://www.pewresearch.org/fact-tank/2018/03/01/defining-generations-where-millennials-end-and-post-millennials-begin/

Dingemanse, M. (2014, February 24). Use of vivid sensory words thrives across languages. *Medical X Press.* Retrieved from https://medicalxpress.com/news/2014-02-vivid-sensory-words-languages.html

Diridon, R. (2018, May 24). Why it's time to get on board with high-speech rail project. *San Jose Mercury News*, p. A6.

Dlugan, A. (2008, March 8). Speech preparation #7: Choreograph your speech with staging, gestures, and vocal variety. *Six Minutes.* Retrieved from http://sixminutes.dlugan.com/speech-preparation-7-staging-gestures-vocal-variety/

Dolinski, D. (2016). *Techniques of social influence: The psychology of gaining compliance.* New York, NY: Routledge.

Douglas, K. M., & Sutton, R. M. (2014). "A giant leap for mankind" but what about women? The role of system-justifying ideologies in predicting attitudes toward sexist language. *Journal of Language and Social Psychology, 33,* 667–680.

Do vaccines cause autism? (2019, April 11). *Johns Hopkins Bloomberg School of Public Health.* Retrieved from http://www.vaccinesafety.edu/vs-autism.htm

Dowd, M. (2008). *Thank God for evolution: How the marriage of science and religion will transform your life and our world.* New York, NY: Viking.

Dunn, M. (2017, November 23). Good night, night: Light pollution increasing in world. *The Mercury News*, p.A8.

Eagan, K., Stolzenberg, E. B., Zimmerman, H. B., Aragon, M. C., Whang, S. H., & Rio-Aguilar, C. (2017). *The American freshman: National norms fall 2016.* Los Angeles: Higher Education Research Institute. Retrieved from https://www.heri.ucla.edu/monographs/TheAmericanFreshman2016.pdf

Eggert, D. (2012, September 7). Jennifer Granholm: "I probably shouldn't have gotten so worked up" in convention speech. *Michigan Live.* Retrieved from http://www.mlive.com/politics/index.ssf/2012/09/jennifer_granholm_i_probably_s.html

Ellen DeGeneres named "most likable woman in Hollywood" to no one's surprise. (2013, September 20). *Huffington Post.* Retrieved from https://www.huffingtonpost.com/2013/09/20/ellen-degeneres-most-likable-hollywood_n_3962566.html

Elliott, L. (2018, January 21). Inequality gap widens as 42 people hold same wealth as 3.7bn poorest. *The Guardian.* Retrieved from https://www.theguardian.com/inequality/2018/jan/22/inequality-gap-widens-as-42-people-hold-same-wealth-as-37bn-poorest

Ellis, A. (1995). Thinking processes involved in irrational beliefs and their disturbed consequences. *Journal of Cognitive Psychotherapy, 9,* 105–116.

Emotions stir engagement in midterm elections. (2018, June 29). *Center for Political Communication.* Retrieved from https://www.cpc.udel.edu/news/Pages/anger,-anxiety-motivate-voters-in-2018.aspx

Engel, P. (2016, January 12). Everyone is raving about a GOP rising star's off-the-charts rebuttal to Obama. *Business Insider.* Retrieved from http://www.businessinsider.com/nikki-haley-state-of-union-response-obama-trump-2016-1

Engleberg, I. (2002). Presentations in everyday life: Linking audience interest and speaker eloquence. *American Communication Journal.* Retrieved from http://ac-journal.org/journal/vol5/iss2/special/engleberg.htm

Erard, M. (2008). *Um . . .: Slips, stumbles, and verbal blunders, and what they mean.* New York, NY: Anchor.

Estrella, C. (2018, December 13). The Oscars might go without a host. *The Mercury News,* p. A2.

Evaluating Internet resources. (2019). *Georgetown University Library.* Retrieved from https://www.library.georgetown.edu/tutorials/research-guides/evaluating-internet-content

Eyewitness testimony is often unreliable and police and lawmakers know it. (2018, May 8). *Los Angeles Times.* Retrieved from http://www.latimes.com/opinion/editorials/la-ed-eyewitness-testimony-20180508-story.html

Fairhurst, G. T., & Sarr, R. A. (1996). *The art of framing: Managing the language of leadership.* San Francisco, CA: Jossey–Bass.

Falling cow injures coffee house customer. (2001, July 12). *Santa Cruz Sentinel,* p. A8.

Famous quotes and authors. (2009). Retrieved from http://www.famous-quotesandauthors.com/authors/albert_einstein_quotes.html

Fang, M. (2016, February 27). GOP presidential field scrambles to attack Donald Trump, deepening the party's split. *Huffington Post.* Retrieved from http://www.huffingtonpost.com/entry/donald-trump-republican-party_us_56d21fe8e4b0871f60eba9ab

Farhi, P. (2010, November 10). Tina Fey accepts the Mark Twain Prize for American Humor. *The Washington Post.* Retrieved from http://www.washingtonpost.com/wp-dyn/content/article/2010/11/09/AR2010110906707.html

Fathi, N. (2009, June 23). Woman's death creates symbol of Iran protests. *San Jose Mercury News,* pp. 1A, 6A.

Feeley, T. H., Anker, A. E., & Aloe, A. M. (2012). The door-in-the-face persuasive message strategy: A meta-analysis of the first 35 years. *Communication Monographs, 79,* 316–343.

Feeley, T. H., Marshall, H. M., & Reinhart, A. M. (2006). Reactions to narrative and statistical written messages promoting organ donation. *Communication Reports, 19,* 89–100.

Feinberg, M., & Willer, R. (2015). From gulf to bridge: When do moral arguments facilitate political influence. *Personality and Social Psychology, 41,* 1665–1681.

Feldman, G., Lian, H., Kosinski, M., & Stillwell, D. (2017). Frankly, we do give a damn: The relationship between profanity and honesty. *Social Psychological and Personality Science, 8,* 816–826.

Festinger, L. (1957). *A theory of cognitive dissonance.* Stanford, CA: Stanford University Press.

Festinger, L. (1977). Cognitive dissonance. In E. Aronson (Ed.), *Readings about the social animal.* San Francisco, CA: W. H. Freeman.

Fields, K. (2017, September 26). Internet plagiarism among college students. *Classroom.* Retrieved from https://classroom.synonym.com/internet-plagiarism-among-college-students-10029.html

Finn, A. N., Sawyer, C. R., & Schrodt, P. (2009). Examining the effect of exposure therapy on public speaking state anxiety. *Communication Education, 58,* 92–109.

Fisher, A. (2016, August 27). 10 business clichés you should eliminate from your vocabulary. *Fortune.* Retrieved from http://fortune.com/2016/08/27/business-cliches-worst/

Folk, S. (2014, February 27). Lighten up your communication: Use humor like Ellen. *The Language Lab.* Retrieved from http://www.thelanguagelab.ca/posts/lighten-up-your-communication-use-humor-like-ellen/

Ford, P. (2001, September 19). Europe cringes at Bush "crusade" against terrorists. *Christian Science Monitor.* Retrieved from http://www.csmonitor.com/2001/0919/p12s2-woeu.html

Foulke, E. (2006). Listening comprehension as a function of word rate. *Journal of Communication, 18,* 198–206.

Francis, J. A. (2018, April). Meltdown. *Scientific American,* pp. 48–53.

Freed, J. (2015). The debt penalty. In L. G. Schnoor & L. Mayfield (Eds.), *Winning orations.* Mankato, MN: Interstate Oratorical Association.

Freeley, A. J., & Steinberg, D. L. (2013). *Argumentation and debate: Critical thinking for reasoned decision making.* Belmont, CA: Thomson Wadsworth.

Frey, W. H. (2018, March 14). The US will become "minority white" in 2045, Census projects. *Brookings.* Retrieved from https://www.brookings.edu/blog/the-avenue/2018/03/14/the-us-will-become-minority-white-in-2045-census-projects/

Friend, Z. (2013). *On message: How a compelling narrative will make your organization succeed.* New York, NY: Turner.

The fringe benefits of failure, and the importance of imagination. (2008, June 5). *Harvard Magazine.* Retrieved from http://harvardmagazine.com/commencement/the-fringe-benefits-failure-the-importance-imagination

Fruciano, M. (2014). How to use gestures effectively. *Effective Presentations.* Retrieved from https://www.effectivepresentations.com/blog/how-to-use-gestures-effectively/

Fruciano, M. (2016, December 20). Why memorizing your speech is bad. *Effective Presentations.* Retrieved from https://www.effectivepresentations.com/blog/memorizing-speech-bad/

Frymier, A. B., Waner, M. B., & Wojtaszczyk, A. M. (2008). Assessing students' perceptions of inappropriate and appropriate teacher humor. *Communication Education, 57,* 266–288.

Full text of remarks from National Rifle Association CEO Wayne LaPierre on gun control debate one week after Newtown school shooting tragedy. (2013, January 6). *New York Daily News.* Retrieved from http://www.nydailynews.com/news/politics/full-text-nra-remarks-gun-control-debate-newtown-article-1.1225043

Gafni, M. (2013, May 12). Is the end nigh for doomsayer radio network? *San Jose Mercury News,* pp. A1, A19.

Gallo, C. (2014, September 25). New survey: 70% say presentational skills are critical for career success. *Forbes.* Retrieved from www.forbes.com/sites./carminegallo/2014/09/25/new-survey-70-percent-say-presentation-skills-critical-for-career-success/

Gallo, C. (2017, May 31). The cognitive cure for stage fright, according to neuroscience. *Forbes.* Retrieved from https://www.forbes.com/sites/carminegallo/2017/05/31/the-cognitive-cure-for-stage-fright-according-to-neuroscience/#38e43960400c

Galloway, L. (2014). Untitled. In L. G. Schnoor, L. Mayfield, & K. Young (Eds.), *Winning orations.* Mankato, MN: Interstate Oratorical Association.

Gardner, L., & Leak, G. (1994). Characteristics and correlates of teacher anxiety among college psychology teachers. *Teaching of Psychology, 21,* 28–32.

Garofoli, J. (2015, May 13). Gavin Newsom crowdsourcing his commencement speech for SF State University. *SFGATE.* Retrieved from http://blog.sfgate.com/politics/2015/05/13/gavin-newsom-crowdsourcing-his-commencement-speech-for-sf-state-university/

Garrand, D. (2018, November 7). Zach Wahls, who went viral defending his lesbian moms in speech, wins Iowa state senate seat. *CBS News.* Retrieved from https://www.cbsnews.com/news/zachary-wahls-who-went-viral-defending-his-lesbian-moms-in-speech-wins-iowa-state-senate-seat-2018-11-07/

Garrett, R. K., Weeks, B. E., & Neo, R. L. (2016). Driving a wedge between evidence and beliefs: How online ideological news exposure promotes political misperceptions. *Journal of Computer-Mediated Communication, 21,* 331–348.

Gass, R., & Seiter, J. (2014). *Persuasion, social influence, and compliance gaining.* Boston, MA: Allyn & Bacon.

Gay marriage polls find personal relationships have major impact on support. (2013, March 21). *Huffington Post.* Retrieved from http://www. huffingtonpost.com/2013/03/ 21/gay-marriage-polls_n_2925240. html?utm_hp_ref=politics

Gazzaley, A., & Rosen, L. D. (2016). *The distracted mind: Ancient brains in a high-tech world.* Cambridge, MA: MIT Press.

Geiger, A. (2017, August 30). Most Americans—especially Millennials—say libraries can help them find reliable, trustworthy information. *Pew Research Center.* Retrieved from http://www.pewresearch.org/fact-tank/2017/08/30/most-americans-especially-millennials-say-libraries-can-help-them-find-reliable-trustworthy-information/

The generation gap in American politics. (2018, March 1). *Pew Research Center.* Retrieved from http://www.people-press.org/2018/03/01/the-generation-gap-in-american-politics/

Ghosh, P. (2014, January 29). Like, uh, you know: Why do Americans say "you know" and use other verbal fillers so often? *IBTimes.* Retrieved from http://www.ibtimes.com/uh-you-know-why-do-americans-say-you-know-use-other-verbal-fillers-so-often-1549810

Glassner, B. (1999). *The culture of fear: Why Americans are afraid of the wrong things.* New York, NY: Basic Books.

Gleicher, F., & Petty, R. (1992). Expectations of reassurance influence the nature of fear-stimulated attitude change. *Journal of Experimental Social Psychology, 28,* 86–100.

Goldstein, N. J., Martin, S. J., & Cialdini, R. B. (2008). *Yes! 50 scientifically proven ways to be persuasive.* New York, NY: Free Press.

Golshan, T. (2017, January 11). Donald Trump's unique speaking style explained by linguists. *Vox.* Retrieved from https://www.vox.com/policy-and-politics/2017/1/11/14238274/trumps-speaking-style-press-conference-linguists-explain

Goman, C. K. (2016, March 31). Is your communication style dictated by your gender? *Forbes.* Retrieved from

https://www.forbes.com/sites/
carolkinseygoman/2016/03/31/is-
your-communication-style-dictated-by-
your-gender/#749e30e3eb9d

Gonzales, A. (2018). Dysfunctional democracy: Gerrymandering as a tool for
erasure. In L. G. Schnoor & L. Mayfield
(Eds.), *Winning orations.* Mankato, MN:
Interstate Oratorical Association.

Gould, S. J. (1981). *The mismeasure of man.*
New York, NY: W. W. Norton.

Govier, T. (2010). *A practical study of argument.* New York, NY: Wadsworth Cengage.

Grace, K. (2000). Unsanitary hotels. In L.
G. Schnoor & B. Wickelgren (Eds.), *Win-
ning orations.* Mankato, MN: Interstate
Oratorical Association.

Grant, K. B., Hiring managers say many
grads not job ready. (2016, May 16).
CNBC. Retrieved from https://www.
cnbc.com/2016/05/16/hiring-managers-
say-many-grads-not-job-ready.html

Greengross, G., & Miller, G. F. (2008).
Dissing oneself versus dissing rivals:
Effects of status, personality, and sex
on the short-term and long-term attractiveness of self-deprecating and
other-deprecating humor. *Evolutionary
Psychology Journal, 6,* 393–408.

Griffin, E. (2012). *A first look at communication theory.* New York, NY:
McGraw-Hill.

Grim, R. (2014, July 2). Two lesbians
raised a baby and this is what they
got—a White House intern. *Huffington Post.* Retrieved from http://www.
huffingtonpost.com/2014/07/02/zach-
wahls_n_5551300.html

Grohol, J. M. (2018). What is catastrophizing? *Psych Central.* Retrieved
from http://psychcentral.com/lib/
what-is-catastrophizing/

Gruber, J. (2001). Heart disease in women.
In L. Schnoor & B. Wickelgren (Eds.),
Winning orations. Mankato, MN: Inter-
state Oratorical Association.

Guay, M. (2018, June 18). The 13 best
presentation apps in 2018. *Zapier.* Retrieved from https://zapier.com/blog/
best-powerpoint-alternatives/

Gun policy remains divisive, but several
proposals still draw bipartisan support.
(2018, October 18). *Pew Research Center.*
Retrieved from http://www.people-press.
org/2018/10/18/gun-policy-remains-
divisive-but-several-proposals-still-
draw-bipartisan-support/

Gutierrez, K. (2014, July 8). Studies con-
firm the power of visuals in eLearn-
ing. *ShifteLearning.* Retrieved from
https://www.shiftelearning.com/blog/
bid/350326/studies-confirm-the-power-
of-visuals-in-elearning

Hall, J. A., & Bernieri, F. J. (2001). *Interpersonal sensitivity: Theory and measure-
ment.* Mahwah, NJ: Lawrence Erlbaum.

Hambrick, David Z., & Marquardt, M.
(2018, February 6). Cognitive ability
and vulnerability to fake news. *Scientific American.* Retrieved from https://
www.scientificamerican.com/article/
cognitive-ability-and-vulnerability-to-
fake-news/

Hannah, M. (2009, June 26). How will Iranian protests change Twitter? *Mediashift.*
Retrieved from http://www.pbs.org/
mediashift/2009/06/how-will-Iranian-
protests-change-twitter177.html

Hare, W. (2009, March/April). What open-
mindedness requires. *Skeptical Inquirer,*
pp. 36–39.

Harold Camping apologizes for faulty
Rapture predictions and retires, report
states. (2011, November 1). *Huffington Post.* Retrieved from http://www.
huffingtonpost.com/2011/11/01/
harold-camping-apologizes-rapture-
predictions_n_1069520.html

Harrison, L. E. (2000). Introduction. In
L. E. Harrison & S. P. Huntington (Eds.),
*Culture matters: How values shape
human progress.* New York, NY: Basic
Books.

Haynes, S. (2019, May 16). "Now I
am speaking to the whole world."
How teen climate activist Greta
Thunberg got everyone to listen.
Time. Retrieved from http://time.
com/collection-post/5584902/
greta-thunberg-next-generation-leaders/

Hensch, M. (2015, October 8). Colbert: McCarthy uses "English-like words. *The Hill.* Retrieved from http://thehill.com/homenews/house/256323-colbert-mccarthy-speaks-english-like-words

Hentoff, N. (1992). *Free speech for me—but not for thee: How the American left and right relentlessly censor each other.* New York, NY: HarperPerennial.

Hickman, V. (2018). When rehab kills: Fraudulent drug treatment centers. In L. G. Schnoor & L. Mayfield (Eds.), *Winning orations.* Mankato, MN: Interstate Oratorical Association.

Hickson, A. (2016, May 18). The one thing 10 faves have in common. *Refinery 28.* Retrieved from https://www.refinery29.com/2016/05/111114/celebrity-quotes-stage-fright-anxiety

Hill, N. (2018). Shut up or get out: How nuisance ordinances fail our communities. In L. G. Schnoor & L. Mayfield (Eds.), *Winning orations.* Mankato, MN: Interstate Oratorical Association.

Hinderliter, D. (2012). Collaborative consumption. In L. G. Schnoor, L. Mayfield, & K. Young (Eds.), *Winning orations.* Mankato, MN: Interstate Oratorical Association.

Hoffeld, D. (2015, April). The science of effective PowerPoint presentations. *Hoffeld Group.* Retrieved from https://www.hoffeldgroup.com/wp-content/uploads/2015/04/Science-of-Effective-PowerPoint-Presentations.pdf

Hoffman, S. (2014, October 7). Why students forget what they've learned & how to increase learning retention. *Reading Horizons Blog.* Retrieved from http://www.readinghorizons.com/blog/review-%E2%80%93-is-it-worth-it

Hofstede, G., & Hofstede, G. J. (2005). *Culture and organizations: Software of the mind.* New York, NY: McGraw-Hill.

Hogan, P. C. (2003). *The mind and its stories: Narrative universals and human emotion.* Cambridge, UK: Cambridge University Press.

Holland, A. (2018). Organ trafficking. In L. G. Schnoor & L. Mayfield (Eds.), *Winning orations.* Mankato, MN: Interstate Oratorical Association.

Holmes, E. A., & Mathews, A. (2005). Mental imagery and emotion: A special relationship? *Emotion, 5,* 489–497.

Horowitz, B. (2002). *Communication apprehension: Origins and management.* Albany, NY: Singular.

Hoshino-Browne, E., Zanna, A. S., Spencer, S. J., Zanna, M. P., Kitayama, S., & Lackenbauer, S. (2005). On the cultural guises of cognitive dissonance: The case of Easterners and Westerners. *Journal of Personality and Social Psychology, 89,* 294–310.

How big is a zetabyte? The size of data is only getting bigger. (2014, January 15). *Auston Institute of Management.* Retrieved from http://www.auston.edu.sg/big-zetabyte-size-data-getting-bigger/

How long would it take to get to Alpha Centauri? (2015, January 14). *EarthSky.* Retrieved from http://earthsky.org/space/alpha-centauri-travel-time

How we got from 1 to 162 million websites on the Internet. (2008, April 4). *Royal Pingdom Blog.* Retrieved from http://royal.pingdom.com/2008/04/04/how-we-got-from-1-to-162-million-websites-on-the-internet

Howard, P. N., Duffy, A., Freelon, D., Hussain, M., Mari, W., & Mazaid, M. (2011). Opening closed regimes: What was the role of social media during the Arab Spring? *Project on Information Technology & Political Islam.*

Hsu, J. (2008, August/September). The secrets of storytelling: Our love for telling tales reveals the workings of the mind. *Scientific American Mind,* pp. 46–51.

Ilakkuvan, V., Turner, M. M., Cantrell, J., Hair, E., & Vallone. (2017). The relationship between advertising-induced anger and self-efficacy on persuasive outcomes: A test of the Anger Activism Model using the truth campaign. *Family and Community Health, 40,* 72–80.

Inman, C. (2010, February 20). Woods' scripted apology perfectly awkward. *San Jose Mercury News,* p. 1D.

Interview: Clifford Nass. (2010, February 2). *Frontline*. Retrieved from http://www.pbs.org/wgbh/pages/frontline/digital nation/interviews/nass.html

Itkowitz, C. (2016, September 15). This Harvard professor explains why we were born to resist working out. *The Washington Post*. Retrieved from https://www.washingtonpost.com/news/inspired-life/wp/2016/09/15/this-harvard-professor-knows-why-you-skipped-the-gym-this-morning-it-is-natural-and-normal-to-be-physically-lazy/?noredirect=on&utm_term=.49b6c3302804

Jackson, B., Compton, J., Thornton, A. L., & Dimmock, J. A. (2017). Re-thinking anxiety: Using inoculation messages to reduce and reinterpret public speaking fears. *PlosOne*. Retrieved from http://journals.plos.org/plosone/article?id=10.1371/journal.pone.0169972

Jaksa, J., & Pritchard, M. (1994). *Communication ethics: Methods of analysis*. Belmont, CA: Wadsworth.

Jamieson, K. H. (1988). *Eloquence in an electronic age*. New York, NY: Oxford University Press.

Jarrett, C. (2016, November 28). The psychology of eye contact, digested. *The British Psychological Society Research Digest*. Retrieved from https://digest.bps.org.uk/2016/11/28/the-psychology-of-eye-contact-digested/

Jemmott, J. B., Jemmott, L. S., & Fong, G. T. (2010). Efficacy of a theory-based abstinence-only intervention over months. *Archives of Pediatrics & Adolescent Medicine, 164,* 152–159.

Jensen, J. V. (1997). *Ethical issues in the communication process*. Prospect Heights, IL: Waveland.

Jiang, J. (2018, May 2). Millennials stand out for their technology use, but older generations also embrace digital life. *Pew Research Center*. Retrieved from http://www.pewresearch.org/fact-tank/2018/05/02/millennials-stand-out-for-their-technology-use-but-older-generations-also-embrace-digital-life/

Jill Bolte Taylor: Neuroanatomist. (2008, March). *TED.com*. Retrieved from http://www.ted.com/speakers/jill_bolte_taylor.html

Jodie Foster speech: Retirement speculation at Golden Globes. (2013, January 13). *Huffington Post*. Retrieved from http://www.huffingtonpost.com/2013/01/13/jodie-foster-speech-retirement-_n_2469530.html

Johnson, D. T. (2016). Juries in the Japanese legal system: The continuing struggle for citizen participation and democracy. *Social Science Japan Journal, 19,* 116–119.

Johnson, S. D., & Miller, A. N. (2002). A cross-cultural study of immediacy, credibility, and learning in the U.S. and Kenya. *Communication Education, 51,* 280–292.

Jones, C. R., Fazio, R. H., & Vasey, M. W. (2012). Attention control buffers the effect of public-speaking anxiety on performance. *Social Psychology & Personality Science, 3,* 556–561.

Jordan, J. J., Sommers, R., Bloom, P., & Rand, D. G. (2017). Why do we hate hypocrites? Evidence for a theory of false signaling. *Psychological Science, 28,* 356–368.

Josephson, M. (2002). *Making ethical decisions*. Los Angeles, CA: Josephson Institute of Ethics.

Julian Castro's daughter punctuates convention speech with hair toss. (2012, September 6). *The Christian Science Monitor*. Retrieved from http://www.csmonitor.com/The-Culture/Family/2012/0906/Julian-Castro-s-daughter-punctuates-convention-speech-with-hair-toss

Jussim, L., Crawford, J. T., & Rubinstein, R. S. (2016). Stereotype (in)accuracy in perceptions of groups and individuals. *Current Directions in Psychological Science, 24,* 490–497.

Kalnis, A. (2018, August 4). ?4U: Is Twitter killing the English language? *Language on the Move*. Retrieved from http://www.languageonthemove.com/4u-is-twitter-killing-the-english-language/

Kamen, S. (2018). A price too high to pay. In L. G. Schnoor & L. Mayfield (Eds.), *Winning orations.* Mankato, MN: Interstate Oratorical Association.

Karia, A. (2015). *TED talks storytelling: 23 storytelling techniques from the best TED talks.* CreateSpace Independent Publishing Platform.

Kavanagh, J., & Rich, M. D. (2018). *Truth decay: An initial exploration of the diminishing role of facts and analysis in American public life.* Santa Monica, CA: Rand Corporation.

Kawatsu, H. (2009, May 25). A mixed jury system for Japan. Paper presented at the annual meeting of The Law and Society, Las Vegas, NV. Retrieved from http://www.allacademic.com/meta/p18168_index.html

Kelp-Stebbins, K., & Schifani, A. M. (2017, August 21). The medium is the masses: Embodied amplification, urban occupation. *Media Fields Journal.* Retrieved from http://mediafieldsjournal.org/the-medium-is-the-masses/

Keohane, J. (2010, July 11). How facts backfire. *The Boston Globe.* Retrieved from http://www.boston.com/bostonglobe/ideas/articles/2010/07/11/how_facts_backfire/

Kingkade, T. (2015, December 17). Florida Atlantic University wants to fire professor who denies Sandy Hook massacre. *Huffington Post.* Retrieved from http://www.huffingtonpost.com/entry/florida-atlantic-university-james-tracyus_56732ee3e4b0b958f655f601

Kirkpatrick, P. (2007). Hunting the wild reciter: Elocution and the art of recitation. In J. Damousi & D. Deacon (Eds.), *Talking and listening in the age of modernity: Essays on the history of sound.* Canberra, Australia: ANU E Press.

Klein, A. (2018). A miracle deterred: The global penicillin shortage and the devastation it leaves behind. In L. G. Schnoor & L. Mayfield (Eds.), *Winning orations.* Mankato, MN: Interstate Oratorical Association.

Klein, R. (2018, February 16). Why school cops won't fix school shootings. *Huffington Post.* Retrieved from https://www.huffingtonpost.com/entry/school-cops-shootings_us_5a8715c8e4b05c2bcaca7c29

Knights, J. (2016). *How to develop ethical leaders. Abingdon, UK: Routledge Taylor & Francis Group.* Retrieved from http://pm-consulting.in/wp-content/uploads/2016/06/Transpersonal_Leadership.pdf

Kolbe, A. (2018, February 26). How reliable is *Wikipedia* as a source of information, and why? *Quora.* Retrieved from https://www.quora.com/How-reliable-is-Wikipedia-as-a-source-of-information-and-why

Konda, K. J. (2006). The war at home. In L. G. Schnoor & B. Wickelgren (Eds.), *Winning orations.* Mankato, MN: Interstate Oratorical Association.

Kopan, T. (2016, February 26). Marco Rubio mocks Donald Trump for "wet" pants. *CNN.com.* Retrieved from http://www.cnn.com/2016/02/26/politics/marco-rubio-attacks-donald-trump-wet-pants/

Kraul, C. (2006, December 20). Renowned for longevity, Ecuadoran town changing. *San Jose Mercury News,* p. 16A.

Krieger, L. M. (2018, March 9). In Twitter-sphere, false information travels fast. *The Mercury News,* pp. 1A, 6A.

Krieger, L. M., & Mattson, S. (2015, July 2). Water usage drops 29%. *San Jose Mercury News,* p. A1.

Kristof, N. (2015, February 7). The dangers of vaccine denial. *The New York Times.* Retrieved from http://www.nytimes.com/2015/02/08/opinion/sunday/nicholas-kristof-the-dangers-of-vaccine-denial.html?_r=0

Kuchinskas, S. (2008, January/February). Conquering fear of public speaking. *WebMD.* Retrieved from http://www.webmd.com/anxiety-panic/features/conquering-fear-public-speaking

Kumkale, G. T., Albarracin, D., & Seignourel, P. J. (2010). The effects of source credibility in the presence or absence of prior attitudes: Implications for the design of persuasive communication campaigns. *Journal of Applied Social Psychology, 40,* 1325–1356.

Lakhan, S. E. (2016, February 8). Training the brain and the startle response. *BrainBlogger.com.* Retrieved from http://brainblogger.com/2016/02/08/training-the-brain-and-the-startle-response/

Lakoff, G., & Duran, G. (2018, June 13). Trump has turned words into weapons. And he's winning the linguistic war. *The Guardian.* Retrieved from https://www.theguardian.com/commentisfree/2018/jun/13/how-to-report-trump-media-manipulation-language

Langeslag, Sandra. (2018, August 30). Effects of organization and disorganization on pleasantness, calmness, and the frontal negativity in the event-related potential. *PLoS ONE.* Retrieved from https://journals.plos.org/plosone/article?id=10.1371/journal.pone.0202726

Larson, C. U. (2012). *Persuasion: Reception and responsibility.* Belmont, CA: Wadsworth.

Leaf, C. (2018, February 22). Why armed guards at schools won't work. *Fortune.* Retrieved from http://fortune.com/2018/02/22/armed-guards-schools-wont-work/

Lecheler, S., de Vreese, C., & Slothuus, R. (2009). Issue importance as a moderator of framing effects. *Communication Research, 36,* 400–425.

Legg, T. (2019, February 1). Catastrophizing: What you need to know to stop worrying. *Health Line.* Retrieved from https://www.healthline.com/health/anxiety/catastrophizing

Lehmiller, J. J. (2017, April 4). Why abstinence pledges don't work. *Psychology Today.* Retrieved from https://www.psychologytoday.com/us/blog/the-myths-sex/201704/why-abstinence-pledges-dont-work

Lennon, R., & Rentfro, R. (2010). Are young adults fear appeal effectiveness ratings explained by fear arousal, perceived threat and perceived efficacy? *Innovative Marketing, 6,* 58–65.

Lese, K. (2012). The kid who cried "Mine": Patent trolls greedy takeover of the technology industry. In L. G. Schnoor, L. Mayfield, & K. Young (Eds.), *Winning orations.* Mankato, MN: Interstate Oratorical Association.

Leshner, G., Bolls, P., & Wise, K. (2011). Motivated processing of fear appeal and disgust in televised anti-tobacco ads. *Journal of Media Psychology, 23,* 77–89.

Levine, K. (2001). The dentist's dirty little secret. In L. Schnoor & B. Wickelgren (Eds.), *Winning orations.* Mankato, MN: Interstate Oratorical Association.

Levitin, D. J. (2015, January 18). Why the modern world is bad for your brain. *The Guardian.* Retrieved from https://www.theguardian.com/science/2015/jan/18/modern-world-bad-for-brain-daniel-j-levitin-organized-mind-information-overload

Lewandowsky, S., Ecker, U. K. H., Seifert, C. M., Schwartz, N., & Cook, J. (2012). Misinformation and its correction: Continued influence and successful debiasing. *Psychological Science in the Public Interest, 13,* 106–131.

Lewis, R. D. (1996). *When cultures collide: Managing successfully across cultures.* London, UK: Nicholas Brealey.

Li, C. (1975). *Path analysis: A primer.* Pacific Grove, CA: Boxwood Press.

Liao, A. (2017, May). What's the most complicated word in English? *Bookstr.* Retrieved from https://www.bookstr.com/most-complicated-word-english

Lilienfeld, S. O., Ammirati, R., & Landfield, K. (2009). Giving debiasing away: Can psychological research on correcting cognitive errors promote human welfare? *Perspectives on Psychological Science, 4,* 390–398.

Lindsey, L. L. M., & Yun, K. A. (2003). Examining the persuasive effect of statistical messages: A test of mediating relationships. *Communication Studies, 54,* 306–322.

Linville, P. W., Fischer, G. W., & Fischoff, B. (1992). Perceived risk and decision-making involving AIDS. In J. B. Pryor & G. D. Reeder (Eds.), *The social psychology of HIV infection*. Hillsdale, NJ: Lawrence Erlbaum.

Littlejohn, S. W., & Foss, K. A. (2017). *Theories of human communication*. Long Grove, IL: Waveland Press.

Lipka, M., & Smith, G. A. (2019, January 24). Like Americans overall, U.S. Catholics are sharply divided by party. *Pew Research Center*. Retrieved from https://www.pewresearch.org/fact-tank/2019/01/24/like-americans-overall-u-s-catholics-are-sharply-divided-by-party/

Lofaso, A. M. (2017). Groomed for exploitation! How applying statutory definition of employee to cover Division 1A college football players disrupts the student-athlete myth. *West Virginia Law Review*, 119, 957–998.

Lucas, S. E., & Medhurst, M. J. (2008). *Words of a century: The top 100 American speeches, 1900–1999*. New York, NY: Oxford University Press.

MacInnis, C. C., MacKinnon, S. P., & MacIntyre, P. D. (2010). The illusion of transparency and normative beliefs about anxiety during public speaking. *Current Research in Social Psychology*, 15. Retrieved from http://www.uiowa.edu/ ~grpproc/crisp/crisp15_4.pdf

Making ethical decisions: The six pillars of character. (2013). *Josephson Institute of Ethics*. Retrieved from http://www.sfjohnson.com/acad/ethics/making_ethical_decisions.pdf

Manjikian, G., & Rusch, E. (2014, September). The voting intentions and opinions of students. *CALPIRG Education Fund*. Retrieved from https://calpirgstudents.org/sites/student/files/reports/Results%20of%20CALPIRG%20Student%20Survey.pdf

Manolaki, A. (2016, August 30). Translating body language signs in different cultures. *Terminology Coordination: European Parliament*. Retrieved from http://termcoord.eu/2016/08/translating-body-language-signs-in-different-cultures/

Maricchiolo, F., Gnisci, A., Bonaiuto, M., & Ficca, G. (2009). Effects of different types of hand gestures in persuasive speech on receivers' evaluations. *Language and Cognitive Processes*, 24, 239–266.

Mason, L. (2016). Why are Americans so angry this election season? Here's new research that helps explain it. *The Washington Post*. Retrieved from https://www.washington post.com/news/monkey-cage/wp/2016/03/10/why-are-americans-so-angry-this-election-season-heres-new-research-that-helps-explain-it/

Mathewson, S. (2016, August 10). How often do meteorites hit the Earth? *Space.com*. Retrieved from https://www.space.com/33695-thousands-meteorites-litter-earth-unpredictable-collisions.html

May, P. (2009, June 22). What's next for Twitter now it's on world stage? *San Jose Mercury News*, p. 6A.

Mayhew, M. J., Rockenbach, A. N., Selznick, B. S., & Zagorsky, J. L. (2018, February 2). Does college turn people into liberals? *The Conversation*. Retrieved from https://theconversation.com/does-college-turn-people-into-liberals-90905

McCoy, S. L., Tun, P. A., Cox, L. C., & Wingfield, A. (2005, July 12). Aging in a fast-paced world: Rapid speech and its effect on understanding. *The ASHA Leader*, pp. 12, 30–31.

McCrae, M. (2019, May 17). More than half of Americans reportedly think we "should not teach" Arabic numerals. *Science Alert*. Retrieved from https://www.sciencealert.com/more-than-half-of-americans-could-be-confused-about-arabic-numbers

McDonald, H. (2015, May 23). Ireland becomes first country to legalise gay marriage by popular vote. *The Guardian*. Retrieved from https://www.theguardian.com/world/2015/may/23/gay-marriage-ireland-yes-vote

McDonald, J. (1998, January/February). 200% probability and beyond: The compelling nature of extraordinary claims in the absence of alternative explanations. *Skeptical Inquirer, 22,* 45–49.

McKerrow, R. E., Gronbeck, B. E., Ehninger, D., & Monroe, A. H. (2007). *Principles and types of public speaking.* New York, NY: Pearson/Allyn & Bacon.

McLaughlin, E. C. (2017, April 20). War on campus: The escalating battle over college free speech. *CNN.* Retrieved from https://www.cnn.com/2017/04/20/us/campus-free-speech-trnd/index.html

McLaughlin, S. (1996). The dirty truth about your kitchen: Using common sense to prevent food poisoning. In L. G. Schnoor (Ed.), *Winning orations.* Northfield, MN: Interstate Oratorical Association.

McLeod, S. (2018, February 5). Cognitive dissonance. Retrieved from https://www.simplypsychology.org/cognitive-dissonance.html

McNiece, M. (2019, May 13). Ryan Reynolds: "Fatherhood is the best thing that ever happened to me. *People,* pp. 76–77.

McNeil, B. J., Pauker, S. G., Sox, H. C., & Tversky, A. (1982). On the elicitation of preferences for alternative therapies. *New England Journal of Medicine, 306,* 1259–1262.

Meacham, J. (2009, August 14). Hitler and health care don't mix. *Newsweek,* p. 9.

Measles cases and outbreaks. (2018, October 6). *Centers for Disease Control and Prevention.* Retrieved from https://www.cdc.gov/measles/cases-outbreaks.html

Measles history. (2018, March 19). *Centers for Disease Control and Prevention.* Retrieved from https://www.cdc.gov/measles/about/history.html

Meet the anti-LGBT hate group that filed an amicus brief with the Alabama Supreme Court. (2015, November 13). *Southern Poverty Law Center.* Retrieved from https://www.splcenter.org/hatewatch/2015/11/13/meet-anti-lgbt-hate-group-filed-amicus-brief-alabama-supreme-court

Menegatti, M., & Rubini, M. (2017, September). Gender bias and sexism in language. *Oxford Research Encyclopedias.* Retrieved from http://communication.oxfordre.com/view/10.1093/acrefore/9780190228613.001.0001/acrefore-9780190228613-e-470

Milbank, D. (2015, September 28). For Rep. McCarthy, the likely new House speaker, words still fail him. *The Washington Post.* Retrieved from https://www.washingtonpost.com/opinions/for-rep-mccarthy-the-likely-new-house-speaker-words-still-fail-him/2015/09/28/67082056-661d-11e5-8325-a42b5a459b1e_story.html?utm_term=.8ac4658578cf

Miller, J. (2013, January 14). Ten wildly varying interpretations of Jodie Foster's Golden Globes speech. *Vanity Fair.* Retrieved from http://www.vanityfair.com/online/oscars/2013/01/jodie-foster-golden-globe-speech-coming-out-reviews

Mirsky, S. (2017, June). Food fright! *Scientific American,* p. 76.

Mitchell, O. (2018). New evidence that bullet-points don't work. *Word Press.* Retrieved from http://www.speakingaboutpresenting.com/design/new-evidence-bullet-points/

Monarth, H. (2014, March 11). The irresistible power of storytelling as a strategic business tool. *Harvard Business Review.* Retrieved from https://hbr.org/2014/03/the-irresistible-power-of-storytelling-as-a-strategic-business-tool

Montana Meth Project. (2019). *About.* Retrieved from https://www.montanameth.org/about-us/

Morgan, N. (2013, April 2). Why you need to change your public speaking style. *Forbes.* Retrieved from https://www.forbes.com/sites/nickmorgan/2013/04/02/why-you-need-to-change-your-public-speaking-style/#8a1273d66360

Morrison, K., & McCornack, S. A. (2015). Rethinking susceptibility: Examining the cognitive and emotional processing of other-directed persuasive fear appeal messages. *Communication Reports, 28,* 103–114.

Mosbergen, D. (2015, May 19). "Have your own standards": Stephen Colbert offers spot-on life advice in Wake Forest commencement speech. *Huffington Post.* Retrieved from http://www.huffingtonpost.com/2015/05/19/stephen-colbert-commencement-speech-wake-forest_n_7310848.html

Motley, M. T. (1995). *Overcoming your fear of public speaking: A proven method.* New York, NY: McGraw-Hill.

Motley, M. T. (2011, January 18). Reducing public speaking anxiety: The communication orientation. *YouTube.* Retrieved from http://www.youtube.com/watch?v=GYfHQvi2NAg

Moyer, M. W. (2016, January/February). Eye contact: How long is too long? *Scientific American Mind,* p. 8.

Murphy, K. (2014, September 30). Voice of free speech still resonates today. *San Jose Mercury News,* pp. A1, A8.

Murray-Johnson, L., Witte, K., Liu, W., Hubbell, A., Sampson, J., & Morrison, K. (2001). Addressing cultural orientations in fear appeals: Promoting AIDS-protective behaviors among Mexican immigrant and African American adolescents and American and Taiwanese college students. *Journal of Health Communication, 6,* 335–358.

Myers, D. (2016). Conservatives, liberals, and the distrust of science. *Teaching Current Directions in Psychological Science, 29,* 35–36.

Nabi, R. L. (2002). Discrete emotions and persuasion. In J. P. Dillard & M. Pfau (Eds.), *The persuasion handbook: Developments in theory and practice.* Thousand Oaks, CA: Sage.

National Archives and Records Administration. (1987). *Kennedy's inaugural address of 1961.* Washington, DC: U.S. Government Printing Office.

National Communication Association reaffirms the importance of preserving free and responsible communication.

(2017, January 30). *National Communication Association.* Retrieved from https://www.natcom.org/press-room/national-communication-association-reaffirms-importance-preserving-free-and-responsible

National Survey of Student Engagement. (2017). U.S. Summary Frequencies. *NSSE.* Retrieved from http://nsse.indiana.edu/2017_institutional_report/pdf/Frequencies/Freq%20-%20SR%20by%20Carn.pdf

National Survey of Student Engagement. (2018). Summary tables. *NSSE.* Retrieved from http://nsse.indiana.edu/html/summary_tables.cfm

Neal, T., & Brodsky, M. S. (2008). Warmth and competence on the witness stand: Implications for the credibility of male and female expert witnesses. *Journal of the American Academy of Psychiatry and the Law Online, 40,* 488–497.

Nevid, J. S. (2011, May/June). Teaching the millennials. *Observer.* Retrieved from http://www.psychologicalscience.org/index.php/publications/observer/2011/may-june-11/teaching-the-millennials.html

Newman, K. (2017, August 15). Why hate groups target campuses—and what to do when they show up. *USA Today.* http://college.usatoday.com/2017/08/15/why-hate-groups-target-campuses-%E2%80%95-and-what-to-do-when-they-show-up/

New survey finds Americans care about brain health, but misperceptions abound. (2013). *The Michael J. Fox Foundation.* Retrieved from https://www.michaeljfox.org/foundation/publication-detail.html?id=484

Nichols, T. (2017). *The death of expertise.* New York, NY: Oxford University Press.

Noguchi, S. (2008, June 25). Lifted lines in grads' speeches. *San Jose Mercury News,* pp. 1B, 5B.

Noonan, P. (1998). *Simply speaking: How to communicate your ideas with style, substance, and clarity.* New York, NY: HarperCollins.

Nordin, K. (2015). 911's deadly flaw. In L. G. Schnoor, K. Young, & L. Mayfield (Eds.), *Winning orations*. Mankato, MN: Interstate Oratorical Association.

Nordquist, R. (2017, April 30). What is identification in rhetoric. *ThoughtCo*. Retrieved from https://www.thoughtco.com/identification-rhetoric-term-1691142

Nordquist, R. (2018, January 4). What are mixed metaphors. *ThoughtCo*. Retrieved from https://www.thoughtco.com/what-are-mixed-metaphors-1691770

Nordquist, R. (2019a, March 13). Non sequitur (fallacy). *ThoughtCo*. Retrieved from https://www.thoughtco.com/what-is-a-non-sequitur-1691437

Nordquist, R. (2019b, April 2). Hasty generalization (fallacy). *ThoughtCo*. Retrieved from https://www.thoughtco.com/hasty-generalization-fallacy-1690919

O'Donohue, W. T., & Fisher, J. E. (2008). *Cognitive behavior therapy: Applying empirically supported techniques in your practice*. Hoboken, NJ: John Wiley.

Ody, B. (2018). Neglected patients: Deliberate indifference in state prisons. In L. G. Schnoor & L. Mayfield (Eds.), *Winning orations*. Mankato, MN: Interstate Oratorical Association.

O'Keefe, D. (2016). *Persuasion: Theory and research*. Thousand Oaks, CA: Sage.

O'Loughlin, M. J. (2016, September 28). Poll finds many U.S. Catholics breaking with church over contraception, abortion and L.G.B.T. rights. *America: The Jesuit Review*. Retrieved from https://www.americamagazine.org/faith/2016/09/28/poll-finds-many-us-catholics-breaking-church-over-contraception-abortion-and-lgbt

Onishi, N. (2007, July 16). Japanese wary as they prepare to join juries. *San Jose Mercury News*, p. 8A.

Onnela, J-P., Waber, B. N., Pentland, A., Schnorf, S., & Lazer, D. (2014). Using sociometers to quantify social interaction patterns. *Scientific Reports*. Retrieved from https://www.nature.com/articles/srep05604#ref15

Otis Blackwell. (2018). *Songhall.org*. Retrieved from https://www.songhall.org/profile/Otis_Blackwell

Palminteri, S., Lefebvre, G., Kilford, E. J., & Blakemore, S-J. (2017, August 11). Confirmation bias in human reinforcement learning: Evidence from counterfactual feedback processing. *PLOS*. Retrieved from https://journals.plos.org/ploscompbiol/article?id=10.1371/journal.pcbi.1005684

Panagopoulos, C. (2010). Affect, social pressure and prosocial motivation: Field experimental evidence of the mobilizing effects of pride, shame and publicizing voting behavior. *Political Behavior, 32*, 369–386.

Paradi, D. (2018). Ten secrets for using PowerPoint effectively. *Think Outside the Slide*. Retrieved from https://www.thinkoutsidetheslide.com/ten-secrets-for-using-powerpoint-effectively/

Parker, K., Graf, N., & Igielnik, R. (2019, January 17). Generation Z looks a lot like Millennials on key social and political issues. *Pew Research Center*. Retrieved from https://www.pewsocialtrends.org/2019/01/17/generation-z-looks-a-lot-like-millennials-on-key-social-and-political-issues/

Passer, M. W., & Smith, R. E. (2016). *Psychology: The science of mind and behavior*. New York, NY: McGraw-Hill.

Patten, D. (2019, February 25). Oscar ratings up from 2018 to 29.6M viewers with hostless show—update. *Deadline*. Retrieved from https://deadline.com/2019/02/2019-oscars-ratings-rise-spike-lee-protest-green-book-abc-1202564523/

Peoples, S. (2013, June 2). Gay marriage win a loss for Catholic Church clout. *San Jose Mercury News*, p. A7.

Perloff, R. M. (2017). *The dynamics of persuasion: Communication and attitudes in the 21st century*. New York, NY: Routledge.

Perry, A. (2017). Alcoholism: The deadliest disease that doesn't get treated. In L. G. Schnoor & L. Mayfield (Eds.), *Winning*

orations. Mankato, MN: Interstate Oratorical Association.

Perry, A. (2018). From life support to end of life support: Providing children with palliative care. In L. G. Schnoor & L. Mayfield (Eds.), *Winning orations*. Mankato, MN: Interstate Oratorical Association.

Pertaub, D., Slater, M., & Barker, C. (2002). An experiment on public speaking anxiety in response to three different types of virtual audiences. *Presence: Teleoperators and Virtual Environments, 11,* 670–678.

Pesce, N. L. (2018, April 27). Stop saying these cringeworthy office phrases "ASAP." *MarketWatch*. Retrieved from https://www.marketwatch.com/story/stop-saying-these-cringeworthy-office-phrases-asap-2018-04-27

Petrovic, K. (2013, March/April). Closing the book on "open-mindedness." *Skeptical Inquirer*, p. 53.

Petty, R. E., & Cacioppo, J. (1984). The effects of involvement on responses to argument quantity and quality: Central and peripheral routes to persuasion. *Journal of Personality and Social Psychology, 46,* 69–81.

Petty, R. E., & Cacioppo, J. (1986a). *Communication and persuasion: Central and peripheral routes to attitude change.* New York, NY: Springer-Verlag.

Petty, R. E., & Cacioppo, J. (1986b). The elaboration likelihood model of persuasion. In L. Berkowitz (Ed.), *Advances in experimental social psychology* (Vol. 19). New York, NY: Academic Press.

Petty R. E., Rucker, D. D., Bizer, G. Y., & Cacioppo, J. T. (2004). The Elaboration Likelihood Model in persuasion. In J. S. Seiter & R. H. Gass (Eds.), *Perspectives on persuasion, social influence, and compliance.* New York, NY: Pearson.

Peyser, M. (2006, February 13). The truthiness teller. *Newsweek*. Retrieved from http://www.democraticunderground.com/discuss/duboard.php?az=view_all&address =364x334537

Phephan, N. (2011). Hospital overcharging. In L. G. Schnoor, L. Mayfield, & K. Young (Eds.), *Winning orations*. Mankato, MN: Interstate Oratorical Association.

Pinker, S. (2015, January 27). Why free speech is fundamental. *Boston Globe*. Retrieved from https://www.bostonglobe.com/opinion/2015/01/26/why-free-speech-fundamental/aaAWVYFscrhFCC4ye9FVjN/story.html

Pires, D. (2018, May 13). "Young people are angry": The teenage activists shaping our future. *The Guardian*. Retrieved from https://www.theguardian.com/society/2018/may/13/young-people-are-angry-meet-the-teenage-activists-shaping-our-future

Poldrack, R. (2010, Summer). Novelty and testing: When the brain learns and why it forgets. *Nieman Reports*. Retrieved from http//www.nieman.harvard.edu/reports/article/102397/Novelty-and-Testing-When-the-Brain-Learns-and-Why-It-Forgets.aspx

Polio vaccine effectiveness and duration of protection. (2018, May 4). *Centers for Disease Control and Prevention.* Retrieved from https://www.cdc.gov/vaccines/vpd/polio/hcp/effectiveness-duration-protection.html

Poole, M. (2009, July 27). A's great Henderson cool at Cooperstown. *San Jose Mercury News*, pp. 1A, 6A.

Poppy, C. (2017, January/February). Survey shows Americans fear ghosts, the government, and each other. *Skeptical Inquirer*, pp. 16–18.

Pornpitakpan, C. (2004). The persuasiveness of source credibility: A critical review of five decades' evidence. *Journal of Applied Social Psychology, 34,* 243–281.

Post-ABC poll: Broad support for gun restrictions, armed guards in schools—January 10–13. (2013, January 16). *The Washington Post*. Retrieved from http://www.washingtonpost.com/politics/polling/postabc-poll-broad-support-gun-restrictions/2013/04/12/c8f74d38-5e95-11e2-8acb-ab5cb77e95c8_page.html

Poston, D., & Saenz, R. (2019, April 30). U.S. will be "majority-minority" in next 25 years. *UPI*. Retrieved from https://www.upi.com/Top_News/Voices/2019/04/30/US-will-be-majority-minority-in-next-25-years/2971556626784/

Powell, T. (2012). It's not the addict, it's the drug: Redefining America's War on Drugs. In L. G. Schnoor, L. Mayfield, & K. Young (Eds.), *Winning orations*. Mankato, MN: Interstate Oratorical Association.

PowerPoint turns 20, as its creators ponder a dark side to success. (2007, June 20). *The Wall Street Journal*, p. B1.

Pratkanis, A., & Aronson, E. (2001). *The age of propaganda: The everyday use and abuse of persuasion*. New York, NY: W. H. Freeman.

Prochow, H. V. (1944). *Great stories from great lives*. New York, NY: Harper & Brothers.

Pull, C. B. (2012). Current status of knowledge on public speaking anxiety. *Current Opinion in Psychiatry, 25*, 32–38.

Quackenbush, C. (2019, January 21). The world's top 26 billionaires now own as much as the poorest 3.8 billion, says Oxfam. *Time*. Retrieved from http://time.com/5508393/global-wealth-inequality-widens-oxfam/

Quastad, D. (2018). Perils of faith-based healing. In L. G. Schnoor & L. Mayfield (Eds.), *Winning orations*. Mankato, MN: Interstate Oratorical Association.

Quick facts: United States. (2017, July 1). *U.S. Census Bureau*. Retrieved from https://www.census.gov/quickfacts/fact/table/US/PST045217

Quinnell, K. (2018, May 22). Executive Paywatch 2018: The gap between CEO and worker compensation continues to grow. *AFL-CIO*. Retrieved from https://aflcio.org/2018/5/22/executive-paywatch-2018-gap-between-ceo-and-worker-compensation-continues-grow

Rabidoux, S., & Rottmann, A. (2017, October 18). Beyond PowerPoint presentations. *Inside Higher Ed*. Retrieved from https://www.insidehighered.com/digital-learning/views/2017/10/18/free-easy-use-online-presentation-tools

Rakestraw, M. (2014, March 13). The art of circumlocution and verbal evasion: Exploring euphemisms. *Humane Connection*. Retrieved from https://humaneeducation.org/blog/2014/art-circumlocution-verbal-evasion-exploring-euphemisms/

Rathe, C. (2017, July 25). Could Millennials reshape global supply chains? *21st Century Global Dynamics*. Retrieved from http://www.21global.ucsb.edu/global-e/july-2017/could-millennials-reshape-global-supply-chains

Rawson, C. (2013). The dreaded "S" word. In L. G. Schnoor, K. Young, & L. Mayfield (Eds.), *Winning orations*. Mankato, MN: Interstate Oratorical Association.

Reid, L. (2013, October 23). UNL study shows college students are digitally distracted in class. *UNL News Releases*. Retrieved from http://newsroom.unl.edu/releases/2013/10/23/UNL+study+shows+college+students+are+digitally+distracted+in+class

Reinsel, D., Gantz, J., & Rydning, J. (2018, November). Data age 2025: From edge to core. *IDC*. Retrieved from https://www.seagate.com/files/www-content/our-story/trends/files/idc-seagate-dataage-whitepaper.pdf

Remarks of Senator Barack Obama. (2008, January 3). *Obama News & Speeches*. Retrieved from http://www.barackobama.com/2008/01/03/remarks_of_senator_barack_obama_39.php

Reynolds, G. (2009, November 18). Phys Ed: Why exercise makes you less anxious. *The New York Times*. Retrieved from https://well.blogs.nytimes.com/2009/11/18/phys-ed-why-exercise-makes-you-less-anxious/

Reynolds, G. (2012). *Presentation Zen: Simple ideas on presentation design and delivery*. San Francisco, CA: New Riders.

Rhodes, N. (2015, January 11). Fear-appeal messages: Message processing and affective attitudes. *Communication Research.* Retrieved from http://crx.sagepub.com/content/early/2015/01/08/0093650214565916.abstract

Rich, K. (2018). Hiding under blue helmets. In L. G. Schnoor & L. Mayfield (Eds.), *Winning orations.* Mankato, MN: Interstate Oratorical Association.

Richmond, V. P., & McCroskey, J. C. (1995). *Communication: Apprehension, avoidance, and effectiveness.* Boston, MA: Allyn & Bacon.

Robbins, M. (2016, January 5). Why Obama cried over gun control. *CNN.com.* Retrieved from http://www.cnn.com/2016/01/05/ opinions/robbins-obama-cry/

Roberts, J. A., & Wasieleski, D. M. (2012). Moral reasoning in computer-based task environments: Exploring the interplay between cognitive and technological factors on individuals' propensity to break rules. *Journal of Business Ethics,* 110, 355–376.

Robinson, K., & Aronica, L. (2015). *Creative schools: The grassroots revolution that's transforming education.* New York, NY: Viking.

Rodriguez, J. (1995). Confounds in fear arousing persuasive messages: Do the paths less traveled make all the difference? Unpublished doctoral dissertation, Michigan State University, East Lansing.

Ropeik, D. (2008, April 13). How risky is flying? *NOVA.* Retrieved from http://www.pbs.org/wgbh/nova/planecrash/risky.html

Rosenbaum, J. E. (2009). Patient teenagers? A comparison of the sexual behavior of virginity pledgers and matched non-pledgers. *Pediatrics,* 123, 110–120.

Rowlands, I., Nicholas, D., Williams, P., Huntington, P., Fieldhouse, M., Gunter, B., Withey, R., Jamali, H.R., Dobrowolski, T., & Tenopir, C. (2008). The Google generation: The information behavior of the researcher of the future. *UCL Discovery.* Retrieved from http://discovery.ucl.ac.uk/177993/

Rucker, D. D., & Petty, R. E. (2004). When resistance is futile: Consequences of failed counterarguing for attitude certainty. *Journal of Personality and Social Psychology,* 86, 219–235.

Rudlin, P. (2014, December 11). Humor easily crosses cultures, but be careful with sarcasm. *Japan Intercultural Consulting.* Retrieved from http://www.japanintercultural.com/en/news/default.aspx?newsID=320

Ruggeiro, V. (1988). *Teaching thinking across the curriculum.* New York, NY: Harper & Row.

Ruiter, R. A. C., Kessels, L. T. E., Jansma, B. M., & Brug, J. (2006). Increased attention for computer-tailored health communications: An event-related potential study. *Health Psychology,* 25, 300–306.

Salomon, A. (2011, September 21). Study shows stage fright is common among working actors. *Backstage.com.* Retrieved from http://www.backstage.com/news/study-shows-stage-fright-is-common-among-working-actors/

Sample size. (2019). *Science Buddies.* Retrieved from https://www.sciencebuddies.org/science-fair-projects/references/sample-size-surveys

Sandburg, C. (2002). *Abraham Lincoln: The prairie years and the war years.* New York, NY: Houghton Mifflin Harcourt.

Sarlin, B. (2016, January 22). Donald Trump tweets apparent neo-Nazi supporter. *MSNBC.com.* Retrieved from http://www.msnbc.com/msnbc/donald-trump-tweets-apparent-neo-nazi-supporter

Sasson, E. (2014, January 14). Jodie Foster's glass closet. *The Wall Street Journal.* https://blogs.wsj.com/speakeasy/2013/01/14/jodie-fosters-glass-closet/

Savitsky, K., & Gilovich, T. (2003). The illusion of transparency and the alleviation of speech anxiety. *Journal of Experimental Social Psychology,* 39, 618–625.

Schreiner, C., Appel, M., Isberner, M-J., & Richter, T. (2018). Argument strength and the persuasiveness of stories. *Discourse Processes,* 55, 371–386.

Schroeder, J., & Epley, N. (2015). The sound of intellect: Speech reveals a thoughtful mind, increasing a job candidate's appeal. *Psychological Science, 26,* 877–891.

Scott, E. (2019, May 6). The definition of relaxation response. *VeryWellMind.* Retrieved from https://www.verywellmind.com/what-is-the-relaxation-response-3145145

Search engine market share United States of America. (2019, April). *Statcounter: Global stats.* Retrieved from http://gs.statcounter.com/search-engine-market-share/all/united-states-of-america

Sedivy, J. (2015, December 16). Your speech is packed with misunderstood, unconscious messages. *Nautil Blog.* Retrieved from http://nautil.us/blog/your-speech-is-packed-with-misunderstood-unconscious-messages

Seim, R. W., Waller, S. A., & Spates, R. C. (2010). A preliminary investigation of continuous and intermittent exposures in the treatment of public speaking anxiety. *International Journal of Behavioral Consultation and Therapy, 6,* 84–94.

Sernoffsky, E. (2017, September 19). Protesters shut down Pelosi news conference on DACA: "All of us or none of us." *SFGATE.* Retrieved from https://www.sfgate.com/news/article/Protesters-shut-down-Pelosi-news-conference-on-12206788.php

Seven tips for making webcam videos look good (and pants are optional). (2017, April 8). *Panopto.* Retrieved from https://www.panopto.com/blog/7-tips-for-making-webcam-videos-look-good-pants-optional/

Sexual harassment in the workplace. (2016, November). *National Women's Law Center.* Retrieved from http://employment.findlaw.com/employment-discrimination/sexual-harassment-what-is-it.html

Shadel, W. G., Niaura, R., & Abrams, D. B. (2001). How do adolescents process smoking and antismoking advertisements? A social cognitive analysis with implications for understanding smoking initiation. *Review of General Psychology, 5,* 429–444.

Shannon, J. (2018, May 26). Near a Nebraska town, cops seize enough opioids to kill over 26 million. *USA Today.* Retrieved from https://www.usatoday.com/story/news/nation-now/2018/05/26/nebraska-cops-opioids-fentanyl-kill-millions/647513002/

Sherif, C. W., Kelly, M., Rodgers, H. L., Sarup, G., & Tittler, B. I. (1973). Personal involvement, social judgment and action. *Journal of Personality and Social Psychology, 27,* 311–328.

Sherif, M., Sherif, C., & Nebergall, R. (1965). *Attitude and attitude change: The social judgment-involvement approach.* Philadelphia, PA: Saunders.

Sherman, E. (2009, March/April). Science and antiscience in America: Why it matters. *Skeptical Inquirer,* pp. 32–35.

Shermer, M. (2013, February 1). What is skepticism, anyway? *Huffington Post.* Retrieved from http://www.huffingtonpost.com/michael-shermer/what-is-skepticism-anyway_b_2581917.html

Shermer, M. (2018, March). Factiness: Are we living in a post-truth world? *Scientific American,* p. 73.

Shimanoff, S. B. (2009). Rules theory. In S. W. Littlejohn & K. A. Foss (Eds.), *Encyclopedia of communication theory.* Beverly Hills, CA: Sage.

Shuler, L. (2019, June 25). AFL-CIO releases 2019 executive paywatch report. *AFL-CIO.* Retrieved from https://aflcio.org/pressreleases/afl-cio-releases-2019-executive-paywatch-report

Sidky, H. (2018, March/April). The war on science, anti-intellectualism, and "alternative ways of knowing" in 21st century America. *Skeptical Inquirer,* pp. 38–43.

Silberman, S. (2019, May 6). Greta Thunberg became a climate activist not in spite of her autism, but because of it. *Vox.* Retrieved from https://www.vox.com/first-person/2019/5/6/18531551/autism-greta-thunberg-speech

Silver, N. (2012). *The signal and the noise: Why so many predictions fail—but some don't.* New York, NY: Penguin Press.

Sma, S., Schrift, R. Y., & Zauberman, G. (2018). The illusion of multitasking and its positive effect on performance. *Psychological Science, 29,* 1942-1955.

Smith, C. (2019, May 11). 30 amazing Wikipedia statistics and facts (December 2018). *DMR Business Statistics.* Retrieved from https://expandedramblings.com/index.php/wikipedia-statistics/

Smith, G. (2015). *Standard deviations, flawed assumptions, tortured data, and other ways to lie with statistics.* New York, NY: Overlook Press.

Smith, J. (2016, August). The job is football: The myth of the student-athlete. *The American Historian.* Retrieved from https://tah.oah.org/august-2016/the-job-is-football-the-myth-of-the-student-athlete/

Smith, S. (2016, February 3). Correction: California drought story. *Associated Press.* Retrieved from http://bigstory.ap.org/article/a455cd6d15ab4206b91dc70abef2b30b/california-weighs-extending-drought-conservation-orders

Smith, S. M., & Shaffer, D. R. (1995). Speed of speech and persuasion: Evidence for multiple effects. *Personality and Social Psychology Bulletin, 21,* 1051–1060.

Soave, R. (2018, March 6). Students at Lewis and Clark College shouted down Christina Hoff Sommers: "We choose to protest male supremacy." *Reason.* Retrieved from https://reason.com/blog/2018/03/06/christina-hoff-sommers-lewis-and-clark

Solomon, D. (2005, September 25). Funny about the news. *The New York Times.* Retrieved from http://www.nytimes.com/2005/09/25/magazine/25questions.html?_r=1

Sonsalla, T. (2017). Racial disparity in cancer care. In L. G. Schnoor & L. Mayfield (Eds.), *Winning orations.* Mankato, MN: Interstate Oratorical Association.

Speech on campus. (2018). *ACLU.* Retrieved from https://www.aclu.org/other/speech-campus

Spitzberg, B. H. (2000). A model of intercultural communication competence. In L. A. Samovar & R. E. Porter (Eds.), *Intercultural communication: A reader.* Belmont, CA: Wadsworth.

Sreenivasan, S., & Weinberger, L. E. (2018, September 18). Fear appeals. *Psychology Today.* Retrieved from https://www.psychologytoday.com/us/blog/emotional-nourishment/201809/fear-appeals

Star, K. (2018, June 10). 6 potential benefits of having anxiety: Positive effects that anxiety can create. *Very Well Mind.* Retrieved from https://www.verywellmind.com/benefits-of-anxiety-2584134

Stephens, K. K., Houser, M. L., & Cowan, R. L. (2009). R U able to meat me: The impact of students' overly casual email messages to instructors. *Communication Education, 58,* 303–326.

Stevens, S., Cooper, R., Bantin, T., Hermann, C., & Gerlach, A. L. (2017). Feeling safe but appearing anxious: Differential effects of alcohol on anxiety and social performance in individuals with social anxiety disorders. *Behaviour Research and Therapy, 94,* 9–18.

Steward, C. (2009, July 24). Rickey takes his speech to school. *San Jose Mercury News,* pp. C1, C5.

Steward, C. (2017, April 4). Henderson relishes his field-good story. *San Jose Mercury News,* p. C3.

Stovall, S. (2012). Juvenile crime from deleterious environmental conditions. In L. G. Schnoor, L. Mayfield, & K. Young (Eds.), *Winning orations.* Mankato, MN: Interstate Oratorical Association.

Strossen, N. (2018). *Hate: Why we should resist it with free speech, not censorship (inalienable rights).* New York: Oxford University Press.

Study: 97% of college students are distracted by phones during class. (2016, February 2). *EAB.* Retrieved from https://www.eab.com/daily-briefing/2016/02/02/study-one-fifth-of-college-students-are-distracted-by-phones-during-class

Sulek, J. P. (2017, September 13). Should free speech cover racist content? *The Mercury News,* pp. A1, A8.

Sullivan, B., & Thompson, H. (2013). *The plateau effect: Getting from stuck to success*. New York, NY: Dutton.

Sullivan, T. (2017). Facilitated communication. In L. G. Schnoor & L. Mayfield (Eds.), *Winning orations*. Mankato, MN: Interstate Oratorical Association.

Sunstein, C., & Zeckhauser, R. (2009). Overreaction to fearsome risks. In E. Michel-Kerjan & P. Slovic (Eds.), *The irrational economist: Future directions in behavioral economics and risk management*. Washington, DC: Public Affairs Press.

Svoboda, E. (2009, February/March). Avoiding the big choke. *Scientific American Mind*, pp. 36–41.

Swann, J. (2019, January 19). Blog: Language: A feminist guide. Blog authored by Cameron, Deborah, Oxford university, U.K. *Journal of Sociolinguistics*. Retrieved from https://onlinelibrary.wiley.com/doi/full/10.1111/josl.12321

Swenson, A. (2011). You make my heart beat faster: A quantitative study of the relationship between instructor immediacy, classroom community, and public speaking anxiety. *UW-L Journal of Undergraduate Research*, XIV, 1–12.

Szalai, G., & Roxborough, S. (2016, February 23). Oscars: How many people watch the ceremony worldwide? *The Hollywood Reporter*. Retrieved from http://www.hollywoodreporter.com/news/oscars-worldwide-tv-audience-867554

Tabuchi, H., & McDonald, M. (2009, August 7). In first return to Japan court, jurors convict and sentence. *The New York Times*. Retrieved from http://www.nytimes.com/2009/08/07/world/asia/07japan.html?_r=1&pagewanted=print

Tan Chin Keok, R. (2010, November 25–27). Public speaking: A case study of speech anxiety in L1 and L2. *Seminar Penyelidikan Pendidikan Pasca Ijazah*.

Tannen, D. (2003, January 5). Hey, did you catch that? Why they're talking as fast as they can. *The Washington Post*, pp. B1, B4.

Tannenbaum, M., Wilson, K., Abarracin, D., Hepler, J., Zimmerman, R., Saul, L., & Jacobs, S. (2015). Appealing to fear: A meta-analysis of fear appeal effectiveness and theories. *Psychological Bulletin*, 141, 1178–1204.

Tavris, C., & Aronson, E. (2016). *Mistakes were made (but not by me)*. New York, NY: Harcourt.

Ted Kennedy's eulogy of brother Robert, St. Patrick's Cathedral, New York City, June 8, 1968. (2009, August 26). *New York Daily News*. Retrieved from http://nydailynews.com/news/politics/2009/08/26/2009-08-26_ted_kennedys_eulogy_of_brother_robert_1968.html

Thibodeau, P. H., & Boroditsky, L. (2011). Metaphors we think with: The role of metaphor in reasoning. *PLOS/One*. Retrieved from http://journals.plos.org/plosone/article?id=10.1371/journal.pone.0016782

Thomson, J. (2008, October 24). A quarter of people fear public speaking more than dying—here's how to beat your fear. *Smartcompany*.com. Retrieved from http://www.smartcompany.com.au/Free-Articles/The-Briefing/20081024

Thrasher, J. F., Carpenter, M. J., Andrews, J. O., Gray, K. M., Alberg, A. J., Navarro, A., . . . Cummings, K. M. (2012). Cigarette warning label policy alternatives and smoking-related health disparities. *American Journal of Preventive Medicine*, 43, 590–600.

Topper, S. (2015, May 29). Public speaking tips: The power of visualization. *Cure Public Speaking Fear*. Retrieved from https://www.curepublicspeakingfear.com/article/7051-public-speaking-tips-the-power-of-visualization

Torres, P. (2016, January 10). Donald Trump talks at a fourth-grade level. *Salon.com*. Retrieved from http://www.salon.com/2016/01/10/donald_trump_talks_at_a_fourth_grade_level_maybe_thats_why_the_fox_news_audience_loves_him/

Total number of websites. (2019, May 5). *Internet Live Stats*. Retrieved from http:// http://www.internetlivestats.com/total-number-of-websites/

Toulmin, S. E. (1958). *The uses of argument*. Cambridge, UK: Cambridge University Press.

The transcript of President Obama's final State of the Union: What he said, and what it meant. (2016, January 12). *The Washington Post*. Retrieved from https://www.washingtonpost.com/news/the-fix/wp/2016/01/12/what-obama-said-in-his-state-of-the-union-address-and-what-it-meant/

Trent, A. (2017). A watery hell. In L. G. Schnoor & L. Mayfield (Eds.), *Winning orations*. Mankato, MN: Interstate Oratorical Association.

Tsaousides, T. (2017, November 27). Why are we scared of public speaking? *Psychology Today*. Retrieved from https://www.psychologytoday.com/us/blog/smashing-the-brainblocks/201711/why-are-we-scared-public-speaking

Tsaousides, T. (2017, November 28). How to conquer the fear of public speaking. *Psychology Today*. Retrieved from https://www.psychologytoday.com/us/blog/smashing-the-brainblocks/201711/how-conquer-the-fear-public-speaking

Tucker, A. C. (2018). $765 billion of medical waste. In L. G. Schnoor & L. Mayfield (Eds.), *Winning orations*. Mankato, MN: Interstate Oratorical Association.

Tufte, E. (2003, September). PowerPoint is evil: Power corrupts, PowerPoint corrupts absolutely. *Wired.com*. Retrieved from http://www.wired.com/wired/archive/11.09/ppt2_pr.html

Turner, M. (2014, September 10). Anger appeals. In *Encyclopedia of health communication*. Thousand Oaks, CA: Sage. Retrieved from http://sk.sagepub.com/reference/encyclopedia-of-health-communication/n29.xml

Turner, M., Bessarabova, E., Hambleton, K., Weiss, M., Sipek, S., & Long, K. (2013, December 17). Does anger facilitate or debilitate persuasion? A test of the Anger Activism Model. *All Academic.com*.

Retrieved from http:// citation.allacademic.com/meta/p_mla_apa_research_citation/0/9/3/2/0/p93201_index.html

Turner, M., Bessarabova, E., Sipek, S., & Hambleton, K. (2007, May 23). *Does message-induced anger facilitate or debilitate persuasion? Two tests of the Anger Activism Model*. Paper presented at the annual meeting of the International Communication Association, San Francisco, CA.

Turner, S. A., & Silvia, P. J. (2006). Must interesting things be pleasant? A test of competing appraisal structures. *Emotion, 6*, 670–674.

Tuttar, J. (2019). Is public speaking really more feared than death? *Speak and Conquer*. Retrieved from https://speakandconquer.com/is-public-speaking-really-more-feared-than-death/

TV or not TV. (1993, April 19). *San Jose Mercury News*, p. 5E.

Twenge, J. M., VanLandingham, H., & Campbell, W. K. (2017). The seven words you can never say on television: Increases in the use of swear words in American books, 1950–2008. *Sage Open*. Retrieved from http://journals.sagepub.com/doi/full/10.1177/2158244017723689

28 distracting mannerisms that must be avoided. (2011, March 29). *Basic Public Speaking*. Retrieved from http://basicpublicspeaking.blogspot.com/2011/03/28-distracting-mannerisms-that-must-be.html

2018 national survey of Catholics in the United States. (2018, February). *Catholics for Choice*. Retrieved from http://www.catholicsforchoice.org/wp-content/uploads/2018/05/2018-National-Survey-of-Catholics-in-the-United-States.pdf

Uncertainty reduction theory. (2019, January 9). *University of Twente*. Retrieved from https://www.utwente.nl/en/bms/communication-theories/sorted-by-cluster/Interpersonal-Communication-and-Relations/uncertainty-Reduction-theory/

U.S. Bureau of Labor Statistics. (2019). Unemployment rates and earnings by educational attainment, 2018. Retrieved from https://www.bls.gov/emp/graphics/2019/unemployment-rates-and-earnings.htm

U.S. Geological Survey. (2015). Earthquakes with 1,000 or more deaths since 1900. Retrieved from http://earthquake.usgs.gov/earthquakes/world/world_deaths.php

Vanoverbeke, D. (2015). *Juries in the Japanese legal system: The continuing struggle for citizen participation and democracy.* New York: Routledge.

Vaughn, D. (2013). The problem with homeless LGBT youth. In L. G. Schnoor, K. Young, & L. Mayfield (Eds.), *Winning orations.* Mankato, MN: Interstate Oratorical Association.

Verlinden, J. (2005). *Critical thinking and everyday argument.* Belmont, CA: Wadsworth/Thomson.

Victory, honor, sacrifice. (Henry H. Shelton address) [Transcript]. (2001, August 1). *Vital Speeches of the Day.* Retrieved from http://www.accessmylibrary.com/coms2/summary _0286_28267884_ITM

Vigen, T. (2015). *Spurious correlations.* New York, NY: Hachette Books.

Villasenor, J. (2017, September 18). Views among college students regarding the First Amendment: Results from a new survey. *Brookings.* Retrieved from https://www.brookings.edu/blog/fixgov/2017/09/18/views-among-college-students-regarding-the-first-amendment-results-from-a-new-survey/

Von Muhlenen, A., Rempel, M. I., & Enns, J. T. (2005). Unique temporal change is the key to attentional capture. *Psychological Science, 16,* 979–986.

Vosoughi, S., Roy, D., & Aral, S. (2018). The spread of true and false news online. *Science, 359,* 1146–1151.

Walker, J. (2013, March/April). Understanding believers' cognitive dissonance. *Skeptical Inquirer,* pp. 50–52.

Wallace, D. S., Paulson, R. M., Lord, C. G., & Bond, C. F. (2005). Which behaviors do attitudes predict? Meta-analyzing the effects of social pressure and perceived difficulty. *Review of General Psychology, 9,* 214–227.

Wang, H-T., Poerio, G., Murphy, D. B., Jefferies, E., & Smallwood, J. (2018). Dimensions of experience: Exploring the heterogeneity of the wandering mind. *Psychological Science, 29,* 56–71.

Warren, C., & McGraw, A. P. (2015). *The humor code: A global search for what makes things funny.* New York, NY: Simon & Schuster.

Weingarten, G. (1994, September 27). I'm absolutely sure: You need a marshmallow enema. *San Jose Mercury News,* p. B7.

Weisinger, H. (2015, October 15). What's your likability quotient? *Psychology Today.* Retrieved from https://www.psychologytoday.com/us/blog/thicken-your-skin/201510/whats-your-likability-quotient

Wells, R., Outhred, T., Heathers, J. A., & Quintana, D. S. Matter over mind: A randomized-controlled trial of single-session biofeedback training on performance anxiety and heart rate variability in musicians. (2012). *PLoS One.* Retrieved from https://www.ncbi.nlm.nih.gov/pubmed/23056361

Werk, N. (2017, December). The power of storytelling in research. *Quirk's Media.* Retrieved from https://www.quirks.com/articles/the-power-of-storytelling-in-research

Westen, D. (2007). *The political brain: The role of emotion in deciding the fate of the nation.* New York, NY: Public Affairs.

Wheaton, S., & Gass, N. (2016, January 5). Obama wipes away tears as he calls for new gun measures. *Politico.com.* Retrieved from http://www.politico.com/story/2016/01/obama-gun-restrictions-217354

Who was Neda? Slain woman an unlikely martyr. (2009, June 24). *CNN.com.* Retrieved from http://www.cnn.com/2009/WORLD/meast/06/23/iran.neda.profile/

Wikipedia: Citing *Wikipedia*. (2017). *Wikipedia.org.* Retrieved from https://en.wikipedia.org/wiki/Wikipedia:Citing_Wikipedia.com/releases/2012/05/120510095812.htm

Wikipedia: Statistics. (2018, July). *Wikipedia.* Retrieved from https://en.wikipedia.org/wiki/Wikipedia:Statistics

Wilson, C. (2008, June 19). Russert gets a final toast from Washington. *USA Today*, p. 2D.

Wineburg, S., McGrew, S., Breakstone, J., & Ortega, T. (2016). Evaluating information: The cornerstone of civic online reasoning. *Stanford Digital Repository*. Retrieved from http://purl.stanford.edu/fv751yt5934

Wiseman, R. (2007). *LaughLab*. Retrieved from www.laughlab.co.uk/home.html

Witt, P. L., & Behnke, R. R. (2006). Anticipatory speech anxiety as a function of public speaking assignment type. *Communication Education, 55*, 167–177.

Witt, P. L., Brown, K. C., Roberts, J. B., Weisel, J., Sawyer, C. R., & Behnke, R. R. (2006). Somatic anxiety patterns before, during, and after giving a public speech. *Southern Communication Journal, 71*, 87–100.

Wong, A. (2018, October 3). Pimples could be good for your grades. *The Atlantic*. Retrieved from https://www.theatlantic.com/education/archive/2018/10/pimples-could-be-good-for-your-grades/572008/

Wong, Y. J., Pituch, K. A., & Rochlen, A. B. (2006). Men's restrictive emotionality: An investigation of associations with other emotion-related constructs, anxiety, and underlying dimensions. *Psychology of Men & Masculinity, 7*, 113–126.

Wooley, J. T., & Peters, G. *The American Presidency Project*. (2017). Santa Barbara, CA: University of California.

Wright, D. B., Memon, A., Skagerberg, E. M., & Gabbert, F. (2009). When eyewitnesses talk. *Current Directions in Psychological Science, 18*, 174–178.

Young, L. J. (2008, April 9). South Korea adopts jury system. *UPI Asia Online. Retrieved from* http://www.upiasia.com/Society_Culture/2008/04/09/south_korea_adopts_jury_system/1409/?view=print

Young, M. J., Behnke, R. R., & Mann, Y. M. (2004). Anxiety patterns in employment interviews. *Communication Reports, 17*, 49–57.

Your guide to education lingo. (2018, August 24). *Concordia University–Portland*. Retrieved from https://education.cu-portland.edu/blog/classroom-resources/education-terminology-jargon/

Yue, X., Jiang, F., & Hiranandan, N. (2016). To be or not to be humorous? Cross cultural perspective. *Frontiers in Psychology*. Retrieved from https://www.ncbi.nlm.nih.gov/pmc/articles/PMC5048456/

Zak, P. J. (2014, October 28). Why your brain loves good storytelling. *Harvard Business Review*. Retrieved from https://hbr.org/2014/10/why-your-brain-loves-good-storytelling

Zandan, N. (2018a, August 1). How to stop saying "um," ah," and "you know." *Harvard Business Review*. Retrieved from https://hbr.org/2018/08/how-to-stop-saying-um-ah-and-you-know

Zandan, N. (2018b, December 21). WSJ: Is this how you really talk? *Quantified Communications*. Retrieved from https://www.quantifiedcommunications.com/blog/wsj-is-this-how-you-really-talk/

Zandan, N. (2019, January 3). Stop saying "um," "ah," and "you know" now. *LiveMint*. Retrieved from https://www.livemint.com/Leisure/pF4IDlhCMxuc06pMCbJXWL/Stop-saying-um-ah-and-you-know-now.html

Zhang, Q. (2005). Immediacy, humor, power distance, and classroom communication apprehension in Chinese college classrooms. *Communication Quarterly, 53*, 109–124.

Zinsser, W. (1985). *On writing well*. New York, NY: Harper & Row.

Credits

Chapter 1
p. 2: Press Association via AP Images; **p. 3:** ©gary yim/Shutterstock.com; **p. 7:** (left) Photo by Rick Rowell/ABC via Getty Images; **p. 9:** © iStock.com/tzahiV; **p. 10:** NICHOLAS KAMM/AFP/Getty Images; **p. 13:** Photo by Cheriss May/NurPhoto via Getty Images; **p. 17:** Press Association via AP Images; **p. 18:** Photo by D Dipasupil/Getty Images for PFLAG

Chapter 2
p. 24: Sipa via AP Images; **p. 25:** © Marcy Wieland; **p. 29** (left): Associated Press/Alvaro Barrientos; **p. 29** (right): © Hongqi Zhang/Alamy Stock Photo; **p. 30:** © Marcy Wieland; p. 31 (left) Courtesy of Zach Wahls; p. 31 (right) Courtesy of Zach Wahls **p. 36:** © Marcy Wieland

Chapter 3
p. 43: (top) Photo by Chip Somodevilla/Getty Images; **p. 43** (bottom): Photo by Michael Nigro/Pacific Press/LightRocket via Getty Images; **p. 46** (top): ©Rawpixel.com/Shutterstock.com; **p. 46:** (bottom) Photo by Patrick ROBERT/Corbis via Getty Images; **p. 48:** © Marcy Wieland; **p. 51:** © Joe Seer/Shutterstock.com; **p. 53:** Photo by Steve Manue/USO via Getty Images; **p. 54:** Associated Press/Evan Vucci; **p. 56:** (top) Associated Press/J. Scott Applewhite; **p. 56:** (bottom) Photo by Brooks Kraft/Getty Images; **p. 58:** Photo by Allison Farrand/NBAE via Getty Images; p.62: © Marcy Wieland

Chapter 4
p. 68: © metamorworks/Shutterstock.com; **73:** © Marcy Wieland; **p. 76:** © Sean Pavone/Shutterstock.com; p.78: © ArtFamily/Shutterstock.com

Chapter 5
p. 84: Photo by David McNew/Getty Images; **p. 87** Photo by Ezra Shaw/Getty Images; **p. 90:** © Marcy Wieland; **p. 92:** © Alfazet Chronicles/Shutterstock.com; **p. 96:** © Marcy Wieland

Chapter 6
p. 103: Photo by Melina Mara/The Washington Post via Getty Images; **p. 105:** Ariel Skelley/

Blend Images/Getty Images; **p.107:** © pathdoc/Shutterstock.com; **p. 109:** Photo by Mayall/ullstein bild via Getty Images; **p. 111:** Photo: Alex Berliner/ABImages via AP Images; p.112: Photo by: Nathan Congleton/NBC/NBCU Photo Bank via Getty Images; **p. 115:** © iStock.com/edhumv; **p. 116:** © Marcy Wieland

Chapter 7
p. 125: © Marcy Wieland; **p. 127:** Sam Owens/The Flint Journal-MLive.com via AP; **p. 135:** Associated Press

Chapter 8
p. 140: iStock.com/creisinger; **p. 151:** ©pablofdezr/Shutterstock.com; **p. 153:** © Marcy Wieland; **p. 154:** © Rich Carey/Shutterstock.com; **p. 156:** © Gary Perkin/Shutterstock.com

Chapter 9
p. 167: © Marcy Wieland; **p. 168:** Courtesy of Don Knuth; **p. 169:** Nicholas Kamm/AFP/Getty Images; **p. 172:** (top) Photo by C Flanigan/Getty Images; **p. 172:** (bottom) ARTHUR EDWARDS/AFP/Getty Images

Chapter 10
p. 176: Carolyn Cole/AFP/Getty Images; **p. 178:** © Marcy Wieland; **p. 182:** © garetsworkshop/Shutterstock.com; **p. 184:** © Marcy Wieland; **p. 187:** © Marcy Wieland; **p. 189:** © Marcy Wieland; **p. 190:** © Sergey Nivens/Shutterstock.com; **p. 192:** © Agenturfotografin/Shutterstock.com

Chapter 11
p. 197: Candorville used with the permission of Darrin Bell, *Washington Post* Writers Group and the Cartoonist Group. All rights reserved; **p. 198:** Associated Press/Victor R. Caivano; **p. 202** Stocktrek/Photodisc/GettyImages; **p. 204** © Tribune Content Agency LLC/Alamy Stock Photo; **p. 210:** (top) © Marcy Wieland; **p. 210:** (bottom) © Marcy Wieland; **p. 213** © iStock.com/Drazen Lovric; **p. 214:** © Marcy Wieland; **p. 216** (top): pick-uppath/Digital Vistion vectors/Getty Images; **p. 216** (bottom): Flying Colours Ltd/Photodisc/Getty Images

Chapter 12

p. 223: Associated Press/The Register-Guard,Chris Pietsch; **p. 225:** Photo by Eamonn McCormack/ Getty Images; **p. 227:** © Marcy Wieland; **p. 229:** © Castleski/Shutterstock.com; **p. 231:** NICHOLAS KAMM/AFP/Getty Images

Chapter 13

p. 236: DOONESBURY ©1985 G. B. Trudeau. Reprinted with permission of ANDREWS MCMEEL SYNDICATION. All rights reserved.; **p. 241:** © Marcy Wieland; **p. 242:** ©OPOLJA/ Shutterstock; **p. 245:** ©Everett Historical/ Shutterstock.com; **p. 247:** DILBERT © (2002) Scott Adams. Used By permission of ANDREWS MCMEEL SYNDICATION. All rights reserved.; **p. 250:** DILBERT © (2002) Scott Adams. Used By permission of ANDREWS MCMEEL SYNDICATION. All rights reserved.

Chapter 14

p. 254: ©SueC/Shutterstock.com; **p. 256:** Photo by Gilles Petard/Redferns; **p. 258:** Associated Press/ Evan Vucci; **p. 259:** Caiaimage/Martin Barraud/ Getty Images; **p. 260:** © Kevin J. Miyazaki 2008; **p. 262:** stevenmaltby/ iStock.com / Getty Images Plus; **p. 264:** Django/Getty Images

Chapter 15

p. 269: John Sleezer/Kansas City Star/MCT via Getty Images; **p. 271:** ©John Gomez/Shutterstock. com; **p. 273:** © Marcy Wieland; **p. 274:** Photo by Volkan Furuncu/Anadolu Agency/Getty Images; **p. 277:** © Marcy Wieland; **p. 279:** *Associated Press/ Charlie Neibergall*; **p. 280:** Photo by Sharon Tshipa/ SOPA Images/LightRocket via Getty Images;

Chapter 16

p. 288: Jack Taylor / Stringer/Getty Images; **p. 291:** © Peter Turnley; **p. 293:** Courtesy of The Montana Meth Project; **p. 295:** Photo by Bill Greene/The Boston Globe via Getty Images; **p. 296:** Associated Press/Steve Helber; **p. 299:** (left) Photo by © Ralf-Finn Hestoft/CORBIS/ Corbis via Getty Images; **p. 299:** (right) Photo by Visions of America/UIG via Getty Images; **p. 301:** © Marcy Wieland

Chapter 17

p. 309: © Jacob Lund/Shutterstock.com; **p. 312:** Robert Willett/Raleigh News & Observer/MCT via Getty Images; **p. 316:** Phil McCarten/Invision/AP; **p. 317:** Photo by Visions of America/UIG via Getty Images

Index

Note: Page references followed by a "*t*" indicate table; "*f*" indicate figure.